Britain, America and the Sinews of War, 1914–1918

Titles of related interest:

War and the State: The Transformation of British Government, 1914–1919
edited by Kathleen Burk

British Economic and Strategic Planning 1905–1915
by David French

British Policy and the Irish Administration 1920–22
by John McColgan

Strategy and Supply
The Anglo-Russian Alliance 1914–17
by Keith Neilson

Britain, America and the Sinews of War, 1914–1918

Kathleen Burk
Department of Humanities, Imperial College, London

Boston
GEORGE ALLEN & UNWIN
London   Sydney

Allen & Unwin, Inc.,
Fifty Cross Street, Winchester, Mass. 01890, USA

George Allen & Unwin (Publishers) Ltd,
40 Museum Street, London WC1A 1LU, UK

George Allen & Unwin (Publishers) Ltd,
Park Lane, Hemel Hempstead, Herts HP2 4TE, UK

George Allen & Unwin Australia Pty Ltd,
8 Napier Street, North Sydney, NSW 2060, Australia

First published in 1985

British Library Cataloguing in Publication Data

Burk, Kathleen
  Britain, America and the sinews of war, 1914–1918.
1. Great Britain – Foreign economic
relations – United States   2. United
States – Foreign economic relations –
Great Britain
I. Title
337.41073   HF1534.5.U5
ISBN 0–04–940076–2

Library of Congress Cataloging in Publication Data

Burk, Kathleen.
  Britain, America and the sinews of war, 1914–1918.
Bibliography: p.
Includes index.
1. World War, 1914–1918 – Economic aspects – United
States.   2. World War, 1914–1918 – Economic aspects –
Great Britain.   3. United States – Foreign economic relations –
Great Britain.   4. Great Britain – Foreign economic relations –
United States.   I. Title.
D635.B87 1984   940.3'1   84–9262
ISBN 0–04–940076–2 (alk. paper)

Set in 10 on 12 point Plantin by Serrite Typesetters
and printed in Great Britain by Billing and Sons Ltd, London and
Worcester

Contents

Acknowledgements

I have incurred many obligations, both institutional and personal, while writing this book, and it is a pleasure to record them.

For access to manuscript collections and permission to quote from them I am indebted to the Controller of Her Majesty's Stationery Office (for material in the Bodleian Library, the India Office Library and the Public Record Office); to the Trustees of the British Library, of the Bodleian Library, of the Imperial War Museum and of the Beaverbrook Foundation; to Churchill College and King's College, Cambridge; to *The Times* Archive; and to Morgan Grenfell & Co. Ltd. For permission to cite papers from collections of which they hold the copyright I am grateful to the executors of the estate of Mr Basil Blackett, Mr David McKenna, Mr A. J. P. Taylor, Viscount Addison and Lord Esher. In the United States I am indebted to the National Archives, the Library of Congress, Yale University, the University of Virginia, Harvard Business School and Amherst College. In Canada I am indebted to Queen's University, Kingston. Finally, I am indebted to Imperial College for providing Susan Buchanan, who deciphered my handwritten emendations and typed the manuscript.

My personal obligations range from the intellectual to the culinary. In its first incarnation this book was a D.Phil. thesis written under the supervision of Mr A. J. P. Taylor. His approach – a detached but kindly interest – was exactly right: stimulating without being over-whelming. I also owe much to Professor H. G. Nicholas, who examined the thesis and who has continued a constant supporter. My third debt of gratitude is to Miss Betty Kemp, who first encouraged me to come to Oxford and who always provided support at the crucial moment.

Friends have helped along the way. I am grateful to Judy Hildesley for early proofreading and to Mike Hildesley for arranging access to the Morgan Grenfell papers for me. Juliet Surridge came to my rescue by reading the final proofs. Peter Ghosh and Philip Williamson read early draft chapters; John Hemery read the Epilogue; and John Campbell and David French both took time to read the entire completed manuscript (and David now shares the responsibility for any mistakes on the military side). More generally, George Peden and I have read and discussed each other's work ever since we were postgraduates together and shared an interest in Treasury papers.

And finally there is my family. My work over the years on Anglo-American relations would have been financially impossible had I not been able to batten on my relatives: my uncle and aunts, Mr and Mrs George Flinn and Miss Mimi Ankney, provided me with room and board on repeated visits to Washington (and Mrs Jo Randolph drove me to and from the National Archives dozens of times), while my cousin Jane Lolachi put me up in Connecticut. My parents provided financial and, joined by my five brothers and sisters, a lot of emotional support, and it is to them that this book is dedicated. My final obligation is of a private nature – but my friends will recognize it.

Kathleen Burk
May 1984

Britain, America and the Sinews of War, 1914–1918

Introduction
Anglo-American Relations, 1895–1918

Between 1895 and 1918, Anglo-American relations were transformed. This transformation was as much a function of British weakness as of American strength: its roots lay in Britain's relative economic decline and the changing power relationships in Europe and Asia. But the weakening of Britain's international position might well have been more gradual had it not been for the First World War, which, while militarily a victory for Britain and her allies, was economically a catastrophe. This same war which drained Britain's resources speeded up America's industrial development, and by 1918 she was, quite clearly, not only one of the Great Powers, but the strongest financially as well. Because Britain had held this very position herself in the years before the war, the new situation was a particularly painful one for her, and the postwar years saw much conflict between the two powers as Britain strove to regain her position in the international hierarchy. But the disparities in resources, population and size were too much for Britain to overcome, given that she had lost so much of her wealth during the war. The First World War, therefore, marks the period when Britain was forced to resign her position of pre-eminence to the United States, although neither country was then aware of the finality of the exchange.

By 1895 British resources were stretched thinly all over the world: she may have had an empire on which the sun never set, but that meant she had to supply and defend an empire whose lines of communication stretched for thousands of miles. British policymakers realised that this empire was secure only so long as she had a dominant navy and so long as sufficient of the other Great Powers did not combine against her.

The foreign policy outlook for the United States in 1895 was very different. Whereas Britain had many potential enemies – France in Africa, Russia in Asia and, soon, Germany in Europe – America felt threatened by no one. She was preoccupied with her own continental-sized territory, and as yet had no overseas possessions. When most Americans looked abroad they saw markets for their exports, not territory to conquer. In the European sense, the United States hardly had a foreign policy, except for the Monroe Doctrine: on this, however, she insisted absolutely. This Doctrine, proclaimed in 1823 by President Monroe, warned that North and South America were no longer open to further colonisation by foreign powers.

The Doctrine was not in fact taken very seriously by the continental European powers, but challenging it would have required the acquiescence of the British navy, and the British usually had little interest in furthering the interests of their rivals. Britain, who in principle had the power to defeat the Monroe Doctrine, chose to respect it by agreeing to resolve the Venezuelan boundary dispute of 1895–7 with American arbitration.[1] The reason for this accommodation was not a British acceptance of the Monroe Doctrine as binding in international law. Rather, Britain was embarking on a policy of settling extra-European problems in order to concentrate her forces nearer home. She could afford to make concessions in the Western hemisphere because while the United States cared about them, Britain did not. On the American side the desire for an amicable settlement of the dispute reflected a growing recognition by its leaders and by the public – the Irish always excepted – of the political and cultural affinities between the two countries.

This favourable American view of Britain was strengthened by the Spanish-American War in 1898. This war made the United States a colonial power, and thus American strictures against British imperialism necessarily lost some of their force. Further, the perceived British role in the war was profoundly important in producing a change in American attitudes towards Britain. It was widely believed in America that Britain had prevented a German-led anti-American coalition from being formed, and that the British navy had prevented the German navy from menacing the American forces in the Philippines; and the Americans, being a sentimental people, were grateful.

The year 1898 also nearly saw an Anglo-French war, and, in the publication of the German Navy Bill, for Britain an ominous harbinger promising a German navy big enough to threaten British naval superiority. The Boer War, beginning in 1899, led to European denunciations of Britain, which were contrasted unfavourably with the relatively muted American response.

Thus isolated and faced with a serious challenge from Germany, Britain had to rationalise her foreign commitments and consolidate her forces nearer the home islands. In order to withdraw forces from the Far

East while still protecting her China trade from Russia she signed the Anglo-Japanese alliance treaty in 1902; in order to protect Egypt and her other African possessions she settled with France in 1904; and in order to protect India and save part of Persia she settled with Russia in 1907.

In the same line were the negotiations over the isthmian canal (the future Panama Canal) with the United States in 1900–1. The question at issue was the revision of the Clayton-Bulwer Treaty of 1850, which provided for joint Anglo-American control of an isthmian canal. The United States wanted it revised. The Spanish-American War of 1898 had demonstrated how desirable such a canal was for the American navy to enable its ships to pass quickly from main naval bases in the Atlantic and the Caribbean to the Pacific. Thus the United States was determined to build an isthmian canal, but she did not want to share control of it with Britain. The British Admiralty argued strongly against giving up the right to joint control on strategic grounds: such a canal would effectively double the striking power of the American navy, and this would threaten Britain's naval position in the Caribbean. Lord Lansdowne, the Secretary of State for Foreign Affairs, disregarded the Admiralty's objections, and by the signature of the Hay-Pauncefort Treaty in 1901 American control of an isthmian canal was assured.

From the American point of view, Britain had conceded supremacy in the Caribbean to the United States. The British point of view, however, was different. Lansdowne and the Cabinet worked on two assumptions, that Britain and America were most unlikely ever to be enemies, and that, by and large, British and American foreign policy objectives were the same, namely, the maintenance of peace and the status quo. Thus, for Lansdowne, the result was not to resign effective British power in the Caribbean to the Americans, but rather to incorporate the United States into the British defence strategy: the United States now took on the defence of the Caribbean and relieved the British navy of the task.

The United States was also coming to share, although not to the same degree, Britain's perception of Germany as a threat to international order. There had been traditional pro-German sentiment in the United States, but this was draining away as a result of a series of incidents, including Germany's predatory activities in China in 1897–8 and the Kaiser's stand during the Boxer Crisis, the allegedly unfriendly manoeuvres of the German fleet in the Philippines in 1898, German participation in a blockade of Venezuela, in insolent contravention of the Monroe Doctrine in 1902, and the German actions during the

Moroccan Crisis in 1905 and the Agadir Crisis in 1911. In a manner that was to repeat itself more than once later in the century, the common external threat brought the two countries closer together.

Thus it was that when Britain went to war with Germany in 1914 the United States was at first benevolently neutral and then a co-belligerent. Throughout this period, America's economic power was vital to Britain, and it is therefore appropriate to compare the economic strengths of the two countries immediately prior to the outbreak of war. In this, it is important to differentiate between financial power and industrial capabilities.

In 1914 Britain was the major international financial power, with the pound sterling serving as the world's primary trading currency. There were at least three important factors making up this financial strength: first, there was the strength of the British economy itself; secondly, there was the extent and the maturity of the British banking system, from the network of country banks able to tap surplus funds in the rural areas to the power and independence of the Bank of England; and thirdly, there was the wealth and expertise of the City of London, demonstrated by its ability to finance trade worldwide. As far as the United States was concerned, it was British funds which had, to a great extent, financed the building of the railways, and it was still in 1914 British funds which financed the moving of the Southern cotton crop to market. The United States did not lack wealth; rather, British firms had traditionally financed such activities, and the United States lacked commensurate experience and expertise in mobilising the funds of its citizenry and funnelling them to where they were needed.

Industrially, the United States was already by 1900 well ahead of Britain in many areas, even in those such as iron and steel, and textiles which for Britain had provided the basis of her industrial revolution. By 1900 as well the population of the United States was more than twice that of Britain, and the continuation of immigration combined with a higher birth-rate ensured that the disparity in labour forces would increase. Qualitatively, there was a difference between American and British industry, in that the former tended to produce cheap goods on machines that could be easily modified to meet changing demands, whereas the latter had greater expertise in producing precision goods, including especially armaments.

In 1914, then, the United States was still very much the subordinate partner in the Anglo-American relationship. She depended on Britain for financial services, for many social and cultural fashions and in general to maintain the standard of Anglo-Saxon civilisation in this age of debased Darwinism. The strategic interests of the two countries were by and large complementary, but this was due more to lack of American interest in many areas of the world, such as Europe, Africa and the Middle East, than to any coherent view of the world. Britain was the experienced World Power, while the United States was merely a potential one.

The major role the United States was destined to play in the First World War was that of economic powerhouse and supplier of munitions, food and money to Britain and her allies. But the organisers of American producers to supply these goods were in large measure not the Americans themselves, but British citizens sent to the United States on missions for this purpose.

It is with this economic role of the United States and with these missions that the book is primarily concerned. By November 1916 fully 40 per cent of British war expenditure was devoted to North American supplies, and the burden nearly destroyed sterling as an international currency. The great political missions, such as that of the Secretary of State for Foreign Affairs, A. J. Balfour, in May–June 1917, were in large part concerned with economics and finance. Sir William Wiseman, the head of British Military Intelligence (MI6) in the United States, wrote in 1917 that 'Nowadays most diplomatic questions at Washington concern supplies, and all questions of supplies when other than mere routine become matters for diplomatic negotiation'.[2] Indeed, supercession of Britain by the United States as the leading financial power can be seen occurring, step by step, in the negotiations between the British Treasury mission and the American government during 1917–18; in the daily dealings of the Treasury mission can be seen the passing of hegemony from Britain to the United States.

These circumstances influenced the British government in its treatment of the American government. For its part, even before it entered the war, the American government tried to use the leverage provided by Allied dependence on American supplies and the American financial market to force changes in British foreign policy. Once America entered the war, the attempts to control became even more direct, and in many cases the British missions bore the brunt of American pressure. Throughout it is apparent that the American government was relatively unprepared, both morally and technically, to face the demands and temptations of a World Power.

The resident British missions in America comprised the representatives of the British government departments which desired to purchase goods or raise finance in America. The War Office was the first to send a representative to America in October 1914, since it had rapidly become obvious that Britain could not itself provide all the supplies needed to equip the new Kitchener army. This particular representative was very soon followed by others, both from Britain and from the other belligerents, with the inevitable confusion and bidding up of prices. Britain attempted to solve the problem by arranging in January 1915 that J. P. Morgan & Co. should act as the sole purchasing agent in America for the War Office and Admiralty, and this eliminated a great deal of the counterbidding. When Lloyd George became the organising minister of the new Ministry of Munitions in May 1915, he determined to exploit American industrial power for the benefit of the Allies, and it was the Ministry of Munitions which sent out to America the first resident mission. By April 1917 this mission had nearly 1,600 members in the United States, and was purchasing munitions for the entire Entente. Its inspectors were in every factory which had a contract with Britain, its agents rode the trains carrying the munitions to port in order to prevent theft and sabotage, and its agents watched the loading of munitions on board ship to prevent time bombs being placed on board. Essentially, the Morgan company negotiated the contracts and arranged for the finance, and the Munitions mission took care of production and delivery. By April 1917 this mission and those of the Royal Commission on Wheat Supplies and of the Board of Trade were together spending $83 million a week in the United States.

Sums of this magnitude were raised only with increasing difficulty. While the United States was neutral they had to be raised privately on the American money market, and this was done in three ways: gold was shipped and used to purchase dollars; American securities, such as shares in American railways which were owned by British citizens, were bought by the British Treasury and sold to Americans in New York; and public loans were issued in the United States, either without any collateral, as with the Anglo-French loan of 1915, or with the use as collateral of securities deposited on loan at the British Treasury, as with the issues of 1916 and early 1917. These public loans became more and more difficult to issue successfully, as the eventual outcome of the war seemed unclear to Americans, and rumours of infighting between the British Cabinet and the generals and newspaper proprietors filtered across the Atlantic. At the same time these operations were of vital importance for Britain, for only by the raising of funds in America could she hope to raise enough dollars, without having to purchase so many with pounds as to depress the rate of the pound and make dollars even more expensive and unobtainable. By contrast, Britain had relatively little difficulty in raising the sums needed in Britain itself, or in the Allied countries, or in the Empire, where Treasury bills could be issued.

In this raising of finance in America J. P. Morgan & Co. were Britain's financial agent (as well as being purchasing agent), since neither the British Treasury nor the Bank of England had the necessary connections or machinery for international financial transactions. In December 1916, however, there was a financial crisis of some magnitude, including a fierce run on the pound, which was precipitated by the Morgan firm, and in consequence the British Treasury lost much of their confidence in J. P. Morgan & Co. They set up a new division in the Treasury to deal with external finance, headed by J. M. Keynes, and in February 1917 sent out their own Treasury mission to reside in New York City, headed by Hardman Lever. Lever was destined to clash swords most actively with American officials as they attempted to control the activities of the Treasury mission and he fought for the power and position of Britain.

A question which arises is, why was all of this activity not placed under the aegis of the British Ambassador, Sir Cecil Spring Rice? The short answer must be that it never occurred to anyone to do so, least of all Spring Rice. The missions had to remain officially unofficial. In the first place, there were problems in international law, which prohibited a belligerent from constructing a supply base in a neutral country. In the second place, because American society was split between those who were pro-Ally, those who were pro-German and those who were highly indifferent, it behooved the British to move carefully, and they worked constantly under the threat of a Congressional embargo on the export of war supplies. Spring Rice's preoccupation was to distance himself from the purchasing missions, although they worked with his goodwill. Finally, the British Treasury refused to work through the Embassy because the Embassy lacked financial expertise and was unable to move with the speed necessary in financial and exchange rate transactions. Spring Rice did not mind, because his domain was relations with the American government. He only began to feel threatened, and to react by harassing the missions, in order to protect his and his Embassy's position, after the United States became a belligerent in April 1917 and the missions assumed official status.

The entry of the United States into the war came as a welcome relief, to say the least, to the British government. Since September 1915 Britain had been guaranteeing the purchases in the United States of the Russians and Italians, and since May 1916 those of the French, and the combined burden of Entente plus her own expenditure had virtually bankrupted Britain in America. Britain's only chance was now to throw herself on the mercy of the American Treasury and beg the Americans to take over the burden of financing the Allies in the United States. No one considered what Britain would do if the American government refused in any measure to do so.

The immediate reaction of the British government to the American declaration of war was to send over a political mission of some stature, headed by A. J. Balfour, and including representatives of the departments with responsibilities requiring them to establish relations with American departments. The purpose of the mission was to ascertain the war-readiness of the American government, to encourage and take advantage of the new partner and to guide her into decisions favourable to Britain with regard to shipping, finance and munitions. The fact that the Americans were not keen to have such a mission come to Washington was deemed of little importance. The Americans, in fact, were almost totally unprepared for war, not knowing how they were to fight, where they were to fight, or with what they were to fight. These were the sorts of questions, of course, that the Balfour mission hoped to answer for the Americans. The mission wanted decisions, and here in some respects they garnered the results of their precipitous descent upon the United States, and a meagre harvest it was. The main impression the mission gathered in Washington was of muddle and confusion. Perhaps it was reprehensible of the Americans not to throw themselves into the arms of the British, but it should not have been unexpected. The American government evinced a sincere desire to help as much as possible, but this was mixed with a large dose of suspicion of the British.

After the return of the Balfour mission to Britain, the Cabinet decided to send out Lord Northcliffe to the United States to weld all of the disparate missions into a British War Mission. This he did, but his arrival was also the occasion for an outbreak of open warfare between the missions and the British Embassy. The British Ambassador, Spring Rice, hated both Northcliffe and the idea of a separate centre of British power and influence in America. He determined to control access to the officials of the American government, and *inter alia* worked to undermine the credit of some of the members of the missions, especially that of Sir Hardman Lever. This was doubly unfortunate, since Lever had his hands full trying to fight off the attempts of the American Secretary of the Treasury, William Gibbs McAdoo, to determine British financial – and eventually foreign – policy.

The question which both the British and the Americans had to confront in the summer of 1917 was, what did the Allies want from the American government, and what were they willing to sacrifice for it? The Balfour mission had announced that the British were desperate for shipping and finance, but over the summer it became clear that all of the Allies also wanted American troops on the Western Front. The main difficulty with the raising of an American mass army was that it would have to be clothed and supplied from scratch. If this were given top priority, what would happen to the stream of supplies currently going to the Allies? Moreover, how would both the Allies and the American army be supplied from the funds available to McAdoo? McAdoo's response was to try to control all official purchasing channels, and he used his financial hold over the Allies to force them to subordinate their purchasing missions to an Allied Purchasing Commission, an arm of the American War Industries Board. The British in fact supported the idea, since the missions were convinced that it was the only way they would get supplies at reasonable prices. As it turned out, the Commission was a poor thing indeed, but the British had to make what they could of the new organisation, since they had cut themselves off from making independent purchases in America. By February 1918 they had lost their financial freedom in America as well, when McAdoo forced them to turn over a very substantial holding of securities in America to the control of the American Treasury.

From a purely administrative angle, the British War Mission was an organisation of some interest. By the end of 1917 it comprised 10,000 members, who purchased munitions, raw materials, food and clothing, saw to its transport and shipment, trained soldiers and airmen, made propaganda forays into the wilds of deepest America, kept an eye on German agents and financed the lot. During the period of American neutrality the missions had remained as unobtrusive as possible so as to escape criticism, but even after the United States became a belligerent, the War Mission was seldom attacked. It was, however, a matter for some comment in Washington that the Ambassador and the Head of the War Mission were continually at odds, and the divided nature of British representation in the United States was only resolved by the recall of both Spring Rice and Northcliffe and the appointment in February 1918 of Lord Reading as Ambassador *and* High Commissioner of the War Mission.

By this time the power of ultimate decision on supplies and finance lay with the Americans. The British in fact became used to their servitude, and tried to convince the Americans to agree to continue the inter-allied organisations for the control and allocation of materials into the postwar period. They felt that this was the only way they could obtain the food and raw materials they needed at a price they could afford. But the Americans absolutely refused. They were the major source of many essential materials and preferred to get the best price possible on the open market; as well, the American government disapproved on principle of the imposition of controls. Further, they did not want to support the Allies in their intention to continue economic warfare against Germany after the war; they wanted to sell to Germany, rather than to treat her as a pariah power. Thus at the end of the war the powers of the American war organisation were terminated immediately, and the British War Mission itself was finally wound up in July 1919.

The intention of this book is to describe a complex structure, built up over four years of war, which involved the British deeply with American industry and finance. Anglo-American relations during the First World War involved much more than American objections to the way in which the Allies blockaded Germany, and President Wilson's peace moves, the issues which were probably most apparent during the war. The financial and commercial relationships were crucial to Britain: without American production and financial aid Britain would have been simply unable, after April 1917, to continue fighting on anything like the scale to which it had become accustomed. The price Britain paid was the loss of its dominant financial position to the United States. The United States for its part had to adjust to meet the responsibilities of an industrial, financial and political World Power; the British war missions attempted to guide the United States during the period of adjustment.

Part One

1914–1917 and American Neutrality: British Relations with Private America

1

British Purchasing, August 1914 to May 1915, and the Appointment of J. P. Morgan & Co.

Britain, in common with the other belligerents, was unprepared for the scale of the war, and for the duration of continual fighting. The assumptions on which British prewar strategic planning had been based were very quickly falsified. British war planning had been based on the assumption that she would utilise her superior naval power and concentrate on supplying her Allies with matériel while blockading the Central Powers and slowly starving them of resources. She would not provide a mass army of her own; rather, Britain's continental Allies were expected to provide the bulk of the land forces with Britain contributing an Expeditionary Force of six divisions (150,000 men), two divisions of which were to remain in Britain for home defence. (In fact, all six divisions of the British Expeditionary Force, plus one cavalry division, were in France by early September 1914.) But very soon after war began, the Secretary of State for War, Lord Kitchener, succeeded in persuading the Cabinet that it was vital that Britain should after all raise a mass army. Kitchener, almost alone in the higher reaches of the government, envisaged a long war, and such was his prestige in the early days that the Cabinet agreed to begin the necessary preparations.[1] In addition, the British army was unprepared for the change in tactics necessitated by trench warfare (as opposed to a war of mobility) and in particular for the enormous expenditure of shells. The result of these strategic and tactical problems was to be a transformation of War Office purchasing practices.

The normal system of buying by the Contracts Department of the War Office in peacetime had been by competitive tender, confined in general to a limited number of approved British suppliers.[2] It soon proved impossible to restrict orders for munitions to known firms, since the need was so great, but the War Office attempted to mitigate the problem by stipulating that firms which had not previously fulfilled orders for the government should work as subcontractors for the approved firms, thereby throwing on their shoulders the task of training the new firms up to the standards necessary.[3] But even with this expansion of the list there were not enough firms to meet all of the orders, and very early on the government had to turn to the United States for further industrial capacity.[4]

There was some anxiety as to the likely American reactions to British orders, but in fact the American government did not hinder the purchase of goods by belligerents. The overwhelming desire of the Administration was to be neutral; and in spite of protests from various groups such as the Irish, the State Department finally issued a circular to the press on 15 October 1914 in which it stated that it had no authority to interfere with the purchase of goods by belligerents, even of munitions, and that in fact it would be highly unneutral for it or for any agency of the government to do so.[5] Besides, there was clearly no point in turning down good business.

Thus the main concern of the War Office was with possible deficiencies in the capacity and productive ability of American firms. British engineering firms were much more used to precision engineering than were American firms, and the question as to whether they could cope with the tolerances necessary in the production of shells or guns was a real one. It was therefore decided to send out agents to inspect likely American firms and to see if they seemed competent. The first agents were sent in September 1914,[6] and in October as a result of a Cabinet decision an agent was sent to place orders.

In the first months of the war, there was understandable anxiety in the British government as to whether Britain could produce enough munitions to supply its expanding army. A Cabinet Committee on Munitions was set up. At the first meeting on 12 October the committee considered the provision of guns, including that of rifles, and decided that there was no prospect of equipping recruits unless special efforts were made. It was decided to send a message to the War Office representative in the United States, instructing him to find out the maximum number of rifles which could be secured from competent firms. The committee wanted 500,000 rifles, but a reply to their inquiry showed that there was little hope for substantial supplies from the USA before September 1915. When the committee met on 21 October Major-General Sir Stanley von Donop, the Master-General of the Ordnance, stated that 781,000 rifles were promised from British sources by 1 July 1915, but the committee decided that this was inadequate and that the army required a further 400,000.[7] It was decided to send a War Office agent to negotiate in the United States, and Lieutenant B. C. Smyth-Pigott and an assistant sailed on 24 October 1914.[8]

Smyth-Pigott took over from Major Farmar, a War Office representative who had gone out in September to see about small arms, and continued Farmar's discussions with the Remington and Winchester firms.[9] Unknown to Smyth-Pigott, however, David Lloyd George, the Chancellor of the Exchequer, was casting around for other means of finding rifles. From the earliest days of the war Lloyd George had searched impatiently for ways of increasing munitions output, although as Chancellor his only direct act was to waive the Treasury's right (and duty) to oversee War Office expenditure on supplies, the point of the waiver being to expedite the placing of orders. Nevertheless, as Chancellor he was acquainted with E. C. Grenfell, senior partner of Morgan Grenfell & Co. and a director of the Bank of England, whose firm was associated with that of J. P. Morgan & Co., the largest investment banking firm in America. Accordingly, Lloyd George contacted Grenfell and early in November 1914, at the Chancellor's request, Grenfell cabled J. P. Morgan & Co. in New York to ask them to inquire of American rifle firms whether rifle-producing capacity could be increased, either by the extension of existing plant, or by the conversion of, say, sewing machine plant for the purpose.[10] J. P. Morgan cabled back that he liked the idea, that he would be glad to get work in that area and that he planned to contact two firms which were friends of the Morgan firm – Remington and Winchester.[11]

The following day, when Smyth-Pigott heard that Morgan's were making inquiries, he cabled the War Office for permission to request Morgan's to desist, on the grounds that the firm and the War Office were competing for the same product.[12] Permission was granted and Morgan's desisted, but Grenfell was outraged at the treatment the firms had received: Morgan's had made the inquiries at the specific request of Lloyd George, and since the War Office had seen a copy of every cable concerning the business, they had had ample opportunity to prevent the investigation.[13] Lloyd George managed to smooth Grenfell's feathers,[14] and Smyth-Pigott placed contracts with both firms to supply 200,000 rifles each.[15] The incident therefore was small and harmless, but it was an example of a major problem with which Britain would have to contend in purchasing in the United States: since there was no one authority to purchase, different departments and agents of the British government – and more importantly the different Allies – were bidding against each other, pushing up prices for goods and causing turmoil in industry as firms fought over the stocks of raw materials and the pool of available labour.[16]

American manufacturers were eager for this business, since some of them were in a desperate financial position after the extremely depressed industrial conditions of 1913 and 1914. Some firms were disposed to undertake munitions contracts without fully realising the inherent difficulties, whether these lay in the manufacturing process itself or in obtaining supplies of raw materials and skilled labour. Unfortunately, the Allied buying agents were not always able, or willing to take the time, to distinguish between those who could deliver what they promised and those who could not.[17]

Another problem was the swarm of private brokers and agents which descended on the British authorities on both sides of the Atlantic. The Allied purchasers were particularly vulnerable in America because of their lack of local knowledge. A broker would realise that the government would require a particular item or raw material, would go to a firm producing it and would persuade the firm to give a commission to the agent if he could arrange for an order to be placed with the firm. Some brokers claimed falsely to be British government agents; in one case,

> it became known that orders were to be placed for a certain kind of cloth; an unauthorised person visited half a dozen of the leading firms in a particular city and told them that he had directions to make inquiries as to the capacity of the mills in the city and had some influence as to the distribution of orders, and by this means he secured promises of commissions from each of the firms in the event of the order being placed there. The orders were duly placed with several of these firms a few days later and the individual who had done nothing except use his intelligence in anticipating probable orders secured substantial commissions.[18]

Further, many agents went to firms, got an option on their production and then offered it to the government, with an additional 10 per cent for themselves. There were great numbers of agents, both with and without official authority, and no one knew how to distinguish the true from the false, since no British government department was notifying the Foreign Office or any other departments of its plans. As one observer noted, 'Neither the Embassy nor the New York Consulate have any knowledge at all on the subject. Agents go over from England apparently without written credentials and without directions to report themselves to any representative of the British Government in America.'[19] Initially, on receiving an inquiry or complaint about a particular man claiming to have government authority, the British Ambassador, Sir Cecil Spring Rice, or the British Consul-General in New York, Sir Courtenay Bennett, was generally able to check on the man only by cabling to London.[20] Spring Rice accordingly tried to get full lists of all accredited agents sent to him, and the War Office at least complied.[21]

In one case it was certainly discovered that the War Office had contracted to buy materials at an unnecessarily high price from a previously unknown agent. This discovery was made by George Macaulay Booth, of the merchant and shipping company Alfred Booth & Co. (which owned a large part of Cunard). Booth had served as an unofficial adviser to members of the War Office and the Board of Trade, and in October 1914, while he was preparing to travel to the United States on a routine trip to look into the New York branch of the family business, he was asked by Kitchener to arrange finance for a contract that the War Office had made with a certain Alfred Fraser for 30,000 winter coats. Fraser had contracted to sell these coats at 37s each, but Booth reported that 'while I was in Boston I made careful investigations and satisfied myself that any large reputable house, acting on behalf of the Government, could have bought these coats at under 24s per coat.'[22]

While he was in the United States the War Office cabled a request that he purchase accoutrements and gun cotton for them, for which he made the necessary arrangements. But probably his most important activity was to investigate the whole problem of agents and to try to bring some order into the purchasing process. He discussed the problem with Spring Rice, an old friend, and he agreed with Spring Rice's growing conviction that a single purchasing agency was vital for the British government.[23]

Spring Rice, in response to the incredible confusion he saw, first suggested to the Foreign Office that Britain channel her purchases through one organisation on 21 October 1914. After talking to Sir George Paish and Basil Blackett, Treasury representatives then in the United States (see Chapter 4), Spring Rice repeated the suggestion, adding that the proposed responsible agent should be a firm of standing on both sides of the Atlantic, such as J. P. Morgan & Co.[24] The Foreign Office passed on the suggestion to the War Office, the Admiralty and the CIR (Commission Internationale de Ravitailement, the London-based organisation which purchased supplies for the Allies in the Allied countries – see Chapter 3), but the immediate response was discouraging: the War Office and the Admiralty both preferred to deal directly with firms or their agents; and the CIR was not placing any contracts in the United States in its own name.[25] Spring Rice continued to argue for such an organisation, but as Lord Eustace Percy at the Foreign Office minuted, 'It is impossible to have "one neck to the bottle" if the War Office insist that their proper course is to deal directly with manufacturers'.[26]

Spring Rice's suggestion that J. P. Morgan & Co. should be made the British government's sole purchasing agent was adopted in January 1915. It is clear that this action by the British government was prompted not merely by Spring Rice (and by those in London more concerned with adequate supplies of munitions than with the methods used to obtain them) but also by Booth, Blackett and Paish, who returned from the United States having witnessed the chaos. What is not entirely clear is just which Cabinet minister formally asked which British or American Morgan partner to take on the responsibility, and when.

When Booth returned to Britain in mid-November 1914 he reported to Kitchener, Sir Frederick Black (the Director of Admiralty Contracts) and the Board of Trade that he felt there was an overriding need for a centralised purchasing agency; he suggested the Morgan firm. Booth, in fact, probably had a further reason for suggesting Morgan's beyond their dominant position in American banking. As a shipowner he would have been aware that the Morgan group controlled substantial tonnage in their International Mercantile Marine combine and he probably calculated that the appointment of Morgan's would ensure use of the ships in the Allied interest.[27]

While Blackett was in the United States he also spent some time, at Spring Rice's request, investigating the conditions of British purchasing. J. P. Morgan reported Blackett's views to Grenfell:

> purchasing matters here for all Allies so completely lack organisation that he [Blackett] looks upon it as immediate necessity that . . . for Great Britain, some central bureau should be

immediately appointed to serve as Government's official representative here, its technical representatives working in cooperation with this central authority. Blackett said that as he saw it we were the logical house for such a relationship; in fact, the only one in America that would command instant recognition and approval.[28]

Morgan also informed Grenfell that Paish had had similar discussions with H. P. Davison (another Morgan partner) and that Paish had already cabled his views to the British government; and further, he asked Grenfell whether he, Morgan, ought to travel over to talk to the British authorities.[29] Grenfell replied that he would talk to the President of the Board of Trade (Walter Runciman) about it, since he could not immediately see the Chancellor.[30] Grenfell continued to talk with various officials, but by 13 November he had to report that he was having difficulties in getting the authorities to agree to Morgan's acting as a central purchasing agency, implying that they balked at paying commission.[31] By 18 November Paish had come out firmly for the appointment of the Morgan firm, and he strongly suggested that a representative of the firm should go to London; this advice was supported by Grenfell, who thought that Davison should sail for England with Paish and Blackett, although he was doubtful if anything would come of it.[32]

Blackett, Paish and Davison sailed for Britain together on 26 November 1914. (All the discussants felt the need for secrecy, and the fact that Davison had also to consult bankers in London about the proposed gold pool – see Chapter 4 – provided a convenient cover-story.) Upon his return to Britain Blackett wrote a memorandum for Sir John Bradbury, Joint Permanent Secretary to the Treasury, in which he enlarged upon the problem and suggested the solution. The great problem with purchasing in America was not so much corruption, as had been feared, but lack of organisation. Everyone agreed that the only satisfactory solution was to establish in New York City some single agency for all British government orders in America. All agents sent out to the United States would present their credentials there and American firms wishing to take up contracts would deal with this agency. He added that the financing of all purchases by the government should be, as far as possible, concentrated in a single banking firm acting with or as the agency.[33] He most probably suggested the Morgan firm when the problem was discussed.

On 16 December Davison had lunch with H. H. Asquith, the Prime Minister, and the Chancellor. He presented to them in writing a proposed purchasing arrangement of which Asquith said he 'approved every word'. Asquith favoured an immediate arrangement with Morgan's covering both the Admiralty and the War Office. Lloyd George and the Treasury officials also came out in support; for Lloyd George (as has been seen) the idea of using Morgan's was not a new one. He now urged Davison to discuss the suggestion that Morgan's should be the British government's purchasing agent with Sir George Gibb of the Army Council. Davison saw Gibb on 17 December and again on 19 December.[34]

Narrow self-interest seems not to have been Morgan's only reason for acquiring the contract. Admittedly, the firm liked the idea of participating in the purchasing for the British government, as J. P. Morgan made clear in his cable to Grenfell of 7 November (cited earlier). But organising all of the purchasing for the British government in the United States was another level of responsibility entirely. Davison was reluctant, apparently feeling that Morgan's were financiers (rather than brokers), were not in fact looking for business and had neither the experience nor the organisation for going into the purchasing field.[35] E. R. Stettinius, who was to run the purchasing organisation for Morgan's, recalled that J. P. Morgan

> did not wish to accept the agency but did so for two chief reasons, in addition to the desire to aid Great Britain and the Allied cause. He realised the inability, under the decentralized and competitive system, of the Allies securing what they needed, and the effect on American economic conditions if the old methods were followed. He knew also that all Europe would condemn America for the cost that would result.[36]

Davison, too, expressed concern about the chaos that had developed in the American market, to the detriment both of the American economy and the Allied purchasers.[37] Morgan's had a sense of corporate responsibility, stemming from their position in American economic life. As the most powerful of the investment banks, Morgan's was the banker's banker, the leader of Wall Street in times of trouble (as in the 1907 panic), and the partners felt that it was incumbent upon the firm to do what it could to straighten things out.

In addition, J. P. Morgan Jr at least had very strong personal ties with

England. He spent six months of the year in England, and moved with ease in its society (his niece, Mary Burns, had married the first Viscount Harcourt). He donated his country house, Dover House, to the British government at the outbreak of war for use as a hospital, and it was to be an anonymous donation by Morgan and Thomas Lamont (another Morgan partner) in 1929 which would enable the National Trust to purchase the land around Stonehenge to save it from development. The British government, in short, could be certain of his loyalty, a commodity felt to be useful at a time when many of the most important investment banks in the United States and merchant banks in London had connections with Germany.

The Morgan organisations were arranged usefully for the government's purposes. There were three interlocking firms, J. P. Morgan & Co. in New York, Morgan Grenfell & Co. in London and Morgan Harjes et Cie in Paris, thereby linking together the two major Allies with what became their major foreign source of supply. (France, in fact, had asked if J. P. Morgan & Co. could find 10,000 horses for them in the United States as early as September 1914.)[38] The senior partners in the London and New York firms owned stock in the other two firms, and because of their leading positions in each country could command both information and credit. Assuming that so unusual a step as to appoint a foreign firm as a central purchasing agent was to be taken, the claims of Morgan's for the position were strong indeed.

The War Office was by mid-December favourably inclined to the suggestion, but it was concerned to know what would be the reaction of President Woodrow Wilson and his Administration to the proposed appointment, and Spring Rice was cabled for his assessment.[39] Spring Rice looked into the problem and talked it over with J. P. Morgan, and concluded that it would not embarrass the Administration, since it was definitely understood that it was a commercial arrangement to increase trade, not a political or diplomatic arrangement. He also felt that Congress need not be feared as long as Morgan's did not try to use their political influence against bills which might be harmful to Britain, and, generally, left all negotiations with the American government to the diplomatic representatives.[40] Late in January J. P. Morgan himself spoke to the President about the matter, and the President had no objections to any action 'in furtherance of trade'.[41]

By this time, however, the War Office had decided to go ahead on the basis of the assurances given by Spring Rice, and on 15 January 1915 a Commercial Agreement was signed between the Army Council and the

Admiralty on the one side and J. P. Morgan & Co. on the other. (The 'Commercial Agreement' referred to J. P. Morgan & Co. as the 'Commercial Agents', but the more descriptive term 'purchasing agents' continued to be used by many of those involved, and will generally be used here.) According to the Agreement, Morgan's would 'use their best endeavours to secure for His Majesty's Government the most favourable terms as to quality price delivery discounts and rebates and also to aid and stimulate by all the means at their disposal sources of supply for the articles required.'[42] For this Morgan's would receive 2 per cent commission of net price of all goods purchased up to £10m. and then 1 per cent upon excess of that. The Army Council declared its intention that all War Office orders, except those of the Remount Commission (which was based in Canada), 'shall be based through the Commercial Agents' and the Admiralty would do the same 'so far as in their opinion they are able conveniently to do so without undue interference with their established channels of purchasing their requirements.',[43] in the United States. These were 'expressions of intention' and

> shall not in any way, however, be binding on His Majesty's Government who expressly reserve the right to make purchases otherwise than through the Commercial Agents if in the opinion of the said Army Council or the Admiralty as the case may be there is good and sufficient reason for doing so. In so far as they may find practicable, and in order to avoid complications His Majesty's Government will keep the Commercial Agents fully posted, as to purchases, if any, made otherwise than through them.[44]

These reservations, not surprisingly, were by mid-1915 the cause of some difficulty between Morgan's and the British government, since upon a number of occasions neither the War Office nor the Admiralty found it 'convenient' to use Morgan's. The immediate effect, however, was a great improvement in the conditions and results of British purchasing in the United States.

While negotiations were going on in London, Thomas Lamont, a partner in J. P. Morgan & Co., approached E. R. Stettinius, the President of the Diamond Match Company, to ask him to take charge of the purchasing for the British government. Morgan's were perfectly aware that they did not contain within their own organisation the technical expertise necessary to purchase, intelligently, items such as shells, shrapnel (a component of some types of shell) and other matériel. In fact, the intention was never that the firm should itself engage in the purchasing. Rather, they established a brokerage arrangement with Stettinius, whereby he set up and ran the necessary organisation, and was paid on a commission basis. The organisation, called the Export Department, was situated on the firm's premises in order that it could avail itself of the influence and financial acumen of the parent firm. By May 1915 it was apparent that pressures on the Export Department had been underestimated and the staff was greatly expanded (it totalled 175 by the spring of 1917). By June 1915 Morgan's had decided that the brokerage arrangement was not a satisfactory way to organise the matter (one possible reason was that Stettinius's commission threatened to exceed the income of any Morgan partner),[45] and they decided to pay the expenses of the department themselves. Absorption was completed when on 1 January 1916 Stettinius became a partner in J. P. Morgan & Co.[46]

Rather than use the Foreign Office channel, the British government communicated with Morgan's through Grenfell's firm in London, an arrangement suggested by Morgan's and urged on the government by George Booth, by now a Deputy-Director of Munitions Supply in the War Office.[47] Charles F. Whigham, a partner in Morgan Grenfell & Co., became Stettinius's opposite number in London. Whigham spent his mornings decoding and reading the cables from New York; his afternoons were taken up with visiting the various governmental departments, where he delivered responses from New York and collected requests for information and for orders to be placed. In the evenings he wrote cables, and encoded them if they were secret, to be sent to Morgan's each night.[48]

The 'amazing, elaborate code' used by Morgan's had been created by Whigham and Stettinius,[49] and its possession was, according to Grenfell, an 'extraordinary' privilege, which had been given to them in a 'fit of broadmindedness' by Lloyd George. It was extraordinary, in view of the strict censorship of all outgoing cables, that the Morgan firms should have possessed a private code. Such a code was denied even to the War Office and the Admiralty, who had to send their messages through the Foreign Office and via the Embassy in Washington and Consulate in New York. This caused frequent delays and consequently the War Office, for example, sometimes asked Whigham to send official War Office messages through their private channels in order to avoid such delays.[50]

Once the Export Department in New York had received and decoded the cables from London, they dealt with inquiries about a wide variety of matériel. The Export Department supplied information on sources of supply, prices, market conditions, the reliability of suppliers and offers to sell. When technical points demanding knowledge of military requirements arose, assistance was obtained from the inspecting officers previously sent to the United States from Britain by the War Office (see Chapter 2). Upon receiving authorisation from London, the department negotiated with the suppliers, secured the best possible terms for the Allies and placed the orders. Finally, the department acted as disbursing agent for paying the suppliers.[51] The department was handicapped, however, by its inability to ask publicly for tenders: to have done so could have caused legal and political problems in connection with America's neutrality (according to international law, belligerents were not to build supply bases in neutral countries) and would have aided German attempts at sabotage. Further, because there was no governmental control over prices and priority, the firm was forced to depend on its own power in the market-place in order to execute orders.[52] This power was justification alone for the British government's choice.

As well as placing the Allies' orders, Morgan's also tried to create productive capacity to handle the orders. The British government financed the extension of company plant, such as for rifle production. Morgan's also brought together combinations of financiers and manufacturers to undertake the responsibility of accepting very large contracts from the British government, an example of which was the Remington Arms Union.[53] This extension of private productive capacity for rifles, powder and shells, and the virtual creation of manufacturing plant for rifle cartridges and for fuses, was to prove vital to America's own war effort in 1917 and 1918.

There was one aspect of the Agreement, however, with which Morgan's proved unable to cope. Clause 6 stated that Morgan's should have general supervision over the shipment of goods, but it soon became apparent that the firm lacked the necessary experience. At the beginning of March 1915 the congestion on American railways of goods awaiting embarkation from the ports to Europe was so great that the railways refused to furnish any additional cars until they were informed of the dates of arrival of steamers. On 23 March 1915 Morgan's told the British government that time and expense would be saved if Britain had its own shipping organisation or employed a firm of forwarding agents. On 26 March at an Admiralty conference of shipping experts it was decided that an American firm of forwarding agents should be employed. Messrs Lunham & Moore, the suggested firm, were reported on by Morgan's as 'highly regarded, believed to be competent, and entirely free from any German affiliation or sympathies'. The firm was subsequently appointed.[54]

The shipping problem was easily solved, but the problem arising out of the reservation clause of the Agreement proved more intractable. The Admiralty, as shown by the lukewarm nature of their commitment in the Agreement, seemingly had little intention of using Morgan's. Spring Rice wrote in mid-March 1915 that 'the Admiralty do not seem to have quite entered into the arrangements . . . for purchasing through a common channel'.[55] In fact, the bulk of the Admiralty orders in the United States to June 1915 were not placed through Morgan's; the firm was not even informed of a number of them.[56]

The response of the War Office was more ambiguous. Occasionally the War Office preferred to place orders through brokers they had previously employed, and the reservation clause (Clause 14) allowed them to do so. This, naturally, encouraged the activities of brokers, activities which caused serious difficulties during the early months of 1915. The markets for raw materials and machine tools were kept in a state of ferment, and it therefore became extremely difficult to place contracts on anything like reasonable terms or to prevent interference with existing contracts. Morgan's protested very strongly and on 11 February 1915 the Director of Army Contracts, U. F. Wintour, gave instructions that no orders were to be placed except through Morgan's without his express authority.[57] Yet, many large American firms continued to approach the War Office through their own brokers, negotiating with Morgan's concurrently and playing the one off against the other. The fact that Morgan's were, in most cases, already in touch with the manufacturers whose offers the brokers submitted made their activities unnecessary, if not mischievous.

Brokers who had previously dealt directly with the War Office resented the Morgan appointment, not surprisingly, and made strenuous efforts to retain their position; in a few cases, where they lacked expertise, Morgan's acquiesced, although 'there is no evidence that any firm persisted in its refusal to negotiate'[58] through Morgan's.

In certain cases direct negotiations between the War Office and the agents of American firms were carried on in London: some corporations, such as the Bethlehem Steel Corporation, had technical experts as well as financial representatives in London and the War Office liked negotiating there, and then directing Morgan's to sign the contract. This often led to the War Office's paying higher prices than were necessary. Morgan's took very strong objection: 'these transactions discouraged their [Morgan's] endeavours to serve the British Government, and impaired their ability to negotiate. If it were generally known that American manufacturers could secure better prices by negotiating direct through their London representatives they would of course be unwilling to negotiate through Messrs. J. P. Morgan & Company.'[59] The large gun orders placed in the United States with the Bethlehem Steel Company in June 1915 were negotiated in London. This gravely prejudiced Morgan's position and there was a great risk of their withdrawal from the Agreement.[60] However, Lloyd George had by now become head of a new Ministry of Munitions and the position of Morgan's became much easier, since he was fully in accord with their attempt to bring order into British purchasing.

The appointment of Morgan's as purchasing agent was a not unmixed blessing for the British government. The firm, the partners in which were largely staunch Republicans, was politically at odds with the Democratic Administration in Washington, a situation which was to prove awkward during the presidential campaign in 1916, and in 1917. Further, the corollary of its leading position in American economic life was that it was seen as a symbol by sections of the Midwest and South of all that was objectionable in the Eastern financial community; the danger was that the British government and Morgan's would be perceived as partners in obloquy. Morgan's was in fact later charged not only with having made excessive profits out of its position, both in commissions and in directing business towards firms in which its partners had an interest, but in having taken a leading role in nudging the United States into an unnecessary war in order to save its financial position.[61] Nevertheless, the British government was generally satisfied with Morgan's performance as purchasing agent, and was very upset when Morgan's resigned their commission after the United States entered the war. (It will be seen in Chapter 4 that Morgan's performance as financial agent was less satisfactory to the British government.)

Money, and especially the amount Morgan's was deemed to have made from its position, formed the gravamen of both the current and the later attacks on the firm. It is difficult to know how important the activities of the Export Department bulked in the firm's accounts. Certainly, it began as an appendage, but equally certainly, it assumed a proportionately more important position. One reason for this, of course, was the scale of purchasing. Kitchener had thought that no more than $50m.'s worth of orders would be placed in the United States;[62] in the event, the total went over $20,000,000,000 within two years.[63] The importance of the Commercial Agency relative to other Morgan interests increased, also, because of the ethical behaviour of the partners; all of them took great pains not to be caught in a conflict of interest, and by and large they sold their stocks in any companies with which they dealt for the British government.[64] The funds realised from these sales were quite probably then used to help Britain finance her purchases: Morgan's advanced funds to Britain at 2 per cent interest in the form of a demand loan, and although part of this was placed with other banks, the partners themselves carried a large part of it (for example, on 22 December 1916 the demand loan amounted to $258m., of which Morgan's alone carried $138m.).[65] The income from this interest, plus the income from the Commercial Agency (according to one report, commission totalled $30m. altogether),[66] doubtless formed a large proportion of the partners' income during the war. On the other hand, this commission may be regarded as a reasonable reward for the risk which Morgan's carried, in that the loss of the war by Great Britain could well have meant financial ruin for them. A principal reason why Morgan's took this risk appears, from private communications between the New York and London firms, to have been a genuine Anglo-American patriotism. And Britain was a satisfied customer.

2
British Purchasing in America: the Ministry of Munitions, June 1915 to April 1917

From the outset of war, Lloyd George had grasped the need to provide greater supplies of armaments at a faster pace than seemed possible by means of the traditional methods. There were two obvious courses of action: existing British suppliers could be reorganised and more tightly controlled, and new sources of supply could be located and developed. Lloyd George supported both courses, but until he became Minister of Munitions in May 1915 he could only support, and not insist upon, any given action. In August 1914 he had no direct control over British munitions, since that was the province of the War Office, and Kitchener jealously guarded his turf. All Lloyd George could do as Chancellor was to remove any financial restrictions on the purchase of war supplies. As for locating new sources of supply: he had lighted on the United States as a new source, and had supported the appointment of J. P. Morgan & Co. as the firm best suited to exploit American industrial production, but here, too, decisive action on his part had to wait until May 1915.

Beginning in September 1914, rumours began to circulate, first in Whitehall, then in Westminster and finally in the world outside, of a growing shortage of munitions. The appointment of the Cabinet Committee on Munitions in October 1914 was one result of that concern, and Lloyd George's membership of that committee served continually to stimulate his interest in the problem. It also should have made him aware of some of the problems involved in manufacturing munitions, but more cynical souls, such as Kitchener and von Donop, doubted whether this was the case. Lloyd George had a touching faith in the ability of any engineering firm – no matter what its previous experience

– to manufacture the most complicated weapon or shell. He also had a strong belief in the powers of exhortation: he appeared to believe that if he brought his powers of persuasion to bear on manufacturers in order to cajole them into agreeing to an earlier delivery date than they had thought possible, then that was the equivalent of delivering the weapons to the Western Front. There is little doubt that Lloyd George's persuasiveness, energy and willingness to trample across lines of command sometimes worked wonders, but there is equally little doubt that these elements in his personality sometimes conjured up illusions of munitions where none could possibly be made to exist.

He had taken part in the discussions about utilising Morgan's to organise the purchasing of war supplies in the USA, and it is therefore not necessary to search far for the inspiration for his Cabinet memorandum of 22 February 1915. In this memorandum, Lloyd George proposed that, in order to increase the supply of munitions, British industrial and manpower resources should be centrally organised.[1] Kitchener reacted to the suggestion with hostility, and it was only on 7 April, after some weeks of simmering antagonism between Lloyd George and Kitchener, that Asquith announced the formation of a committee (known as the Treasury Committee) which had 'full authority to take all steps necessary' to utilise the resources of the country to provide munitions for the army and navy.[2] The committee however turned out to be totally useless, since Kitchener refused to delegate any of his authority to supply the army to a mere civilian committee.

This deadlock between Lloyd George and Kitchener was only resolved by the events of May 1915. Admiral Lord Fisher, the First Sea Lord, resigned on 16 May 1915 in protest against the Dardanelles policy of Winston Churchill, the First Lord of the Admiralty. This triggered off a political crisis, the result of which was the reconstruction of the government as a coalition. During the same week, the 'Shells Scandal' blew up. Incited by Sir John French, the Commander-in-Chief of the British Expeditionary Force in France, *The Times*'s Military Correspondent (Lieutenant-Colonel Charles à Court Repington) wrote that British forces had been unsuccessful in the Battle of Festubert because of a shortage of high explosive shells. His dispatch was printed on 14 May and was the first in a series of articles published by the Northcliffe press attacking the government, and especially Lord Kitchener, for their supposed inaction in overcoming the shortage of munitions. The campaign did not destroy Kitchener, but it certainly brought the problem of munitions to a fascinated public's attention.[3]

A result of this combination of circumstances was the establishment of a new department of state, the Ministry of Munitions, with Lloyd George as its head. (It was necessary that it be a separate department, rather than part of the War Office, in order that it might wield executive authority.) Lloyd George and likeminded supporters took advantage of the temporary fluidity of the political scene to work for the establishment of the new department.[4] The Shells Scandal, by making the public anxious about the shortage, created an atmosphere conducive to a novel solution. Lloyd George knew better than anyone the need to grasp the hour, and on the day the new ministry was established, 26 May 1915, he whirled into his new office and began to organise. Statutory authority only caught up with him on 9 June 1915, when the Ministry of Munitions Act received the Royal Assent.

As Munitions Minister Lloyd George was soon once more concerned with the state of the American market. He wrote that 'From what I hear we can enormously increase the American output, and what is almost equally important, we can expedite it'.[5] The obvious move would have been to inquire from Morgan's whether American capacity could be increased and deliveries quickened. But Morgan's were now the proper channel, and Lloyd George instinctively evaded them as earlier he had evaded the War Office and approached Morgan's. He decided to send a small mission to the United States to look into the situation, without considering whether or not this would undermine Morgan's position, and on 12 June 1915 he asked D. A. Thomas if he would undertake the task. Thomas was somewhat reluctant – on returning from an earlier government mission to supervise the shipment of munitions from the United States to Britain he had narrowly escaped drowning when the *Lusitania* was torpedoed – but he finally agreed to go.[6]

Thomas was a Welsh coalmine-owner and Liberal politician (a longtime colleague and sometime rival of Lloyd George).[7] More to the point, he had considerable business interests in the United States: he thus knew his way around and would not be dependent upon Morgan's for advice. On 23 June Lloyd George explained to the House of Commons his intentions in sending Thomas:

in consequence of the great importance of the American and Canadian markets and of the innumerable offers which I have received, directly and indirectly, to provide shell munitions of war...it was very desirable that I should have someone there who...should be able to represent the Munitions Department in the transaction of business there and find out exactly the position...I propose to ask Mr D. A. Thomas to go over to America for the purpose of assisting us in developing the American market...Mr Thomas will co-operate with Messrs. J. P. Morgan & Co....with a view to expediting in every way the supply of munitions. While invested with full powers he will, no doubt, act in consultation with the authorities at home, except in cases of special urgency.[8]

The other members of the mission were Major-General R. H. Mahon of the War Office, an artillery expert, and R. H. Carr, the Secretary to the mission.[9] The group sailed on 26 June 1915.

They arrived in New York on 15 July. The original intention had been to proceed immediately to Canada, but this was postponed when it was belatedly learned that the Canadian Prime Minister had just left for Britain, and the first three weeks were spent in New York instead.[10] Although Spring Rice met Thomas at the boat and they had a long discussion on the problems involved, Thomas felt that the less direct contact he had with the Embassy the better, for it was his intention to conduct the business of the mission as quietly and unofficially as possible. Both he and Spring Rice feared that the cry would be raised in the United States that the mission had come over to organise American industry in the British interest, and since Lloyd George had announced in the Commons that the duties of the Thomas mission entailed precisely that, it would have been astonishing if there had not been some American reaction. But Thomas and his two colleagues kept their heads down, doing everything possible not to offend – publicly – against American neutrality,[11] and there was no lasting harm done by the announcement.

Thomas was specifically charged with ascertaining the possibilities in the United States for supplying heavy guns and ammunition, machine guns and rifles, and with taking any necessary steps to increase the supply at the earliest possible moment.[12] More generally, however, according to Lord Eustace Percy, Thomas's business in the United States was mainly to arrange with Morgan's methods of placing orders,[13] while Sir Edward Grey, the Secretary of State for Foreign Affairs, later minuted that he had been sent to the United States mainly to inquire into complaints there *against* Morgan's.[14] Lloyd George assured H. P. Davison (then in London), however, that Thomas's intention was to co-operate with Morgan's. Thomas himself confirmed this to Davison, when he talked with him before sailing from London. Davison was pleased with Thomas, characterising him as a 'clean cut business man' who appreciated the importance of centralisation.[15] Morgan's fears of interference with their attempts to centralise purchasing were thus quietened.

Thomas spent the first three weeks in New York familiarising himself with Morgan's, meeting manufacturers and investigating cases of complaint or offers of matériel. He decided that as far as the actual business of negotiating for and purchasing of munitions was concerned, Stettinius and the Export Department of Morgan's were extremely efficient, and that there was no question as to the soundness of the decision to appoint a single agent. The weakness of the Export Department lay in its arrangements for investigating whether firms tendering offers had the technical ability to carry out the orders, and for following up contracts and expediting deliveries. Thomas observed that the last functions might perhaps have been regarded as falling to the British military inspectors (who had previously been sent out by the War Office and the Admiralty to specific firms to advise on technical points, to inspect materials and to pass goods delivered for shipment), but that, owing to the enormous area which they had to cover and to the inadequacy of their numbers, it was impossible for them to do much in that direction without detriment to their main function.

Thomas discussed these difficulties with Stettinius, who agreed with him about the weakness of the facilities for investigating possible new plant; he urged Thomas to obtain the assistance of additional experts from Britain. This Thomas was loath to suggest to the British government, since he was fully aware that there was a shortage of suitable experts. Thomas determined to see whether, by enlisting the services of the representatives of the Ministry of Munitions and the War Office who were already in the United States, he could form a satisfactory organisation to carry out this work. Moreover, the desirability for other reasons of drawing together the various independent representatives of the government then engaged on separate missions was in itself obvious to Thomas: *someone* ought to know who they all were and precisely what they were all doing in the United States. The new organisation would be complementary to the Export Department at Morgan's, in that it would undertake the technical duties which Morgan's agreed were necessary, but which they were neither equipped nor eager to carry out.

On 12 July 1915 he formed an Advisory Committee drawn from British government representatives already in the United States, the principal functions of which were to examine the facilities of new firms seeking contracts for munitions, and to investigate charges against Morgan's to the effect that responsible manufacturers declined to act through the firm. Further, the committee provided Thomas with permanent and effective representation in the United States during his frequent absences in Canada. He appointed as chairman of the committee Lieutenant-General L. T. Pease, who had virtually completed an investigatory mission for von Donop. Other members of the committee were H. Japp, President of the firm S. Pearson & Son of Canada, who was helping the Ministry of Munitions to speed up deliveries ordered from American manufacturers, and J. P. Sneddon, a consulting engineer, who was assisting Morgan's by advising on the capacity of plants.

With the increasing importance to the Ministry of Munitions of speeding up deliveries, and of obtaining accurate and systematic information on the progress of contracts and the outlook with regard to future deliveries, it became necessary to expand considerably the scope of the committee, which, on 5 September 1915, was enlarged by Thomas into the British Munitions Board. Pease continued as chairman, while Lieutenant-Colonel C. E. Phipps, head of the British Inspectorate in the United States (see below), was appointed deputy chairman. Japp and Sneddon continued on the new Board, and Thomas added F. W. Abbot, an English construction engineer with wide experience in the United States and elsewhere, and Captain B. C. Smyth-Pigott, the inspector of small arms, who had paid his first visit to the United States for the War Office in 1914. It was devoutly hoped that the Board could eliminate the overlapping of the various officials who were representing the British government in the United States and paying independent visits to manufacturers.[16]

The work of the Board fell naturally into three sections: the New Work Section handled new work, investigating the ability of new firms tendering for munitions contracts; the Follow-Up Section did just that, watching orders on contracts already placed, both before and after deliveries had begun; and the Record Section was responsible for statistics and for drawing up formal progress reports, sent fortnightly to the ministry. There were in addition two inspection departments which were not, strictly speaking, under the administrative control of the Board, the one (under Phipps) being responsible for guns and ammunition, the other (under Smyth-Pigott) being responsible for small arms. By mid-October 1915 the organisation was working reasonably smoothly, and the division of functions between Morgan's and the Board was quite clear: Morgan's negotiated contracts for munitions and paid for them, and the Board watched the production and arranged for transport and shipment.[17]

Thomas fell ill, and entered hospital in early November, where he remained until he sailed; he arrived back in Britain in mid-December 1915.[18] Upon his arrival he presented to Lloyd George a report which described his activities and made some recommendations. He advised that General Pease be placed in charge of all the technical officers representing the ministry in the United States, so that his position would be seen as that of the ultimate technical authority representing Britain in the United States. He advised that the inspection staff should be increased and that Colonel Phipps, the head, should transfer his headquarters from Bethlehem Steel Company to New York City, to keep him from being associated with one firm, and to facilitate co-operation between Phipps, Pease and Stettinius. He supported Morgan's in advising strongly against the ministry's dealing with agents of American firms in London such as those representing the Bethlehem Steel Company, on the grounds that it severely damaged Morgan's position as British agent, and thereby led to higher prices for British government contracts. He suggested some redistribution of those contracts from the East to areas such as the South and Midwest: the resources of the big industrial firms in the East were already so heavily drawn on that there was now little room for expansion, and it would be politically astute to place contracts where feeling against the Allies (or against Morgan's) was extant or in danger of building up. However, he felt – in common with Morgan's – that if it were at all possible, the ministry should refrain from placing any further munition orders in the United States at all, since the capacity of currently capable firms was fully taken up, there were growing labour problems stemming both from a scarcity of skilled labour and from pro-German agitation, and there was the growing difficulty of finding finance. He then reported on his efforts concerning guns, rifles and machine guns.

Finally, Thomas recorded his high opinion of Pease's work, and stated that he had 'no hesitation in saying that the representation of the Ministry of Munitions in the United States may with the utmost confidence be left in his hands'.[19] However, on returning to Britain, he found that Lloyd George, without consulting him, had already appointed E. W. Moir as Pease's successor. It is clear that Lloyd George could hardly have withdrawn his invitation to Moir, but the fact that Pease was in the United States originally at the behest of von Donop would hardly have recommended him to Lloyd George. It was von Donop's empire, after all, that Lloyd George had usurped, and many elements in the War Office remained unreconciled to the new order. Pease therefore returned to Britain after Moir had taken up his duties in the United States.[20]

Early in November 1915, presumably upon receipt of the news that Thomas had gone into hospital in the United States, Lloyd George had contacted Moir and asked him to go to the United States as the Ministry of Munitions' representative there. Moir was a civil engineer and contractor, a partner in S. Pearson & Son and the Controller of Munitions Inventions in the ministry. Moir wrote back on 6 November, accepting the responsibility, and stating the conditions of his tenure: that he would possess plenary power and refer to nobody but Lloyd George, that he would have full authority to make such contracts through Morgan's as he thought necessary, and that while he would not deal with highly technical questions, he would control the staff of the inspecting departments, which did.[21] Three days later Moir withdrew his letter, since his eldest son had just been killed on the Western Front; but Lloyd George convinced him that he was needed, and on 22 November Moir agreed to go.[22]

He sailed for the United States on 13 December 1915. Spring Rice was not at all happy about the substitution of Moir for Pease, and in January 1916 he wrote to Grey complaining of Moir's attitude and temperament. He felt that Moir was 'putting up the back of all American business men with whom he comes into contact'; he had an abrasive personality and he tried to bully the Americans. Most importantly, he and Stettinius, the head of Morgan's Export Department, did not get along, and Britain could not quarrel with Stettinius without also quarreling with Morgan's, an event which Spring Rice believed would be disastrous.[23] Considering Spring Rice's close relationship with J. P. Morgan, it is probable that he was conveying Morgan apprehension, as well as his own fears that Moir would needlessly disturb Anglo-American relations.

Grey passed Spring Rice's letter on to Lloyd George, who had Sir Frederick Black and Eric Geddes, members of the ministry's Munitions Council in London, comment on it. Black, who was Director-General of Munitions Supply, wrote that Spring Rice was reacting to Moir's forceful personality. He felt that Morgan's had feared that Moir had been sent out to supersede them, but that they were now reassured on that point; they knew that Moir would act as a progress agent for the ministry, in replacement of Pease but with a stronger organisation. He stated that Moir's recent letters had shown that his only criticism of Stettinius and Pease was that they had not fully realised the importance the ministry attached to getting trustworthy information about probable deliveries, and not merely accepting assurances that contractors were doing their best. Moir was doing what he had been sent out to do: to form a practical judgement about the future progress of deliveries from manufacturers. Geddes, the Deputy Director-General of Munitions Supply, felt that Moir should have the substance of Spring Rice's complaint placed before him, in a letter which, at the same time, showed that the ministry had full confidence in him. As well, Lloyd George himself should talk to J. P. Morgan and try to reassure him.[24]

The fact that there was considerable friction between Morgan's and Moir (see note 24) was very apparent when Lloyd George saw Stettinius and Morgan during their visit to Britain. They seemed convinced that Moir intended to place orders with new firms independent of the Export Department, and in an interview with Lloyd George in early March 1916 offered to give up the agency. Lloyd George decided against accepting this and wrote to Moir on 9 March that there must be closer co-operation between his agency and Morgan's; all firms offering supplies should be referred to Morgan's, and Morgan's should receive a copy of all official reports.[25] He suggested that there should be a conference between Moir, Stettinius and Morgan; this took place upon the return of the latter two men to the United States. Moir wrote to Lloyd George on 31 March that they were now working in harmony, although he could not forbear from defending his own conduct.[26]

Moir's attitude can probably be ascribed to the immensity of the task he had been set. Upon his arrival in New York, he found that 'from the production and shipping point of view...the American supplies were in a very unsatisfactory position.'[27] He turned to the production side first, redistributing the functions of the British Munitions Board: he combined the New Work and Follow-Up Sections and allocated the responsibility for different classes of munitions, such as shells or small arms, to separate individuals, who jointly formed what was afterwards known as the Progress Department, under the direction of Moir with Japp as chief of staff. The functions of the Progress Department (or

Quantity Inspection Department, as it was sometimes called) were to expedite delivery in every way by visiting the factories of contractors and subcontractors and, where needed, suggesting changes. They pointed out inefficient plant, suggested new sources of supply, helped contractors obtain additional plant and generally did what they could to help contractors produce the largest quantity of whatever they were producing as quickly as possible.[28]

The aims of the Progress Department were found to conflict with those of the other major department working to produce munitions: the Military Inspection Department, the overriding concern of which was the *quality* of goods produced. Thomas in his report had already reported unfavourably on the position of Phipps as head of the Inspection staff, and Pease and Morgan's had agreed with him. Now Moir echoed Thomas's complaint that the headquarters of the staff should not be in a firm which had to be inspected (Bethlehem Steel), and that Phipps as head should be travelling and inspecting the inspectors, instead of doing proof-butt work. Moir in addition disliked the quasi-autonomous position of the Inspection Department, feeling that all branches having to do with munitions in the United States ought to be under the control of the representative of the Ministry of Munitions (as the Ministry of Munitions felt about War Office munitions activities in Britain). He felt that the staff very much resented, as military men, any civilian interference in the inspection of munitions. The administrative outposts of the Lloyd George and Kitchener empires were in fact engaging in the same demarcation disputes as their counterparts in London. Lloyd George backed Moir and decided that the Military Inspection Department should be reorganised and its headquarters transferred to New York, with General F. F. Minchin being sent out to take over its supervision under Moir. Minchin arrived on 14 April 1916 and shortly thereafter the headquarters were moved to New York. Moir reported on 9 May that the new arrangements were working well and that closer touch between the quantity and quality departments would increase efficiency.[29]

The other problem Moir had to consider was that of the arrangements for transporting the finished munitions, both by rail and by sea. Luneham & Moore, an American forwarding firm, had been appointed by Morgan's to take charge of forwarding arrangements, but a backlog of supplies had once again built up. By February 1916 it was necessary to move 90,000 tons of freight monthly for the Ministry of Munitions alone. A major difficulty was that Luneham & Moore shipped 90 per cent of the freight from New York, and on 16 February, for example, 20,000 tons of freight had accumulated there.[30] By late March Lloyd George was writing testily to Black that the transport problem in the United States 'Seems to be very unsatisfactory. I should like to know what Mr Moir is doing to improve matters. It seems to me to be specially one of the objects he was sent out to America for.'[31] Moir had formed a Traffic Department under E. J. Karr to assist Luneham & Moore and to deal with the railroad transport of materials to the ships. The ministry, in response to a cable from Moir, sent out a Mr Fellowes to help, and pressed the Admiralty to provide more shipping.[32] On 31 March Moir replied to Lloyd George's inquiry:

> the whole difficulty has been the lack of ships...I have been pushing Messrs. Luneham & Moore to make use of other ports, which they have been doing in some measure...Mr. Fellowes... has been going around with...Mr. Karr...visiting the various ports in the country and the railroad companies, trying to find additional facilities for shipping and railroad transport....[33]

By 1 April he wrote that he had nearly finished organising a department to handle the forwarding of goods, but was awaiting Fellowes's conclusions.[34] When he acted upon them, the result was that many ports in addition to New York were utilised, and the congestion of munitions was eased.[35]

By mid-May 1916 Moir had decided that his presence in the United States was no longer required, on the grounds that the machinery he had created was sufficient to carry on the work of producing and shipping munitions in the United States, and that he could supervise the American Section of the Ministry of Munitions (as it was called in London) from London. Lloyd George was at first reluctant to allow Moir to leave the United States, on the curious ground that his organisation contained a number of departments with separate heads. He, or someone, was presumably afraid that if Moir returned to London, the organisations he had welded together in the United States would break up into warring factions. Moir arranged to resuscitate the British Munitions Board, which had never been dissolved, composed of himself as President and Japp and Minchin as Vice-Presidents, with a selection of the chief men in each department as a committee. Japp and Minchin were to alternate as chairmen of meetings, and each would continue in his own sphere – Japp concerned with production and forwarding, and Minchin with design and inspection. Moir stated that both men were in accord with the arrangement. Lloyd George then reluctantly acquiesced in Moir's return.[36]

Upon his return to London, Moir continued to control the American Section of the Ministry of Munitions. He and Lloyd George were still concerned about the shipping arrangements and one of Lloyd George's first instructions to him upon his return was to go to the Admiralty and try to convince them to establish 'some Admiralty control in the United States for the shipment of munitions.'[37] What control there was over merchant shipping was exercised by the Admiralty Transport Department – a situation which persisted until the establishment of the Ministry of Shipping in December 1916. Since the Admiralty Transport Department had no representative in the United States, it was necessary to cable London for a decision, with a concomitant loss of time every time a question arose over the provision of a ship to carry munitions. As a result of a conference with Moir held on 20 June 1916 the Admiralty sent Lieutenant Connop Guthrie to the United States with the power to decide on the spot questions which had hitherto been referred back to London. To encourage co-operation, his offices were located close to those of the Shipping Department of the Ministry of Munitions in New York. The result was a much smoother shipping procedure with a better distribution of freights over the different ports.[38] After he had been there for some months Guthrie strongly recommended replacing Luneham & Moore with an *ad hoc* organisation he proposed to form. The Foreign Office, however, vetoed the idea on the basis that Britain should not appear to contravene the American neutrality laws – and especially should not do so just before the presidential election in November 1916 – since this might prevent Britain's placing of a loan in the American money market.[39] The shipping arrangements thus continued as they were until 1917.

In the area of production, the natural conflict between quantity and quality continued, and Christopher Addison, Parliamentary Secretary to the Minister of Munitions, reported in September 1916 that Minchin, head of the Military Inspection Department in New York, was opposed to Moir's interfering in design questions.[40] In October Minchin resigned, in order to spend more time on his work with the Anglo-Russian Sub-Committee (see Chapter 3) and Colonel L. R. Kenyon was appointed the chief of inspection.[41] But conflict between the War Office and the Munitions representatives continued, and in

December 1916 George Booth felt constrained to write to Addison (now Minister of Munitions) to protest about the situation. He stated that the nature of the Ministry of Munition's representation in the United States was unsatisfactory; that everyone agreed that the American Section had to have a chief administrative head, but that Moir was alone in thinking that the head could reside in London. He continued:

> The present position concerning interdepartmental work, is really pathetic. Japp telegraphs to his chief, Moir, to complain that Kenyon does not give him information; Moir sees Holland who cables out to Kenyon saying please give Japp all the information he requires; Kenyon telegraphs back to Holland that he is giving Japp all the information he requires....[42]

In short, Moir was out of touch with the American situation.[43] But in spite of this appeal, nothing was done until the entry of the United States into the war in April 1917 forced changes on the organisation.

The year 1916 grew increasingly difficult for the ministry and its purchasing mission. For one thing, the dollars necessary to pay for the munitions and supplies were becoming harder to find. But even more worrying, British relations with the United States were deteriorating, in particular over the Royal Navy's habit of stopping American merchant ships and hauling them into port. Here their cargoes might be confiscated, on the grounds that they were bound for an enemy belligerent, or at the very least held up. The enraged American exporters urged Congress to impose an embargo on the sale of munitions to the belligerents – in reality, given British command of the seas, to the Allies – and this threat became a very real one.[44] Another worry during the spring and early summer was the threat of an American war with Mexico: if war came, the American government would almost certainly commandeer any munitions being produced in order to equip her own under-supplied forces, thereby depriving Britain and the Allies of vital supplies.[45] In July 1916 relations became very difficult indeed, as the events of the month piled one on top of another. First, on 18 July the British government published a blacklist of American firms which they accused of trading with the Central Powers; the uproar stimulated by this publication in the United States can be imagined. Secondly, on 22 July came the unresponsive reply of the Foreign Office to the protest made by the American government on 24 May, in which the Americans objected to British interference with the mails; many American businessmen were convinced that the British were using the threat of German espionage as an excuse to steal American commercial secrets. And thirdly, on 28 July the British government executed Roger Casement for his part in the 1916 Easter Rising in Dublin, which enraged Irish-Americans and put intense strain on Anglo-American relations. Britain got off very lightly, in fact, since the main response of the Administration and the Congress was to amend a Revenue Bill to include a 12½ per cent Direct Profits Tax on the gross incomes of munitions manufacturers; the Bill became law on 8 September 1916.[46] The manufacturers, of course, immediately passed on the cost to the British government, although the government fought hard to prevent this.[47] Finally, in December 1916 came the Federal Reserve Board's warning to investors to beware of foreign (that is, British) issues, which for a time threw all of British finance and thereby purchasing in the United States into turmoil (see Chapter 4).

The purchasing mission itself, however, seems to have had little to do with the formulation of overall purchasing policy against this background. Thus, after Lloyd George's direction to his subordinates in May 1916 that the Ministry of Munitions was to make whatever purchases were deemed necessary without worrying about the cost,[48] the mission simply executed the minister's instructions with the greatest dispatch and economy possible. It was assumed that the Americans would not cut their own throats by prohibiting the trade which was so profitable for them; if a threat arose, it was left to the diplomatic representative to handle it. The mission confined itself, for example, to finding enough steel to buy for shipbuilding, to placing contracts for large guns at less than ruinous prices,[49] or to procuring adequate supplies of rifles.

The problem of rifles was especially intractable for the ministry and its mission. Addison wrote in May 1916 that deliveries of American rifles were unsatisfactory in both quality and quantity;[50] and by early June, out of one million rifles ordered in the United States, and now overdue, only 480 had been delivered.[51] By September, with 200,000 out of 1,600,000 delivered, the question arose as to whether Britain should give notice that the late deliveries would neither be accepted nor paid for, since the contracts allowed this notice to be given before the end of that month. Morgan's objected, saying that it would cause very serious difficulties, but the ministry decided to send in the notices.[52] Difficulties were caused, and by mid-October rifle contractors had decided that they would not go on manufacturing for the British government unless the government was prepared to take over the past liabilities incurred in relation to the contracts and also to protect the contractors against future losses. (The manufacturers were disheartened by the difficulties of manufacturing to the high standards required by the inspectors, by the repeated changes in design and by the relatively small proportion of rifles accepted.)[53] Morgan's was reluctant to recommend this, but they considered that if the government did not do so it would be impossible to arrange any more loans in the United States, and without these dollar loans it would be extremely difficult to pay for the supplies which Britain needed. Reginald McKenna, the Chancellor of the Exchequer, felt that the government was being black-mailed, but – with the financial difficulties constantly in his mind – he felt that they would have to pay. The Cabinet was livid, and there was some discussion about taking over the firms and putting in British nominees to run them. The Cabinet realised that if they told the firms to do their worst (that is, cease production) they would get neither rifles nor money, but they were reluctant to accede to the proposal as it stood.[54] It was not until December 1916 that an agreement to guarantee the financial viability of the firms was worked out and full production was resumed.[55]

The idea of taking over important suppliers and running them with British nominees was not a new one, and Britain was in the process of doing so when the above discussion took place. Britain and Russia were co-operating in taking control of the Eddystone Ammunition Company, although by leaving the same officials in outward control, Britain felt able to assure Robert Lansing, the American Secretary of State, in answer to his inquiries, that that was not in fact the case. Spring Rice was extremely worried about the probable consequences to Britain's position in the United States if it were discovered that Britain was contravening the neutrality laws so blatantly. If Lansing did discover this, he did not pursue the issue.[56]

By and large, however, the American Section of the Ministry of Munitions was quite above-board in its operations. As the needs of the Allies expanded in 1916, so had the mission, until by April 1917 it employed nearly 1,600 members in the United States. Its inspectors were in every factory which had a contract with Britain, its agent rode the trains carrying the munitions to port in order to prevent thievery and sabotage, and its agents watched the loading of the munitions on board the ships to prevent time bombs being placed aboard. Its relations with Morgan's were amicable. Its success as an organisation lay in its simultaneous efficiency and unobtrusiveness; even when Anglo-American relations were most strained, neither the Administration nor the Congress singled it out for attack.

3
Purchasing and the Allies, 1914–1917

Britain's duties as a member of an alliance went far beyond the provision of a mass army to fight on the Western Front or of the Royal Navy to command the oceans. Britain had also to provide vital supplies to her allies, and often the wherewithall to pay for them. Her importance as the wholesaler of the Entente stemmed primarily from two factors: in the first place, since she had been neither invaded nor occupied, her mines, fields and factories remained in working order, while those of important parts of, for example, France and Russia did not; and secondly, the British merchant shipping fleet was the largest in the world (although it grew increasingly smaller through attacks by German submarines), and this gave Britain access to world markets. Accordingly, she took the prime responsibility for providing supplies from the earliest days of the war. With such provision, however, came the extension of controls: the initial reason was to keep prices down, but controls also served to moderate the profligate spending of certain of the Allies, spending which was carried out by means of British credit. Two of the most important categories of supplies were munitions and wheat.

From the earliest days of the war Britain had controlled the purchases of the Allies in Britain. On 5 August 1914 France proposed to Britain that the latter should take over the purchasing of supplies for the French government in Britain in order to prevent bidding and a consequent rise in prices. A conference was arranged by the Foreign Office on 10 August. It was decided that there should be a small consultative committee, based in London, of two or more representatives of the French government who would act as buyers, together with representatives of the Admiralty, the War Office and the Board of Trade. Consequently, the Commission Internationale de Revitaillement (CIR) was established on 17 August 1914 with staff from the Board of Trade to do the clerical work. Belgium and Russia joined the CIR in September, and with the entry of other Allies into the conflict they were invited to participate; the CIR eventually covered all purchases in Britain and the Empire, and most purchases in the Allied countries and in most of the neutral countries, for France, Belgium, Russia, Serbia, Portugal, Japan, Italy and Romania. The United Kingdom was in fact the chief source of supply for the Allies. The CIR examined offers made by manufacturers and suppliers, considered Allied needs, consulted the British government about the availability of transport and finance, and either placed the orders or indicated the firms to whom they should be given. Large numbers of orders needed to be placed abroad, however, and whenever possible they were placed in the Empire.[1] The Allies were on a basis of equality in the CIR, the purchasing commission for the Allies in the Allied countries, but this was not necessarily the case where purchasing in the United States was concerned.

The position of France was somewhat different from that of the other Allies, in that France tried, for as long as possible, to maintain herself in a position of equality with Britain as far as purchasing and paying for supplies was concerned. Keynes, in fact, commented in March 1916 that Britain had only one ally, France, and that the rest were mercenaries.[2] From the beginning of the war France maintained separate purchasing missions in the United States, but she co-operated with Britain in that her purchases there were placed through Morgan's, which firm also acted as the financial agent for France in the United States.[3]

France, Britain and Russia held in Paris on 2–5 February 1915 the first joint financial conference of the war. Here, France agreed to share equally with Britain in the support of Russia, and all three agreed to pool their resources to assist their other allies.[4] Britain and France continued their co-operation with the Anglo-French Loan Mission to the United States in September–October 1915 (see Chapter 4). In September 1915, as well, the two countries signed an Agreement to establish an Inter-Allied Munitions Bureau, theoretically to co-ordinate purchasing in all neutral countries, but for the time being only in the United States. The Bureau was to concern itself only with those articles for which there might be 'injurious competition'.[5] The Bureau itself was not to purchase in the United States – both countries already used Morgan's – but was intended to co-ordinate their orders from London. The Agreement also stipulated that the purchasing missions in the United States would meet frequently and would consult with one another and with Morgan's.[6] Presumably the Bureau served to eliminate whatever friction there had been over purchasing in the United States.

The Anglo-French attempt at maintaining a position of equality for France had failed by May 1916, when Britain had to take over the financing of French purchases in the United States (see Chapter 5). By April 1917 Britain financed French purchases not only in the United States but also in Britain and the Empire, as well as supporting the French exchange. Yet, apart from grain, which was handled by the Wheat Executive for all of the Allies (see below), all contracts for France were placed in France's name, and Britain exercised no supervision over them and expressed no criticism of them.[7]

This was not necessarily the case with the other major Allies, Italy and Russia. Italy received by August 1915 a subsidy from Britain of £2m. a week,[8] and by September of that year, according to the Treasury, Italy would, without British help, have been unable to finance necessary imports of munitions and food.[9] Keynes used this lever in November and early December 1915 to attempt to force the Italians to concede some kind of supervision to Britain over Italy's chaotic purchasing activity, carried on by means of British credit. The best he could achieve was the incorporation of a clause into a loan agreement which provided for their representatives in the United States to act in consultation with British officials to avoid ruinous competition.[10] By April 1917, however, as Keynes wrote,

At first the money [provided by Britain] was expended by the Italian Government independently of the British Government. As time has gone on an increasingly large part of the orders has been placed through British government departments. Independent purchases are still made in France and Switzerland out of British credits and to a certain extent in the United States, the last-named being limited by the independent resources which the Italian government have been able to raise in New York. Orders elsewhere, including the great bulk of the North American purchases, are placed, as a rule through the British government departments, and only after previous approval by the British Treasury.[11]

If the Italians caused some difficulty, the Russians were even worse. In the early months of the war their agents had been among the most troublesome in bidding up prices for supplies in the United States.[12]

Britain was able to achieve some control over Russian activities through the medium of the CIR, in that as a result of the request of Russia in May 1915 for help in obtaining supplies in the United States, most Russian munitions orders were placed through the Ministry of Munitions.[13] Further, Keynes grabbed the chance presented in September 1915 by negotiations for Russian shipments of gold to the United States to persuade the Russians to agree to a procedure whereby all Russian purchases made on British credit would first be examined and approved by Russian and British representatives in London.[14] (Yet that did not prevent independent Russian orders. In one typical case, the Russians asked the Treasury to approve an order for locomotives, which the Treasury subsequently rejected. Russia nevertheless placed the order in the hope and expectation that Britain would accept the *fait accompli* and supply the necessary finance and tonnage.)[15]

At the same time as the gold agreement, Russia proposed to send a commission to the United States to place new contracts and to supervise contracts already made. The War Office welcomed the plan, except that it insisted that orders should be placed through Morgan's.[16] Accordingly, Russia set up a purchasing commission in the United States, headed by General Sapojnikoff, with representatives from the Ministries of War, Marine and Commerce. The appointment of Sapojnikoff was unfortunate, since one thing on which the British and certain Russians in the United States could agree was his lack both of ability and judgement.[17] In order to supervise contracts, Russian inspectors were appointed to the factories executing Russian contracts, and this immediately led to such difficulties that Morgan's felt constrained to register a protest: the standards of the inspectors were so high, and their inability to settle questions promptly so endemic, that the progress of work was being much delayed.[18] The complaint was passed on to Russia, and after some discussion it was decided in December 1915 to appoint a member of the British War Office, Colonel W. Ellershaw, to the Russian purchasing commission, which then became known as the Russian Commission.[19] This was a unique arrangement in the Alliance, since for no other ally was it necessary for Britain to keep a purchasing watchdog in the United States. It was, however, possibly the only way to reconcile the nearly irreconcilable: Russia wanted as large a provision of supplies as possible, to be financed in the main by Britain, with the minimum restrictions imposed on her freedom to place orders, while Britain needed to ensure that her ally received vital supplies without Britain herself being irrevocably crippled financially. Ellershaw was accompanied by T. S. Catto, a principal owner of the American-Levant Line, Limited, who arranged for the railway transport and shipment to Russia of munition orders.[20]

In spite of the Commission, the Russian inspectors continued to cause great difficulty, as Spring Rice reported in June 1916: 'Military Attaché reports very serious condition in Russian purchases of ammunition here and failure of Russian inspectors to pass finished material on frivolous grounds. Stettinius and Minchin both consider situation very grave and think a radical change of personnel absolutely necessary and extremely urgent.'[21] To try to resolve a problem which had been hampering production for a year, and which the large orders for shell recently placed for Russia had exacerbated, Britain negotiated an Anglo-American Agreement for Co-Ordination and Acceleration of Deliveries in July 1916. A major provision was the establishing of an Anglo-Russian Sub-Committee, to be based in New York, which was to control all matters relating to the execution of all orders placed in the United States for Russia, and which would include two representatives of Britain.[22] General Minchin soon thereafter resigned from the Ministry of Munitions organisation in order to deal with inspection for the sub-committee. Complaints about the inspectors dropped off thereafter.

By April 1917, as Keynes wrote,

> a very complete and elaborate machinery had been established for the purpose of supervising and criticising Russian demands. As time has gone on an increasing number have actually been placed through British government departments... The elaboration of such a system has been a matter of considerable difficulty. But it is now working well upon the whole. No order is now placed on behalf of the Russian government...which is to be financed out of British credits, except with the prior approval of the Treasury.[23]

Keynes added that, to mitigate the harshness of the system of supervision, the Russian government were given a monthly credit of £4m. to be at their disposal without supervision or criticism.[24]

By April 1917 Britain had, through the use of her financial power and through the exploitation of the undoubted efficiency of Morgan's and the purchasing missions in the United States, brought the purchasing of the Allies under nearly as strict a control as that of the British government departments themselves (and considering the case of the Ministry of Munitions, perhaps even more so). The organisational structure worked well until, under American pressure in the summer of 1917, it was subsumed within larger inter-allied bodies.

British attempts to control the purchasing of munitions by the various allies was a messy business, involving as it did separate and firmly held views as to the types and amounts required of weapons and ammunition. Wheat was easier. For one thing, wheat was wheat, with no need to argue over the calibre required; but beyond that, the organisation established by the British, from purchasing to shipping, was so obviously efficient that the Allies were happier to join efforts with the British.

Britain was very much dependent on imported wheat, and there had been recurring fears that an enemy would try to starve her out in time of war. Within the first week of war a Cabinet Committee on Food Supplies was set up, and the committee immediately instructed the Royal Navy to divert British grain-carrying ships from enemy to British ports and to take over the cargoes. The reaction, however, demonstrated the danger inherent in such activity: American grain dealers were outraged, and they threatened to suspend all shipments to Britain unless the Royal Navy stopped seizing their property. The British dependence on American grain (and American goodwill in general) meant that she had little choice but to give in, and on 20 August 1914 the Admiralty was instructed to stop diverting the grain-carrying ships.[25]

If Britain was not to be allowed to seize grain openly, perhaps she could accumulate it secretly. In November 1914 the Cabinet committee set up a Grain Supplies Committee whose brief was to build up a reserve stock of 1½ million tons of wheat and ½ million tons of flour; the intention was to release these supplies slowly on to the market during 1915 in order to prevent too great a rise in prices. The idea was to utilise the normal channels of trade, and thus the contractors Ross T. Smyth & Co. were used as purchasing agent. However, if the plan was to be successful, it had to be secret, or prices would rise anyway. Walter Runciman, in fact, lied to the House of Commons in an attempt to keep the government's activities secret, insisting on 17 February 1915 that the British government had rejected the idea of buying wheat on its own account.[26] But the news leaked out in March, and the upshot was a grain 'importers' strike'[27] which lasted for some weeks. In the end the government had to withdraw from the market and hope that success at the Dardanelles would release Russian wheat on to the market,[28] but in fact only timely purchases of Indian wheat averted a crisis in 1915.[29]

But wheat prices continued to rise – they rose by 80 per cent in the first twelve months of the war[30] – and the activities of international speculators were being encouraged by competitive purchasing by the Allies. The Cabinet Committee on Food Supplies therefore decided in early 1916 to establish an International Joint Committee at the Board of Agriculture, to be chaired by Sir Henry Rew, which was to co-ordinate all purchases for the British reserve stock, for the Italian government and for the War Department of the French government. Messrs Smyth acted as purchasing agent for the committee, and Portugal and Belgium subsequently appointed representatives. Yet the French Department of Commerce, which purchased wheat for civilian requirements, refused to work through the joint committee and continued to compete actively in the world's markets.[31]

By midsummer of 1916 objections to government intervention were fading away, and official circles certainly supported a more forthright governmental policy. The poor harvest of autumn 1916 brought matters to a head, but there was a concatenation of causes which led to a reversal of policy. In the first place, there was a likelihood of crop failure in both North and South America, which would ensure a world deficit of wheat; secondly, even if the wheat were available on the world market, the German submarine campaign was steadily depleting the amount of tonnage available to carry the wheat; and thirdly, Britain's growing financial straits made it more and more difficult for the private trader in wheat to purchase exchange (to pay for foreign wheat) at reasonable rates. In these circumstances, the grain trade became unable to maintain the normal system.[32] Finally, a change in policy was encouraged by the growing political crisis, in which 'the demand for a more positive food policy became one of the main spearheads of attack on the Asquith coalition.'[33]

The Board of Trade and the Board of Agriculture therefore made representations to the Cabinet Committee on Food Supplies in September 1916, and it was decided that the government must now assume the responsibility for importing wheat. Thus, on 10 October 1916 the Royal Commission on Wheat Supplies was appointed, with Lord Crawford, now President of the Board of Agriculture and Fisheries, as the chairman.[34] It was soon found that control could not be confined to wheat and flour, and on 27 October the powers of the

Commission were extended to 'other grains',[35] and on 25 April 1917 to 'all pulses and all substitutes for wheat, pulses and their products.'[36]

The Commission was presumably modelled on the Royal Commission on Sugar Supplies, which had been set up in August 1914 (with full control over the trade) in that its conduct, in view of the technical nature of the business, was left as much as possible in the hands of those with the necessary commercial experience. In the case of sugar, purchases were negotiated by members of the Commission in daily touch with the market, and brokers representing every export market laid their offers before the Commission, and, if business resulted, were paid by the producers.[37] There was always a sufficient supply of sugar to be bought, however, which was not the case with wheat, so that it was vital to the latter case to eliminate competition as much as possible. Therefore, rather than use the usual procedure of sending cables to American shipping houses – which stimulated competition – it was decided to appoint representatives in the United States 'to purchase as near to the farmer as possible'.[38] A new firm, the Wheat Export Company, was set up in New York to represent the Commission, under the direction of the only two British grain firms which were already operating and resident both in London and New York. These were Ross T. Smyth & Company, which had been acting as a purchasing agent for the British government on and off since 1914, and Samuel Sanday & Company, and they provided the Commission with a fully equipped agency, as well as with a channel of communication similar to that of the Ministry of Munitions with Morgan's in New York via Grenfell. As the work increased it was necessary to appoint a member of the Commission to take charge of each of the chief exporting countries. The Wheat Export Company of New York was only one of several the Commission set up (there was another in Canada, for example), and since the circumstances governing the purchase and shipment of supplies varied so greatly between the different countries, no uniform method could be adopted; it was therefore necessary to invest each Commissioner with considerable powers both of negotiation and of local organisation.[39]

In New York the President of the Wheat Export Company was G. F. Earle, an Englishman who had spent his entire career exporting grain from the United States with the Sanday firm, and who headed the grain-purchasing department of the new company. Serving as chairman and first vice-president of the company was H. T. Robson, also English, a partner in the Smyth firm and a member of the Wheat Commission. He had been in charge of grain purchases for the British government in the Argentine in 1914–15, and in charge of purchasing grain in the United States and Canada for the International Joint Committee on behalf of Britain, France and Italy in 1916.[40] As the scope of purchases grew, so did the organisation, and other experienced grain men were sent out to help.

The primary reason for the growth in the Wheat Export Company in New York was that by the end of 1916 it was empowered to purchase for France and Italy as well as for Britain. Previous to the establishment of the Commission a joint committee representing France, Britain and Italy had purchased a limited amount of wheat, as noted above, but the growing difficulties of supply and finance led, at the instigation of France, to the formation of the Wheat Executive, which was to meet the Allied requirements by purchasing, allocating and transporting all cereals. By this time the most serious shortage was that of ships, and since it took three times as much tonnage to ship the same amount of wheat from Australia as from North America, the bulk of purchasing for the Wheat Executive fell to the Wheat Export Company of New York.[41]

The Wheat Executive was set up at the same time as the new Ministry of Food, which Lloyd George intended should control the importation and production of all foodstuffs. The new ministry

confronted existing bodies [the Wheat and Sugar Commissions] occupying positions of some independence. Their relations to the Ministry were not clearly defined for some time and they regarded control by the Ministry with some suspicion. Friction of a rather indeterminate character occurred from time to time, and though the right of the Ministry to control was not denied, the exercise of this right was, to say the least, not welcomed.[42]

It was decided to keep the Wheat Commission (and also the Sugar Commission) separate from the ministry, although all coercive power and administrative finance came from the ministry. (The official history, in fact, considerably understates the case when it refers to conflict, and the separation of the Commission from the ministry set the stage for a real battle in 1917–18. Sir John Beale became chairman of the Commission in August 1917 and he immediately, and continually, objected to his position's being interpreted as one of administrative subordination to the Permanent Secretary to the Ministry of Food, Ulick Wintour. The conflict was only resolved in September 1918 by

Wintour's forced resignation and Beale's assumption of Wintour's former position as Permanent Secretary.)[43] In the event, the purchasing mission to the United States, the Wheat Export Company, remained relatively untouched by the infighting in London.

The wheat-purchasing mission for Britain and the Allies, then, was in the form of a commercial company, staffed by men who made the grain trade their business. It acted in a commercial manner, and in fact, later in 1917, it cornered the American wheat market, with remarkable results in forcing down the price.[44] It will be seen in Chapter 7 that the American Administration was so impressed with the ability and efficiency of the Wheat Export Company that, after American entry into the war, it attempted to convince the British government to make the company the purchasing agent in the United States for all foodstuffs for the Allies.

The Allies, perhaps, were slightly less taken with the whole experience. While usually appreciating the need for common purchasing, and while recognising the efficiency of the British organisations involved, they resented the situation in which British power plus Allied need had landed them. As well, many of the Allied politicians and some of the Allied officials suspected that their own requirements were sometimes sacrificed to those of Britain, who controlled the bulk of the finance and the shipping. But an alliance is an unwieldy mechanism at the best of times, and when it is joined by what was in effect several cartels, it is not surprising if the outcome included frequent skirmishing.

4
Financial Relations, 1914–1915: the Growth of British Dependence

The international position of Great Britain and her Empire in 1914 had two main supports: the first was her command of the sea, based on the size and strength of the Royal Navy and the merchant shipping fleet, and the second was her command of international finance, symbolised and supported by the strength of the pound sterling. The financial and trading power exercised by the City of London was based on experience and expertise, and on a sophisticated banking system, one able to tap funds countrywide through a system of country and urban banks, and which centred on the experience and self-confidence of the Bank of England. The pound acted as an international medium of exchange, and the USA was not the only country to look primarily to London for short- and long-term trading and investment capital.

Given this background, it is arguable that one of the most important long-term results of the First World War for Britain was her exchange of position with the USA as dominant and subordinate financial powers. Over the four years of war, there was a growing British dependence on American finance. The reason for this was simple: being forced by circumstances to purchase munitions, food and other supplies in the USA, she was also forced to find the dollars to pay for them. This put an increasing strain on the sterling/dollar exchange. Thus Britain had, over the period of war, two separate but related problems: she needed to find the funds both to pay for supplies and to support the rate of the pound.

While the USA remained neutral, the American government did not make loans or grants to the British government and Britain came increasingly to look to the private money market in New York for the necessary funds. A theme of the period 1914–15 was a growing realisation on the part of the British that their own resources were not going to be sufficient for their needs, and that if Britain was not going to sink more and more deeply into financial trouble, she would have to try to tap American funds to pay for American goods. Neither the British government nor the Bank of England possessed the machinery for financial transactions in the USA, and J. P. Morgan & Co. were employed as financial agent. Ordinarily, any necessary financial transactions were carried out by Morgan's on behalf of the British government, but if events warranted it, special financial missions were sent out. During the period 1914–15 there were three such missions. The circumstances of the first of these, the Paish mission in October 1914, shows Britain acting as unquestionably the dominant financial power, perhaps for the last time. The mission was sent out in response to the request of the American Secretary of the Treasury for aid in resolving the financial crisis caused by the outbreak of war. The second and third missions, in the late summer and autumn of 1915, were motivated directly by Britain's increasing need for dollars.

From 1865 to 1914 the USA had been the single most important area for British long-term foreign investment, constituting almost 21 per cent of the new overseas issues in the British capital market; by 1914 the estimated aggregate of British funds invested totalled over £835m.[1] In July of that year, when war seemed imminent, panicky foreign investors urgently began selling these American securities in New York, intensifying a process which had been going on for several years, as European bankers built up their gold reserves. The scale now, however, was totally different, with the USA losing $45m. worth of gold in the single week ending 1 August. In addition to the gold drain, there was a second problem: the withdrawal of British facilities for capital and credit. The threat, and then the onset, of war had caused major crises in the main financial centres of Europe, which eventually spread to London. This had immediate ramifications for Americans, who regularly borrowed in London to finance short-term obligations. London was the centre of the international money market, and with its bankers refusing – or, with the paralysis of the foreign exchange market, unable – to lend, there was no immediate way to move the Southern cotton crop to market or to finance other exports, the proceeds of which annually paid short-term American obligations abroad. These obligations, estimated at $350m., stemmed largely from tourism.[2]

The Secretary of the Treasury, William Gibbs McAdoo, moved to alleviate the situation in several ways. On 31 July he agreed with the governors of the New York Stock Exchange that the Exchange should not open that day, in order to prevent the dumping of securities which would ensue with the – then imminent – closure of the London Exchange. Further, he had to deal with the breakdown in the rate of exchange (it had risen as high as $7 to the pound compared with the normal $4.86). In the days of the Gold Standard the rate was presumed immutable, but the implication was that gold could be shipped. With the safety of the sea lanes uncertain, insurance rates shot up astronomically. On 19 September 1914 delegates from the clearing banks and the Federal Reserve Board (which governed the twelve Federal Reserve Banks) met with McAdoo and they decided to set up a gold pool of $100m. to aid exchange by guaranteeing the nation's maturing obligations, and which would serve also to restore confidence and strengthen American credit. The government also decided to set up a War Risk Insurance Bureau to insure cargoes refused by private insurers. By mid-November 1914 the price of sterling exchange had fallen once more to par, and on 22 January 1915 the gold pool was terminated.[3]

The most visible problem arising from the lack of credit and the fall in exchange was that of moving the cotton crop, and here, after unsuccessful attempts to convince the South that it was a problem best handled by Southern banks, McAdoo bowed to pressure. The Treasury joined with New York bankers and the Federal Reserve Board to set up a Cotton Loan Fund of $135m. on 30 November 1914 to loan to producers at 6 per cent.[4]

Finally, McAdoo proposed to the British Ambassador, Spring Rice, that Britain send over a special agent to consider the problems of exchange and cotton, a suggestion which Spring Rice encouraged. Rumours that some sort of visit was being mooted had clearly been circulating in American financial circles, since two days earlier Morgan's had cabled to Morgan Grenfell that the New York partners had heard that the Bank of England wanted to send a representative to the USA to discuss the problem of settling American debts in London. Grenfell cabled back that the rumour was without foundation, and since he was one of the directors of the Bank, his reply was taken as authoritative. It was, so far as the Bank was concerned, but less than a week later the firm had to admit that a mission *was* going out to the USA. The Chancellor had decided to send Sir George Paish and Basil Blackett to confer with McAdoo. Paish had been editor of *The Statist* until his resignation in August 1914 to act as financial adviser to Lloyd George, and Blackett was a first-class clerk in the Financial Division of the Treasury. Grenfell thought that the whole idea was unsound, on the grounds that the Germans would claim that Britain was seeking financial help, and his disapprobation clearly influenced his New York partners. He thought that it was very important that the public should know that the journey was being made in response to McAdoo's request. Nevertheless, he commended Paish to J. P. Morgan, describing him as impracticable but honest (and pro-Morgan), and the two men sailed for America in early October 1914.[5]

They found in America a financial community webbed with complex hostilities. Between the Administration and bankers there was dissension and distrust: during the 1912 elections Wilsonian 'New Freedom' rhetoric had castigated massive aggregations of 'illicit' power in a few private institutions, among which figured the large New York banks; the bankers themselves resented the scope of the new Federal Reserve Act, which set up the Federal Reserve banking system, and particularly the aspect of governmental rather than private control; and more personally, both McAdoo and John Skelton Williams, the Comptroller of the Currency, had suffered at the hands of the New York financial community in their business affairs.[6]

The Federal Reserve Act had been the most recent battle-ground, with the members of the Federal Reserve Board only sworn in on 10 August 1914, while the new Federal Reserve Banks did not open until 16 November. It was uncertain who would control the Board (a problem not resolved for some years); McAdoo asserted the Treasury's overlordship while the Board perceived itself as independent of the Treasury and with the potential to develop into a Supreme Court of Finance. The Board itself was split over basic policies, with Paul Warburg, Adolf Miller and Frederick Delano generally acting in opposition to the Wilson Administration group of Charles Hamlin, Williams and McAdoo, leaving W. P. G. Harding often holding the balance. This split became of some moment to Britain later on in the war, since Warburg was pro-German and very influential; although an American citizen, he had been naturalised only in 1911, and his brother was head of the Hamburg branch of his bank, Kuhn, Loeb & Company.[7]

Yet in the event it was Secretary McAdoo who had the greatest influence on the development of American financial policy. President Wilson seldom concerned himself with finance, and McAdoo consequently was allowed a much freer hand to formulate Treasury policy, both foreign and domestic, than for example the Secretary of State was allowed in foreign policy. He had a personality of force and charm, but his drive to amass power in the Treasury – in his biographer's view, a major theme of his tenure[8] – and the methods he utilised tended to alienate even close supporters. Charles Hamlin, one of the members of the Federal Reserve Board who tended to support McAdoo, wrote in December 1917 that 'As a man...in spite of his brilliance, he was vindictive, rather treacherous, vain conceited & wildly jealous of anyone with him receiving any credit.'[9] Before the United States entered the war his primary goal was to assert Treasury control over the money market; after April 1917, if Colonel E. M. House, President Wilson's unofficial adviser, is to be believed, it was to assert Treasury control over the government.[10]

McAdoo's ambitions to dominate the situation were apparent to the British mission. Blackett felt that he wished to be 'the saviour of the financial situation'; the New York bankers, conversely, clearly did not welcome the mission, being either lukewarm or forthrightly hostile to the London visitors. Morgan's and their colleagues possibly took their cue from Grenfell, while other New York bankers, according to Blackett, were disinclined to ask favours of Britain.[11] McAdoo, however, was now publicly committed to making some sort of agreement with Britain.

The first week of the Paish mission's visit (16–22 October 1914) was taken up with preliminary meetings with the Reserve Board and with Hamlin and Warburg as a sub-committee of the Board. The discussion centred around the security to be given for a prospective British gold loan (to be utilised as a hedge against the gold drain). Britain asked first for the gold and then for American government obligations in the form of Treasury bills to be pledged as security, while the United States proffered some of the surplus cotton: both notions were eventually quashed. The first general meeting, held at McAdoo's invitation, took place on 23 October, and was composed of McAdoo, the Federal Reserve Board, fifteen bankers, and Paish and Blackett. The bankers felt that there was no need for special measures to deal with commercial exchange (although they were somewhat worried about a possible further European sale of American securities), but – Blackett perceived – McAdoo clearly did not wish them to return to London empty-handed after coming out at American invitation. Therefore a committee of bankers was appointed to discuss with the Reserve Board and Paish and Blackett whether any settlement could be proposed to the British.[12]

Paish met with Hamlin and Warburg and three New York bankers on 24 October and conceded that Britain would accept Treasury bills rather than gold as security for the gold loan.[13] Discussion continued on other technical points, and then on 30 October the meeting took place between Paish and Blackett and the committee appointed on 23 October. Much to McAdoo's dismay the bankers reported, yet again, that no special measures need be taken (other than to encourage Britain to buy American cotton – and the prevailing low price would probably encourage this anyhow), but at the urgent request of Warburg and McAdoo this memorandum was withdrawn. The following day Paish and Blackett were presented with a new scheme, which the Morgan partners thought had been drawn up solely by Warburg; after some hesitation they agreed to put it forward to the British government. (Hamlin felt that it was so favourable to the United States that he was sorry that it had not already been cabled to London.) Briefly, the plan was that there could be a revolving credit of £20m. to be administered through the Bank of England and British banks which would guarantee purchases of exchange to facilitate exports. Paish made the further concession that instead of requiring American government obligations as security, Britain would accept first-class stock exchange collateral and the guarantee of a private banking syndicate rather than insist on a guarantee's being backed by the American government or the Federal Reserve Banks. Nothing was to be done immediately, however, and the gold pools would continue to handle the foreign exchange situation; then when the New York Stock Exchange reopened, the credit, if necessary, could be utilised.[14]

Paish cabled the proposal to the Treasury and the Bank of England. But while he was awaiting his instructions, McAdoo was losing his ardour: around 14 November he told Hamlin that financial matters had so improved that it would not be harmful if the whole proposal were dropped.[15] On 20 November Paish, Hamlin and McAdoo met and Paish explained that the Treasury was so busy with war measures that he had not yet received any instructions; McAdoo assured him that he was in no hurry. In fact, for McAdoo as for the British, events were becoming distinctly embarrassing.[16]

Fortunately, on the same day the Treasury representatives received instructions to return to Britain to discuss the proposal. Blackett for one welcomed the recall – although he feared that McAdoo was disappointed – since the talks he and Paish had held with Benjamin Strong, Governor of the New York Federal Reserve Bank, J. P. Morgan and other leading bankers had left no doubt that their departure would be welcomed.[17] This opened the way to a resolution of the problem, however, as Strong suggested in a letter to McAdoo: H. P. Davison, a partner in the Morgan firm, would be travelling to London on the same boat with Paish and Blackett; he could get in touch with James Brown, partner of the New York banking firm Brown Bros, who was then in London, and together they could take up negotiations with Paish and the London bankers. He had discussed this with Paish who quite approved.[18] Paish himself wrote to McAdoo on 25 November that since the commercial situation had righted itself, the need for the bankers' committee plan had appreciably diminished since their arrival, but that it would facilitate the reopening of the New York Stock Exchange and the restoration of business to normal conditions by removing anxiety about the gold drain.[19] Most important of all, no one would lose face.

This in fact was the line urged upon the British Treasury by Blackett. He argued that bankers would be glad to see the plan agreed on both sides for use in an emergency; besides, private negotiations and an agreement of that nature would enable the Treasury to escape from a thoroughly awkward situation, one which had to be resolved in order to ensure good relations in the future.[20] Negotiations, therefore, meandered on, but on a private basis – and the plan was never carried out.[21]

Was the whole mission, then, an exercise in futility? In immediate terms, most certainly; Spring Rice even thought that it had given offence, since the American bankers, he felt, had resented the attempt to replace a 'gentleman's agreement' on the retention of gold with a definite arrangement.[22] Paish, however, disagreed, on the grounds that the crucial consideration had been the need to reassure the American bankers, and this had been accomplished. In a memorandum written after his return and widely circulated, he argued first that his wide discussions in America had convinced him not only that the Allies had the overwhelming support of the United States, but that this support could be utilised to enable the Allies to gain access to the economic wealth of America. He added (with some prescience) that France and Russia had immediate need for credit there, but that if the war were a protracted one, by 1916 even the resources of Britain would be strained; they all would need to buy goods on credit and pay with securities. As he put it, 'Such a transaction would place at the disposal of the Allies not only all of their own income but would enable them to draw upon the surplus wealth of the United States as well'. He felt that the bankers' committee scheme was desirable, therefore, because it would allay fears which might otherwise lead to the Allies' being prevented from selling securities and placing loans in the United States in 1915 on the grounds that these Allied transactions might cause a great flood of gold to leave the USA.[23] He was concerned here with the steps which France and Russia would probably have to take – but before the year was over Britain would be forced to do so as well.

In December 1914, for the first time since the war had begun, the rate of exchange in New York went against Britain. Other than in the Treasury, there was little response in the government to what was the beginning of a slide both in the rate of the pound in the United States and in the confidence of the American business and financial community in British ability to maintain it. It was not until nine months later that the Cabinet realised that it must take steps to support the exchange or else watch the structure of British credit crumble.

The fact that the internal financing of the war was being accomplished reasonably easily may have made it more difficult for the government to recognise how serious a problem the growing weakness of the pound might be. On 17 November 1914 the Chancellor had presented his first War Budget, which doubled the income tax and supertax and raised duty on beer and tea; on the same day he issued the first War Loan, for £350m., and it was very quickly oversubscribed. In addition, the government issued Treasury bills, usually for periods of three or six months, and, when there was too much short-term paper on the market, three- or five-year Exchequer bonds to mop up all the excess liquidity; the bonds and bills were issued to bridge the gap between successive War Loans (the second War Loan was issued in July 1915). Further, gold continued to be produced in the Empire, although it was largely left on deposit in the producer countries. There was thus no shortage of money to supply the Allied armies with those goods which could be procured within the Empire; it was the growing demand for foreign exchange, that is, dollars, to pay for the goods from America which was beginning to cause problems.[24]

The need to keep up the rate of exchange of the pound to the dollar was seldom openly questioned.[25] Britain had to buy on the world market and therefore had to maintain the rate in order that imports should not become dearer through a declining pound. It was true that the German exchange against the British and neutral currencies had fallen,[26] but because Germany controlled a compact area which produced most of her wartime requirements, she had little need for foreign exchange except to pay for supplies bought in the contiguous neutral countries, and for those she was willing to pay a premium. But there was a more important reason for Britain to maintain the pound: her prestige as a Great Power was tied up inextricably with the prestige of the pound as an international currency. As part of British propaganda the comparison had been drawn between the mark and the pound, the one losing and the other maintaining its value, and it was believed that loss of confidence in the pound would be tantamount to a major Allied defeat in battle.[27] Yet the pound had been in a position of supreme power relative to other currencies for so long that apparently it was difficult for members of the government to realise that its problems were very real; domestic and military topics probably seemed of more immediate concern.

The fight to keep confidence in the pound soon centred in the USA. Because of its supplies of food and raw materials such as wheat, cotton, petroleum and copper, and because of its actual and potential manufacturing capacity, the USA became the greatest foreign source of supply for Britain during the war. Already in 1915 the volume of imports from America was 68 per cent greater than in 1913.[28] Therefore the downward drift of the pound caused some concern in the government – if only amongst Treasury officials.[29]

The rate of exchange of the pound in New York deteriorated steadily through the spring and summer of 1915. The fall had begun by December 1914, and when by 15 February 1915 it had reached $4.79½ (from $4.86), E. C. Grenfell was moved to place the situation before the Treasury. Grenfell urged the government to take measures to shore up exchange, suggesting as one move the issuing of a British government loan in the United States, and J. P. Morgan & Co. in fact arranged with a group of New York bankers to make a temporary loan to the Bank of England in New York to steady exchange whilst preliminaries were settled to issue such a loan.[30] But nothing came of it, for, as Grenfell telegraphed to Morgan and H. P. Davison on 19 February 1915,

> Governor of Bank of England and I find it is impossible get authorities take any action in comprehensive manner on Exchange question at present (stop) Chancellor of the Exchequer and colleagues so fully occupied other matters that cannot give proper attention to this matter, and we think Exchange position may have to become worse before proper remedies taken. This may appear to you very foolish procedure but from your own experience dealing with Government officials you will

understand it is often impossible make them appreciate a difficult situation, especially on such complicated matter as Exchange. H. P. Davison knowing mentality of Chancellor of the Exchequer will specially appreciate our difficulty. . . .[31]

The situation continued to deteriorate, and by April the pound was down to $4.80. J. P. Morgan was in Britain, and on 1 April he had lunch with the Chancellor. Lloyd George asked him to find out whether Morgan's could place a long-time loan for $100–150m., with the proceeds to be used to control the exchanges. A rise in the stock market later in the month, however, encouraged the government to pull back, since they were in any case disinclined to borrow money in the USA at a rate more than 1 per cent higher than would be the case in Britain. By June the rate was just above $4.77, and Davison in New York wrote to Grenfell to warn him that the New York partners were very apprehensive about exchange conditions: they felt that the British authorities *must* have some solution in mind and they wanted to know what it was. Davison travelled to London himself where he conferred with the London partners and the Governor of the Bank of England on 23 June; they all agreed that something must be done, but what? The solution seemed to be a British government loan in New York, and Morgan's were asked to sound out the prospects amongst their associates. The answer – which was, in short, that the prospects were not very good – should have shaken the equilibrium of the authorities, but nothing was done to arrest the gradual slide in the value of the pound.[32]

By July the situation could no longer be ignored. On 20 July 1915 Grenfell informed the War Office that Morgan's in New York could not buy more dollars without forcing the rate below $4.77, and that there were munitions orders to pay for;[33] Reginald McKenna, the new Chancellor of the Exchequer, was forced to tell the Cabinet on 22 July that because of this inability to buy exchange, a contract entered into by Britain for Russia in the United States could not be completed.[34] At the request of the Bank of England, Morgan's in New York arranged a loan of $50m., which was guaranteed by $40m. in American securities provided, at the request of McKenna, by the Prudential Assurance Company, and £5m. in gold shipped by the Bank of England.[35] This provided the money for the down payments needed immediately and thereby gave temporary relief until, as Morgan's thought, more comprehensive arrangements could be made to meet the situation.

However, on 14 August Grenfell again had to write to Lloyd George at the Ministry of Munitions and inform him that the proceeds of that loan were nearly gone, that the rate of exchange had dropped to $4.70¼, and that to cover payments due the following week totalling $17m., Morgan's had only $4m. in hand.[36] The fear that Britain literally would not be able to pay her bills finally galvanised the government, and at the Cabinet meeting on 18 August 1915 it was agreed that American securities would be purchased by the government from their British owners for resale in New York, and that £100m. in gold (to which sum France and Russia would be asked to contribute, since Britain was guaranteeing a substantial amount of their purchases in the United States) would be shipped to America.[37] On 22 August the Chancellor led a small group to Boulogne for discussions with the French, where it was decided to send a joint mission to the United States (the Anglo-French Loan Mission) to attempt to raise a loan on the private market.

In order for the projected mission to succeed in raising such a loan, however, it would be vital to maintain the value of the pound during the negotiations, or the certain outcome would be a very public failure for the Allies. 'Maintaining the value', however, meant shipping gold to enable Morgan's to purchase pounds in New York to support the rate. Where was this gold to come from? The Treasury knew that Britain alone could not supply all the gold which might be necessary, since gold stocks in Britain had traditionally never been very high (particularly in comparison with some of the continental countries such as France) and the Treasury had already been financing its allies for nearly a year. The Treasury knew, however, that the Bank of France had managed to increase its gold stocks by about £40m. during the period 1913–15; further, at the meeting in Paris of the Allied Finance Ministers in February 1915, the decision had been taken to pool financial resources. It was natural, therefore, for the Treasury to look covetously at the gold stocks of its allies: if British credit was used to guarantee French and Russian purchases, French and Russian gold ought to be used to support British credit. As J. M. Keynes, a member of the Finance Division of the Treasury, wrote on 19 August, France and Russia ought not 'wastefully to hoard' their huge reserves: 'the right policy...is to commandeer the gold, in effect, for government purposes and then *use* it.' After some discussion, therefore, each country agreed to hold $200m. in gold in readiness to ship as necessary to the United States week by week in order to maintain the exchange rate during the negotiations. Russia would be asked to contribute $200m. as well, and the proceeds of the loan would be apportioned in proportion to the amount of gold each country had contributed.[38] On 25 August the Cabinet agreed to the proposal, and decided to send Lord Reading, the Lord Chief Justice, as the head of the mission. (Reading had once worked in the City, and for some years had taken an interest in financial problems. On the outbreak of war Lloyd George had given him a room at the Treasury, where, until McKenna became Chancellor, he had spent part of each day dealing with financial problems.) The other members of the mission were Sir Edward Holden (Chairman of the London City and Midland Bank), Sir Henry Babington Smith (ex-Treasury official and President of the National Bank of Turkey) and Basil Blackett;[39] the French decided to send M. Octave Homberg of the Quai d'Orsay and M. Ernest Mallet, a well-known private banker and a regent of the Bank of France.[40]

Blackett had noted as early as 5 January 1915 that it might soon be useful for Britain to borrow in the United States, and the Treasury had, during the spring and summer, considered borrowing as one of its three main options in the fight to maintain the rate of exchange (the other two being shipping gold and selling American securities).[41] When the idea of a loan was canvassed, however, two separate questions arose: would the American government allow it, and would American bankers subscribe to it?

The American government's position had been established in the early days of the war, when in August 1914 the French government had asked J. P. Morgan & Co. to float a $100m. loan in the United States. Morgan's inquired as to the Administration's attitude, and the Administration refused to approve the loan in order to protect the gold reserve. However, the Secretary of State, William Jennings Bryan, possibly went further than the President intended (the President was at that time stricken by the death of his wife) by adding in the official statement that 'in the judgment of this Government loans by American bankers to any foreign nation which is at war is [*sic*] inconsistent with the true spirit of neutrality.'[42] The policy was restated publicly in a letter to Senator William J. Stone of Missouri on 20 January 1915 and in a statement in the press on 31 March,[43] although there had in fact been some softening of the Administration's position.[44] A semi-public policy reversal was only begun in August, however, when James B. Forgan, the President of the First National Bank of Chicago, wrote to a member of the Federal Reserve Board on 17 August inquiring as to the attitude of the Administration towards the flotation of a large British loan in the United States. A positive response was urged by both McAdoo and Robert Lansing, now Secretary of State (Bryan had resigned in June 1915 over the second Lusitania Note), but at first the President would only say that the government would take no action either for or against the loan. But the New York bankers refused to commit themselves to such a loan without explicit assurance from the government.[45] So on 6 September Lansing wrote another letter to Wilson in which he argued clearly and forcefully that the belligerent governments be allowed to float loans in the United States. He did not mention the problem of exchange – although McAdoo was disturbed about it[46] – but concentrated on the balance of trade. In the period 1 December 1914–30 June 1915 American exports had exceeded imports by nearly a billion dollars, and it was estimated that for the final half of the year the excess would be a further $1¾ billion. Furthermore, it was estimated that European banks had about $3½ billion in gold, and to withdraw any considerable amount would disastrously affect the credit of the European nations, resulting in general bankruptcy. If the European countries could not pay for these goods they would have to stop buying them and the American export trade would shrink proportionately, resulting in 'restriction of outputs, industrial depression, idle capital and idle labor, numerous failures, financial demoralisation, and general upset and suffering among the laboring classes.' At the outset, the policy of discouraging loans had been sound, because popular sympathy had not crystallised in favour of one side or another; now it had done so and the purchase of bonds could not further increase partisanship and bitterness. Therefore, the practical reason for the policy had disappeared, and it should not stand in the way of the national interest when the economic situation was so acute.[47] To these arguments the President agreed,[48] and the way was clear, as far as the American government was concerned, for the efforts of the Anglo-French Loan Mission. Yet the President still refused to announce publicly that this was the case. (McAdoo, however, had already taken measures on his own to let important New York bankers understand the position.)[49] Nevertheless, he probably allowed Lansing to intimate as much to the press, since on 14 September a 'highly placed administration official' was quoted to this effect.[50] However, when the British Cabinet on 25 August had decided to send the mission, they could hope that the Americans could be persuaded to change their minds.

Assuming this were effected, the second question would still be unanswered: would a loan floated by Britain and France be attractive to the American financial public? By all accounts the outlook was gloomy, if not yet disastrous, and the longer Britain took to decide on a loan the more so it became. Wall Street was well aware of the scale of British commitments in the United States and expectations of a loan had been rampant at least since early June 1915. In mid-June Davison travelled to London, where he remained until 10 July, and where he joined Grenfell in discussions with the Treasury on the need for a loan (see above). While he was there the situation in the United States worsened: it was felt that Britain had probably overstayed her hand, and because of the German victories in Russia and the rumours of in-fighting between British politicians, generals and newspaper-owners confidence in her ability ultimately to finance herself and her allies had declined.[51] Upon his return to the United States he wrote to Grenfell that 'Since my return I have made careful inquiry into the *Loan* situation, and am greatly disappointed and surprised to find a markedly unfavourable change toward the placing any important amount of a loan, even of *Great Britain*'. His only suggestion was that a loan in some form could be made upon a large amount of American securities, if they could be made available.[52]

There the matter rested until August 1915, when the rate of exchange became so bad that a considerable number of contracts for exports were cancelled.[53] The Exchange Committee, headed by Lord Cunliffe (Governor of the Bank of England), was directed by the Treasury to look into the question of raising a dollar loan, and Morgan's were asked to advise on the amount likely to be obtainable on the security of British and French government notes. The answer that Morgan's telegraphed on 18 August caused intense anxiety: the probable maximum that could be raised was $100m. on one-year 5% notes, and the governments needed ten times that much.[54] Furthermore, at this point no one knew whether the American government would even allow any loan to be raised there. Nevertheless, the situation was serious; and in the circumstances the governments decided to dispatch the Anglo-French Loan Mission in the hope that a direct approach by the two governments involved, rather than through Morgan's as agents, would overcome American financial doubts.

The mission sailed on 1 September 1915 and immediately internal difficulties arose. Another passenger on the ship was Sir Ernest Cassel, ostensibly going out to the United States on private business, but apparently as an unofficial member of the mission. Although naturalised in 1878, he had previously been a German citizen, and even his membership of the Privy Council did not shield him from vicious attacks by sections of the press and the public caught up in wartime anti-German fever. One member of the public so caught was Holden, and he joined the French members of the mission in complaining hotly of Cassel's presence. Reading decided to bring matters out into the open at one of the daily meetings of the mission, and he thought that this had cleared the air; the French were conciliated, but Holden remained resentful, refused to recognise Cassel, and generally made it impossible for Cassel to aid the mission in the United States. (This had unfortunate results, because Cassel had links with the most important German-American bank in the United States, Kuhn Loeb & Co., and Reading apparently had counted on his convincing the bank to help with the loan.)[55]

The difficulty over Cassel having seemingly been settled, the mission utilised the remainder of the voyage to decide its preliminary negotiating position: they would try for an unsecured loan (that is, one based on no collateral) of £200m. – and in no case would settle for less than £100m. – at 4½ or 4¾ per cent interest, but at the last resort, 5 per cent.[56] As it turned out, the last resort arrived fairly early on in the negotiations, but it took some hard arguing by Morgan's to convince them of this. The relationship of the British government to Morgan's was, in fact, one cause of their difficulty, but the mission had good reason for maintaining it.

One result of Theodore Roosevelt's 'trust-busting' and Wilson's 'New Freedom' rhetoric had been that the term 'Money Trust' was now part of the political currency; J. P. Morgan Senior (who had died in 1913) had been the most active – or at least the most conspicuous – of the financial manipulators, having amongst his accomplishments the formation of US Steel, and his firm was identified in many minds with irresponsible power. The Wilson Administration was one group which distrusted Morgan's; another was the large group of banks and investment companies not numbered amongst Morgan associates. The jealousy of the banks was a common theme of English commentators in the United States, as was the hatred of the Midwest, the South and the West for the New York banks and for Morgan's most of all.[57] Holden probably realised something of this, since he had had dealings with Frank A. Vanderlip, President of the National City Bank, a rival of Morgan's; and Blackett most certainly did from his experiences with the Paish mission. But the British government was beholden to

Morgan's for the help already given, and Morgan's position as pur-chasing agent would have made it almost impossible to shake them off, even had it been desirable. As it was, J. P. Morgan Junior, now head of the firm, contacted Reading while the ship was still at sea and suggested arrangements which made it quite obvious that the mission was to be primarily in Morgan's hands – although the profit was to be prestige rather than money, since Morgan's accepted no additional commission other than that of a member of the syndicate eventually set up. Morgan wired that he had arranged to meet the mission at the ship, and to have them meet a number of prominent men in the afternoon of their arrival and at dinner in the evening;[58] the pace remained much the same for the term of the visit.

The mission spent the first few days in preliminary investigation and the perusal of the press. As a result they decided to emphasise the need of the Allies to issue a loan in order to maintain the exchange; this would facilitate American exports to the Allies and enable the British to purchase essential foodstuffs.[59] At no time during the visit was the need to purchase munitions mentioned, although the mission steadfastly declined to promise not to purchase such commodities.[60] As well their investigations made them aware of the universal expectation that the loan would be secured with American securities as collateral – and Reading moved swiftly to disabuse Morgan's of that notion.[61] The next day (14 September 1915) he told Morgan's that they wanted the loan to be for £200m. The major points of the British position were now revealed, and the negotiations would begin the following day.[62]

The mission was ensconced in the Hotel Biltmore, and there the bankers gathered for discussions; these proved quite difficult and were deadlocked more than once. This was an attempt by the British to appeal to members of a foreign public. The discussions with Morgan's and the other bankers concerned the terms on which a syndicate would underwrite the issue of the bonds. This would ensure that the British government would obtain the necessary funds, but of course this would leave the bankers with the risk that they would have to hold the bonds themselves if they were unable to sell them to the general public. During the discussions the mission kept one thought firmly in mind: no matter what the terms, there must be a loan, and it must not fail. The fact that a substantial public loan could be raised by Britain in the United States must be demonstrated beyond question. And in fact, whenever a concession needed to be made, it was invariably justified on this ground.[63] By 17 September Morgan's and the other bankers had made an offer – a loan for three years at 5 per cent interest – which the mission refused. But in the general atmosphere of goodwill Morgan's agreed to share in the syndicate at the same price as all the other under-writers without any special payment as managers and to associate others in the management of the loan.[64] Unfortunately, that goodwill was quickly dissipated: on 18 September Morgan's offered a five-year loan at 5 per cent with the option for the bondholders in four years to convert into 15–25-year bonds at 4½ per cent, the price to the syndicate to be 97½, and the amount to be £100m. The French were still insisting on £150m., however, and delay caused by their insistence 'took the gilt off the gingerbread' to quote Blackett.[65] Late in the afternoon of 18 September the Chancellor telegraphed to Reading instructing him to accept the offer of £100m., and the French were overborne.[66] On 21 September the Chancellor agreed to the terms of a five-year loan at 5 per cent, the upper limit of interest the British would consider.[67]

Morgan's meanwhile were taking soundings amongst their associates, and the results were so disquieting that they were forced to revise their offer of 18 September: at a price to the British government of 97½ they could not form a syndicate for more than £50m., but if the price were lowered to 96 for sale to the public at 97½ they might be able to form one for £100m. and were prepared to try. The mission insisted that the net price not be lower than 97½ and deadlock ensued. Reading telegraphed the situation to the Chancellor, suggesting the formation of a Trust company financed by the British to take part in the syndicate, and asking whether he would sanction the lower price requested by Morgan's. He added that he felt that Morgan's had genuine fears for the success of the loan and were not simply manoeuvring for better terms, citing the German-American opposition (there were threats to withdraw deposits from banks which took part in the loan) and the outraged reaction to the British Prize Court judgement which had condemned a number of ships carrying meat packed in the Midwest. He emphasised the need to decide quickly.[68] There was no response from the Chancellor, and after a conference of bankers at J. P. Morgan's library, Reading had to telegraph terms which were slightly better for the syndicate – the loan was to be issued to the public at 98 – and to request authority to accept the terms, since the position was becoming imperative.[69] Finally on 25 September the Chancellor telegraphed his agreement.[70] Reading immediately replied, stressing yet again the need to make the issue attractive in case further loans proved to be necessary; he added that he would try to make arrangements for additional credits.

Then he gave suggestions for the press announcement in Britain, emphasising that there should be no adverse comment, because it would immediately be quoted in American papers, and some time would elapse before the underwriting contract was signed and the loan issued to the public.[71] Later in the day he found time to write two letters to the Chancellor, one to go by the Foreign Office bag and one to be carried by Cassel on his return to Britain. In the former he elaborated on the difficulties of the mission, and admitted that the bedrock was that Americans, including many who were friendly to Britain, were genuinely nervous about the result of the war. New York and Boston were pro-Ally, and sympathy opened the door, but then 'finance looks to hard facts'. Not only should the loan not fail, but it should rise a little, and therefore he wanted to announce another loan, this raised on securities, while still in the United States (in order that the public could see that Britain could pay her bills).[72] But it was in the confidential letter carried by Cassel that he spoke plainly and said that no one had realised just how bad the situation was – the difficulties had been 'stupendous', and he mourned the fact that Holden by his prejudices had made them worse than they might have been.[73] (Blackett in fact felt that Holden had been wholly responsible for the price's being 96 rather than 97½, writing to the Treasury that 'He was far more concerned for his own prestege [*sic*] and for securing himself the position of being able to say that failure was due to our not following his advice than he was for making the Mission a success.')[74] Altogether it made a doleful assessment. The following day Reading telegraphed that Morgan's and the mission had agreed on the essential terms.[75]

But negotiations were by no means completed. Two further important concessions made by the British were that money paid in in the various districts should remain on deposit in the local banks until required by the Treasury, and that all the proceeds were to be spent in the United States.[76]

McKenna presented the whole bundle of terms to the Cabinet on 28 September, which discussed the matter at some length, in particular, presumably, the rate of interest: though nominally 5 per cent, with the discount to the underwriters and the charges and commissions it worked out at nearly 6 per cent – far higher than the rate obtaining in Britain. But McKenna undoubtedly made known to the Cabinet the difficulties which had faced the mission, and as the Prime Minister wrote to the king, 'The Cabinet with some reluctance sanctioned this plan, as the best available in the circumstances'.[77] It was then necessary

for Parliament to pass a Bill legalising the joint Anglo-French responsibility for the loan, as well as the waiver of income tax on payment. In
spite of Reading's urgings of special efforts – nothing could be signed
in the United States until the Bill was passed – it was 14 October before
the Royal Assent was received.[78]

Meanwhile in the United States there were details of the machinery
for the handling and servicing of the loan to be worked out. It was
decided, on the advice of the Governor of the Bank, that the bonds
would be printed in the United States.[79] It was also decided that rather
than hire an accounting firm to audit the loan accounts, Britain would
send someone out.[80] There was some spirited discussion over expenses
and publicity (with Holden manifesting great hostility to Morgan's) and
over the payment of coupons: the mission felt that they should be
payable into several of the leading New York banks as well as into
Morgan's. The mission considered that it would be undesirable,
because of jealousies in the United States and possible criticism in
Britain, to appear to be too much in Morgan's hands, and since Britain
might wish to return for further loans, they should keep the principal
New York banks favourably inclined. Morgan's felt that because their
assistance with the loan had been given without extra remuneration, the
usual course should be followed and the coupons should be made
payable at their house exclusively; they felt that the mission's
proposition was a public slight to them.[81] The Chancellor agreed with
the mission, writing that it would be impossible to avoid criticism in the
House of Commons if Britain appeared to be giving a monopoly to a
particular firm: 'I should like to be in a position to say that Morgan's
had throughout the proceedings shown every desire not to acquire any
exclusive position or privilege for themselves'.[82]

While the various details were being worked out, Reading busied
himself with meeting as many influential Americans as possible, particularly at small private luncheons or larger dinners, such as were given
for him by leaders of banking and commerce in Chicago and by the
Pilgrim Society in New York. He also met with Colonel House three
times, when they went over the political, military and economic
problems of the war at great length, as well as the obstacles to Britain's
finding finance in the United States, which were fresh in Reading's
mind. House arranged a brief meeting with the President for Reading,
which he combined, in a visit to Washington, with taking a seat on the
Bench of the Supreme Court.[83]

But amidst all this gaiety, Reading attempted to work out other ways in which Britain could raise money in the USA. He suggested to the Chancellor that he consider dollar bills of exchange or a loan on American securities, and he also collected information on the feasibility of dollar acceptances. It was decided that the first suggestion was impracticable and the last not attractive to American bankers, but that it would be possible to raise a loan of some magnitude on securities.[84] Discussions continued after the mission returned to Britain on 16 October 1915, and it was eventually decided that the borrowing should be done by London banks dealing with American banks, rather than by the government directly. This was decided on the basis that the banks could do it more gradually, that they could negotiate more freely and that they did not commit the British government. This last was an important point, for if once the government borrowed in the United States on collateral, they could never again borrow without it, and the Treasury certainly contemplated further unsecured loans such as the one just raised. By mid-November the arrangements were completed, and Reading for one felt that £300m. could be raised in this manner in the following twelve months.[85]

But the fact that it was felt that this money had to be raised was a judgement on the achievement of the mission. In fact, the consensus was that the mission itself was a success but that the loan was a failure. Although there was some grumbling that the underwriters got too much, the fact that they had agreed to underwrite $500m. – a staggering amount to the Americans – was considered to be due to the ability of the mission. The geographical distribution of the underwriters, however, is a clue to a major reason for the failure of the loan: although they comprised 1,570 banks and institutions, only one major Chicago bank was a member of the syndicate, and support for the loan was generally lacking in the Midwest, South and West. These were areas of German and Scandinavian settlement and of the strongest isolationist sentiment, and it was the efforts of those people, as well as of organised pacifists, Irish immigrants and anti-Russian Jews (German-Jewish banks included some of the most important in the United States), backed by the Hearst press, which prevented the loan from selling successfully to the public. On a more prosaic level, Americans were not used to foreign loans and distrusted them; they were also used to collateral security and to interest of 5½–6 per cent on the most unimpeachable stock, whereas to the Treasury an interest rate at that level would have implied the failure of British government credit. A further technical factor was that by law no United States National Bank could lend more than 10 per cent of its capital and surplus to any one person or institution (although the authorities had announced that no proceedings would be taken against banks if they did not strictly adhere to the 10 per cent limit).[86] The success of the mission lay in the fact that it had convinced 1,570 banks and financial houses, often against their previous financial judgement, that Britain was good for $500m. and that the public would buy that amount's worth of bonds; the failure of the loan lay in the refusal of the public to do so.

This was so in spite of the impressive propaganda effort made, with speeches and public statements of support. In the Midwest, for example, the Hearst press and the pro-Irish and pro-German organisations 'paralyzed efforts to distribute the Anglo-French bonds.'[87] It was quickly obvious that public response was poor, and by 27 October 1915 only $4m. worth of bonds had been sold. Homberg, who had been one of the French members of the mission, wanted to have the bonds quoted on the New York Stock Exchange, but Reading argued that it would be difficult to do so with any advantage: since the sales were so poor, it would scarcely be possible for the market price to be over 98, and a price under 98 would stop sales to the public. Homberg as well as the British continued to worry (by 20 November only $11m. had been sold), and late in November he sent a memorandum to the British in which he pointed out that on 14 December the syndicate would come to an end, that the public was not taking up the bonds and that something would have to be done to maintain Allied credit. His suggestion was that someone should buy the bonds on behalf of France and Britain.[88]

Sir Paul Harvey (Treasury representative in the United States – see below) spoke to Davison and Morgan's on 30 November on these lines. Davison stated that the Allied governments should support the market on 15 December 1915 since, in the absence of any good military news, speculators would hold off until they thought that the bonds had fallen to their natural price. Harvey thought that that was the natural interest of the syndicate, but Davison replied that since Morgan's had pressed the banks to buy the bonds, they could not ask them to put up the money to maintain the price. He added that Morgan's was willing to advance funds in the form of a 4 per cent demand loan to support the bonds and would hold the bonds as security. Harvey consulted Vanderlip of the National City Bank, who came up with an alternative plan, but one which was less advantageous to the British.[89] When Harvey next met with Davison and J. P. Morgan they objected hotly to Harvey's discussions with Vanderlip. Harvey replied that Davison had been so cold and unhelpful at their previous meeting that they should not be surprised that he had turned elsewhere for advice. The problem was that Morgan's was 'intensely sore' over what they considered had been their cavalier treatment by the mission and the British government – they felt that they had been used and then tossed aside. They cited as examples the facts that the loan account had been centralised at the National City Bank and that coupons had not been made payable exclusively at Morgan's. Harvey answered that the latter point was still open. The storm cleared the air, and Morgan's repeated their offer to send support money at 4 per cent, although when Davison read out to Harvey his cables to Grenfell, Harvey pointed out that he had suggested 4 per cent interest to him but 4½ per cent to Grenfell.[90] The agreement which the Treasury confirmed with Morgan Grenfell & Co. on 10 December was along the lines suggested to Harvey: Morgan's were to advance the funds on fourteen-day call at 4 per cent up to $25m., and to purchase the bonds at 95, which they would hold as security for the funds.[91]

In spite of this support, however, the loan failed to rise. The British hope had been that those persons making large sums out of the Allies would buy the bonds; in fact the results would have been disastrous if six companies with large contracts from the British government had not bought $100m. (Dupont, Bethlehem Steel and Westinghouse together bought $70m.). But by and large this hope had not been realised: when the syndicate ended on 14 December 1915, $187m. worth of bonds were still unsold and had to be taken by the underwriters, and only $33m. had been sold to ordinary non-institutional investors.[92] The report of a Cabinet committee considering the financial effort in late January 1916 pointed out that in spite of large government purchases of its own bonds the American price had already fallen from 96 to 94.[93] The British attempt to float a large, unsecured, public loan in the United States had met with failure, and a year would pass before, out of desperation, another was considered.

While the mission was still in the United States, it had been decided, because of some dissatisfaction with Morgan's procedures, that a representative of the Treasury was needed on the spot to administer the proceeds of the loan. Blackett wrote to Sir John Bradbury, Joint Permanent Secretary at the Treasury, that although Morgan's had behaved very well, they were 'certainly open to criticism for their want of organisation and slip-shod methods'. Therefore he felt that it was absolutely essential that someone representing the Treasury should be in New York to operate upon the Treasury account when the proceeds of the loan were paid in.[94] Reading repeated to the Chancellor that someone would have to remain in the United States to represent the Treasury, and the Chancellor agreed; however, he felt that he could not spare Blackett from his work in London. It was eventually decided to combine two necessary tasks, that of operating the account and that of auditing the loan operation, and to send out Sir Paul Harvey to act with Blackett.[95]

Harvey was Chief Auditor of the National Health Insurance Scheme, and formerly Financial Adviser to the Egyptian government. His new duties were to supervise all the arrangements made in relation to the Anglo-French loan and 'all other operations' in the United States; he was authorised to issue instructions on behalf of the Treasury and to operate on any accounts standing in the name of the Treasury. He arrived at the end of October 1915.[96] Harvey was the first Treasury representative sent out because of dissatisfaction with Morgan's as the American agent of the Treasury. Later, in 1917, the Treasury would send out a permanent mission under S. Hardman Lever to take over the financial duties in the United States until the end of the war (see Chapter 5), but Harvey was presumably meant to stay only as long as the Anglo-French loan required any administering.

Until the imbroglio with Morgan's in December, his time was largely taken up with just that: he made arrangements for calling up the loan deposits in the banks, he paid out money on the Treasury account, he tried to forecast the needs of Britain and to arrange for gold and securities if they should prove necessary, and he tried to mediate between Homberg and Davison, who apparently did not trust each other. Blackett remained to help until 23 November,[97] but thereafter Harvey apparently had no subordinate, and with the press of work it is no wonder if the 'suspicion and hostility'[98] of Morgan's was enough to cause a polite explosion. Morgan's felt that because of their aid the government should accede to their wishes, but the representative of the Treasury would be the most unlikely person to do so if he felt it would hamper future financial operations. And as the year ended and the orders of the Allies in the United States continued to mount, there was little doubt that further financial operations in 1916 would be required.

5

Financial Relations, 1916–1917: the Slide to Disaster and the Advent of the Treasury Mission

The period January 1916–April 1917 saw the inexorable growth of British purchasing in the USA. This made it increasingly necessary to raise dollars to pay for the goods, and 1916 saw a series of British loans issued in New York, money for which Britain was forced to pay ever-higher rates of interest. These interest rates reflected both the decreasing faith in ultimate Allied victory and the increasing attraction of domestic American investments. But the British attempts to raise finance in the USA were complicated by the fact that Britain and the USA clashed over a number of foreign policy issues. The climax came in December 1916, when the misjudgements of Morgan's and the restless attempts to mediate by President Wilson together caused a sterling crisis of some magnitude. The British Treasury sent out S. Hardman Lever to take over the responsibility for British finances in the USA, and he spent most of his time until the USA entered the war in April 1917 trying to keep Britain from having to default on her debts.

The Treasury had lost control over the spending departments, and especially over the Ministry of Munitions, long before 1916. Lloyd George, when Chancellor, had himself given a *carte blanche* to the War Office, when in October 1914 he had suggested that since it was not possible to insist on Treasury control in regard to departmental contracts (which often had to include abnormal financial conditions), such contracts should throughout the war be concluded without reference to the Treasury.[1] In May 1916 Lloyd George, now Minister of Munitions, clashed with McKenna, when the latter attempted to curtail the free-spending habits of the War Departments. Lloyd George believed that the American manufacturers would make their own arrangements for financing war orders if the alternative was to lose them,[2] and that in the last analysis the American government would step in to guarantee the orders. Christopher Addison, his Parliamentary Secretary, wrote:

> Lloyd George let himself go on the view of the Treasury pundits as to the ability of this country to pay... He said that he absolutely declined even to discuss the proposition that American manufacturers who carry out, say, $30 billion worth of contracts yearly – often on the most uncertain credit – would decline to supply goods on the credit of the British Empire; the Russian Empire; the French Republic and the Italian Kingdom all joined in one guarantee... He said that we were to place whatever orders we thought were necessary, not more, of course, and let the Treasury raise their question in the Cabinet, if they wanted....[3]

McKenna did raise the question in a paper laid before the Cabinet on 19 May 1916 on British financial liabilities in the United States. With regard to commitments already entered into, Britain had to find $434m. by 30 September. McKenna stated that he was looking into the possibilities of raising another unsecured loan and using South as well as North American securities; but he hoped that the Cabinet would back him in an appeal to the War Departments not to enter into any new commitments in the United States (during the previous three months the new commitments had totalled $282m.)[4] until he knew the outcome of his investigations. Morgan's added their own appeal to Lloyd George,[5] but no decline in spending resulted.

A growing difficulty was the need to carry the Allies on Britain's back. Addison wrote in his Diary on 8 May that 'Ribot [French Minister of Finance] was over here last week almost in tears, saying that they themselves could not find in America what would be accepted as payment and that we must take on their commitments there, as well as our own, the Russians' and the Italians'... Allies' orders amount to nearly ½ of the sum mentioned about [$1,200,000,000 to be found by the end of September, if all orders were delivered].'[6] McKenna decided that Russian needs in particular could be scrutinised for economies,[7] leading Lloyd George to charge that the Russians were being deprived of matériel. McKenna rebutted the accusation on 5 July,[8] and the end of the argument coincided with Lloyd George's move to the War Department to replace Lord Kitchener, who had gone down with the

Hampshire on 5 June 1916. The Cabinet-level argument, however, did not prevent Keynes's attempts to control Allied purchases made with British funds (see Chapter 3).

In an attempt to relieve the strain on British finances at this juncture, J. P. Morgan & Co. came up with the idea of quietly organising a corporation, all of the capital officers and personnel of which would come entirely from Morgan's, and which would borrow money on the New York money market, using British government securities in their possession as collateral. The sums raised, plus the corporation capital of $10m., would then be loaned to the British government, either on demand or for periods of three, six, or nine months or longer. By this means Morgan's hoped to be able to borrow and continue borrowing a considerable amount, perhaps $200m. Such a corporation, to be called the American and British Loan Corporation, would relieve the immediate situation, and in addition would help to fill the gaps between formal loan issues. The Governor of the Bank of England thought the idea a very good one, and encouraged Morgan's to go ahead. Morgan's did so, and by 2 August were on the point of filing the formal organisational papers. At the last moment, however, the whole project was cancelled. Morgan's were driven to this decision because of the poor showing of a French loan which they had underwritten, a loan which had been offered on terms which Morgan's had assumed would be very attractive to the market. The indifferent success of the French loan meant to Morgan's that the New York market's assessment of Allied financial prospects was worse than they had realised.[9]

The moral Morgan's drew from the episode was that the needs of the Allies, and in particular Britain's, were so large that the only course that would serve would be a major borrowing by the British government itself. Morgan's suggested that Britain arrange at once to borrow in New York $250–300m. for a period of two years, the loan to be secured by collateral. The hope expressed was that if the issue was successful, the market demand for British paper would be immensely strengthened and the plan for the American and British Corporation could then be put into operation to carry the situation with demand loans.[10] The British government, of course, would have preferred a straight loan without borrowing on collateral, such as had been the case with the 1915 Anglo-French loan; their fear was that having once borrowed on collateral, they would not again be able to borrow without it. But under the circumstances, they felt that Morgan's were the best judges of the matter, and agreed.[11] A loan of $250m. was issued in late August at

5 per cent interest, with the money to be available to the government on 1 September, and it was secured by $300m. worth of Canadian, American and other foreign securities; it was due to mature in only two years.[12]

Britain was fortunate in being able to raise the loan, because relations between Britain and the United States were by now fraught with tension. There was growing American disgust and anger with the shipping blockade, heightened by the British cable and mail censorship. The British response to the 1916 Easter rising in Dublin, and particularly the decision to execute the leaders, was viewed with dismay by pro-Ally Americans and with real hatred by the politically important Irish-Americans. Finally, in an incredibly maladroit move, Britain published on 18 July 1916 a blacklist of some eighty-seven American and 350 Latin American firms accused or suspected of trading with the Central Powers.[13] President Wilson wrote to Colonel House on 23 July that 'I am, I must admit, about at the end of my patience with Great Britain and the Allies. This blacklist business is the last straw... I am seriously considering asking Congress to authorise me to prohibit loans and restrict exportations to the Allies.'[14] House agreed that 'Their stupidity is beyond belief', and he encouraged Wilson in his move to let Spring Rice know what Britain could expect if she did not change her methods.[15]

By the autumn, therefore, relations between the two countries were in a decidedly delicate state. Congress was threatening reprisals, although the Foreign Office thought the possibility of their application remote.[16] Worse, however, was the threat that Spring Rice conveyed to London late in September that the President was considering mediation between the belligerents, at a time when it would be most disadvantageous to the Allies (the Battle of the Somme had failed to dislodge the Germans). Without consulting either the Prime Minister or the Foreign Secretary, Lloyd George decided to forestall Wilson, and summoning Roy Howard of the United Press, gave on 28 September 1916 an interview which outlined the substance of the policy of the 'Knock-Out Blow' – that Britain would fight to the finish and that there could be no outside interference.[17] Fearful of the American reaction, the Foreign Office called together an interdepartmental committee on 30 September to consider how far Britain was dependent on the United States; the statements of the various departments were printed for the Cabinet on 6 November, and the conclusions were alarming. The Ministry of Munitions procured a large percentage of its guns, shells, metals, explosives and machine tools from the United States; the Army Department considered that there was no substitute for American supplies of oils and petroleum, nor for that of preserved meat; the Board of Trade stated that for cotton, for foodstuffs, for military necessities and for raw materials for industry, the United States was 'an absolutely irreplaceable source of supply'; the Board of Agriculture emphasised the dependence of Britain on the United States for grains; and finally, the Treasury stated baldly that 'Of the £5,000,000 which the Treasury have to find daily for the prosecution of the war, about £2,000,000 has to be found in North America' and added that there was no prospect of any diminution without a radical change in the policies of the Allied War Departments. The Treasury expressed, in its conclusion, the only action possible for the government: 'the policy of this country towards the U.S.A. should be so directed as not only to avoid any form of reprisal or active irritation, but also to conciliate and to please'.[18]

The Treasury was even more acutely conscious than the other departments of the precariousness of its position relative to the USA. Back in August, because of growing pressure by France on Morgan's to issue French loans in the USA, Morgan's had suggested that a conference should be held in London to sort out Allied finances. Davison and then Morgan sailed for London in September, and from 3 to 10 October 1916 a Joint Anglo-French Financial Committee met with the Morgan partners to consider the financial position and prospects of the Allied powers, and especially of Britain, in the USA.[19] The report of the committee was presented to the Cabinet by McKenna on 24 October, who introduced it by writing that

> We ought never to be so placed that only a public issue in America within a fortnight stands between us and insolvency. Yet we are quickly drifting in this direction... If things go on as present, I venture to say with certainty that by next June or earlier the President of the American Republic will be in a position, if he wishes, to dictate his own terms to us.

The committee began by stating that in the period May to September 1916 Treasury expenditure in the United States had been at the rate of $207,500,000 a month; a conservative estimate of requirements for the period October 1916 to March 1917 was $250m. a month, assuming that there were no further orders from the Ministry of Munitions nor any extraordinary need to support the exchange. Assets to meet this could only be found from the sale of securities, from gold and from loans. The first of these resources, which had yielded $300m. in the previous five months, had to be regarded as negligible for the future and the remnants should be retained for use as collateral. As for gold, the Treasury had managed to build up a secret reserve of £100m. (probably from gold from South Africa), but they expected to have to expend half of it in the next six months. That left a deficit of $1,250,000,000 to be met by the issue of loans in America at a rate of $200m. a month, when to raise $80m. a month had required the most persistent efforts. The committee put the position to the Morgan representatives, who did not conceal their dismay – the New York firm cabled on 10 October that 'Your confidential information as to requirements of Allied Governments is staggering. It is far from clear how they can possibly be met'. The conclusion of the Morgan representatives in London was that 'By the use of every available device, and possibly at the cost of postponing payments by bank overdrafts, we [Britain] shall still be solvent on the 31st March. They cannot tell us how this result shall be achieved'. In other words, Britain would start the following financial year with her devices exhausted, the American market congested with Britain's issues and the gold reserves diminished by at least one-half. The main problem in the United States was the pace of borrowing:

> The question is whether the money can be turned over in America and brought back to us in the form of loans as fast as we are spending it. Between each loan and the next we live on an overdraft with our bankers. Each time the overdraft grows heavier, and the longest interval we can spare between the successive loans grows less. The maximum overdraft we can secure is limited by the financial capacity of New York and by the peculiar banking laws of the United States.

The only concrete suggestion which the committee could come up with was to look beyond New York to the 'great investing public' out in the Middle and Far West.[20]

During a committee meeting on 6 October, Lord Reading had raised the possibility of attempting another unsecured Anglo-French loan, ideally to be issued in November.[21] While discussions went on, arrangements were meanwhile made in late October for Morgan's to float another secured loan in the USA, this one for $300m. at 5½ per cent, maturing in three and five years.[22] It was finally decided that while an unsecured loan would probably be possible in due course, it could hardly be contemplated before 10 January 1917,[23] and this became the working date. But even this tentative plan had to be abandoned due to the intervention of the most serious financial crisis with which Britain had had as yet to deal, a crisis for which Morgan's, as British financial agent, were to some degree responsible.

H. P. Davison had been one of the Morgan partners consulted by the Anglo-French Financial Committee in London in October 1916, and shortly after he returned to the United States he began to lay the groundwork for the contemplated unsecured loan, stating in conferences in New York and Chicago that such a loan was being considered and that the time had come when such loans should be accepted as direct obligations of Britain and France, without the need for collateral. Davison reported that the reaction of the bankers had been very favourable, but the reaction in the hostile press was that Britain was becoming short of collateral and that she would soon flood the United States with gold and then go off the gold standard. In the meantime Britain required dollars for December to finance an overdraft of $175m. and it was decided to attempt to issue short-term, unsecured Treasury bills, which would be bought by American banks and repeatedly renewed. (Davison, again, had been very encouraged by the bankers' reception of this idea.)[24] Davison, inexplicably, proceeded to acquaint Warburg with the details of this intention (the only explanation given was that Warburg was the New York representative on the Federal Reserve Board – but he was notoriously pro-German), and Crawford reported that Warburg encouraged Davison to reveal this intention to the whole Board. Davison's own explanation for meeting the Board was less conspiratorial: that in view of the Board's interference with a recent French acceptance credit, Morgan's thought that he should meet the Board.[25] The advance notice to Warburg did allow him time, if it was necessary, to whip up opposition to the plan. Davison met with the Board on 19 November 1916, where he stated that Morgan's intended to issue the Treasury bills, without limit but possibly to an amount as high as $1 billion, and as fast as the market could absorb them. Frederick Delano attempted to moderate the suggestion by saying he saw no objection to $100–200m., but this Davison brushed aside. He emphasised several times that Morgan's desired no ruling from the Board, but merely wished to tell them the facts. He implied a threat by saying that the Federal Reserve Banks must take the bills or trade would stop, but pulled back quickly in shock when the reaction was that perhaps a recession was preferable to loading up the banks with securities which, although liquid in form (that is, short-term), might have to be refunded into thirty- or forty-year bonds. The Board was, as well, worried about the American dependence on war trade. After lunch W. P. Harding was instructed to say that although the Board would have nothing to say in regard to private investment in the bills, they might have to issue a word of caution to member banks. Davison replied that no present action was contemplated. Davison then saw the President and presumably acquainted him with Morgan's intentions.[26]

Morgan's apparently attempted to forestall the Board by allowing an article to appear in the press on 24 November announcing the probable offer of the bills, and saying that the banks would probably take $1 billion. Harding rang Morgan's in New York and said that the Board had understood from Davison that no immediate action was in contemplation, and that they might have to issue a statement warning banks of the danger of investing in such bills. Thomas Lamont, a Morgan partner, said that the article went too far, that the amount of the loan would not be unlimited but would only be $10–15m. for 60–90 days, and that it would not be issued before 1 December – and that if the Board issued such a warning they might have to withdraw the issue.[27] Although Morgan's did not appear to take Harding's threat seriously – the partners sent a 10 a.m. cable on 24 November to Morgan in London stating that 'It hardly seems probable that the Federal Reserve Board will issue any statement on this point'[28] – an announcement on the lines of Lamont's reassurances was issued the following day. But Morgan's were losing control of the situation, and at a meeting on 24 November between the partners and the Governor of the Federal Reserve Board of Washington, the Governor warned them that the Board might decide that 'this form of obligation is so undesirable for American Banks as to compel them in the near future to issue some public statement to that effect.'[29]

The threat was carried out. The Board drafted a warning to be inserted in the *Bulletin*, the organ of the Federal Reserve Bank system, cautioning banks against investing too heavily in short-term foreign securities, and Harding took it to the President for his approval. The President not only approved the action of the Board but felt that the announcement should be stronger – that this kind of security was not liquid and could therefore prove very embarrassing if there was a change in American foreign policy – and that the warning should extend to the private investor as well as to the member banks. The

Board strengthened it, and issued it to member banks on 27 November, and it appeared in the press on 28 November 1916.[30] Wilson's addition was the core of the matter:

> The Board deems it, therefore, its duty to caution the member banks that it does not regard it in the interest of the country at this time that they invest in foreign Treasury bills of this character.
>
> The Board does not consider that it is called upon to advise private investors, but as the United States is fast becoming the banker of foreign countries in all parts of the world it takes occasion to suggest that the investor should receive full and authoritative data – particularly in the case of unsecured loans – in order that he may judge the future intelligently in the light of present conditions and in conjunction with the economic developments of the past.[31]

The reaction was strong and immediate. The price of Allied bonds and American war stocks tumbled on 28 November, and Morgan's that day had to buy nearly $20m. worth of sterling to maintain the exchange rate.[32] The opinion in the New York financial community was that by warning the private investor the Board had overstepped its boundary, and that any warning it might have felt the need to issue to banks could have been conveyed in private.[33] Within a week values in the securities market had fallen by $1 billion.[34]

Morgan's were defiant at first, saying that they intended to go ahead with the Treasury bills, although they were convinced that sales would now be negligible at the start. However, they changed their attitude after communicating with McKenna, and on 1 December they announced that they had decided not to go ahead with the issue.[35] On the diplomatic front Sir Richard Crawford, Commercial Attaché at the British Embassy in Washington, and Spring Rice remonstrated with Harding and other members of the Board, accusing them of gratuitously destroying Britain's credit in the United States, and they attempted to convince the Board to modify or retract its statement.[36]

As Governor of the Board, Harding was their target, and Crawford talked to him on 30 November. Harding said that he had not liked the reference to the private investor, that it had originally referred to quite another matter and that its inclusion had been prompted by Warburg. As far as the intimation to the banks was concerned, there was no objection to a moderate issue, but Davison had stated that Morgan's intended to feed up to $1 billion into the market, and the Board had feared that Britain would not be able to redeem such an amount and would have to refund the short-term bills into long-term bonds. Crawford insisted to Harding that the Board should explain that the reference to private investors did not refer to British bills. Harding agreed, and suggested that Crawford should talk to the Secretary of State, who would hint as much to the Board.[37] Crawford talked to the Counselor of the State Department, Frank Polk, the following day, and Polk talked to Lansing and then gave the desired sanction to the Board.[38] The Board then issued a statement to the effect that 'they did not want to reflect on the credit of any Government but only wished to warn persons in smaller communities who did not understand "real values".'[39] Harding followed this up by emphasising, in a speech made in Boston in mid-December, that in its statement the Board had not intended to attack the credit of any country, either openly or covertly. He also told Crawford privately that the Board would not again interfere in matters of this kind and would raise no objection to the floating of a further loan.[40]

By this time, unfortunately, the damage had been done. Britain was now precluded, Morgan's felt, from raising any loan at least until January 1917. This would have been bad enough if the government had had only to consider paying for orders – it had been necessary to find $38m. in the previous week alone[41] – but now exchange was in dire straits. The London Exchange Committee panicked and recommended the suspension of specie payments, but the Cabinet remained firm and instructed Morgan's to continue to support the exchange rate of the pound.[42] By mid-December the situation was perilous. John Maynard Keynes, then a Treasury official, wrote in 1939 a memorandum describing it:

> I remember in particular a terrific run at the end of 1916, when the daily requirement...ran for a short time in excess of $5 million, which in those days we considered simply terrific. Chalmers and Bradbury never fully confessed to ministers the extent of our extremity when it was actually upon us, though of course they had warned them, fully but unavailingly, months beforehand of what was coming. This was because they feared that, if they emphasised the real position, the policy of the peg might be abandoned, which, they thought, would be disastrous. They had been brought up in the doctrine that in a run one must

pay out one's gold reserves to the last bean...in the circumstances they were right.[43]

The Asquith Coalition government fell in the midst of all this,[44] and at the first meeting of Lloyd George's new War Cabinet Chalmers was called to report:

'Well, Chalmers, what is the news?' said the goat [Lloyd George]. 'Splendid,' Chalmers replied in his high quavering voice, 'two days ago we had to pay out $20 million; the next day it was $10 million; and yesterday only $5 million.' He did not add that a continuance at this rate for a week could clean us out completely,...[45]

The only step the government could take – besides paying out to the last bean – was to stop the placement of any orders in America, which McKenna had done immediately. This was intended not only to spare exchange, but to make the Americans realise what repercussions the destruction of British credit would have on their own employment and trade.[46] In time, there were signs that the measures were beginning to bite.[47]

But amidst the shock, the government wanted to know why the American government had acted as it did. They were willing to accept the fact that there were good banking (rather than diplomatic) reasons for the Board's actions:[48] the Board feared for the liquidity of the banks,[49] especially in view of Davison's statements about 'feeding the market',[50] and they desired to build up their gold reserves in place of so much paper.[51] But then Spring Rice ascertained and informed the government that the State Department had approved of the warning, and the question became, Was the President behind it? Spring Rice wrote that 'intimate friends of the President have given the most positive assurances that he knew nothing whatever about it'.[52] There was no clear answer to this until February 1917, when Harding told the British that the President had directly influenced the Board's warning.[53] But at the meeting of the War Committee on 28 November 1916, when the action of the Board was first considered by the government, Grey had stated that he thought that the President was behind it,[54] and apparently the government acted on that assumption.

What were the motives of the President? Ever since the beginning of the war, his constant desire had been to bring the war to an end by

mediation, with himself acting as mediator. His motives were humani-
tarian, but his ruthless treatment of the British in this particular episode
illustrated his feeling that by this time relations with Britain were more
strained than with Germany.[55] At the time the action of Morgan's – and
Warburg[56] – afforded him the opportunity to apply pressure, he was
fresh from his electoral triumph and thereby secure in power. There is
no doubt that he still smarted from Lloyd George's attempt, in
September 1916, to forestall an earlier peace move; if the pressure were
not seen to come directly from the President it would be harder to
counteract. And in November 1916 the Allies had few points more
vulnerable than credit in the United States. The President – along with
others in the Administration – was certain that peace was imminent;[57]
the Allies should be forced to accede to mediation; only supplies and
credit from the United States kept them going; undermine this credit
and there would be no choice left.

An incident which the British did not know about illustrates that in
fact the primary concern of the President was not the liquidity of the
banks. John Skelton Williams, the Comptroller of the Currency, had
been investigating the general financial condition of the banks, and,
perhaps smarting from what he considered a slight on their solvency,
produced shortly after the warning a statement intended for the
Bulletin, in which the banks were congratulated for presently carrying
less than $250m. worth of short-term foreign paper. The Board refused
to sanction it, since it would have denied that there had been any reason
for the warning.[58] (When they had issued the warning the Board had
genuinely thought that liquidity was a more serious problem than was
in fact the case.) Williams then sent it to the President, requesting that
it be released, but the President replied by asking that he do nothing
about the statement: 'I am not sure what indirect effect the publication
might have on some of our foreign relations.'[59] In fact Grey's assessment of 28 November, that he 'wondered whether Policy was really at
the back of the statement of the American Bank group... President
Wilson believed that the War could be wound up now on reasonable
terms, but those terms we should regard as unsatisfactory and
inconclusive. Dr Wilson, however, intended to bring pressure to
bear',[60] was substantially correct.

Another point of discussion by the British was the degree of
culpability of Morgan's. The government was inclined to put blame
where it appeared due, and Morgan's, and especially Davison, had few
defenders. Arthur Willer, *The* (London) *Times*' correspondent in

Washington, expressed what was doubtless in many people's minds when he sent this comprehensive indictment to his Editor:

> That firm [Morgan's] had undoubtedly done good work, especially in regard to purchases: but it has in the broader sense been provincial, unstatesmanlike, and selfish. The most unpopular house in the country, the personification for the radical West of the malign money power of Wall Street, it has done nothing to propitiate either the people or the politicians. Nor has it done anything to advertise the solidity of the borrowers upon whose reputation the success of a loan must ultimately rest. Ever since the first large loan it seems to have been solely concerned with making as much for itself as possible . . . Independent bankers and bond houses have been discouraged from helping us right and left. The one idea has been to keep things in their own acquisitive hands and to let the future take care of itself. . . Western financial opinion has been usually ignored and when noticed, insulted.[61]

There is no doubt that Morgan's showed deficiencies in judgement. They had actively campaigned for the Republican candidate, Charles Evans Hughes, and against the President during the autumn, in spite of their acknowledged position as British agent. They had been cavalier in their treatment of the Board, and when it had reacted, they had been publicly defiant, until instructed to do otherwise by the British. More personally, Davison had shown defects of personality such as to prejudice friend and foe against him: Spring Rice, a close friend of J. P. Morgan Junior (Spring Rice had been best man at his wedding), said Davison 'had all the aggressiveness of the older Morgan without his genius and that he was always inclined to slop over',[62] and that he had no judgement.[63] Delano, a member of the Board, described him as 'too proud' to accept guidance.[64] The Foreign Office minuted that the conduct of Morgan's had been 'over-bearing and ill advised' and that Davison's especially had been 'injudicious'.[65] Further, they took up Spring Rice's complaint that neither he nor Crawford had been consulted by Davison: they had 'more than once pointed out . . . that Morgan's cannot be regarded as a substitute for the proper diplomatic authorities in conducting negotiations likely to affect our relations with the United States. The history of this incident points the moral and I feel strongly that we ought to rub it in when sending a copy of this despatch to the Treasury.'[66] The Foreign Office then conveyed to the

Treasury Spring Rice's suggestion that Crawford, as commercial attaché at the Embassy, should take care of financial negotiations.

The Treasury response was distinctly cool. Sir Robert Chalmers, Joint Permanent Secretary at the Treasury, told a member of the Foreign Office that the Treasury were satisfied with Morgan's and that Crawford was well-meaning but not very helpful.[67] Sir John Bradbury, another Joint Permanent Secretary to the Treasury, wrote on 13 January 1917 to A. J. Balfour, now Secretary of State for Foreign Affairs, that there were 'very great practical difficulties' in associating the Ambassador with purely financial negotiations between London and New York – that there was often a need for instant decisions, and that it was impossible to forecast future trends, since the situation changed from day to day. There were also disadvantages in a division of responsibility. But the Foreign Office's point regarding the unsuitability of entrusting Morgan's with negotiations had evidently struck home, because in the same letter Bradbury announced that the Treasury intended to send its own financial mission to New York.[68]

The man chosen to head the Treasury mission was S. Hardman Lever. Although British, before the war he had been a partner in a firm of chartered accountants in New York and had therefore an 'expert knowledge'[69] of American conditions. After the outbreak of war he had joined the Ministry of Munitions as Assistant Financial Secretary, and then had moved to the Treasury (much against the will of Christopher Addison at Munitions)[70] as Financial Secretary. The purposes of his mission were to make a general survey of the British financial position in North America, and to investigate certain questions regarding the supply of munitions. Spring Rice was informed that his visit was informal and that no public announcement was to be made. He was due to arrive in mid-February 1917, accompanied by Andrew McFadyean as his Private Secretary.[71]

Although the occasion of Lever's being sent out to the USA was Treasury dissatisfaction with Morgan's, the firm in fact welcomed his mission, Grenfell assuring the Chancellor that 'I thought personally that no better person could be chosen'.[72] The New York partners were 'delighted to have him',[73] and he was certainly considered to be a Morgan friend. But the change of government and the advent of the Lever mission did change the relationship between Morgan's and the British government, since the Treasury now, naturally, looked primarily to Lever rather than to Grenfell for advice. Grenfell had not anticipated that this would be the case, writing on 11 December 1916 that he had 'no reason to believe that our relations with the new Government will not be just as perfect as with the past'.[74] But by mid-March he recognised that 'Since the 1st January and the organisation of the new Government there has been distinct indication of a desire on the part of the Authorities to work less closely with us and since the departure of Lever all cables have been sent direct, in fact it has been very difficult to get answers from the Authorities to your enquiries through us.'[75] Morgan's, not surprisingly, were 'considerably disturbed' by Grenfell's cable, apparently interpreting the cooling of relations as stemming from Lever's activities in some way; they had, after all, 'dealt with Sir Samuel Lever in the most confidential way', and were alarmed at their possibly harbouring a viper (Lever had an office at Morgan's).[76] Morgan Grenfell rushed to reassure Morgan's of Lever's good faith; the difficulties came rather 'from action or inaction of some of the permanents',[77] by whom they meant Sir Robert Chalmers, one of the Joint Permanent Secretaries to the Treasury.[78] Morgan Grenfell were concerned that they were no longer used as before to smooth the way for and advise both sides; but if the relationship with Lever was working well, they were 'completely satisfied'.[79]

The first months of 1917 were a time of turmoil. Britain's finances had never recovered from the devastation wreaked upon them in December 1916. The Treasury was forced to scrabble for finance wherever it was to be found; a loan of $50m. was issued in Japan for credit in the United States,[80] and Bethlehem Steel, at least, was persuaded to take Treasury notes in payment for orders.[81] Meanwhile her overdraft at Morgan's grew larger, and it was decided to attempt another secured loan.

The government had decided to make the deposit of British-owned American securities with the Treasury compulsory,[82] so that for a time there was sufficient to serve as collateral. But the outlook for a loan, even by mid-January, was not at all encouraging; even the success of the Third War Loan in Britain served only to maintain what level of confidence there was in the United States, while its failure would have had a disastrous effect on opinion.[83] The British Government was careful to sound out Administration opinion, and this time Crawford, rather than Morgan's, conducted the negotiations.

Crawford met with McAdoo and Harding on 25 January 1917. McAdoo stated that the United States was likely to make heavy demands on the banks to meet the Treasury deficit and to finance American military 'preparedness'. Thus he would like some advance warning about loans the British government was considering issuing in the United States. Crawford readily agreed, and offered any information McAdoo desired about the loan Britain was proposing to issue. On 26 January Harding told him that the interview had been most satisfactory and that Britain need fear no difficulties concerning the loan.[84] The loan was duly issued that week, for $250m. at 5½ per cent, maturing in one and two years.[85] With such attractive terms, the issue was quickly oversubscribed.[86]

Then everything changed. Germany declared unrestricted submarine warfare, and the United States severed diplomatic relations with Germany on 4 February 1917. British representatives began to receive hints of future American financial aid,[87] and it was at this juncture that Lever arrived. He was ordered to proceed immediately to Washington to take over any financial discussions.[88]

Lever, however, remained a week in New York, talking to people and assessing the situation before proceeding to Washington.[89] He arrived there on 19 February, called on Spring Rice and then met and talked with Crawford for some time. Crawford gave Lever a 'full and illuminating survey'[90] of financial affairs. He described the personal friction between Davison and McAdoo, which had intensified their political differences. He considered that a major cause of problems between Britain and the United States in this sphere – and a major cause of the Reserve Board Crisis – was the lack of information received by the Administration on proposed British loans. In fact, Davison's professed view was that the only way to deal with the Board was to give them no information until it was too late for them to intervene – a procedure which Crawford felt (and Lever agreed) courted disaster. Finally, Crawford described his own policy as one of cultivating good relations with officials, especially with Harding, to the success of which Spring Rice had earlier testified.

Lever then lunched with J. P. Morgan, and as a result of the morning's talk with Crawford, he urged Morgan to keep in his own hands (and away from those of Davison) the conduct of the negotiations which were to take place in the afternoon. Morgan was to see McAdoo about a proposed notice that it was hoped would be issued by the Federal Reserve Board approving of National Banks' investing in British Treasury bonds.

In the afternoon Lever saw Polk, the State Department Counselor, who spoke of his desire to do anything to help the Allies, and who praised Crawford highly. Lever's own impression of Crawford was highly favourable, and he ascribed wholly to his work the formation of a bridge between Morgan's and the American Treasury.[91] He was therefore quite happy to leave negotiations in Washington, largely concerned with the possible statement by the Board, in Crawford's hands, with the addition of an occasional trip to Washington by himself.

Lever in fact had his hands full in New York attempting to keep Britain solvent. Even with the cancelling of orders caused by the December 1916 crisis, Britain was, during February, spending an average of $83m. a week in North America.[92] Britain hoped to issue a $250m. unsecured loan – hence the talks with the Board in order to remove the obstacle of their previous warning. Beyond that, the financial situation was one of stagnation. Ever since the severance of relations, no one wanted to invest and bankers were reluctant to lend, since everyone was waiting to see how the international situation would develop and what American policy would be. Unfortunately, Britain still had to pay for orders, and the overdraft at Morgan's grew larger. The British agreed to pay 6 per cent for short-term funds, and some money trickled in.[93] But by the beginning of March the situation was 'very critical',[94] and Lever felt that the time had come to start selling some of the securities Britain had deposited with Morgan's as collateral for the overdraft, the only way, he believed, to reduce what was becoming an appalling sum (by 6 April 1917 it totalled $345m.).[95] The need for a large public issue was overwhelming.

The British were proposing to issue a loan for $250m. at 6 per cent interest. They wanted it to be unsecured, but they were willing to deposit 20 per cent of the sum in gold in Ottawa, to be available for those who wanted to redeem the bonds before maturity and were thereby willing to accept a lower rate of interest.[96] They wanted the Board to issue a statement approving the issue as one in which the Banks could properly invest, and in fact encouraging the banks to do so as a means of financing the export trade.[97] The Board had approved such a statement by the end of February, but McAdoo caused it to be held up pending the decision of Congress as to whether or not American merchant ships should be armed.[98] During the discussions there were suggestions for 'trades' of a character which would become familiar to British negotiators later in the year: in return for loan facilities Britain should provide gold shipping facilities for the United States, she should help provide wood pulp which Canada was threatening to embargo, she should have Morgan's lobby senators for the passage of a bill the Administration desired.[99] At the end of the discussions a favourable statement was issued on 9 March, but as it turned out, no loan was issued, since at the request of the Administration Britain left the loan market clear for the Administration's own issue, the Liberty Loan. But the statement, accompanied by some judicious purchasing by Morgan's of Anglo-French Loan and British loan securities to encourage the market, made the outlook for British finances brighter than for some time.[100]

Lever now sent a comprehensive assessment of the position to the Chancellor, now Andrew Bonar Law, on 9 March 1917. He was convinced that Morgan's was the only firm who could in future handle the British situation. Presumably this was partly because of Morgan's position as the bankers' banker, but he also recognised that some of the problems arose because Morgan's had many enemies working with them who did not give wholehearted co-operation. Lever felt that Britain's financial difficulties were attributable to the fact that the 1915 Anglo-French Loan had been underwritten so widely that there was no one left to buy it; further, that collateral (secured) loans could, and should, have been avoided, and that the January 1917 collateral loan, with its conversion privilege (that is, earlier issues could be converted to the new issue without the lender giving new money), had placed British credit on a basis from which it would be difficult to recover. In short, Lever disagreed with some of J. P. Morgan & Co's judgements, but felt that Britain needed to utilise Morgan power in the money market. The only means by which recovery could ensue, he concluded, was by an improvement in the market for the various British issues, and this could be obtained mainly, if not solely, by the actions of the Administration. Investment had come to a standstill and little would happen until the Administration made up its mind as to its policy.[101]

Thus the point had been reached where Britain no longer had control over her external financial affairs, but was at the mercy of events and the American government. While Britain waited for the Administration to decide between peace and war, Lever cobbled up one expedient after another to stave off disaster, and Britain struggled on, sometimes with little more than a week's money in hand for American payments. By mid-March the Chancellor asked for an assessment of the position, and the conclusion was that the Treasury, with all expedients, could see little more than a month ahead.[102] The British government existed on tantalising promises of help which began to filter through, as it became obvious to the Americans that Germany was not likely to forgo submarine warfare and that the United States would most likely soon be at war. Harding, at McAdoo's instigation, suggested in a speech on 21 March that in case of war the United States should lend the Allies $1 billion, taking Allied bonds in exchange.[103] Lever was able to report a radical change of sentiment in the Midwest and West in favour of financially aiding the Allies.[104] But the need was inexorable, and by the end of March it was decided to sell more securities and to ship more gold.[105] Finally, on 2 April 1917 the President asked Congress to recognise a state of war between the United States and Germany.

That same day the Chancellor reported to the Cabinet on the financial situation. On 1 April Britain had $490m. worth of securities in the United States, but this was balanced by an overdraft of $358m.; there was $87m. in gold, making a net total of $219m. actually in New York, but expenditure was at the rate of $75m. a week, so it would only last three weeks. Beyond that, the only visible asset was £114m. in gold in the Bank of England and the Joint Stock Banks. It was truly as he said:

> The Cabinet would therefore see that on the face of it our position was a very black one indeed. The British Government had been deliberately going ahead with the knowledge that danger in this direction was in front of them which we might be unable to face. We had felt that the use of our gold and all our other resources would carry us on as long as possible.[106]

Britain has come to the end of her resources, and in the euphoria engendered by the entry of the United States into the war, it was fully anticipated that the American government would take over the burden of financing the purchases of the Allies in the United States.[107] No one considered what Britain would do if the American government refused in any measure to do so.

Part Two

1917–1918 and the Love–Hate Relationship: British Relations with Public America

6

The Balfour Mission,
April–May 1917: the
American Giant Awakens

Once the United States had declared war in April 1917 British reticence about their purchasing activities in the United States could end. There was no immediate change in the activities of the resident missions, however, partially because events in the United States – and in the Wilson Administration – were so confused that no one could predict what direction American war preparations would take. This confusion the British government found intensely frustrating. Time had been wasted waiting for the American government to decide to declare war, during which the British had consciously tried to refrain from putting overt pressure on the Americans, while resources of supplies, ships and men were dwindling. The USA, it was felt, needed to be shocked into awareness of the need to get their country organised for war. What the British therefore decided to do was to send a political mission of some stature to the United States. The Balfour mission was sent in an attempt to ascertain the war-readiness of the American government and to encourage and take advantage of the initial enthusiasm of the new partner.

The mission was composed of seven different departmental missions – one each for blockade matters, shipping, wheat, munitions, the army, the navy and the Treasury – and was presided over by the Secretary of State for Foreign Affairs, A. J. Balfour, whose duty it was to charm the American people into suppressing any distrust of Britain and to inspire them to plunge into the joint war effort. The mission came to discuss war problems with an Administration totally unprepared for such discussions, and spent such a short time in Washington that the results were uneven. Balfour was nearly an unalloyed success – even the moderate Irish-Americans liked him – but the level of accomplishment of the departmental missions varied greatly, with, for example, the wheat mission accomplishing nearly everything it had set out to do, and the shipping mission achieving virtually nothing.

From the moment when diplomatic relations between the United States and Germany were severed on 3 February 1917, the British government considered that American entry into the war was certain.[1] At the same time, it was considered politic that no hint of this attitude should be given publicly. This did not prevent the various governmental departments from drawing up memoranda on aid from and co-operation with the USA, against the day when the 'overt act' by Germany required by President Wilson before he would ask for a declaration of war should occur. There were several such acts, and on 2 April 1917 the President asked Congress to recognise a state of war between the United States and Germany. On 3 April Lloyd George read out to the Imperial War Cabinet a report of the statement, and after some discussion the Cabinet agreed on a proposal that had been earlier considered: that the British government should send a special mission to the USA, with (it was hoped) the political effect of inspiring the new partner to great efforts. The Cabinet instructed Balfour to sound out the American Ambassador, Walter Hines Page, that afternoon on the acceptability of the plan to the American government; Page, a noted Anglophile, immediately assured Balfour that it was a splendid idea.[2] On 4 April Balfour reported back to the Cabinet, and it was decided that the head of the mission must be of very high status (in order to flatter the Americans) and that he should be accompanied by representatives of the Admiralty, the War Office, the Ministries of Munitions, Shipping and Food, and the Bank of England.[3]

It was decided on 5 April that Balfour should head the mission, and only then was a serious attempt made to ascertain whether the President would welcome such a mission, since it was very well understood in London that Page had little real influence in Washington because of his notorious Anglophilia. Sir Eric Drummond, Balfour's Principal Private Secretary, cabled Colonel House on the matter that afternoon, and House sent the cable on to the President. House was well aware of the President's probable response, and he tried to smooth the way first by describing Balfour as the most liberal member of the Cabinet, and secondly by emphasising that it would be a great service to the relations between the two countries if the President could talk to Balfour personally.[4] The President was, in fact, most reluctant, as he wrote to House on 6 April: 'The plan has its manifest dangers. I do not think that all of the country will understand or relish. A great many will look upon the mission as an attempt to in some degree take charge of us as an assistant to Great Britain.'[5] He recognised the advantages of such a mission, however, adding that 'it will serve a great many useful purposes and perhaps save a good deal of time in getting together';[6] but he did not give a final answer, and House wrote to him again on 8 April, stating that he was afraid that it would give offence unless he could answer Drummond's cable soon. The President finally acquiesced, and House thereupon cabled Drummond on 9 April accepting the proposal.[7]

The various departments then chose their representatives. To tend to the needs of Balfour, the Foreign Office sent Drummond, later the Earl of Perth, who was brother-in-law to the late Duke of Norfolk and a prominent Roman Catholic layman, and Ian Malcolm, MP, who were respectively Balfour's Principal Private Secretary and his Parliamentary Private Secretary, as well as Cecil Dormer, who was in charge of travel arrangements. The Admiralty sent Rear-Admiral Sir Dudley deChair, who had been naval attaché in Washington in 1905–6, and Fleet Paymaster V. A. Lawford. The War Office sent General G. T. M. Bridges as head of the military mission, and he was accompanied by Major H. H. Spender-Clay, MP, who had been on Bridges's staff in France; Lt-Col. C. E. Dansey, a member of the General Staff, whose province was Military Intelligence; Col. T. H. Goodwin of the Royal Army Medical Corps; Lt-Col. Langhorne, Royal Artillery; Lt-Col. F. K. Puckle, whose speciality was supplies and transport; Capt. T. Heron of the Ordnance Department, whose speciality was lines of communication; and Lt-Col. Lionel Rees of the Royal Flying Corps. The Ministry of Munitions sent W. T. Layton, Director of Requirements and Statistics Branch of the ministry; C. T. Phillips, of the American and Transports Department; P. M. Amos, chairman of the Priority Committee; and Capt. Leeming. The Royal Commission on Wheat Supplies of the Ministry of Food sent A. A. Anderson and H. D. Vigor, respectively vice-chairman of and secretary to the Wheat Commission. To deal with war trade and blockade matters, the Ministry of Blockade sent as head Lord Eustace Percy of the Foreign Office, who was acknowledged – at least in London – as possessing special expertise on American affairs; A. A. Paton of the Ministry of Blockade; S. McKenna of the War Trade Intelligence Department; F. P. Robinson of the Board of Trade; and M. D. Peterson of the Foreign Trade Department. Geoffrey Butler, an ex-Cambridge don working in the News Department of the Foreign Office, took general charge of information and publicity. The Treasury representatives would be Sir Hardman Lever and Andrew McFadyean, who were already in the United States, and the Bank of England was represented by its Governor, Lord Cunliffe.

While those selected were preparing for the journey, the Cabinet discussed the proposals for various forms of assistance which the mission would ask the American government to render the Allies, and on 10 April Balfour asked the Cabinet to decide specifically on instructions for his guidance in the United States. Briefly, the Cabinet decided on the following: (1) Balfour was to draw the President's attention to the need to develop fully American shipbuilding capacity. Further, he was to explain the difficulty of inducing neutral vessels to continue in Allied trade, and to ask whether American vessels plying the coastal trade could be directed into this trade and their place taken by neutral vessels; (2) he was to urge the United States to send a few trained troops to the Western Front immediately, both to show the flag in Europe and to give the Americans a stake in the war. He was to emphasise the need for large drafts of men as soon as possible and to offer aid in training them (the hope was that they could be sent to join Allied units); (3) at the request of the Minister of Munitions, he was to stress the importance of the United States Army's adopting British patterns of guns; (4) at the request of the Shipping Controller, he was to urge the importance of releasing surplus supplies of wheat; (5) he was to stress the importance of increasing the output of, and reducing civilian demand for, steel, and to warn against recruiting steelworkers and other skilled workers into the army; and (6) he was to inquire into the importance of the Irish question in Anglo-American relations and telegraph the results of this inquiry to the Cabinet.[8]

The mission departed from Liverpool on 13 April 1917, after being held up for some hours by reports of German submarines sighted in the Irish Sea, and arrived at Halifax, Nova Scotia, on 20 April. There the mission boarded a train for the journey to the United States, and on 21 April, on the Maine border, they were met by the official reception committee. Balfour gave a press conference in the railway car – timed to appear in the Sunday morning papers – and arrangements were made for the mission to arrive in Washington, DC, on Sunday afternoon, 22 April.[9]

In the meantime, the American government was preparing for the missions (the French government had decided to send one as well, and it would be in the United States at the same time as the British one). Breckenridge Long, Third Assistant Secretary of State, was in charge of the mundane arrangements, and he went so far as to offer the use of his house in Washington as the residence for the British (the offer was accepted).[10] Colonel House was repeatedly consulted on the arrangements until, as he wrote in his diary on 21 April, 'I am sick unto death of it and have more than half a notion to avoid it'.[11] House did not really mean this, however, in view of the fact that he agreed with Sir William Wiseman that it was up to him to ensure Balfour's success with the President.[12] Wiseman was the head of British Military Intelligence in the United States, but with a cover as a member of the Ministry of Munitions there. More important in this connection, he was rapidly becoming Colonel House's and the President's link with the British government, in their efforts to bypass the two unsatisfactory ambassadors.[13] Wiseman visited House on 15 April, and House noted that

> We discussed . . . a plan by which I could see him [Balfour] before he saw anyone else. Wiseman thinks I should give him a survey of the attitude of the U.S. He told me what Spring Rice had in mind to say to Balfour and he thinks this should be neutralised. What a task it is to work against such erratic and uncertain influences. Sir William thought I should guide Balfour as to what he should say to the President and not allow him to drift on the rocks. . . .[14]

Consequently House joined the mission's train in New York City at 9 a.m. on 22 April, and rode with them as far as Baltimore, while he and Balfour talked together for an hour. Knowing the President's tendency to delay making a decision, House advised Balfour to be entirely frank with the President about the needs of the Allies – and if anything to exaggerate rather than to minimise the difficulties involved, so that the President would feel it was necessary for the country to 'go in up to the hilt'.[15] He advised Balfour not to discuss peace terms with the President, since he suspected that differences would be bound to arise. The two men agreed enthusiastically that their countries should stand together for a 'just peace'.[16] More prosaically, they discussed the drawbacks of the Ambassador, Spring Rice, but House urged Balfour not to replace him: his subordinates, especially Wiseman, Crawford and Commodore Gaunt, the naval attaché, were working in such close harmony with American officials that it would be unfortunate to disturb existing relations by bringing in a new ambassador. Finally, House agreed to go to Washington in a few days.[17]

The mission arrived in Washington that afternoon. Thereafter, the days were taken up with a constant round of technical conferences and public events, the latter to a large extent being dominated by Balfour (although General Bridges and Admiral deChair, as heads of the military and naval missions, sometimes joined him). The purpose of these public events was to generate mass public support for American aid for the Allies and general enthusiasm for the joint waging of war. The mission was entertained at a large dinner at the White House on 23 April; it travelled to Mount Vernon with the French mission on 29 April to lay a wreath on George Washington's tomb; Balfour addressed a joint session of Congress, which the President attended, on 5 May; the mission visited New York City for several days, during which time the mission was fêted at several civic banquets and Balfour (on 13 May) made an unpublicised visit to ex-President Theodore Roosevelt; the mission visited Richmond, Virginia, on 19 May as a token appearance in the South; and finally on 25 May most of the mission departed for Canada.[18] (During all of this activity, Balfour still managed to play tennis 'many afternoons', when, partnered by Malcolm or Drummond, he played Frank Polk and David Houston, the Secretary of Agriculture.)[19]

Balfour was the political leader of a largely technical mission. He 'kept general touch, alert for any point where a word from him might lessen difficulties, but never attempting to interfere with the course of technical negotiations'.[20] His duty was to impress the American public with his statesmanship and amiability – and, by extension, that of the British nation – and he spent his time making speeches and press statements directed towards that end. Further, Balfour undertook several long conversations with House and the President, singly and together. Balfour's first discussion with House, on 22 April, has been noted above. His first discussion with the President, at which Secretary of State Lansing was also present, took place on the morning of 23 April in the White House. As far as Balfour was concerned, the most important statement by the President was that he did not think it expedient to bind himself by treaty obligations to the Allies, although he would throw himself wholeheartedly into the war and see it through to the finish. No questions of detail were discussed – in fact, Balfour felt that they were 'rather sedulously avoided' by both the President and Lansing. Balfour felt that this was not surprising, since 'it is quite clear that not very much has been attempted and nothing completed by way of reforming and expanding organisation required to deal with the problem of a great war'.[21] The President himself was rather displeased with the discussion, telling House that it was not satisfactory because 'Lansing has a wooden mind and continually blocked what I was trying to convey.' He wanted another conversation with Balfour, with House present, and he suggested a family dinner at the White House, with a conference afterwards.[22]

House saw Drummond on 26 April, and the two decided that House should see Balfour again before he saw the President at the family dinner on 30 April, so that House 'might know how to guide the conversation and make it effective and harmonious'.[23] Accordingly House met with Balfour and Drummond on 28 April, when they talked for over an hour. The main topic was possible future peace terms to be imposed on the Central Powers, assuming that Germany would be decisively defeated. Then House inquired as to what treaties had been signed by the Allies on the division of spoils, and Balfour told him. House's reaction was 'that it was all bad and I told Balfour so. They are making it a breeding ground for future wars.' Balfour agreed 'with enthusiasm' to House's suggestion that the United States should keep clear of any promise so that it could exert an influence 'against greed' at the peace conference.[24]

Future peace terms formed the main topic of after-dinner conversation between the President, House and Balfour on 30 April. As House wrote,

> The ground we covered was exactly the same as Balfour and I had covered in our conference Saturday. I did but little talking, but tried to steer the conversation so as to embrace what Balfour had said to me and what the President and I had agreed upon in former conferences... The conclusions arrived at were exactly the conclusions which Balfour and I had reached in Saturday's conference....[25]

House and Balfour met again on 13 May. They discussed German and Austrian peace terms, which discussion House reported to the President in a letter that day. What he did not mention – nor record in his diary – was that he had developed the idea of a secret Anglo-American defensive naval alliance. Balfour, however, leapt on the idea, and it was the object of some discussion in the Cabinet, but nothing ultimately came of it.[26]

Balfour had two more meetings with the President. He called on Wilson on 17 May to say goodbye before the mission left for Richmond. On 21 May the President paid Balfour the compliment of calling on him to say a final goodbye and the two spoke for an hour. There is, apparently, no record of either conversation, but presumably they covered topics of interest to both – the peace terms, the submarine situation and Russia, where the course of the revolution was causing the Allies grave concern about her ability to remain in the war.[27]

Another topic with which Balfour had been concerned during his visit to the United States was the Irish question. When the United States had entered the war Wilson had realised that the problem of Ireland could bar effective co-operation with Britain. On 11 April 1917 a message written personally by the President was telegraphed to Page for him to convey to Lloyd George, which stated that 'the only circumstance which now seems to stand in the way of an absolutely cordial co-operation with Great Britain . . . is the failure so far to find a satisfactory method of self-government for Ireland.'[28] Lloyd George and the Cabinet had already evidenced their concern by charging Balfour with the task of investigating the importance of the Irish question in the United States.[29] Balfour spoke to Lansing, who told him that the effect of the Irish question on American opinion was a significant cause of current hostility to Britain.[30] On 3 May Balfour met a group of Irish-Americans, all of whom were moderates committed to home rule, and firm supporters of Wilson's war policy. The Americans stressed the unacceptability of partition and Balfour stressed the problem of Ulster. The more active and extreme Irish-Americans were not present, and Balfour may not have appreciated their importance when he cabled to Lloyd George on 5 May that the Irish question 'is apparently the only difficulty we have to face here, and its settlement would no doubt greatly facilitate the vigorous and lasting co-operation of the United States Government.'[31] This was, of course, just what the President had written on 10 April. Balfour later attended a dinner to meet Irish-American politicians,[32] and Drummond held a series of meetings with Catholics (which meetings House felt 'must be watched with care'),[33] but Balfour apparently did not change his assessment of 5 May.

Balfour, then, spent his time in the United States either discussing questions of high policy or showing the flag. Only rarely did he participate in the technical discussions, after the opening, rather formal, session of each of the missions.

The main task of the representatives sent by the Ministry of Blockade was to convince the American government to join wholeheartedly in the enforcement of the economic blockade procedures developed by the Allies over the three years of war. The negotiations were not to be undertaken by the mission alone, but in conjunction with the Embassy, and the decisions taken on what proposals to put forward to the Americans would, in fact, be 'subject in every particular to the advice of the Embassy, who are the only people competent to judge the situation'.[34] In view of the friendly relationships between subordinate officials on each side described by House to Balfour, particularly between Crawford and Polk, the Counselor of the State Department,[35] this was probably a wise arrangement.

The terms of reference of the mission were (1) to arrange adequate control over all American exports to countries contiguous to Germany; (2) to arrange machinery for preventing American exports from reaching unfriendly firms in neutral countries; and (3) to utilise the British/American monopoly over coal to direct ships and to control shipments for Allied use. Soon after the arrival of the mission in Washington, the members met with representatives from the Embassy (primarily Crawford and J. Broderick) to discuss and agree on the proposals to be put before the American government. They decided to urge (1) that the United States adopt a blacklist of enemy-associated firms in Latin America, and place under control enemy firms in the United States; (2) that the United States join with the Allies in using its economic power to force the neutral countries to conform to Allied requirements – for example, to force Spain to send more iron ore to Britain for munitions and to force neutral shipping out of harbour and into the carrying trade for the Allies; (3) that the American government be represented on all blockade bodies in London, and waive all past American claims for damages to shippers and exporters; and (4) that the Navicert system, by which the Embassy certified American ships as carrying non-contraband goods, be continued. They decided not to press censorship questions, to leave coal and oil questions to be handled separately, and to do the same with finance, on account of the latter's technical nature. It was also decided to propose that joint Anglo-American sub-committees be set up on various topics to draw up reports and present them to a joint committee comprising senior members of the mission and of the interested American departments.[36]

The first formal meeting was held on 4 May, when Balfour and the blockade mission representatives met Lansing and his assistants. The Americans agreed to the setting-up of the proposed sub-committees, and a series of meetings was held by the subordinate officials to discuss the substantive proposals.[37]

The third point which the mission had decided to urge – that the

American government be represented on all blockade bodies in London – was soon partly accepted by the Americans. On 5 May Lansing wrote to the President strongly supporting the appointment of a representative to the War Trade Intelligence Department in London, which collected information on firms doing business in neutral countries, so that the United States would have access to the information. The President replied two days later that it was a 'very useful suggestion', providing that Lansing could find the right man.[38]

On 7 May the Embassy forwarded to the State Department a long memorandum on the assistance Britain hoped would be provided by the United States in the joint struggle to force the neutrals to accede to Allied demands concerning shipping and exports;[39] but the next day, when Polk met with Percy, Crawford and Robinson, he warned them that the United States would not be able to go as far as the British government wished them to go.[40] Further to this meeting, Crawford sent Polk on 11 May memoranda containing information on methods already used by Britain to control neutral tonnage, in particular through the supply of bunker coal, and suggesting how American co-operation could improve this control, especially now that the Allies and the United States controlled 'practically the whole coal supplies of the world'.[41]

Polk's warning notwithstanding, negotiations proceeded with some dispatch. Balfour by 8 May could cable to London that policy would be settled by the time the mission returned,[42] and on 10 May Willert could write to his Editor that 'the best thing that has happened is the surprising willingness of people here to co-operate with us over the blockade. I dare say that not much of this will be allowed to get into print but as things are going now, it looks as if we shall get everything we want. This applies both to the actual blockade and the coal situation.'[43]

On 14 May joint sub-committees which had been set up on export licences and on statistics and sources of information submitted their reports to the Secretary of Commerce, William Redfield, and Lansing. The report on export licences dealt mainly with British desires, and that on statistics with aid that the United States Diplomatic Service could render, assuming the former report was accepted.[44] On 17 May L. H. Woolsey, the Law Adviser in the State Department, drew up a memorandum which embodied the points made by the American representatives in the discussions with the British, and which summed up the American response to the British requests: the United States would not assist in the blockade of neutral countries (which the

American government felt was contrary to neutral law), but would co-operate on the basis of the right of the United States to control its exports to any country, neutral or belligerent. The government was unwilling to force neutrals to send tonnage through the submarine zone for the benefit of the United States or of the Allies, beyond insisting that they carry their own supplies to and from the belligerents. The government would issue export licences to American ships, which would no longer come under the British Navicert system. The American government would insist on an equal voice in bunker control, and would not refuse coal to persons merely on the ground of enemy association or nationality, without reasonable ground for believing that the coal would be used for the direct benefit of Germany. The United States would agree on a coal 'whitelist', but would not accept the British and French blacklists in their entirety. The government would appoint representatives on the various British and Allied blockade committees, on the basis that arrangements were not to be concluded without the approval of the United States.[45]

These reservations arose from the reluctance of the American officials completely to abandon their positions of three years by immediately agreeing to procedures which they had previously condemned as illegal. Also, they could not accept mere nationality as proof of wrong-doing, since German-Americans made up the largest non-English-speaking group in the United States, and there was no proof of its disloyalty.[46]

After the American government had stated its position, Polk suggested to Crawford, on 18 May, that they should each put on record any outstanding points so that they could be cleared up. Polk submitted a list of minor proposals, such as the removal of all persons in the United States from the blacklist and relief of American ships from the bunker conditions, virtually all of which were agreed to by the British and embodied in a memorandum by Woolsey on 23 May.[47] Crawford, for his part, feeling that there was for the moment little more to discuss in regard to pressure on neutrals concerning export trade and shipping, stated that the British could now only leave the American government to evolve its policy. He thought that although there were some divergent views on trading with the enemy, these would probably turn out to conflict more in principle than in practice. He still urged that the United States join Britain in enforcing new bunker conditions, and suggested further discussions of bunker control before the mission departed.[48] As a result, Woolsey read a memorandum to Percy in which the American government unofficially accepted one of the two alternative proposals for bunker control which the British had put forward.[49]

Thus when the mission left Washington for Canada on 25 May (leaving Percy and Peterson behind to help the Americans set up the necessary machinery to enforce trade restrictions and a blockade), the British were, by and large, satisfied with the agreements that had been reached. The negotiations had been hampered by the fact that Congress had not yet passed the Trading with the Enemy Act and the Espionage Bill, and therefore no one had known just what powers the Administration would possess to carry out a war trade policy (although agreements had been based on the assumption that these two bills would be passed in the proposed form). They felt that the American government was fully convinced of the need to keep all supplies of military value from reaching the enemy, and although the USA could not agree to adopt the British Navicert system, probably because it was administered by British officials, they planned to replace it with their own stringent system of export licences. No formal agreement was reached on bunker control, but the mission was convinced that the USA recognised the importance of keeping coal out of the hands – and ships – of the enemy, and would in fact largely go along with the British practice, if not principle, while reserving their position.[50] With the exception, then, of the vital problem of neutral shipping, the British blockade mission achieved the substance, if not the appearance, of the goals which they considered to be most important.

The shipping mission, like the blockade mission, was concerned to force neutral tonnage into Allied service, but in addition the mission intended to do all it could to encourage American shipbuilding. The shipping mission began with extremely high expectations, but a combination of circumstances and personalities ensured that it achieved almost nothing.

On the day Britain received word of the President's speech to Congress, Sir Joseph Maclay, the British Shipping Controller, produced a memorandum setting out the urgent need for shipping, and suggesting what aid the USA could furnish. Rather than wait for the departure of the mission, the memorandum was communicated to Page and he cabled it to the State Department, so that the American government was early apprised that, in Maclay's words, 'The most vital thing for the Allies at present is the provision of shipping.'[51] The British need seemed self-evident, and Lord Eustace Percy was not alone in his belief that 'We must assume that we can in the next few weeks put forward the most drastic proposals of co-operation without fear of offending or inconveniencing the United States Government.' As far as the shipping problem was concerned, he felt that the British government 'need only ask to get the full co-operation of the American Shipping Board in directing tonnage into the needful trades and in bunker policy'.[52] The shock was correspondingly greater when, after the first informal meetings with William Denman (the Chairman of the United States Shipping Board), the British realised that he was virulently anti-British.

The Ministry of Shipping sent as its representatives on the mission Arthur Salter, Director of Ship Requisitioning, and Thomas Royden of the Cunard Company, but the ship they were on collided with a British cruiser in the Mersey, and they only arrived in the United States after the rest of the Balfour mission had departed. In the circumstances Robinson of the blockade mission took the lead in negotiating with the Shipping Board, joined on occasion by Percy, Alan G. Anderson, the Wheat Commission representative in the mission, and by T. Ashley Sparks, T. S. Catto and Cannop Guthrie, all Ministry of Shipping representatives in the United States. (Sparks, as General Manager of Cunard, was disqualified from diplomatic discussion, and Balfour impressed Anderson for this work.) The first meeting of the British shipping experts took place on 26 April. Robinson, Anderson, Sparks and Catto were present, and they decided that since Britain supplied shipping for France and Russia, any tonnage provided by the United States for either of these allies could only benefit Britain, and therefore it should be suggested that this be done. Further, they decided to recommend that the United States step up shipbuilding and put controls on the chartering of neutral shipping by private citizens. Memoranda embodying these suggestions were duly sent to the State Department.[53]

Informal meetings were held with Denman and his officials in the first days of the mission's stay in Washington. Denman asked for information of various sorts – how British, including colonial, shipping was employed, how Allied shipping was employed, for statistics of tonnage losses, for example – and the British cabled to London time and again for particulars he requested.[54] On 1 May the first formal conference was held, attended by Balfour, Drummond, Anderson, deChair, Lansing, Denman, Redfield and Polk, among others.[55] The discussion may have been heated, because when on 7 May Denman requested another conference with Balfour, Lansing delayed his approval until 10 May.[56] Meanwhile, the Cabinet was sending increasingly desperate requests to Balfour for American help with shipping, with accompanying statistics showing higher and higher tonnage losses.[57] These were conveyed to the American government, who, as Balfour informed London, realised the gravity of the situation,[58] but the hostility of Denman prevented progress. That earlier optimist, Percy, finally wrote that

> Crawford thinks Balfour should be merely civil and polite to Denman and promise him to do anything possible. I'm afraid I don't agree. We have been jollying Denman along, and the only result is that he thinks he has been jollying us along. The time has come when Mr Denman must be shown that we are not going to continue to talk until we have some proof that the talk is not merely academic.
>
> I would suggest that Balfour should take the initiative of cross-questioning him on what he had done up to date – what are the Board's construction plans...etc?....[59]

That, of course, was the nub of the matter: the British could have borne with any chauvinistic unpleasantness – in fact, some had been expected – if only there had been any signs of early results in the matter of shipping. Denman was convinced that the British were keeping their merchant marine out of danger in order to force American vessels to take greater risks, so that at the end of the war, Britain would remain the major merchant sea power. The Shipping Board had control over all neutral ships in American waters, and the British found it impossible to get Denman to agree to their being put into immediate service for the Allies. Further, the construction of new ships was delayed because Denman and his subordinate, General Goethals of Panama Canal fame, feuded constantly and publicly over whether the Shipping Board should build steel or wooden ships. Just before the mission left, Goethals was given extra authority over shipbuilding, and the British, who found him an energetic, practical man, hoped for an improvement in shipbuilding performance.[60]

While the mission was in Washington, Denman spent no little time attempting to convince Balfour to turn over British shipbuilding orders in American shipyards to the United States. During the previous year, when the German submarine campaign had begun to take serious toll of British shipping, T. Ashley Sparks had come to the United States and placed as many contracts as possible for ships with American yards. Denman tried to get Balfour to turn the contracts over to the government voluntarily, but Balfour, in a written undertaking, agreed only to turn them over if the American government made a formal request to this effect; in any case, as he pointed out, the government could commandeer them if the British government refused to turn them over. The mission assumed, from Denman's dissatisfaction with Balfour's undertaking, that Denman must feel he could not win the sanction of the State Department and Congress. (As it turned out, this was a miscalculation.) At any rate, Balfour thought that Denman was assured of his good faith, but after the mission had left Washington for Canada, both Percy and Crawford wrote frantic letters to Balfour in which they warned him that Denman was saying that Balfour (presumably when First Lord in 1916) had deliberately filled up American yards with orders on 'slow time' to prevent the American mercantile fleet from being built; they felt that he should immediately write to Colonel House denying the slander. Drummond did so, and he later received word that House had laid the rumours to rest.[61] The incident illustrates the ineradicable prejudice of Denman which prevented the mission from accomplishing anything. Presumably the President might have modified Denman's approach, but he tended not to interfere in the doings of departments – except the State Department – unless a situation became so awful that he had no choice. In this case he did not grasp the nettle until the Balfour mission had departed, when he asked for the resignations of both Denman and Goethals and appointed Edward Hurley as chairman.

The final report on the shipping mission, written by Robinson, summed up the difficulties involved and the consequent lack of achievement:

The authority at present charged with the responsibility ... with merchant shipping is the Federal Shipping Board. This Board contains one shipowner, but, otherwise, the members have no practical knowledge of shipping matters. The Chairman, Mr Denman ... with strong anti-British prejudices, is far the most important member, and keeps the greater part of the business in his own hands. In these circumstances ... great difficulty was experienced in arriving at any satisfactory understanding with the United States Government in regard to shipping matters.

The results achieved may be summarised by saying that the serious urgency of the tonnage problem has been brought home to the United States authorities...Mr Denman...does not, however, realise the importance of immediate action... He is aiming rather at spectacular action on a large scale at some time in the future...

It seems likely...that some difficulty will be experienced in securing co-operation between the Ministry of Shipping and the Shipping Board. This difficulty is, however, entirely due to the personality of Mr Denman....[62]

The near total failure of the shipping mission can be contrasted with the success of the wheat mission. The occasion of the Balfour mission was seized upon by Lord Crawford, Chairman of the Wheat Commission, and Lord Davenport, the newly appointed Food Controller, as a chance to send out representatives (Alan G. Anderson and H. D. Vigor) under the best possible auspices to 'clear up a number of outstanding difficulties'.[63] The special objects of the mission in the United States were (1) to emphasise the prime importance of food as a war need; (2) to examine the Commission's local machinery (the Wheat Export Company); and (3) to establish touch with any Food Controller appointed in the United States.[64]

Before leaving, Anderson and J. Beale of the Wheat Commission had talked to the Shipping Controller about a possible wheat shortage: in February, North American shipments of wheat had fallen without warning from a promise of 260,000 tons to 120,000 tons. While on board ship, Anderson brought to Balfour's attention the question of establishing priority for wheat shipments over those of munitions; Layton of the Ministry of Munitions demurred at this suggestion, and Balfour cabled to the Cabinet for a decision. Upon arrival at New York, Anderson learned that France, Italy and Britain had all taken alarm about food, and consequently the Shipping Controller had offered a substantial increase in tonnage for wheat, achieved by decreasing the amount for munitions. Therefore, one further task of Anderson's was to find enough wheat to fill all the ships now available.[65]

Vigor spent the greater part of his time while in the United States inspecting the Wheat Export Company's procedures (which he and Anderson decided were quite efficient), travelling around to the different wheat exchanges and working with the different branches of the Department of Agriculture,[66] while Anderson was responsible for most of the negotiations.

On arrival in the USA Anderson and Vigor stayed in New York for a short period while the rest of the mission went to Washington. In New York, Anderson met with Layton, George Booth (on another mission for the Ministry of Munitions to facilitate the production of Russian munitions), Connop Guthrie, the head of the Ministry of Shipping mission in the USA, and Robson of the Wheat Export Company of New York, and they discussed the possibility of providing the necessary extra wheat. They decided that there would be great difficulty getting enough wheat to port to fill all of the extra tonnage: the problem was the organisation of Allied internal traffic in the United States. They all agreed that Allied demand on the American railroads should be concentrated in Guthrie's organisation; as things were, Guthrie routed Allied wheat shipments, Japp of the Munitions mission routed British munitions, and Russian, French and Italian missions all routed their own munitions – and the American railway system was in a state of chaos.

Anderson decided that the real problem was the independence of the Allies, but that if he could get the Ministry of Munitions to give responsibility to Guthrie for routing munitions, the Allies would have less excuse to demur.[67] The Wheat Commission accepted the suggestion with alacrity,[68] and when questioned, so did the Railway Executive, the committee of American railway heads who were attempting to organise the system for war purposes.[69] Layton changed his mind several times, due to the known desire of his ministry to maintain a separate organisation, but finally on 3 May Anderson got him to dispatch a message to Addison advocating the concentration of all traffic under Guthrie.[70] It appears probable that Addison resisted so long because of personal antipathy towards Guthrie,[71] but finally, upon the return of the mission to London, Anderson learned that a scheme for a Traffic Executive controlled by Guthrie had been approved and was being implemented.[72] Thereafter, all routing of grain and munitions for the Allies was under the control of one organisation from the producer to the Allied countries.

Anderson's other main task was to establish contact with Herbert Hoover, soon to be in charge of the United States Food Administration. Hoover, who had been in charge of the Belgian Relief Commission, arrived in Washington on 6 May, and within a week the President had asked him to take charge of food matters. Because of Congressional opposition the Food Administration did not formally come into being for three months, but the British assumed that Hoover would be in charge of food matters and acted accordingly. There was some fear that

Hoover and Houston, the Secretary of Agriculture, would clash, but although they did not agree on policy – Hoover favoured much more national control than Houston – Houston supported Hoover,[73] and they were 'both keen to help' the Allies.[74] Hoover proposed to set up a Grain Executive which would purchase all wheat in the United States at the elevators, and which would sell all the wheat available for the Allies to the Wheat Export Company at cost plus charges; for its part the Wheat Export Company would agree to purchase all wheat offered. The Wheat Commission strongly approved the scheme, but its implementation had to wait until Hoover received his powers from Congress in July 1917.[75]

Anderson also attended meetings in Washington on shipping and on food supply.[76] As well he and Robson visited Chicago from 9 to 13 May at the invitation of the Chicago Board of Trade, during which visit a lucky coincidence enabled them to achieve another desire – lower prices:

> Our great demand upon North American wheat had skied the price up from 155¢ a bushel in October 1916, to 297¢ a bushel in May 1917, and if traders were allowed to gamble in futures there seemed no reason why the top should ever be reached. On the other hand, we did not want to check production, or to hamper even for a time the flow of wheat to the seaboard. Supply was the first consideration, taking precedence even of price.[77]

Wild speculation in futures (along with Wheat Export purchases to fill the extra tonnage) had caused the rise, and when the British reached Chicago,

> the bubble burst and we had our chance [to stop the trade in futures]. The wheat traders of Chicago had sold in several consecutive months much more wheat than existed and during our visit they discovered that someone had definitely cornered the market on a scale which had never before been achieved.
>
> Our hosts of the Board of Trade, after some hours of suspicion of one another, reached the true conclusion that we were the culprits, . . .[78]

Anderson and Robson easily convinced the traders that the object was not to ruin them – the Allies merely needed the wheat to survive. The arrangement decided upon was that traders who had sold short would be allowed to purchase actual wheat as it came to the elevators in order to liquidate their commitments, while the exchanges would be closed to trading in futures for the duration of the war. This brought the price down, and within a few months the Allies bought at fixed prices from only one source in the United States, the Grain Executive.[79]

Anderson and Vigor, then, had reason to congratulate themselves on the outcome of their mission. They had confirmed that the Wheat Executive Company was efficient, they had helped to reorganise Allied internal traffic, wheat prices had been brought down and the importance of the need for food had been emphasised. Finally, the American government organisation being established to control food was headed by a man who both admired the organisation set up by the British in the United States and was prepared fully to co-operate with it, to the satisfaction of both sides.

The munitions mission, like the shipping mission, actually achieved very little, but in this case it could be ascribed rather less to personal prejudice towards the British on the part of the Americans and rather more to the political realities of the situation. The overriding concern of the Ministry of Munitions was that the production being carried on for the British and the Allies in the United States should not be interfered with, and to this end the earliest and most important requirement, the ministry felt, was that the American forces utilise British patterns for guns, rather than adopt their own.[80] In this, the mission was only partly successful.

Before departure, Addison and Layton, the head of the munitions mission, drew up a list of points to impress on the Americans, and later on board ship this list was further discussed by the mission to determine which points should be emphasised.[81] These points were largely accepted by Newton Baker, the American Secretary of War: as the basis for discussions. The subjects to be considered, then, were (1) American gun and shell patterns, (2) the nature and extent of Allied requirements, especially those of Russia, (3) the protection of Allied contracts and priority in labour, materials and transport, (4) the organisation in the United States of purchasing for the Allies, and (5) the control of prices.[82]

When Layton first arrived in the United States, he spent some time in New York inspecting the ministry's organisation there and (as described above) helping to restructure the internal transport system.[83] He then proceeded to Washington for the general strategy meeting of the whole mission and to begin talks with American officials. He rapidly discovered that in some cases, groundwork had already been laid by Lever.

Lever, before joining the Treasury, had been Assistant Financial Secretary to the Ministry of Munitions. On 10 April Crawford, Spring Rice and Lever had called on Polk, and Polk had stated that 'their [the American] munitions departments would welcome any information or help which Lever might be able to give them from his Ministry of Munitions experience and that Lever should communicate with General Crozier, Chief of Ordnance, or Mr Scott, Chairman of the Advisory Council to the Committee of National Defense . . . [Lever] explained that he was already in touch with Crozier'.[84] Thereafter Lever met with Scott or Crozier several times, describing Ministry of Munitions' methods for purchasing materials and munitions, and discussing future price policies towards the Allies in the American markets. He also discussed purchasing with Bernard Baruch, the future Chairman of the American War Industries Board.[85]

Lever, also prior to Layton's arrival, began discussions on the question of the British rifle plants in the United States. As a result of the rifle crisis in late 1916 the British government had taken over several American rifle plants, and the American government now wished to purchase them from the British. The British government was perfectly willing to sell them, and therefore negotiations largely turned on the matter of price, which was settled on a basis of an American governmental payment of $9m. for the plants, with the British government taking any machinery not set up. (Baker gave his final approval to the agreement on 15 May 1917.)[86]

Lever, then, took care of a substantial amount of the preliminary information-giving before Layton and the rest of the mission arrived in Washington. The first formal meeting of the munitions (and military) mission with the American government officials was held on 5 May, the British being headed by Balfour and the Americans by Baker. Although much of the discussion was concerned with troops (see below), Balfour also urged that serious consideration be given to use by the American forces of British gun patterns, since additional types of guns and ammunition would adversely affect the supply situation. Baker referred the matter to General Crozier of the Ordnance Department and the General Staff for their consideration.[87] The members of the mission advanced three major reasons for American adoption of British patterns: bulk supplies of guns and ammunition could be secured much more rapidly if only British types were ordered; there would be great military advantages in uniformity of material on lines of communication in France; and if, for any reason, lines of communication over the Atlantic were cut when American troops were in France, the troops could draw munitions from British production and supplies. General Bridges, the head of the military mission, put forward the same considerations in a letter to General Scott, the Chief of the General Staff, and in a letter to his successor, General Bliss.[88] The British did not realise that General Joffre, of the French military mission, was simultaneously advising Baker to use American guns.[89] In the end, Baker decided in favour of the recommendations of General Crozier and the Ordnance Department, a decision which Layton learned about from Baker in a few minutes' conversation on the day of his departure from Washington: recognising that it would only be possible to secure bulk output of rifles and guns from the factories developed by the British government, the Ordnance Department decided to use British guns, for the most part – rebored to take American ammunition. (Layton estimated that this would mean a six-month delay.)[90] Fundamentally, Baker and the War Department would have preferred to use American guns, but had they made that choice, the first American troops to go to France would have been unarmed.[91]

The second subject to be discussed by the mission with the American officials was the nature and extent of Allied requirements, especially those of Russia, which Balfour brought to Lansing's attention in a letter on 7 May.[92] The American government was particularly interested in Russia and was sending a mission, headed by Elihu Root, a former Secretary of State and distinguished Republican elder statesman, to give aid and advice to the infant Russian republic. The British attempted to convince the American government that strict control should be kept over Russian purchases and supplies, but while the mission was in Washington, the Americans decided, for political reasons, to send railway stock to Russia, although there was, as yet, no tonnage in which to send it; the Americans did concede, however, that the British position was desirable in principle.[93]

The third subject for discussion was the protection of Allied contracts from commandeering by American government departments, and priority in labour, materials and transport for them. In the days immediately following the American severance of relations with Germany, the British government had asked for and received official assurances that Allied contracts in the United States would not be interfered with.[94] Yet, as Layton wrote in early June, 'The plans of the [American] departments are apt to be laid without considering their reactions, and we have already had preliminary warnings from our officers of the harmful effect on our supplies which may be produced by efforts of manufacturers to satisfy the demands of the Ordnance Department.'[95] The working of the priority system in Britain was explained to various American officials by Amos, chairman of the Priority Committee, but, as Layton wrote, 'in this, as in other matters, we have been greatly hampered by the absence of fixed responsibility which made it very difficult for us to make our representations in the right quarters.'[96] The day before the mission departed, Balfour wrote to Lansing pointing out that the entry of the United States as a belligerent meant that she was now competing with the Allies for goods, and urging co-ordination to avoid delays in the execution of orders and transport.[97] A Priority Board had been established, but on the day the mission departed Baker told Layton that the 'necessary decisions' had not yet been taken as to its functions.[98]

The fourth subject for discussion was the organisation in the United States for purchasing for the Allies. Because of the well-known and often-expressed dislike of the Administration for the Morgan firm,[99] it was considered that the American government might require an alternative method of purchasing for the Allies. Morgan's realised this as well as anybody, and on 4 April wrote to British government departments suggesting that they take up with the American government the possibility that the American government might itself purchase for the Allies in place of Morgan's.[100] The Administration considered this possibility,[101] and Layton felt that the course would have many advantages: 'it would be the surest way of placing on the American Government the responsibility of securing deliveries and handling as a whole all questions of priority . . . while it would be a simple matter of negotiation to retain those firms which have proved their capacity to produce the special requirements of each Ally.' As Layton noted, however, Morgan's organisation appeared to be the only machinery in the United States available for handling so large a task, and 'political reasons' prevented its absorption by the government as it stood.[102] Stettinius, the head of the Morgan organisation for the Allies, gave a memorandum to House – which House sent on to the President – recommending that the Allies retain their purchasing missions in the United States, which would co-operate with an American governmental prices and priority board.[103] Crawford broached the subject of the continued use of Morgan's by Britain to McAdoo, one of Morgan's staunchest detractors, on 15 May, and McAdoo answered that 'he had no objection to offer'.[104] Thus, as the time drew nearer for the mission to leave Washington, it seemed that the only feasible method would be for the Allies to retain the Morgan agency, and that American governmental control should be limited to 'a visa sufficient to enable the American Treasury to justify Allied expenditure to Congress'.[105] As Layton wrote on 5 June, however, 'it is realised in Washington that it would leave the Allies worse off than before America entered the war, since it gives no help to them in the matter of prices, and leaves them with the responsibility of getting deliveries, while it lays them open to the competition of the American munitions programme without establishing any means of co-ordinating the two sets of demands.'[106] And finally, with the express intention of bringing matters to a head and forcing the American government to make a decision, on 24 May Morgan's gave notice to the British government to terminate their role as negotiators of new contracts, although they offered to continue to execute contracts already negotiated.[107]

The fifth and final subject of discussion was the control of prices. What the British wanted was for the Allies to be able to purchase American raw materials and manufactured goods on the same terms as the American government, at prices much lower than the market prices for such goods. The American government resisted this idea strongly. Lever brought up the idea in his preliminary talks with McAdoo, Crosby and Baruch, but they all felt it would be impossible to effect.[108] The difficulty was that the producers, such as copper producers, were putting up fierce resistance on the grounds that they could not afford to give the same prices to the Allies as they had agreed to for the American government;[109] in the case of steel, in which the British government was especially interested, the American government itself was finding extreme difficulty in persuading the companies to agree to sell steel to them at less than market prices.[110] Balfour and the munitions mission finally felt constrained to write to the Secretaries of State, Interior and Commerce, pointing out that the United States was dependent on the British Empire for wool, rubber, tin, jute, ferro-manganese, plumbago and tonnage accommodation, and purchases by the American government of these commodities appeared to stand on the same footing as purchases by the Allies in the United States.[111] Baker, in fact, was convinced by the arguments put forward by the mission in conference, and he wrote to the President on 28 May urging the fixing of prices on an identical basis for the Allies and the American government.[112] The President was apparently convinced, but he had yet to enforce his conviction on his Administration; as Layton wrote, 'we have been repeatedly informed indirectly that the President will not hear of any suggestion that the Allies should be given less favourable terms than the American Government, but we have not been able to get any assurance that this is the official policy.'[113]

In his final report on the mission, Layton described the confusion reigning amongst those in the American government responsible for munitions. There were an extremely large number of boards, committees and departments whose co-ordination was a matter of great difficulty. Most had been appointed after the United States entered the war and their functions had not been distinguished. Progress was also seriously handicapped by the fact that Congress insisted that every item of expenditure must be brought before the Appropriations Committee. To sum up,

> the mission arrived before the Administration had had time to organise any effective control of American industrial resources, or to make any adequate delegation of authority. Hence none of the leading munitions questions between the two Governments have been brought to a definite conclusion, and it has only been possible to advance negotiations a stage or two. For the rest it has been possible to help those who are likely to have control of munitions to a better appreciation of the nature and magnitude of their task, and to tell them of the methods that have proved successful at home.[114]

Although General Bridges joined with the munitions mission in its attempt to convince the War Department to adopt British gun patterns, the major preoccupation of the military mission he headed was troops. British and French losses on the Western Front, and in particular the losses in 1916 on the Somme and at Verdun, had exhausted their manpower resources. Thus, the main objects of the mission were to persuade the United States to send immediately a Regular Army division in order to raise Allied morale, and as soon as possible thereafter to send drafts of partly trained men to be trained in Europe and then fed into British or French units. Of these objects, however, the mission succeeded in achieving only the first.

When the mission arrived in Washington on 22 April, Baker asked that discussions on military policy be deferred until the passing of the Army Bill then before Congress.[115] Because conscription was having a ragged time in Congress (Champ Clark, the Speaker of the House of Representatives, equated conscripts with convicts), Bridges, at a press conference, spoke very strongly in favour of compulsion. The other members of the mission thought that he had 'really messed it up', but the press, instead of being outraged, characterised him as a 'bluff soldier who did not know how to mince words', and he was asked to address the appropriate Senate committee on the same subject.[116]

On 29 April the Army Bill passed, with Bridges claiming some of the credit, and on the same day the Chief of the General Staff, General Scott, asked Bridges to let him have, in writing, his views on future co-operation of the American military forces in Europe. Bridges had met with General Joffre of the French mission when it arrived in Washington on 26 April, and they had agreed on the policy of urging the immediate dispatch to France of a *regular* division, followed as soon as possible by conscripted reinforcements, whose training would be completed in France,[117] and Bridges wrote to General Scott on 30 April that 'The sight of the Stars and Stripes on this continent will make a great impression on both sides... To this end I would like to see one of your regular divisions sent to France at once'.[118] The letter was read by both Baker and the President. On 2 May Bridges met with Baker for a long conference during which Bridges urged that the regular army division should co-operate with the British because of the similarity of language, but Baker told him that co-operation would most likely be with the French, and 'He [Bridges] seemed entirely satisfied and apparently had been directed not to stress this point.'[119] (The British had decided not to press this matter because Britain was being successful in its negotiations with the Americans on naval matters and because 'the French are a little touchy'.)[120] Thus it was decided early on that the Americans would send a division of the Regular Army as a token of the future, and that it would co-operate with the French.

The other questions about troops were, what was to follow, and when. What the British wanted, as Balfour made clear at the 5 May conference between the mission and representatives of the War Department and General Munitions Board, was for the United States to send large drafts of men who were only partly trained to the Western Front. There they would be more efficiently trained due to the exigencies of war than they could be in the United States, and fed into British and French units; their early arrival might well decide the outcome of the war. Bridges put the arguments to House, and Balfour sent a last plea to Lansing just before the departure of the mission.[121] But General Bliss, now Chief of the General Staff in succession to General Scott (who had been sent to Russia with the Root mission), set out the position as the General Staff saw it:

> The gentlemen belonging to these Missions at first were very reserved in their conferences with us. At first they laid stress only on the desirability of having a small body of troops go to the European theatre of war for the mere purpose of producing a moral effect . . . on the . . . Entente Allies. As they began to speak more unreservedly they let it appear that they wanted also to produce a moral effect upon our own people . . . It was not long before they said quite openly that we would not feel that we were in the war until we were well 'blooded' . . .
>
> The General Staff still feels that we should train and equip and prepare a formidable force before going across, but as the foreign gentlemen spoke more freely it became evident that what they need and want is *men*, whether trained or not . . .
>
> I feel France and England should stand fast and wait until our reinforcements can come and give a shattering blow.[122]

Baker accepted this argument, and very large detachments were not sent across until the shock of the German offensive in March 1918.

Although the French were awarded the first detachment of Regular Army troops, the British were successful in obtaining specialist auxiliaries, about which there were a number of meetings between various military mission members and their opposite numbers in the War Department in the first days of the mission's visit. Bridges in his report of 29 April was hopeful for the success of these talks, and on 3 May Baker secured the President's approval to a plan to send a number of railway battalions to man the supply line in France, medical units, including six base hospitals, and trained and untrained pilots and mechanics for the Air Service.[123] In addition, on 10 May the President approved the sending of companies of foresters to work in the French forests to fell timber for the trenches and soldiers' quarters. All of these auxiliaries were to wear American uniforms and to be paid by the United States and would later be transferred to the American army when it was organised and sent over.[124]

While Bridges was holding discussions about troops, each of the other members of the military mission gave lectures or attended talks in connection with his own speciality. Lt-Col. Langhorne, for example, visited the War College on 30 April and 2 May and gave lectures on heavy howitzers and the establishment of Divisional Ammunition Columns respectively. Lt-Col. Puckle discussed supply and transport problems with members of the War College. Lt-Col. Rees arranged for American air personnel to be trained in Canada, and visited aeroplane factories. Colonel Goodwin made all the arrangements for the medical aid being sent by the American government. Lt-Col. Heron lectured on lines of communication, and Major Spender-Clay lectured on Staff Duties. Lt-Col. Dansey held talks with the War Department on military intelligence; and the General Staff, which decided to establish an Intelligence Branch modelled on that of the British, requested that Colonel Dansey be left behind to help to organise the Branch, despite unexpected opposition from the Departments of State and Justice and the Treasury, as well as from Colonel House.[125] Even Bridges, in his spare time, gave a series of lectures at the War College on 'The Mounting of a Modern Battle'.[126]

The military mission, then, did a good deal of educative work in the higher reaches of the American army, which was unused to modern forms of warfare, and whose battle tactics had been largely formed by the Indian wars. Also, Bridges convinced Baker that the Chief of the General Staff, General Scott, was far too old for his post, and was instrumental in having him replaced by General Bliss, who was not much younger but who possessed much greater ability.[127] The mission secured the agreement of Baker and the President to the immediate sending of a division of the Regular Army to France, as well as the specialist auxiliary detachments. But they failed to convince the War Department to adopt British gun patterns, or to send large drafts of semi-trained troops to boost manpower on the Front. The mission was reasonably pleased with the outcome of their endeavours, but this might not have been so had they realised just how long the Allies would have to wait for American troops.

The main goal of the naval mission was, quite simply, to obtain the loan of as many American destroyers as possible in the shortest time. They were needed to help in the fight against German submarines which were sinking increasing numbers of Allied merchant ships, a situation which was causing grave concern to the British government.[128] In this, the mission, which was led by Admiral deChair, was quite successful.

Immediately after Congress recognised a state of war, Vice-Admiral Browning, Commander-in-Chief, North America and West Indies, began talks with the Navy Department over the provision of destroyers, and by 12 April agreement had been reached for the dispatch of six, with possibly another twelve to follow soon thereafter.[129] When the mission reached Halifax on 20 April, therefore, deChair found that 'my work was much facilitated'.[130] On 23 April he met with Josephus Daniels, the Secretary of the navy, who was accompanied by Admiral Benson, the Chief of Naval Operations, and Rear-Admiral Fletcher, but, in spite of Browning's groundwork, he immediately ran into difficulties: the navy was reluctant to send any more destroyers out of American waters. DeChair argued that eighty ships a week were being sunk by submarines, but this only served to harden the Americans; they felt that if the destroyers were sent, enemy submarines might cross the Atlantic (as they had done previously) to menace what would be undefended American coastal waters. Negotiations went on day after day, until the Assistant Secretary of the navy, Franklin Roosevelt, was won over, and he helped to persuade his colleagues of the necessity of sending a further thirty-six destroyers. DeChair experienced some difficulty in persuading the Americans to send all the destroyers to British waters, instead of sending some to assist French patrols, but he eventually convinced the Americans of the danger of dispersing the destroyer force. Therefore, on 25 April the first flotilla of six boats was dispatched to Queenstown, on 8 May and 13 May each a further six, and on 1 June a further thirty-six arrived.[131]

The immediate situation was much eased, but the naval mission was also concerned with the future construction of destroyers. The British argued strongly for giving priority in American shipyards to the construction of small craft for anti-submarine work, that is, destroyers and patrol boats. The Americans, conversely, were more concerned with building capital ships. The reason given was the fear of a postwar clash with Japan in the Pacific, where the United States had growing interests, but there was also some concern about postwar relations with Britain, whose mastery of the seas some naval men – and civilians – were determined to supplant.[132] A very few destroyers were begun, but by 14 May, as Balfour cabled to Lloyd George, 'Large US programme for capital ships makes construction of any considerable number of additional destroyers impossible. We have suggested abandonment for the present of capital ships but fear of Japan is so great both in the Navy Department and elsewhere that we have made no progress.'[133] What

Balfour did was to talk to Colonel House about the problem, and House developed the idea of a secret, Anglo-American defensive naval alliance, which, because Britain would guarantee naval aid to the United States if Japan attacked, would release the American navy from its obligation to build capital ships. Balfour sent it on to Lloyd George,[134] but nothing came of the idea because of the President's dislike of secret treaties (and the Congress would never approve an open one of this nature), and the Anglo-Japanese alliance. At any rate, in early July the American government reached a unilateral decision to postpone the capital ship programme for the duration of the war, and to begin immediately the construction of a further two hundred destroyers.[135] Thus, although the naval mission had not achieved its goal before departing from Washington, its arguments prevailed soon thereafter.

While in Washington deChair sometimes joined Balfour in his various public ceremonies. He also twice answered questions before the Naval Affairs Committee of the House of Representatives in secret session. He and his colleagues met daily with members of the Navy Department to answer inquiries, discuss inventions and arrange for other aids, such as mines, buoys and gun mountings.[136]

All in all, the naval mission was accounted a success. The reception of the British by the American naval officers had been much friendlier than expected; as Balfour wrote, '[Admiral Benson] was supposed to be anti-British, and [Daniels] to be incapable of taking wide view of naval policy. But no sign of these short-comings visible in the policy actually adopted.'[137] The Navy Department – in common with most of the other American departments – was in 'hopeless confusion',[138] but after initial resistance the department bowed to the arguments of the mission and the logic of submarine destruction and provided the aid required.

The head of the financial mission, Sir Hardman Lever, found himself with, loosely, three sets of problems. First of all, as the Treasury representative in the United States, he had to continue to find the funds to pay for the purchases of the Allies. Secondly, he had to contend with Lord Cunliffe, Governor of the Bank of England, in his attempts to continue in the United States his struggle with the British Treasury for the predominant voice in setting financial and especially exchange policy. And thirdly, he had to secure the promise of funds over the long term from the American government.

As described earlier, expenditure by Britain in the United States in April 1917 was in the order of $75m. a week. In March arrangements had been nearly completed for the issuing of a $250m. unsecured loan by the British, but it was not carried through at the request of the American Treasury, which wanted the field clear for its own Liberty Loan bond issue. Therefore, the overdraft at Morgan's grew, and Morgan's began to show signs of restiveness. On 9 April Lever, Crawford and J. P. Morgan met with Governor Harding of the Federal Reserve Board, at McAdoo's request, to discuss the needs of the Allies. Lever told Harding that Britain would require $500m. 'as quickly as possible', and in view of the overdraft it would not last more than thirty days, but that second and third instalments of the same amount would last sixty days each. He also pointed out that the immediate need was largely the result of French and Russian commitments assumed by the British government. Lever then spoke privately with Harding. He told him that in order to meet immediate needs, presumably including the overdraft, Britain proposed to issue a loan based on Canadian Pacific Railroad stock. He said that Britain would prefer not to issue it if 'temporary accommodation' could be extended by the American Treasury pending the Liberty Loan. Harding sounded out McAdoo on the question, but McAdoo replied that Britain should go ahead with the loan.[139]

A few days later Lever received disturbing reports from brokers and bankers that the issuing of the CPR loan might be construed as anti-Administration, in that it was 'deranging the plans'[140] for the Liberty Loan. Lever telephoned to Lamont of Morgan's, who agreed to send a special messenger with a letter to McAdoo that night, pointing out the possibilities and again asking him if he was willing that the loan should proceed.[141] Lever learned two days later that McAdoo desired that the issue not proceed, and that the British government carry on for sixty days, when the Liberty Loan would be completed. Lamont asked McAdoo how the British government was expected to finance their requirements in the meantime, and his reply was that 'that was their hunt'. McAdoo sent word to Spring Rice that the issue should not proceed because Britain could get the money more cheaply later from the American Treasury; and in the circumstances Lever had no choice but to cancel the issue.[142]

Fortunately for the British, McAdoo was not always quite so unhelpful. On 17 April Lever and Crawford had a long interview with him, detailing 'the situation in New York and the nature of our necessities', and after a long discussion McAdoo agreed to assist Britain as soon as the bond bill (giving the Treasury the right to make foreign loans) was passed, by making a temporary short-term loan of $150m. to $200m.[143] Lever received $200m. on 25 April, which was payable on 30 June, but he had had to agree that it would not be paid into Morgan's.[144]

In the meantime the Balfour mission had arrived in Washington. Lever called on Balfour on 23 April, and then he had a long conference with Cunliffe to explain the situation in the United States to him. Although he and Lever attended some of the conferences with McAdoo or Oscar T. Crosby (the Under Secretary of the Treasury) together, for the most part Cunliffe had independent duties. He spent some time acquainting the members of the Federal Reserve Board with the details of the British War Loans and war financial policy in general.[145] He then decided to make a tour to meet bankers and officials of some of the Federal Reserve Banks. McAdoo asked Hamlin to accompany him, and on a trip which lasted from 5 to 9 May (Cunliffe had to be in New York on 10 May with the rest of the mission), they visited Richmond, St Louis, Chicago and Cleveland. On 15 May they visited Boston.[146] At all of these stops Cunliffe explained fully the workings of the three British War Loans, and he was 'able to reassure many on the point which was causing them some anxiety . . . namely, as to the effect that the subscriptions to their Victory Loan of 2,000,000,000 dollars [that is, the Liberty Loan] would have on their deposits.'[147] Cunliffe incurred Hamlin's disgust before the visit was out because he refused to visit the Atlanta and Philadelphia Reserve Banks; he preferred to spend the time fishing in Florida. Hamlin wrote that 'He has missed a great opportunity to help his Government and I am very sorry . . . He told me he caught four fish in Florida, one weighing 125 pounds. His devotion to fishing has been at the expense of his Government.'[148]

Lever had his own difficulties with Cunliffe. He seemed to lose few opportunities to undermine British Treasury policy – sometimes in Lever's presence. On 25 April he expressed to Hamlin his sympathy with the Federal Reserve Board's action of December 1916, which had nearly wrecked British finances.[149] On 26 April, during a conference with Lever and McAdoo, Cunliffe supported McAdoo in his contention that the British government, rather than the American government, should advance the money for a Russian contract with Westinghouse.[150] On 29 April Davison of Morgan's rang, and Lever discovered that Cunliffe had been saying that 'plainly the British Government would have to issue some loans independently of the American Government' – which McAdoo had specifically, with reference to the CPR loan, asked Lever not to do.[151] On 2 May, at the first formal conference between the mission and the Treasury, attended by both Balfour and McAdoo,

> The requirements of Great Britain ... were discussed. McAdoo
> stated that the requirements of the Allies were so great that he was
> going to have difficulty in meeting them. Cunliffe interjected a
> remark that we could help out by selling Scheme B securities.
> McAdoo seemed surprised to hear that we still had American
> securities ... to sell. Lever ... did his best to change the subject by
> a reference to the securities forming the collateral to our loans.
> It was pointed out to McAdoo that we required $50m almost
> immediately. The Governor in reply to a question said that the
> 8th or 10th May would be early enough. Lever, however,
> supported by Balfour, insisted that we should require this not
> later than the 5th. McAdoo agreed.... [152]

Worst of all, as far as immediate problems were concerned, were
Cunliffe's attempts to force the British Treasury to ship gold to keep up
the exchange; the Treasury was trying every expedient possible to avoid
shipping any more gold. While he was in New York Cunliffe publicly
stated that he felt that the British government should ship more gold. It
was obvious that Cunliffe was trying to force the Chancellor's hand,
and equally clear that he could not be publicly corrected in the United
States.[153] He even went so far, when he and Lever had an interview with
McAdoo, as to make it 'plain that he was in favour of continued gold
imports into America'.[154] The Chancellor and Lever commiserated with
each other, but little could be done except to make it clear that
Cunliffe's views were his own and not those of the British
government.[155]

The major problem with Cunliffe's various offers of help to the
American Treasury was that they interfered with Lever's attempts to
make a case for massive long-term financial aid from the United States
to Britain. Ambassador Page on 6 April had transmitted a memorandum from Balfour to Lansing in which the financial needs of Britain
were expressed as being second only to shipping needs;[156] McAdoo
therefore probably was not surprised at Lever's statement to Harding of
Britain's needs on 9 April.

The estimate given to Harding for McAdoo on 9 April had covered
only British needs, and not those of the Allies. The British assumed that
the American government would take over payments for the Allies
dating from the American entry into the war; and France by 2 May had

agreed with Britain to reimburse Britain for payments dating from 1 April out of advances from the American Treasury.[157] There was more difficulty with Italy and Russia. The British Treasury had by 6 May received assurances that the American Treasury accepted the principle that the Allies should reimburse Britain for money spent on their account in the United States since 1 April 1917, using funds provided by the American government, and by 9 May Italy had agreed to reimburse Britian for such sums (in fact, Italy secured her advance from the American Treasury on that understanding).[158] Unfortunately, Crosby, the Treasury Under Secretary in charge of foreign loans, began to make difficulties, and told the Italians that the more they paid out to Britain now the less they would receive from the United States in the future.[159] Lever informed Balfour of the difficulty he was having with Italian repayments. It was arranged that Crosby and Lever should come to see Balfour, and 'At this interview Balfour told Crosby that he had clearly understood, and Crosby did not dispute this, at the interview with McAdoo [on 2 May] that the United States Government would take care of these payments.' [160] Crosby desired more information on the payments made for Italy. Lever disliked giving such information 'in principle', and he suspected that it was all a means of putting pressure on Britain to export more gold to the United States, a 'policy in which they are supported by public utterances of Cunliffe'.[161] The Chancellor gently rebuked Lever on 22 May: 'It does not seem to me unreasonable of US Treasury to ask details of Italian repayments. Generally speaking I feel we ought to be ready to furnish quite frankly any information asked for. They have some ground for suspicions in present case as Italians made suggestions to us for including pre-April expenditure, which of course we refused.'[162] Lever provided the required information to Crosby, and on 28 May Crosby gave his formal approval to reimbursements by Italy and Russia to Britain out of funds provided by the United States; that same day Lever received the first payment from Italy.[163]

In the case of Russia, however, the arrangement did not operate in the manner intended. The United States advanced $100m. to Russia in May, but instead of reimbursing the British, the Russian government instructed their Ambassador in Washington to pay nothing out of the credit to Britain in respect of contracts placed for the Russians through Morgan's.[164] Russia continued to refuse to give authority to any of its representatives in the United States to commit Russia financially, and Crosby said that he could not find anyone to deal with. (Lever also felt that the uproar in Russia – the aftermath of the February Revolution – made the American Treasury less ready to assume Russian obligations.)[165] The matter was not settled during the Balfour mission's stay in Washington; in fact, the Russian provisional government did not directly recommend that the American government reimburse Britain until 3 November 1917, four days before its downfall, and two years later the United States and Britain were still negotiating over the matter.[166]

Another element in the problem of financial aid for Britain was the ignorance felt by the American Treasury in the face of the huge sums Britain said she required. As McFadyean described McAdoo and Crosby,

> McAdoo, a Wall Street failure with designs on the Presidency, presides over the Treasury with more than an eye on his personal ambitions and on politics. He and the Administration...cut themselves away from the best financial advice which they could require by their political and personal hostility to New York finance and financiers. Crosby is a gentleman and honestly pro-Ally, but his experience of finance is limited, I believe, to the directorship of a street-car company, and his vision is correspondingly circumscribed... In their inexperience and their fearfulness they are incapable of any wide outlook or real grasp, and take refuge in red tape and petty detail.[167]

This lack of a wide outlook was obvious, as far as Lever was concerned, in nothing so much as the American Treasury's reaction to the run on the pound which occurred during the mission's stay. Crosby and McAdoo (aided by Cunliffe) kept urging Lever to bring down more gold from Ottawa, and Morgan's compounded the problem by refusing to buy any more sterling exchange unless they had cash in hand (apparently they could borrow no more from other banks).[168] The main reason for the drain, according to the Chancellor, was the heavy shipments of wheat, bought at unprecedented prices in order to fill the extra tonnage provided by the Shipping Controller; a subsidiary reason was that American banks were withdrawing their sterling balances from London in order to purchase Liberty Loan bonds.[169] But whatever the reason, the British found it difficult to convince the Americans that it was vital to support the rate of exchange; and in immediate terms, that it was legitimate to use funds provided by the American government to do so. The fear, apparently, was that McAdoo would not be able to convince Congress that it was a 'war purpose'.[170] The problem of the support of exchange was not resolved during the mission's visit, and the lack of agreement led to a crisis of some magnitude during the summer of 1917.

With these difficulties, Lever attempted to persuade McAdoo and Crosby to promise a stated amount of aid to Britain, whether it was $2,000m. to last until the end of December 1917[171] or – a later estimate – $1,100m. plus the $400m. overdraft at Morgan's.[172] On 2 May, at the first formal meeting of the mission with Treasury officials, McAdoo agreed to advance $200m. in three instalments in May.[173] However, in negotiations over the course of the month, he refused to promise any more. He required more and more specific information, which Lever gave to Crosby in a statement on 22 May.[174] What McAdoo objected to was the assumption of the Allies that they had only to ask for money and it would be given; as Crawford reported to Lever, 'McAdoo had sent for him the day before and complained that some of the Allies were approaching him in a manner which suggested that they thought them- selves to have a right to loans, which was not the view which he took.'[175] McAdoo's general approach to aid to the Allies is illustrated by a letter he wrote to the President:

> The so-called 'Bond Bill'... which authorises the Secretary of the Treasury, with the approval of the President, to purchase...the obligations of foreign governments...provides...that the Secretary of the Treasury...may 'enter into such arrangements as may be necessary for establishing such credits,' etc. I inserted this language for the specific purpose of enabling this Government to impose such terms and conditions upon the borrowing Powers as would give us potential voice in the use of such credits.[176]

When by the time the mission was departing McAdoo had still not promised further financial aid, the Chancellor cabled to Balfour that 'Lever's telegrams seem to indicate doubt about getting necessary funds from US Government for purchases in US. I know how completely you realise that failure in this direction would now mean complete disaster and I wonder whether it is possible for you to get assurances from President to relieve us of this anxiety.'[177] Balfour conveyed the cable to

Lansing and McAdoo, to be sent on to the President,[178] and presumably this appeal had some effect, since funds were provided for June. But it was a close-run thing.

The financial mission, then, managed to gain short-term funds to cover immediate necessities, and Lever, apparently, managed to neutralise Cunliffe's somewhat mischievous statements; but the mission was unable to persuade the American Treasury to provide a long-term schedule of financial aid for the British government. McAdoo preferred to keep control over disbursements to the Allies, in order that the Allies would be more amenable to pressure.

What, then, were the achievements of the Balfour mission? Most observers agreed that it was a personal triumph for Balfour, and that the publicity engendered by the mission greatly encouraged the American public's growing feeling of involvement in the war and helped to diminish anti-British feeling.[179] As Willert later wrote,

> What counted was that Balfour and his staff had temporarily changed the outlook towards Great Britain. In Washington the grievances and misunderstandings, personal and other, generated during American neutrality had disappeared. Throughout the country irritation over Ireland had been kept within bounds and the distrusts of Great Britain and her Empire temporarily diminished. British foreign affairs had been shown to be in the hands of a statesman with a sympathetic grasp of the importance of America; Washington officialdom had been introduced to a group of Englishmen who were forthcoming and easy to work with.[180]

The inspirational purpose of the mission was achieved and this was not unimportant. But what of the practical effects? Judged by the list of requirements drawn up by the War Cabinet it was not wholly successful: (1) American vessels had not yet been diverted from coastal into Allied trade, and although presumably the President realised the need for shipbuilding capacity to be developed, there had been no progress when the mission departed; (2) the United States had agreed to send a Regular Army division to the Front as soon as possible, but not to send large drafts of semi-trained men to be fed into Allied units; (3) the United States refused to adopt, unchanged, British gun patterns; (4) a sufficient quantity of wheat to fill the available tonnage was being sent to the Allies; (5) nothing had been done to reduce civilian demands on steel, although the Conscription Bill would ensure that skilled workers would not be used as soldiers; and (6) Balfour confirmed what the British government – and everyone else – already realised about the importance of the Irish question in Anglo-American relations. Willert, when writing to his Editor in July 1917, was scathing:

> It was a paradoxical affair, that mission: it was advertised to be practical and not political. A.J.B. [Balfour] was a brilliant success politically...practically, the mission was not a great success. Cunliffe, as you will realise, muddled finances. Bridges, besides behaving like an undignified bounder socially, failed to do much with the War Department... DeChair, through no fault of his own I am sure, failed to get the Navy Department to work out a policy. They are today working from hand to mouth.[181]

Willert was a bit harsh, considering what was achieved by the blockade, wheat and even naval missions, as well as the smaller accomplishments of the military and financial missions.

Even so, the reach in most cases had exceeded the grasp, and there was general agreement on why this was so. Drummond cabled to Cecil soon after the arrival of the mission in Washington that

> Difficulty has been that we found Administration here in really what was state of chaos. As a result it has not been possible to initiate any formal discussions... We have been told actual arrival of Mission has been of immense service as it has led to appointment of committees to control and deal with all the subjects which Mission wish to discuss...
>
> I do not think that we can force the pace more at present and it might be dangerous even to do so....[182]

Further, the Administration really had no idea of what it wanted of Britain, and the members of the mission found it very difficult to discover just who to deal with.[183] The British sometimes found a certain lack of total commitment to the war amongst the officials; as McFadyean reported, 'Apropos of some obvious measure of co-operation Burlinson, the Postmaster-General, recently remarked that they "were not so far into the war as that".'[184] But one reason for the diffidence of the officials was their apprehension about the reaction of Congress,[185] apprehension which was not misplaced, since no department was immune from ferocious investigations into its activities.[186] Also, co-operation was held up in some cases by the anti-British feeling of officials, especially from Denman of the Shipping Board, as well as by the simple American desire to do things their own way.

But what the British tended to forget in their reports was the fact that the American government had neither requested nor welcomed the mission. The idea had been wholly British, and only reluctantly had the President acceded to the idea. There is no doubt that the arrival of the mission not only facilitated co-operation between the two belligerents, but also forced the development of the United States' own war organisation; but the British should not have been quite so surprised when the United States did not react in the ways a seasoned belligerent might have done.

7

The Northcliffe Mission, June–November 1917: the Imposition of American Control

During the latter half of 1917 the relationship of the British government to the American government changed appreciably. As long as the United States was only the most important of the neutral powers, the Allies had had to take account of her wishes, but in the final analysis could ignore her. Now that the USA was a belligerent power (even if she insisted that she was an 'Associate' rather than an 'Ally'), she could insist upon, or decline to allow, courses of action about which the other Allies might have different ideas. The need to co-ordinate American military and diplomatic plans with those of the other Allies in a systematic manner finally led in early 1918 to the establishment of the Supreme War Council; in her own sphere – the American production and financing of war matériel – the American government moved even earlier to impose central co-ordination and control over the activities of the Allies.

On a small scale, then, the changing nature of the Anglo-American relationship was exemplified by the transformation in organisation and powers of the British missions in the USA. (This was even more manifest in the changing Anglo-American financial relationship, which will be discussed in Chapter 9.) Before the USA entered the war the missions had acted as private organisations, with neither help nor hindrance from the American government; during the Northcliffe period the American government moved to control the activities of the missions, so that by December 1917 almost nothing could be either purchased or paid for by the missions in the USA without the permission or the aid of the USA. The implications for the relationship between the two governments was soon obvious: the British were now very much dependent on the Americans, rather as the French, Russians and Italians had been on the British.

Nevertheless, the missions retained their importance, since the Americans refused to take over the detailed purchasing and shipping of the required materials. The British government, however, decided that it was necessary to establish a unified control over the various missions. During the period of American neutrality, the disorganisation of the British missions in the United States had been common knowledge amongst British officials: the missions had been sent out independently and not even the Foreign Office or the Embassy knew how many there were or what they were all doing. Once the United States was a belligerent Britain presumably no longer had to remain quite so unobtrusive in the United States, and the idea of sending out a responsible Head who would bring all the missions together was a natural one, although it is unclear who first proposed the idea. On 31 May 1917 Lord Northcliffe, owner of *The Times* and the *Daily Mail* and critic of the British government, accepted the post of Head of the British War Mission, which was to comprise all of the departmental missions in the United States. Northcliffe made certain administrative changes, and he improved communications among the missions in the United States and also between the missions and London.

It was during Northcliffe's period as Head of the British War Mission that the American government began to insist that purchasing and financing by the Allies should be co-ordinated by the creation of inter-allied bodies (the Inter-Allied Council and the Allied Purchasing Commission). Northcliffe played a credible part in the negotiations for the inter-allied bodies, but his experience with the financial negotiations during yet another crisis was not so happy. Northcliffe as well as others realised his incompetence in this area, and he was instrumental in convincing the British government to send Lord Reading out to supersede him.

During Balfour's visit to the United States, he and Colonel House had discussed the inadequacy of Spring Rice as Ambassador, which was epitomised by the fact that Spring Rice no longer had access to the President,[1] and Balfour could see for himself that Spring Rice was a detriment to Anglo-American relations because of his growing nervousness and lack of balance. (Among other habits, he saw German spies and German sympathisers everywhere, not excluding the American government, and this sometimes led to imperceptive dispatches.) Consequently on 5 May 1917 he wrote to Cecil:

> Please tell P.M. that result of my experience here leads me to the conclusion that Spring Rice has done excellently here, but there is still work to be accomplished which falls quite outside ordinary diplomatic responsibilities... Grey has peculiar qualifications...and if he were to come as Special Envoy during the war I believe he could perform services of incalculable benefit to the two countries. So thinks also Colonel House....[2]

He added, in a separate cable to Cecil, that if Grey could not come, it was probably better to make no change.[3]

On 11 May Cecil cabled to Balfour that the War Cabinet had 'after some hesitation' agreed to the proposal and that a letter was going out to Grey that evening.[4] Grey, however, was reluctant, and the War Cabinet did not try to persuade him, as 'the P.M. Curzon and Milner were averse from the appointment partly because they think him too pacifist and partly because the P.M. wants to send a businessman.'[5] In a draft of a cable to Balfour (but not in the cable as actually sent) Cecil wrote that Lloyd George 'though he has not said so to me...is thinking of Northcliffe.'[6]

Although there was some suggestion of Austen Chamberlain's going out,[7] Cecil was right about Lloyd George's ultimate intention. As Sir Maurice Hankey, the Secretary to the War Cabinet, wrote in his diary on 24 May 1917,

> Interesting discussion at morning War Cabinet on subject of the articles on the submarine question in the Times and Daily Mail, and all Northcliffe press...Ll.G. very angry about it... He is now trying to persuade the War Cabinet to send Northcliffe to America to coordinate the purchases, transport arrangements &c of the various Depts. This, of course, is really a dodge to get rid of Northcliffe, of whom he is afraid. I am certain N. will not accept it, even if he is asked....[8]

(Hankey was quite right about Lloyd George's fear of Northcliffe. A month later, Lloyd George admitted to C. P. Scott, the Editor of the *Manchester Guardian*, that Northcliffe had been sent because 'it was essential to get rid of him. He had become so "jumpy" as to be really a public danger and it was necessary to "harness" him in order to find occupation for his superfluous energies. I had to do this, said Lloyd George [,] "if I was to avoid a public quarrel with him"....'[9])

Balfour had requested that no decision about a change in diplomatic representation be made until his return to Britain,[10] and the War Cabinet noted this; but on 25 May 1917 the Cabinet decided that the request

> need not deter a decision with regard to a business man being appointed as the Head of all the Missions representing the different Departments concerned, such as the Admiralty, the War Office, the Ministry of Munitions, the Shipping Controller, and the Food Controller.
>
> It was pointed out that these Missions were at present without a responsible Head, with the result that there was some conflict of interests ... Although the person selected would no doubt have a great deal to do with Americans, his primary duty would be to control our own operations, including recruiting, production, purchasing, manufactures, transport, and the priority of the various claims.[11]

The War Cabinet decided that Northcliffe was a suitable man for the position, and instructed Hankey to notify Balfour and Spring Rice and ask for their views.[12]

Balfour was appalled. In his reply to the War Cabinet he agreed that the British missions to the United States needed co-ordination and that there were defects in the American government's administrative organisation, but he expressed 'grave doubts' about their choice. He wrote that if Americans 'picture Northcliffe other than a newspaper proprietor, it is probably as rigorous hustler and loud-voiced propagandist; one who will tell Americans what to do.' He added that the government of the United States was the President and it would be all-important to find out what he thought of the proposition.[13]

The Cabinet instructed Cecil to ask Page, the American Ambassador, for his views, and when Cecil reported on 30 May that Page was 'enthusiastically in favour of the suggestion' the Cabinet decided that Lloyd George should 'invite Lord Northcliffe to proceed to the United States of America, not as a diplomatic representative, but as the Head of the Mission representing the different Departments concerned, for the purpose of co-ordinating their action.'[14] The next day, Lloyd George reported that he had offered the post to Northcliffe, who had accepted.[15]

That same day Spring Rice called on Colonel House with copies, which he had just received, of the War Cabinet–Balfour correspondence about the appointment of Northcliffe. Spring Rice was exceedingly upset, and asserted that if Northcliffe came out he would go home. House told him that 'I thought he and I could take care of Northcliffe if he came, and I suggested that he, the Ambassador, should merely "sit tight" and let Northcliffe do the rest.'[16] The implication, of course, was that Northcliffe would hang himself with no help from Spring Rice. Later that day, House wrote to the President, enclosing the cables from Balfour, and asking him to confirm Balfour's statement that it would be better not to send anyone at present.[17] Wilson telegraphed that 'Action mentioned in your letter of yesterday would be most unwise and still more unwise the choice of the person named.'[18] But it was too late, in spite of a warning sent by the Secretary of State to Page;[19] and House concluded, in a letter to the President, that Northcliffe would have to be tolerated:

I am sorry that Northcliffe is coming. I thought Balfour's cable had headed him off... In Balfour's cable he urged that they ascertain your wishes either through Page or through me. They concluded to use Page since he was more convenient. Wiseman tells me that Page approved his coming and thought he would be acceptable to you... It is to be remembered that Northcliffe comes apparently with your approval and of course expects to be cordially received. I am afraid his visit may stir up the anti-British feeling here that at present is lying dormant.[20]

Northcliffe, unmindful of all this (Lloyd George had told him that Balfour wished him to go to America immediately),[21] had begun preparing for his mission. Hankey could not have been alone in being surprised when Northcliffe accepted the mission, but Lloyd George appealed to his patriotism and to his conviction that he understood and could communicate with Americans. He accepted reluctantly, but began interviewing heads of departments on their problems in the United States, while Hankey, at the behest of the War Cabinet, drafted his instructions.[22] The War Cabinet approved the Terms of Reference the same day:

The War Cabinet have decided that...[Northcliffe]...shall be appointed with direct responsibility to them as Head of a British War Mission, comprising the existing Departmental missions, so that by generally supervising and coordinating their action he may prevent overlapping and secure better results. He will have full authority over all the Departmental missions... His primary duty will be to control our own operations... He will determine the priority of conflicting claims...it will be necessary for the Head...to establish...the friendliest possible relations...with the representatives of our Allies in the United States... On questions of importance arising directly out of his Mission the Head of the Mission will have the right to communicate directly with the Prime Minister... The Head...will keep the British Ambassador at Washington generally informed of the main lines of his action, and will profit by the Ambassador's advice and assistance, whenever these may be required.... [23]

It was the last quoted point in his instructions which was to give Northcliffe his most intractable problem during his stay in the USA. His interviews with the departmental heads had possibly prepared him to some extent, because he wrote to Lloyd George on 2 June warning him that if Spring Rice interfered and made mischief, he (Northcliffe) would return and tell the Foreign Office and the War Cabinet why. [24] But judging from the reaction, nothing had prepared him for the insulting manner (as he considered it) in which he was greeted on his arrival in New York on 11 June 1917.

The difficulty was that he was *not* greeted, at least by anyone from the Embassy or Consulate. The reason given by Spring Rice was that the Embassy had not been notified of the date of Northcliffe's arrival for reasons of security; Northcliffe, however, found this hard to believe, since hordes of newspapermen had been there to meet him. (Spring Rice did have some excuse, since Lloyd George's staff had not notified the Foreign Office, and thus Spring Rice had not known the date for certain. Yet there is no doubt that Spring Rice had not put himself out in the matter.) Northcliffe was 'angry beyond words', according to House, [25] and sent an ultimatum to Lloyd George to the effect that if his treatment in the United States did not improve (and if Lloyd George did not rectify some ungrateful remarks he had made in the House of Commons about the mission), he would instantly return and tell the world why. [26]

This was followed by an even more unfortunate incident. Spring Rice invited Northcliffe to dine in the Embassy on 15 June, while Northcliffe was in Washington to meet the Secretary of State and other officials. Northcliffe arrived a bit early, at Spring Rice's request, and was shown into the study. Spring Rice immediately accused Northcliffe of being his enemy, said that Northcliffe had tried to harm him through the pages of *The Times* and said that he would not be received by Lady Spring Rice. Northcliffe turned to leave, but Spring Rice caught him by the hand, saying, 'We have got to work together, whatever we may feel about each other.' The two shook hands, and fortunately the French Ambassador was then announced.[27] The Foreign Office heard about the occurrence and Drummond wrote confidentially to Percy, who was still in Washington, asking him about the situation.[28] Percy replied on 22 June, saying that the confrontation on 15 June had been one of Spring Rice's 'incalculable actions'. Northcliffe now realised the need for caution, and intended to stay in New York. But, Percy added, 'Main point is that there has been and will be no friction over business – nothing affecting Public Service... For the rest we must make up our minds to ignore personal friction which there must inevitably be between those who will always be fools and those who will never be gentlemen. Only thing to do is to minimise personal contact.'[29] This was, in fact, the only melodramatic incident recorded. For the rest, Spring Rice behaved in countless petty ways to undercut the mission, while Northcliffe for his part behaved with commendable restraint. In fact, Northcliffe had the sympathy and admiration of most observers in this, whether or not they agreed with other of his actions. Yet, Spring Rice's behaviour was not inexplicable: he was after all fighting for the authority and prestige of his Embassy and his own position. As one student of the situation has put it, 'Although any envoy mission poses some threat to ambassadorial prestige, an ambassador can usually survive a single, well timed visit by a skilled executive agent; i.e. one with a specific purpose and well-defined plan of action and who does not stay overlong; otherwise he runs the risk of being a co-ambassador and the ambassador has trouble re-establishing his position.'[30] As far as Spring Rice was concerned, that was precisely what was happening.

The upshot, however, was to nullify immediately the section of Northcliffe's instructions which directed him to 'profit by the Ambassador's advice and assistance'.[31] Fortunately for Northcliffe, there was an alternative source of aid to whom he could turn – Colonel House.

House had already decided to do what he could. He wrote in his diary on 9 June that

> Wiseman and I decided to make the best of it and try to guide Northcliffe so as to make his visit a success rather than a failure which it bids fair to be. Arthur Willert . . . is a dependable fellow and is in sympathetic touch with both Wiseman and me. He is to be his [Northcliffe's] right hand man. When we discussed Northcliffe's coming with the Ambassador it was our intention to let him run amok, but after enjoying the thought of this, Wiseman and I decided the matter was too serious and that we should help when we could.[32]

House smoothed the way for Northcliffe to see the President by writing to him on 12 June that the British government had given Northcliffe the widest possible powers and it would therefore seem necessary to give him proper consideration; he added that Northcliffe would ask for an interview through the Embassy.[33] The President was not eager – 'I don't believe in Lord Northcliffe any more than I do in Mr Hearst'[34] – but he agreed to see Northcliffe on 18 June. Northcliffe found the President 'cordiality itself'.[35]

House helped Northcliffe time and again, over the Ambassador, over oil, over finance, but to do so he needed information. Northcliffe gladly gave House whatever memoranda and cables from the British government he thought would help, but he did not realise that as well, House had access to his private cables to the War Cabinet, through the agency of Wiseman. As the head of Military Intelligence, Wiseman had established his own cabling arrangements with London, providing secure and rapid transmission, which from the beginning Northcliffe used for his more confidential and urgent cables. Wiseman and House worked together to foster closer Anglo-American relations. Thus they rapidly developed the habit of consulting together over Northcliffe's cables to see what he was saying to ensure that London would not gain an inaccurate view of events and attitudes in the United States. For example, as House wrote in his diary for 30 June 1917,

> Sir William [Wiseman] has just phoned that Northcliffe was satisfied with his interview with the President, and is writing out a report to be cabled to his government. When this report is ready to be cabled it will be phoned to me, so I may be apprised of its

contents. Northcliffe does not realise how he is being moved on the chessboard, and how carefully he is being watched to keep him from making mistakes.[36]

It is unclear whether the British government realised just how close an eye House was keeping on Northcliffe, but there is no doubt that they took House at his own valuation, appealing directly to him through Wiseman whenever there was an acute crisis, such as the one in July over finance (see Chapter 9). In fact, there were occasions when House felt that they asked his advice when they ought not to have done so: for example, on 25 August 1917 Cecil cabled to House asking whether Spring Rice should be left in Washington, whether he had the confidence of the President and if not who should replace him as Ambassador, and whether Northcliffe should remain.[37] House's reaction was that Cecil's cable was 'astounding' and made him 'feel fearful' that they asked his opinion on such matters.[38] Even so, for the British government, not wholly trusting either of their two representatives, it was endlessly useful that he was there, apparently omnipotent.[39] Fortunately, House grew quite fond of Northcliffe, felt that he was doing his best in a difficult situation and therefore put himself out to help him.[40]

Northcliffe set to work immediately upon his arrival to meet the heads of the missions in the United States, to learn what the missions were doing and to bring them into closer contact with each other. He was impressed with the quality of the mission heads, but on the whole he felt that the staffs were too large, and over the period of his stay in the United States they were reduced. Northcliffe found that the various missions worked almost entirely independently of each other, with no direct communication between them, and in some cases the heads did not even know each other; he instituted regular meetings of the heads. Because of his differences with Spring Rice, Northcliffe did not set up his headquarters in Washington, in spite of the urgings of Wiseman, Willert and others that he do so. Instead he took offices in New York, arguing that it was the financial and industrial centre of the United States, and that he could make flying trips to Washington when they were necessary. The New York offices of the British War Mission (BWM) comprised the Production and Inspection Departments of the Ministry of Munitions mission; the Russian Transportation Committee; the Ministry of Shipping mission; the Wheat Export Company; the Anglo-Russian Committee; the Treasury mission; eventually the

Ministry of Food mission; the recruiting mission; the Remount Department; and other smaller, sometimes temporary, missions, such as a leather-purchasing mission. Northcliffe brought over staff from the *Daily Mail* to provide the secretarial assistance, and Andrew Caird, editor of the *Daily Mail*, was the general administrator.[41]

Northcliffe in fact found that there was too much to do in Washington to be taken care of by occasional visits, so he opened up BWM offices there and put C. B. Gordon, the head of the Ministry of Munitions mission, in charge as Vice-Chairman of the BWM. (This was an unfortunate choice, as Gordon was impatient and irascible and not easily given to negotiation; he was eventually replaced in this capacity by Sir Frederick Black.)[42] Willert, *The Times* correspondent in Washington, was swept up by Northcliffe into the BWM, and named its Secretary with an office in Washington. Most of the missions kept people in Washington, such as Blackett for the Treasury, and Royden and Salter for the Ministry of Shipping, and their duty was to negotiate first with the officials of the American government, and later with the Allied Purchasing Commission (see below) for supplies and priority in purchasing.[43]

Northcliffe found that the activities of the BWM were hampered by the length of time it took for his cables to be considered in London, and by the lack of co-ordination of instructions sent out by the various departments in Whitehall. He decided in early July to send C. T. Phillips back to London to set up a central office which would handle all cables to and from the United States. He arranged with Western Union Telegraph in the USA that all cables bearing his name coming to the BWM, and all cables bearing his name going to the War Cabinet, would have priority. He then bombarded London with complaints and exhortations, urging the departments to expedite their cables and to co-operate in setting up the Phillips office. Finally in mid-August he learned that this was being done, and that thenceforward one office in London would be responsible for co-ordinating cables and maintaining a comprehensive file on work in America.[44]

Northcliffe left most of the day-to-day work to the missions and concentrated on meeting American officials and leaders in finance and industry, on publicity work and on high-level negotiations during crises. Because of McAdoo's disinclination to talk to Lever, he engaged in financial negotiations until his admitted lack of knowledge of finance made it an impossible task (see below and Chapter 8). As well he took part in negotiating the setting up of the Allied Purchasing Commission.

Gradually, however, the greater part of his time came to be spent on writing articles and giving interviews, and on travelling; he also indulged in covert propaganda which, apparently, he thought no one noticed, and which sometimes gave offence to the Americans. (For example, he wrote a series of magazine articles criticising President Wilson; fortunately, they were not published.) His staff, in fact, began to complain quietly that Northcliffe no longer did any of the work, but spent all of his time travelling. However, since he was neither a businessman nor a financier, and the members of his staff were experienced at their work, it was probably just as well that he stayed away from the daily routine. There was, after all, little harm done – and possibly some good obtained in awakening the American public to the needs of the war – since Willert and Wiseman were able to keep him from engaging in activities which would have made his recall imperative.[45]

During Northcliffe's period in the USA the Allied missions were forced to change their purchasing procedures and join together in inter-Allied organisations. In doing so, each lost its independence, with the ultimate decisions being taken by an organisation of the American government. The new inter-allied organisations were shaped largely by the desire of McAdoo, the Secretary of the Treasury, to have an authority which he could cite to the Congress when the scale of the loans to the Allies was questioned. In response to American concern about the size and frequency of loans to the Allies, the Balfour mission, in agreement with the French Commission under Tardieu, had drawn up proposals for the establishment of an Allied Conference in London or Paris to consider the applications which the Allies proposed to make to the USA; the approved programmes would then be submitted to the American government by a committee of the Allies in Washington. On 25 May 1917, after the departure of the mission, a conference was held at the Treasury between the Americans and the French and British at which the memorandum agreed between the French and British was discussed.[46] McAdoo apparently took over the scheme as his own, and on 30 May 1917 he informed a conference of the French and British representatives of the principles which he felt should be adopted by the Allies in purchasing military supplies in the United States: contracts for raw materials should be closed at prices set by a Commission to be appointed by the President, which Commission would also determine the priority of contracts, and there should be

An inter-allied body with plenipotentiary authority upon which U.S. would be represented to be constituted in London or Paris to frame a programme of military requirements determine quantities and priorities with special reference to shipping space available from time to time. This body to transmit so much of the programme as calls for supplies from U.S. sources to this country for action.[47]

On 4 June Tardieu, the French High Commissioner in Washington, Crawford, Phillips (Ministry of Munitions representative who had come out with Balfour) and Crosby conferred and decided on a draft Agreement for an Inter-Allied Council (I-AC).[48] This draft was considered by the War Cabinet on 8 June, and referred to Lord Curzon for his decision.[49] On 30 June Curzon submitted a report setting out a scheme for the I-AC, which the War Cabinet accepted on 5 July 1917.[50] Meanwhile, McAdoo was becoming impatient, and on 12 July he cabled Page to tell the British government that 'before any engagements beyond the month of July can be discussed' an understanding on an I-AC (and Purchasing Commission) should be reached.[51] In other words, unless the Allies quickly agreed to the new procedures, McAdoo would refuse any more loans. On 19 July 1917 Spring Rice forwarded McAdoo's written proposals for an I-AC and on 20 July the Foreign Office directed Spring Rice to give to McAdoo the British government's scheme that had been approved on 5 July. This scheme had meanwhile been submitted to the Allies, but they were still considering it.[52]

Spring Rice on 21 July 1917 cabled an appreciation of McAdoo's problems to the Foreign Office:

On 15 August the last payments promised or practically promised will be made, McAdoo with a view to future payments must submit proposals to Congress for a new loan or authority to make advances. When he does this he must have in hand means of proving that he possesses (?machinery) for fixing needs of Allies and distributing supplies under satisfactory guarantees.[53]

Essentially, McAdoo was in political difficulties because of the scale of loans to the Allies, especially to Britain. He had exalted political ambitions which made it imperative for him to prove that he was keeping tight control on the spending, and that the loans were being used only for military supplies. He believed that an Inter-Allied Council, with a suitably 'distinguished'[54] membership, would provide credibility for the requests. He therefore used his financial hold over the Allies to force them to accede to this proposal.

In London, the Admiralty, Treasury, and Ministry of Shipping fought to be excluded from the purview of the I-AC. On 5 July, the day it considered McAdoo's proposals, the War Cabinet turned down the Admiralty's first bid to have the purchase of ships and oil remain under the direct control of the Admiralty. The Admiralty persisted, however, and it was decided that the Admiralty could retain control until the new organisations were working. The Treasury and Ministry of Shipping both insisted that they could not submit to the dictates of I-AC. The Ministry of Shipping felt that it was not a suppliant in this case, and further, since the provision of shipping was a hand-to-mouth matter calling for rapid decisions, Britain, which controlled the bulk of the world's shipping, must keep direct responsibility for it. Without a doubt there was also the consideration that this was Britain's only real lever over the Americans, and it would be lunatic to give up her sole means of influence. The Treasury considered that some of the most pressing financial problems, such as the maintenance of exchange and payments for supplies contracted for before the United States entered the war, would not fall within the scope of the I-AC, and in general, that the Chancellor must retain the right to deal with the Secretary of the Treasury directly. The War Cabinet agreed with these arguments, and McAdoo finally acquiesced in both of these reservations.[55]

After further negotiations the Foreign Office notified Spring Rice on 29 August 1917 that Britain and France accepted the 4 June draft Agreement for the I-AC, substantially as modified by Curzon. For Britain there were to be three separate bits of machinery – the I-AC, the Allied Purchasing Commission in Washington and a British Priority Committee. The Priority Committee would determine, having regard to finance and tonnage, the priority demands for supplies from the various departments of the British government; it would be a high-level committee, chaired by Austen Chamberlain. When the list of demands had been drawn up, the committee would submit it to the I-AC, which would decide the order of priority of the requests of all the Allies; once this was decided, the programme would be submitted to the Allied Purchasing Commission in Washington for its decisions on which of the Allied needs could be filled, where and at what price. The decisions would be passed on to the Allied missions in the USA, which would actually negotiate the contracts and carry them out. Curzon reiterated that the I-AC had been imposed on Britain by the American government for political reasons, and he expected it to be largely honorific, perhaps meeting monthly. He took account of McAdoo's expressed desire for a distinguished statesman and a distinguished military man as two of Britain's representatives, and he stated that since membership would not take up too much time, Britain could afford to appoint General Smuts and Lord Buckmaster to the I-AC. Austen Chamberlain would be the third representative and would handle most of the actual work.[56] The War Cabinet on 26 September 1917 accepted the details of Curzon's scheme for Britain,[57] and meanwhile Russia and Italy had agreed to the proposals.[58] The I-AC was not properly set into motion, however, until mid-December 1917 when, under pressure from Crosby (in Europe for an Allied conference), it was constituted as the Inter-Allied Council for War Purchases and Finance.

The Allied Purchasing Commission (or Inter-Allied Purchasing Commission, as it was sometimes called) was intended to receive the programme of the I-AC and direct its execution in the USA. McAdoo called for such an organisation in the same conference with Allied representatives on 30 May 1917 in which he called for the I-AC, and by 7 July he had a draft Agreement ready which he submitted to the Allies for their consideration.[59] On 12 July, to encourage negotiations, he warned the Allied representatives that there would be no more money until a Purchasing Commission was agreed upon.[60] The British were quite amenable to the idea, because they hoped that a Commission would fix prices, especially for raw materials; they were currently being quoted, for example, up to 8½¢ a pound for steel instead of the 2½¢ a pound that one steelman admitted would be a fair price.[61] The British learned that they would be excluded from any other purchasing channel, and were encouraged to expect controls on prices.[62]

The Allied mission representatives in Washington held a series of conferences on the Allied Purchasing Commission. (Spring Rice insisted on attending these conferences with Gordon and R. H. Brand, a partner in Lazard Bros and Deputy Chairman of the BWM, whether or not Northcliffe was there, and insisted on speaking French, much to the discomfiture of Gordon, who did not understand the language. The French Ambassador did not attend. Both Northcliffe and Tardieu protested to their respective governments that Spring Rice was holding up the proceedings.)[63] On 24 July 1917 the Foreign Office instructed Spring Rice to accept the general lines of McAdoo's proposal, and on

26 July the Allied mission representatives agreed together to accept McAdoo's outline in vague terms and to ask that he enter into negotiations with them on the powers of the Commission.[64] On 28 July, however, McAdoo himself suffered a sharp disappointment when the President announced the formation of the Commission: McAdoo had wanted a single Commission which would purchase for both the American government and the Allies, but the President created a War Industries Board of three men, which had as one of its constituent parts an Allied Purchasing Commission.[65]

Over the next three weeks the scope and powers of the new Commission gradually emerged. The War Industries Board (WIB) would be made up of Bernard Baruch, in charge of raw materials; Robert Lovett, in charge of determining priorities; and Robert Brookings, in charge of finished products. These same men would also constitute the Allied Purchasing Commission, on which they would cover the same responsibilities. On 8 August 1917 Spring Rice ascertained that the WIB would have no legal coercive powers, but that the President had general powers to take over any industrial firm necessary to prosecute the war, which he would exercise on the recommendation of the WIB. On 9 August he understood that the WIB would be able to fix prices, from which the Allies would profit; but on 19 August Gordon learned from Crosby that the Allied Purchasing Commission would not be able to fix prices, and would have no power to do so even if, eventually, the WIB was given that power.[66] Nevertheless, the British government had no choice but to sign the Purchasing Agreement and hope for the best, and Northcliffe signed on 25 August 1917.[67]

A general description of the workings of the Commission was written in 1923 by Grosvenor B. Clarkson, an American who had been intimately connected with the birth of the WIB:

> Owing to the difficulties inherent in the situation of a great industrial nation transforming its productive organization to meet the requirements of war...the task of the Inter-Allied Purchasing Commission would have been hard enough at best. But being without any more real authority in the beginning than any other part of the War Industries Board at that time, it was placed in a very awkward position. There was nowhere else for the commercial and industrial representatives of the Allies to go in their quest of action... Yet the...Commission and the War

Industries Board had no authority. All the Commission could do was to argue, beg, and implore the army, navy, and Shipping Board people to let the French have this, the British that, the Italians something else, and so on. It was a maddening position.[68]

The great difficulty was the habit of the American military authorities of taking what they wanted with no thought for the needs of the Allies already in the field, but the Board made 'every effort...to secure precedence for the requirements of the Allies in all the days the American armies were training' until needs could be met according to the common effort when all the Allies had armies in the field.[69] A decision by the Commission was a decision by the WIB. The members of the Commission met regularly with the representatives of the Allies' missions in Washington. According to Clarkson,

> These meetings, daily at first and semi-weekly later, soon became judicial conferences...Each national representative stated the position of his country with regard to an article or commodity and then the conference discussed the relative importance of need with the common cause the sole criterion as judgment. It was no unusual thing for the representative of one nation, after hearing the presentation of the position of another nation, to waive or postpone his own applications.[70]

It is possible that the unanimity and effectiveness gained in the memory – Willert wrote on 19 September 1917 that the Commission was a 'farce'[71] – but the British had to make what use of it they could, since there was no alternative channel of supply.

The Ministry of Munitions mission in the United States, while sharing in the general uncertainty of all the missions consequent on the upheaval described above, had, in addition, to cope with the withdrawal of Morgan's from the purchasing contract, whereupon the mission had to set up its own purchasing department at short notice. In addition, an oil supply crisis in Britain forced Northcliffe to set up an Oil Committee made up of munitions and shipping mission people to locate oil tankers. Underlying the frequent crises was the continuing struggle of the mission during the entire period to obtain the goods it needed at reasonable prices, a struggle particularly acute where steel was concerned.

When Addison, the Minister of Munitions, learned that the North-cliffe mission had been decided upon, he consulted with E. M. Moir, head of the American Department of the ministry, and they decided (contrary to Moir's earlier position) that the munitions mission in the United States needed a resident Head. They appointed C. B. Gordon, a former vice-president of the Bank of Montreal and currently vice-chairman of the Imperial Munitions Board, who was in London at the time. After arranging with Northcliffe's assistant, Andrew Caird, that Caird should meet the people in Munitions and other departments and learn some of the problems before joining Northcliffe in the United States, Gordon arranged to travel out with Northcliffe.[72] He assumed charge with little difficulty, in time setting up his headquarters in Washington.

At the end of May 1917, when discussing the setting-up of an I-AC and a Purchasing Commission, McAdoo had stated that all the existing machinery of the missions engaged in purchasing, inspecting, and so on, should be maintained, with the exception of the Morgan organisation: he was insistent that Morgan's should no longer sign contracts for the Allies.[73] As earlier described, Morgan's had the same idea, and in mid-July suggested that they should gradually hand over to the munitions mission all of their staff that the mission required and should remain only as the financial agents.[74] They renewed the argument a week later to Northcliffe, insisting that they wanted to be relieved of making purchases and of making payments for previous purchases. Morgan's in fact continued ready to help the British government with its purchasing and financing in the USA: it was simply that in view of the political climate in Washington, with the Administration's dislike of Morgan's, they judged that it would be embarrassing to the British government to continue as before.[75] The Ministry of Munitions, however, was more concerned with expediting the flow of munitions to Europe than with political complications in distant Washington, and insisted that no change should be made in Morgan's functions pending the decision to establish an I-AC in London.[76] There the matter rested for the moment.

At the end of August Morgan's took decisive action. As Northcliffe cabled to Balfour for the War Cabinet on 29 August 1917,

> Morgan's termination of purchasing came more suddenly than we
> expected and was produced, in my opinion, by two factors: first,
> irritation of Stettinius against Gordon who, though able and

industrious, is brusque in manner, and secondly, the political factor which was, to use Stettinius' own words, 'Morgans do not mean to be a target for every peccant politician in Congress'. . . We cannot replace Stettinius who is a genius but he has privately assured me of the benefit of his continued advice.[77]

One suggestion Stettinius made was that the munitions mission 'should have Sir Frederick Black as negotiator for us with the Government Committees at Washington [instead of Gordon]. He regards that part as the most dangerous difficulty of all. Negotiations with the sub-committees dealing with all various materials of war require great patience here.'[78] Northcliffe regarded Gordon as a major cause of the dislocation, adding to Balfour that 'I think strongly worded cable should be sent to Gordon calling attention to the very great responsibility imposed upon him'.[79]

There followed a hectic two days as a new Ministry of Munitions Purchasing Department was spatchcocked together with men from the mission's Production and Inspection Departments.[80] On 1 September 1917 Gordon wrote to Winston Churchill, who had replaced Addison as Minister of Munitions, describing the new organisation. The Export Department at Morgan's would be maintained to supervise and carry out current Allied contracts, but the general supervisor at the Morgan organisation, W. H. Marshall, would now work with the mission's Purchasing Department in New York. The difficulties of the mission had been greatly increased by the setting up of the Allied Purchasing Commission in Washington (the Agreement for which had been signed on 25 August), because it was now necessary to set up an organisation in Washington to negotiate with the Commission. Gordon in fact anticipated some difficulty: permission both to make inquiries and to purchase goods had to be obtained from the Commission in Washington, while negotiations about terms, inspection, delivery, and so forth had to be settled with firms who had their headquarters in New York.[81]

By November 1917, when Northcliffe returned to Britain, the mission organisations had settled down to a reasonably satisfactory routine. The staff in Washington conducted all preliminary negotiations with the Commission for permission to make inquiries concerning all supplies on behalf of all departments, not only for the Ministry of Munitions. The staff of the munitions mission acted as the BWM when negotiating priority matters with the WIB; that is, they negotiated the priority of delivery of all materials and supplies (except food) for the

Ministry of Munitions, the Admiralty, the War Office, the Board of Trade, and for all the Dominions and Dependencies. Finally, the staff of the mission in Washington negotiated export licences for raw materials.

After the necessary initial permission to make inquiries had been obtained from the Allied Purchasing Commission in Washington, the Purchasing Department in New York negotiated with the firms for the terms of contracts, which were then sent back to Washington to be approved by the Commission. After final permission was obtained, which could take some time if priorities of supplies or delivery had to be hammered out, the munitions mission's Production and Inspection Departments in New York would supervise the production of whatever was being bought, at the end of which the Ministry of Shipping mission in New York would arrange for the rail and ocean transport.[82]

Northcliffe also found it necessary to set up a special Oil Committee, made up of representatives from the munitions and shipping missions. He had not been in the United States three weeks when an acute shortage of oil for the Admiralty had necessitated a midnight cable from Balfour and a hurried interview with the President before the crisis was resolved.[83] At that time he formed a committee made up of Caird, Royden and Sparks of the shipping mission, and William Boyd, Scottish-born partner of a New York shipping firm who had newly volunteered to help the shipping mission, and who handled most of the detailed work.[84] In mid-September 1917 Northcliffe institutionalised the arrangement, placing Caird in charge of an Oil Committee made up of the above men plus Sir Frederick Black of the Admiralty;[85] this was just in time for a new crisis, that of a shortage of oil tankers in which to transport oil which the Admiralty urgently needed. In spite of an appeal to the American government to requisition the necessary tankers, by November 1917 they were still not forthcoming, a situation which caused Black to write a bitter memorandum to the Prime Minister in which he charged that British trading interests were to be sacrificed rather than American oil or tanker interests.[86]

Oil tankers were just one of many needs which the munitions mission found it difficult to meet. Steel was also vital to the British and was extremely difficult to purchase. The mission was caught between the desire of the steel producers to push prices as high as possible (the American government being at first unable to impose uniform, lower prices on steel), and the refusal of the American government to allow the British to use American government loans to purchase at the high prices. (Northcliffe in fact grasped the nettle and placed an order for steel at the high price prevailing, and the American government acquiesced.)[87] Steel prices were later fixed, but the mission was repeatedly frustrated, over copper, over shells, over rubber boots, over any number of supplies.[88]

The Ministry of Munitions mission during the Northcliffe period, in short, suffered a transformation in which it lost its independence of action. Before the entry of the United States into the war it had had difficulties in obtaining goods – and in paying for them – but at least it had made its own decisions. By November 1917 this was no longer the case.

When Northcliffe came to the United States the only permanent resident mission of the Ministry of Food was the Wheat Export Company of the Royal Commission on Wheat Supplies, which had been absorbed by the newly created Ministry of Food in December 1916. The position of the Wheat Export Company did not change during the Northcliffe period, although the company had to adjust to working with the new Food Administrator, Herbert Hoover, but other areas of food procurement became subject to the same centralising forces as munitions. Hoover insisted that first all hog products, and then all foods, should be purchased for the Allies by one organisation, and in September 1917 the Allied Provisions Export Commission was set up for this purpose.

Early in June 1917 Hoover approached H. T. Robson of the Wheat Export Company and asked whether the company could take over the purchase of meat products for the Allies, since he was quite perturbed at the high prices caused by the competitive buying of the Allies. Robson wrote to Anderson, vice-chairman of the Wheat Commission, that it was 'impossible', but suggested that Anderson pass on the word that Hoover would welcome more definite control of meat buying in the United States.[89] Hoover renewed the suggestion in July, and Spring Rice was forced to inquire what British policy was, since Hoover was threatening to use export prohibition to enforce his policy.[90] He renewed the threat in an interview with Royden of the shipping mission on 17 August 1917, over two months after he had first requested action from the British.[91]

The British were, in fact, moving to comply with Hoover's wishes, even though they were not keeping him informed of it. On 23 August 1917 the Foreign Office informed Northcliffe and Spring Rice that an

Inter-Allied Meats and Fats Executive was to be set up. According to Lord Rhondda (formerly D. A. Thomas of the Ministry of Munitions, now the Food Controller), it was to deal with animal products and foods not dealt with by any other inter-allied authority (except vegetable oils and fats); all Allied purchases of such products were to be concentrated in the one organisation.[92] Rhondda further informed Northcliffe on 31 August that he would be sending representatives to set up a permanent buying organisation for the Meats and Fats Executive and to make arrangements generally for food from North America other than wheat.[93] At the end of September 1917 the Ministry of Food mission, headed by Owen Hugh Smith, went out to the United States.[94]

The mission, after consultation with Northcliffe and Hoover, set up an Allied Provisions Export Commission (APEC) and the French and Italian missions in the United States appointed representatives to it. The procedure decided upon was for the APEC to submit a programme of supplies needed to Hoover, which once approved would have the automatic sanction of the Allied Purchasing Commission of the WIB. The APEC acted as agent for any Allied country wishing to purchase; that is, if, for example, France desired to buy cheese, the APEC negotiated the purchase and closed the contract, and the French representative then signed the contract and arranged for the necessary finance and tonnage. Competition was thereby avoided, but only French credit was involved. Hoover later requested that the APEC act for Portugal and Belgium as well. The work of the APEC was divided between two departments: one acted as the representative in North America of the Ministry of Food, in which capacity the mission closed contracts for British government requirements, and the other as the representative of the Inter-Allied Meats and Fats Executive in the United States.[95]

By November 1917 the mission had only been established a month, and it still had outstanding problems. One was that products covered by the Agreement for the Meats and Fat Executive were still being imported into the Allied countries on private account, causing much competitive buying. Another was that there was still no price control for many food products in the USA although Hoover was working out a scheme to control the supply and prices of hog products (the most important items of purchase for the mission) according to which the Allies' needs would be purchased on the same basis as those of the American army and navy. At any rate, the mission had the inestimable advantage of having the American Food Administrator on its side; as

Owen Hugh Smith wrote, 'Hoover has showed every wish to assist the Commission in every way possible and to allow them, so far as possible, to have the food products they require.'[96]

When Northcliffe arrived in the United States there was no resident British military mission with the general duty of liaison with the American government. During June and July 1917 the question as to whether or not there should be such a mission was much canvassed, and the compromise decision was taken to post to the Embassy a new military attaché and assistant military attaché, both of whom had seen action. Once they were established in Washington they encouraged the American government to ask that other military aid be sent out from Britain.

In June 1917 there were three War Office missions resident in the United States. In February 1917 a British and Canadian Army Recruiting Mission had been established in New York City under the leadership of General W. A. White. Since the United States was still neutral it had had to work somewhat circumspectly, although it acted with the acquiescence of the American government. By June 1917 it was able openly to recruit British citizens in Canada and the USA. The War Office had in August 1914 established a Remount Commission which, although its headquarters were in Montreal, maintained a number of purchasing depots in the United States, such as in Atlanta, Georgia, and Des Moines, Iowa. The Royal Army Medical Corps had, since the Balfour mission, maintained a staff of three in Washington. All of these War Office missions were brought under the wing of the British War Mission when Northcliffe went out to the USA.[97]

Soon after Northcliffe's arrival the question arose as to whether there should be a military mission in Washington to give information and aid to the American government in raising and training a citizen army at short notice. Conflicting advice came to the British government on this question: Spring Rice argued against such a mission, saying that it was better to let the French take the lead in this matter, and that if the American government wanted such a mission they would request one,[98] while Page and Northcliffe independently argued that such a mission would be welcome.[99] Secretary of State Lansing seemed to favour the idea,[100] but Secretary of War Baker did not, as he wrote to Colonel House on 18 July 1917: 'Now the so-called "doctrine" of the English and the French differ. There are many important respects in which their experts disagree... In order to avoid misunderstandings, it has seemed to me from the beginning, better for us to have our own doctrine'.[101]

On 28 July 1917 Spring Rice reported that although the American government still did not want a military mission, it would greatly appreciate a more energetic British military attaché; Wiseman on behalf of the British approached House and he confirmed that it would be advantageous if the present attaché were replaced by someone with recent military experience. On 24 August 1917 Wiseman cabled to House that a new military attaché had been appointed.[102]

The new military attaché was Maj.-Gen. J. D. McLachlan and the new assistant attaché was Lt-Col. the Hon. Arthur C. Murray, both of whom had seen action in France; they travelled out in September on the same boat as Lord Reading (see Chapter 8).[103] Their coming seemed to coincide with a change of heart in the American War Department; as Murray wrote to a friend, 'Whatever may have been the feeling some months ago, they [the American military authorities] are now fully and completely alive to the difficulties of creating and organising an immense Army, and ask for information on every conceivable point.'[104] On 19 September 1917 Page conveyed a request from Baker to the British government for 167 officers and 165 NCOs to come out to the USA to help train the American army, and in October the British Military Mission (Instructional), headed by Brig.-Gen. G. F. Trotter, went out to the States. The mission included experts in machine guns, gas warfare and bayonet training, who immediately went their separate ways to the thirty-three divisional training camps in the USA.[105] The mission remained under the command of the military attaché in the Embassy, and did not come under Northcliffe and the BWM. In January 1918, at the request of the War Department, an artillery mission headed by Maj.-Gen. Sir John Headlam also went out to the USA.[106] The War Office made a further contribution later in 1918 when it sent a number of invalided officers out to help in the American Liberty Loan drives; these officers retailed their experiences at the front in four-minute speeches in theatres and at outdoor rallies.[107]

During the Northcliffe period, the Ministry of Shipping mission had to deal with important questions of high policy as well as with routine arrangements for shipping goods. The two main policy questions, which put some strain on Anglo-American relations, were (1) whether the American government could be prevented from requisitioning ships being built in the USA under contract for Britain, and (2) whether the

USA could be brought to assign the same high priority as would Britain to concentrating her resources of steel and manpower on building merchant ships. Questions of this sort were largely dealt with by that part of the mission which worked in Washington, with negotiations being handled by Thomas Royden, while in New York, Capt. Connop Guthrie, the head of the mission, directed the operational headquarters.

The mission headquarters in New York had separate departments for inland and ocean transport, which handled all British supplies from the USA and also French and Italian grain supplies, with branch offices and agencies in ten places. The Inland Transport Department had two sections, one for grain and its products for Britain, France and Italy, and one for munitions for Britain. A Traffic Executive with representatives of Britain, France, Italy and Russia co-ordinated the internal munitions traffic of the Allies. (Guthrie was Director of the Traffic Executive.) The Ocean Transport Department also had two sections, one dealing with the liners and one for 'tramp' transport. There was in addition an Oil Department, which was under the direction of the Oil Committee, and a Troop and Passenger Department, which arranged for the accommodation of American troops in British liners and generally supervised the passenger accommodation of the liners.[108] A member of the shipping mission, T. S. Catto, represented it on the Russian Transport Committee in New York, which since 1915 had been responsible for internal routing to seaboard and shipment to Russia of all supplies purchased in the United States by Britain for Russia. The committee was responsible for negotiating with the British Ministry of Shipping for steamers for the shipments. Although the financial responsibility of Britain for Russia had ceased by November 1917, the shipping responsibility could not, since Russia did not have the necessary steamers and the few which she had were under the control of the British Ministry of Shipping.[109]

The New York headquarters of the mission, then, determined the actual transportation arrangements; the Washington office served as the link with the American government. The representatives were Thomas Royden and Arthur Salter, who had come out in June 1917 as late members of the Balfour mission (Salter returned to London in late September 1917). They were immediately confronted with the question of whether the American government would requisition for its own use the British ships being built in the USA. They were fighting an unequal battle against the US Shipping Board, however, in view of the letter which Balfour had given to Denman, which pledged that Britain would give up the ships if the United States requested that she do so. Nevertheless, the Ministry of Shipping decided to fight for the ships. Royden did what he could, trying to weaken the resolve of the Shipping Board, but even Denman's enforced resignation in the last week of July did not help; Royden and Salter saw the President on 26 July 1917 and he assured them that he supported the action of the Shipping Board, although he agreed to consider the matter.[110] Royden heard from the Embassy on 25 July that the Shipping Board had decided to go ahead and requisition all ships built or building for foreign owners *except* those which had certificates or provisional certificates of registration. To try to save those being built for the Cunard Company, 170 vessels in all, he sat up into the small hours issuing provisional certificates of British registry for them, arguing that 'Even if ultimately the United States Government refuse to accept such certificates as not meeting requirements they will give us a basis on which to fight United States Government's right to requisition them.'[111] The general requisition order was issued on 3 August 1917, but the British government continued to fight for the ships. Maclay, the Shipping Controller, on 20 August asked for one last strong appeal to the American government, and Northcliffe appealed to House on 25 August. Yet Balfour and Cecil both argued against pushing the matter, since the USA had the legal right to commandeer the ships, and Britain might obtain better terms if she appealed to the American sense of justice and goodwill. Balfour had sent a letter in that sense to Page on 16 August, and the War Cabinet decided on 24 August that that was the most which could be done.[112] The appeal was unsuccessful, however, because, as House wrote to the President, 'The difficulty confronting us which they do not appreciate is Denman and the anti-British element here. Balfour agreed with Denman...that these ships could be taken over, and if the new Shipping Board adopts a different course, Denman will probably make an attack.'[113] A member of the State Department put it more crudely when he wrote that Denman would 'crucify us if we give up those ships'.[114] In the event they did not, although by the end of October, out of 171 contracts for steamers, Britain had secured eleven and was trying to bring pressure for nine tankers; but the Shipping Board had already taken delivery of four and told the British that they had no chance of receiving the remaining vessels.[115]

The other question dealt with by Royden and Salter was what Salter described as 'the principal objective of persuading America to organise a vast ship-building programme.'[116] While the Balfour mission was in the USA the War Cabinet had tried to create the proper sense of urgency in the American government by bombarding it with statistics of losses due to submarines, but there had been no immediate result. The War Cabinet for itself grew more and more worried, until on 9 August it decided

> in view of necessity for maintaining tonnage as far as possible, that they would devote to shipbuilding all the steel plates that could be used, although this decision involves a reduction in the amount of shell produced. They further decided to release men from munitions works and from the Army to provide the necessary labour. Prime Minister regards the rapid production of ships as absolutely the first war necessity today.[177]

Meanwhile in the United States Royden and Salter had decided

> after a full study of our prospective needs and resources, that what was needed [from America] was six million tons a year. It was a vast requirement . . . for America which had never built on a large scale . . . But . . . we believed that it was just possible. We had at first a skeptical though friendly reception, but at last a sympathetic hearing, and in the end the always latent American enthusiasm for aiming high if you aim at all was fired. After many soundings we came to the conclusion that if the British Cabinet made a formal appeal for this figure . . . it was likely to succeed.[118]

Salter returned to London in September and put the case to the War Cabinet. The result was a personal appeal by the Prime Minister sent through Wiseman to House for the President.[119] Eventually the United States did pledge itself to build the six million tons of shipping per year, but due to political difficulties and sheer bad management the programme did not really begin to show results until mid-1918.[120]

In terms of policy decisions, in short, Britain lost one fairly quickly but gained the more important one at a later date: she lost most of the replacement tonnage which had been ordered in 1916, but she convinced the USA to take the decision on shipbuilding policy which ensured that by late 1918 the Allies would not be hampered by lack of ships. With regard to the major day-to-day work of the Ministry of Shipping mission – the transportation of supplies and men within and from the USA to Europe – the mission was as successful as could be expected in the circumstances. The prime obstacle in its work was the sheer disorganisation of the American railway network which was not rectified until it was nationalised in January 1918 for the duration of the war.

On the whole, then, the constituent elements of the British War Mission during the Northcliffe tenure adjusted more or less successfully to the new regime of American control, and got along with their American opposite numbers. The glaring exception was the Treasury mission. There were arguments between Lever and McAdoo over the size and frequency of American loans to Britain, over the use of American funds to maintain the exchange rate of the pound and over whether or not the American Treasury should pay off the British overdraft with Morgan's. The details will be discussed in Chapter 9, but the upshot in this context was that by 9 July 1917 McAdoo absolutely refused to receive Lever, on 10 July House and Wiseman agreed that Lever must be replaced and on 13 July the President told Wiseman the same thing.[121]

Who, then, was to negotiate with the American Treasury? Blackett had arrived on 11 July, but McAdoo considered him a minor Treasury official not of the status to confer with him or Crosby on equal terms. Spring Rice and Crawford took care of the later negotiations over exchange, but as a member of the State Department wrote, 'Spring Rice is not a financier and Crawford is worn out'.[122] Northcliffe equally was not a financier, but the Treasury formally named him its accredited representative,[123] and he moved to replace Lever in talks with McAdoo and Crosby. In one sense this was fortunate, since McAdoo liked and admired Northcliffe – in his memoirs he wrote that he had 'met few men with such quick comprehension as Northcliffe; it was never necessary to explain everything twice. He reminded me more of the higher type of American business executive than any foreigner I have ever known.'[124] On the other hand Northcliffe frankly admitted to House that he knew very little about finance, a perception which was corroborated by Benjamin Strong, the Governor of the Federal Reserve Bank in New York City.[125] Unfortunately McAdoo was not that knowledgeable either – Strong felt that 'McAdoo's trouble is that he does not understand the matter himself and is not willing to delegate authority to others'.[126] By his refusal to see Lever McAdoo had lost his chance to talk to the only technically competent British representative available, and Strong was brought in by House and Wiseman to explain things to McAdoo – and from the American point of view.[127] But this could only be a temporary expedient.

House, Wiseman and Northcliffe discussed the situation on 16 July and the conclusion they came to was that the British government would have to send over Lord Reading to negotiate with McAdoo.[128] The following day Northcliffe cabled to Lloyd George, Balfour, Reading and Bonar Law that

> [House] strongly urges important British official, liberal in politics, preferably ex-Cabinet Minister, of high financial ability, a personality well known to American public and press, come to Washington for 3–4 months to arrange whole future financial relations of the United States and Great Britain about which I and others here are very anxious. . . . House . . . named Reading and said he was in every way best qualified. I earnestly hope . . . Reading will . . . come here for period named.[129]

Since there had been complaints by the Americans about the number of British officials with whom they had to deal, the Chancellor understandably did not see how sending yet another was going to help matters.[130] He balked, as well, at sending this particular official. When Stamfordham, private secretary to the king, queried the choice of Reading, pointing to 'the accusations recently made against him in a London financial newspaper',[131] Bonar Law replied that 'The considerations mentioned by you about Reading have weighed very much with us and in my case have seemed so important that I have been so unwilling to adopt this suggestion that I have been the cause of delay in doing it.'[132] These accusations stemmed from memories of the Marconi Scandal in 1913, and they made the Prime Minister, as well as the Chancellor, 'quite afraid to utilize his services',[133] according to Lord Rothermere. Further, the Chancellor's permanent officials at the Treasury wanted someone from their own ranks to go, rather than an outsider (this attitude caused Wiseman to cable to Northcliffe that the 'Treasury do not understand American situation'),[134] and the Chancellor himself felt that if a politician had to be sent, it should be a Unionist rather than a Liberal.[135]

There was the question of Northcliffe as well: some members of the War Cabinet were afraid that they would arouse Northcliffe's wrath if they sent Reading out to replace him. Wiseman was in London in August and argued the case for sending Reading. He allayed the War

Cabinet's fears of Northcliffe by cabling Northcliffe to send a cable insisting on Reading's coming to the USA. Northcliffe had, in fact, been indefatigable in urging the British government to send Reading out, whether from patriotism or from the realisation that the situation was such that otherwise no one was likely to come out of it with any credit.[136] The Chancellor finally decided that the fact that all sources stated that Reading would be *persona grata* with the American government was decisive, since 'in present circumstances that is the essential thing'.[137] On 24 August he told Wiseman that he had decided to ask Reading to go out to the USA on a special financial mission, on 30 August the War Cabinet agreed, and on 5 September 1917 Reading and Wiseman sailed for America.[138]

Northcliffe remained in the United States after Reading's arrival, but he decided to return to London in November with Reading. The truth was, he yearned for England. There had been hints all through the period of his mission that he was not entirely happy with his task – House felt in June that he found the duties 'irksome',[139] Spring Rice reported in July that he was 'tired of business'[140] and Northcliffe himself in August revealed that he disliked the social part of his duties. He also disliked the situation in which he found himself:

> It is a curious experience to a man of 52 years of age to be transplanted to an entirely different country...to have only partial authority over thousands of people connected with the Mission when before he has been accustomed to absolute authority; to be 'up against' British forces here which ought to be working with him but are working against him, and the Allies who are each for themselves and the devil take the hindermost.[141]

By September he had decided that he wanted to return to England for a month at the end of November, and he wrote to his brother, Lord Rothermere, asking if he would come out to take his place for that period. Rothermere agreed, but Wiseman heard about the plan and warned the Foreign Office, which scotched the idea.[142] On 27 September Northcliffe cabled Lloyd George that he wished to come home for a 'short visit' in November.[143] He also suggested that Sir Frederick Black should, during his absence, act as his deputy as Head of the BWM, and the War Cabinet agreed.[144] Reading and Northcliffe sailed for Britain on 3 November 1917.

He did not return to America. He wrote to Balfour at the end of November in terms which certainly suggested that he meant to return, but on 6 December 1917 he was so unsure that he asked the advice of House, who was also in London. On 14 December he told Balfour that he had still not decided whether or not to return to the United States. On 3 January 1918 he wrote to Caird that Reading would be going out to America as High Commissioner while he remained in London for two or three months to organise the British end of the BWM, to be established in Crewe House. He saw its main purpose as giving effect to Reading's recommendations from the United States. By the end of January he was letting friends in Washington know that he would be remaining in London as Chairman of the BWM.[145] A close associate, Sir Campbell Stuart, later wrote that while in the USA Northcliffe's mind had been turning to war propaganda; that sort of thing was obviously more to his taste than being an administrator, and on 7 February 1918 he was appointed Director of Propaganda in Enemy Countries.[146]

8
The Reading Missions, September–November 1917 and February–November 1918

Lord Reading journeyed to the USA twice during 1917–18 on behalf of the British government: the first visit was meant to be – and was – temporary, while the second visit was meant to be – and was not – semi-permanent. In both cases the main problem was the failure of British representatives already in the USA adequately to carry out their duties. This was not the first time this had occurred during the war, of course, and previous chapters have detailed failure and rescue. But by the autumn of 1917 such inadequacy was of acute concern. Lever's fights with McAdoo threatened American financial support of Britain, while Spring Rice's deteriorating mental and physical health, along with Northcliffe's growing indifference to his work in the USA, threatened to undermine British attempts to knit together American and British wartime and postwar interests and politics. The British Cabinet, after some disagreement, designated Lord Reading to save both situations.

Lord Reading came to the USA in September 1917 primarily because of the impasse reached between the American Treasury and the British Treasury mission. He remained for two months, during which time he overcame American resistance to providing funds to be used outside the USA, and also obtained the promise of funds for three months in advance. As well, he helped to persuade President Wilson to send the House mission to Europe to attend an Inter-Allied Conference.

Reading's other duty during this mission had been to survey the state of British representation in the USA, and he returned to Britain convinced that it must be changed drastically. The problem was that despite the success of Northcliffe, as Head of the British War Mission, in organising the individual missions into some semblance of a whole, the British government was still left with a vital split in its organisation. While the USA was neutral and the missions were acting as private organisations, the British Embassy had not usually involved itself with the missions and their activities. Once the USA was a belligerent, however, the Ambassador continually attempted to control all policy discussions which took place between the British and the Americans in Washington, attempts which led to frustration in some of the missions and a state of armed truce between the Ambassador and Northcliffe. On going out to the USA in September 1917, Reading had suffered from the Ambassador's ill-will, and his and Northcliffe's return to Britain in November 1917 was the signal for the British government to take the decision which had been brewing in London for some months: to recall the Ambassador and to send out one supreme British representative to head both the Embassy *and* the British War Mission. Reading was chosen for the post, and with his return to the USA in February 1918 all of the British representatives were finally, after three-and-a-half years of war, brought under unified control.

Once Reading had arrived in February with his dual portfolio, he did not often interfere with the running of the departmental missions. However, he did make the final decision on who could come out and join them, and he similarly exercised close control over which speakers were sent out from Britain to lecture to the Americans. He was a success as High Commissioner of the War Mission, but he returned home in July 1918 because he felt he was less successful as Ambassador. Nevertheless, Lloyd George and he finally decided in October 1918 that he must go back to the USA, but this plan was soon abandoned in order that Reading might attend the meeting of the Supreme War Council in Paris at which peace terms were to be discussed.

The British government had taken over a month to decide to send Reading to the USA, although Reading knew nothing of this, since he had apparently not been given his copy of the cable of 17 July 1917 in which Northcliffe had conveyed the American desire that Reading be sent out. He accepted the task promptly when requested, agreeing to embark at a few days' notice,[1] on the condition that his powers and responsibilities were clearly and widely defined.

The War Cabinet decided on 22 August to ask Reading to go out to the United States.[2] The Chancellor talked to Reading on 24 August; as he reported to the Prime Minister,

I saw him [Reading] this morning and found him very ready to go . . . and it is definitely arranged that he will go, probably at the end of next week . . . As I felt sure would be the case when Reading had more time to think about it he became alarmed at the indefiniteness of his position – that is, he does not know where he would stand in relation both to the Ambassador and Northcliffe.[3]

Northcliffe had cabled to the Chancellor that Reading should come out with 'full powers'[4] and the Chancellor had cabled back for a fuller explanation.[5] Northcliffe answered on 25 August:

It is essential in order to avoid annoying this very touchy Government by cable delays that Reading should have wide power . . . [to take] immediate decisions. He will find himself in strange political atmosphere, difficult to convey to you by telegram, and if he has not great deal of authority he will be much hampered in his negotiations.[6]

The same day, Cecil cabled to House, asking his advice on Reading's powers. As described above, House was astounded to be asked such a question by the British, but he did his best to reply, stressing the need for Reading to have 'entire authority over financial questions'.[7] The Chancellor argued that 'Reading ought to go, if he is to be of use, in a position strong enough to be regarded as *the* representative of the Government while he is there',[8] and, as Cecil wrote to Balfour,

Reading was very insistent that he would not go unless he was given sufficient powers to overrule both Spring-Rice and Northcliffe in his own department, if he found it necessary to do so. He pointed out that, though he hoped and believed no such exercise of authority would be necessary, yet, if he had not it as an ultimate resource, he might be put in an impossible position. He is, rightly I think, insistent on his dignities as Lord Chief Justice, both because of what is due to the Office itself, and even more because he regards as his main asset in America the fact that he is a great British 'swell'.[9]

The War Cabinet, on 28 August, therefore gratified Reading's wish 'to be granted special plenary authority to deal with all financial questions without constant reference to His Majesty's Government', and that this should be made clear in a telegram to Spring Rice.[10] This cable stated that Reading will have the full authority of the War Cabinet to negotiate with the United States Government and to decide on behalf of the British Government any question that may be raised. Though primarily concerned with finance he will be authorised to deal with any subject which he considers desirable for the proper discharge of his mission.[11]

It will be recalled that the motive for the Reading Mission was the financial tangle in the USA. However, the opportunity was too good to lose, and Reading was given further tasks. Northcliffe cabled the suggestion that Reading 'should examine diplomatic war mission and propaganda situations in United States',[12] and it was certainly part of his mission to survey the whole field of British representation in the USA and report back to the War Cabinet.[13] More important for the future conduct of the war, Lloyd George decided to use Reading to present to the President a scheme for an Allied War Council whose intended function was to produce for the alliance a new war strategy laying less emphasis on the Western Front: the awful example of the Third Battle of Ypres, known to the soldiers as Passchendaele, was currently in front of his eyes.

The Reading entourage was relatively small. Reading wanted 'some knowledgeable official to go with him'[14] and Lloyd George at first suggested that Hankey should go, but he then decided that he could not spare Hankey, whom he told to nominate someone. Hankey nominated Colonel Ernest Swinton, who is credited with inventing the tank, and who was Assistant Secretary to the War Cabinet under Hankey himself. The Treasury sent J. M. Keynes, who was head of the 'A' division and therefore in charge of inter-allied finance. It is unclear whether Reading requested his help, or whether the Treasury imposed him upon Reading. At any rate, Reading found him extremely useful: the intent had been for Keynes to accompany Reading on the voyage and then turn around at New York and come back, but Reading implored the Treasury to let him stay for a further ten days.[15] Reading was also accompanied by his wife.

Reading arrived in New York on 11 September 1917 and went straight to Washington. He immediately ran into the problem the Chancellor had foreseen – that of too many representatives. The problem was largely, although not wholly, Spring Rice. Northcliffe wrote that 'Reading was treated on arrival exactly as I was',[16] by which he probably meant that Reading was subjected to a whispering campaign in Washington which was stimulated by Spring Rice, and in which Reading's Jewishness played a predominant role. Further, Spring Rice was dilatory in arranging a meeting with the President for Reading, and Reading had been in Washington well over a week before the interview took place. It should be added that Spring Rice's explanation was that the President was away, and that House held Spring Rice and the State Department both responsible for the embarrassing position in which Reading found himself.[17]

Further difficulties were caused by Reading's desire to save Spring Rice's feelings. As Keynes wrote in a Memorandum for the Chancellor, 'Lord Reading . . . was unceasing and indefatigable in his efforts to spare the Ambassador's susceptibilities in every way possible and do nothing possible to impair his position.' But Reading's 'unwillingness to assert himself' only led to a situation wherein 'Nearly a week after our arrival he [Spring Rice] had still failed to notify Lord Reading's position and powers and finally only did so at Lord Reading's express dictation.'[18]

The result was unsatisfactory. Spring Rice reported that Secretary of State Lansing

> thought the mission would be very useful but he wished it [the cable detailing Reading's powers] kept secret and desires to give the impression that the mission is purely financial. Public opinion might be affected if it were generally known that such extended powers had been given to Reading, as people are very sensitive to any suspicion of exercise of English influence here.[19]

This could well have been true, although there were no feelings more sensitive than those of Spring Rice. Apparently the Foreign Office followed Spring Rice's advice, with unfortunate results; as Wiseman wrote,

> In order to avoid hurting the feelings of Spring Rice or Northcliffe the full importance of Reading's mission and his credentials were not made public. I now think this was a mistake. The impression got about Washington . . . that Reading was nothing more than a Treasury representative; indeed, that he really came out to settle the question of the Morgan overdraft. He has found it rather difficult to rectify this and it has made his position difficult.[20]

It is unclear what Wiseman meant by the reference to Northcliffe, since Northcliffe had urged that Reading be given full powers. Indeed, in the same cable, he remarks that 'Northcliffe accepted his coming very well'.[21] Yet House wrote in his diary on 16 September 1917 that he and Wiseman 'have the greatest difficulty in keeping the Ambassador, Reading and Northcliffe on amicable terms',[22] and the following day the War Cabinet discussed 'the great difficulty of having, as it were, three Ambassadors...in America at the same time'.[23] Nevertheless, most observers felt that Reading and Northcliffe got on very well, that Northcliffe helped when he could and that Reading accepted his help at face value; it was only later that Willert, for example, discovered that Reading had never trusted Northcliffe as much as he had thought at the time.[24]

Reading immediately set to work on the financial problems, two of which generated the most discussion during his visit: the question of whether American advances could be spent outside the USA, symbolised by the question of payments for Canadian wheat, and the British desire to have an agreement setting out the amount of the American loans in advance.

Lever opened the question of the use of American credits abroad when he wrote to Crosby on 23 August 1917: the Canadian wheat crop was shortly coming on to the market and the Wheat Commission wished to buy the surplus for the Allies, which would reduce the Allied need for American wheat; would the American Treasury agree to the use of some of the advances made to Britain to pay for some portion of this wheat? Crosby in his reply of 28 August, while not flatly refusing, emphasised that if at all possible, Canadian wheat purchases should be settled without reference to the American government.[25] In the first week of September, Crosby again hinted strongly that there would be no help with Canadian wheat.[26] The Chancellor responded with an urgent cable to Lever setting out the result if the Americans held to this position: 'Position as regards Canadian wheat in particular is causing anxiety. Unless Wheat Commission are authorised to make purchases within few days result will be dangerous shortage in U.K. food supplies by end of year, a condition of affairs which submarine situation makes it imperative to avoid.'[27] Yet a cable from Lever to Chalmers makes it clear that the British were already using American funds to purchase Canadian wheat: 'In spite of risk of objection being raised later I agree that in all circumstances we may continue to make payments from New York funds.'[28] Possibly the Treasury wished to make such purchases on a much larger scale – or they hoped that the Americans would never notice. This was how the position stood when Reading arrived in Washington.

Lever immediately apprised him of the situation: 'Canadian wheat. On Reading's arrival yesterday I furnished him with full information on this subject and pointed out that...this ranked as a most pressing matter.'[29] The problem for Britain in Canada, as in the USA, was the need to purchase exchange: the need to buy Canadian dollars was threatening the pound to such an extent that British purchases of Canadian products were becoming problematical – in fact, the purchase of cheese had ceased in June 1917, thereby throwing the Canadian cheese industry into turmoil.[30] Reading met with McAdoo on 13 September to discuss the situation, and again on 18 September. At the latter meeting Reading proposed that since it was imperative that the British government know by 19 September whether the Wheat Commission could purchase the Canadian wheat (because of the need to arrange for shipping), and since the American government was reluctant to commit itself to a large expenditure of money without a detailed examination of the position, the American government should place $50m. at the disposal of the British government for the purchase of Canadian wheat without prejudice to its future policy (that is, the action would not be used by the British government as a precedent).[31] McAdoo telephoned his acquiescence, and Crosby finally confirmed that the USA would supply the $50m., although he registered his disapproval of the transaction.[32]

Reading was quick to gain further concessions. As he reported to the Chancellor,

> I have explained to Crosby our intention subject to his acquiescence to employ $15mil. monthly of credits he gives us for various Canadian purchases. He is not prepared to agree in principle to use of US credits for Canadian purchases. But I gather that he is prepared to overlook payments within above total provided we are able to make out that our Canadian contracts involve directly or indirectly expenditure in US to this amount.[33]

Crosby in fact considered that it was improper to use American credits voted by the Congress to purchase goods abroad, basing his conclusion on his interpretation of the bill authorising the Liberty Loans and on McAdoo's assurances to the House of Representatives' Ways and

Means Committee that the proceeds of the loans to the Allies would not be used outside the USA.[34] (His successor as Assistant Secretary of the Treasury, R. G. Leffingwell, a future partner in J. P. Morgan & Co., later called his reasoning 'an exposition of the law by a civil engineer' and asserted that Crosby was absolutely wrong.)[35] And in fact, by the end of October the American Treasury was assuming that about $60m. a month from its advances to Britain were being used for outside purchases.[36]

Reading travelled to Canada for three days to persuade a group of Canadian bankers to float a loan to help finance the wheat crop, since the American Treasury had insisted that Canada must do more to help itself. After talking to the Canadian Cabinet and the principal Canadian bankers, he reported to the Chancellor on 6 October 1917 that 'Estimate of exportable wheat and oats is about $350mil. U.S. Treasury have already agreed to advance $50mil. for October... White and bankers have agreed to lend $100mil. to HMG, ½ this year and ½ next spring, for 2 years... This proposition to be contingent upon U.S. Treasury finding the balance of $200mil.'[37] Reading returned to Washington and discussed the situation with Crosby on 8 October: 'Crosby is disinclined to give promise beyond immediate necessity. I have pressed for decision and explained Canada's promise conditional only... He is consulting President... This case challenges policy of U.S. Treasury as to payments abroad and is for us good ground of attack.'[38] On 12 October the two men went over the proposition, and Reading finally extracted a promise from Crosby that the USA would advance the $200m. Reading must have been somewhat surprised when he received a letter from Crosby dated 17 October wherein Crosby stated that Reading might have had $200m. in his mind, but Crosby had had only $150m. in *his*, and the latter figure would stand – although the British could apply for more later if necessary. Reading agreed, and, after representations from Hoover, the Food Administrator, further agreed that half of the wheat surplus destined for the Allies would go through American flour mills, which were running at only half capacity.[39]

This last point is an example of Reading's attempt to apply the policy of 'reciprocity', as he suggested to the Chancellor on 18 September: 'Would be of considerable value from political point of view if in any arrangements I conclude with McAdoo, provision could be made whenever possible for reciprocity of treatment, so that he could make public statements that United States Government gets some set off to the advances of the Allies.'[40] The Chancellor agreed to this proposal 'if you find it will help you in your negotiations with McAdoo' and informed Reading that he was inquiring of the departments what arrangements would be practicable.[41] A week-and-a-half later Reading requested that the Chancellor expedite the list of supplies with which the Ministry of Munitions and the War Office thought they could help the USA, for the reason that 'I am doing everything possible to get United States Government to look at question of supplies to their own departments and to Allies as a whole' and it was necessary to show that the British government was prepared to do the same.[42] An arrangement was made for Australian wool to be supplied to the American government at the same price as to the British government, but this was apparently the only arrangement of this sort made during Reading's visit.[43]

Reading adopted (in contrast with Lever) a policy of candour towards McAdoo, who was greatly appreciative: 'it was a great relief to me to have a man of his fine ability, common-sense and good judgment with whom to discuss the complicated questions that were constantly arising... Our relations were soon established on a plane of complete candour and confidence.'[44] In particular Reading proposed to the Chancellor that he should 'communicate to McAdoo full text of any financial agreements you may make with the Allies which in any way affect dollar finance. I propose to treat McAdoo and Administration with complete frankness.'[45] The Chancellor agreed to a policy of candour towards the USA and assured Reading that he would supply him with any agreements that were made. This soon upset the French, who objected to Reading's showing McAdoo previously secret Anglo-French concords.[46] At the cost of French uneasiness, Reading gained American confidence; and a feeling of trust was essential if the USA was to view the Anglo-American war effort as a partnership.

The most nerve-racking part of Lever's duties had probably been his repeated attempts to convince the American Treasury to promise – in advance – to pay a regular agreed sum to Britain, thereby enabling the British Treasury to plan ahead. Lever never succeeded, but Reading's frank approach undoubtedly helped him to convince McAdoo to make such a promise. As will be described in Chapter 9, there had been a major crisis in July and August caused by British attempts to get enough funds to cover exchange and other expenses. The Chancellor therefore instructed Lever to await Reading's arrival before submitting new estimates to McAdoo. Consequently, when Reading arrived on 12

September Lever insisted to him that Britain must be promised further credits by the end of the week.[47]

During his first four days in Washington Reading talked to Lever, Spring Rice, Northcliffe, Lansing and McAdoo about the situation; he then cabled to the Chancellor on 15 September his impression that

> we shall have some difficulty on obtaining dollars required apart from question of how far U.S. credits will be available for Canada or exchange. On points of principle trust will be possible establish friendly relations and satisfactory arrangements but in fixing aggregate of credits as distinguished from method of employment McAdoo may be soon against practical difficulties which no good-will can overcome. He is getting his measure through Congress but own government's expenditure is budgeted on colossal scale . . . His power to finance this is problematical and advances to Allies will suffer first . . . War Cabinet ought to be aware that continuance of British Departmental expenditure on present scale is probably impossible.[48]

He added that he would request a $50m. supplement (for Canadian wheat) to the usual request of $185m. for September, but he warned that Lever had been asked to reduce the demand below even the latter figure.[49]

As might be expected, the question of exchange soon arose. One factor in the American response was the desire of McAdoo, and probably others, to replace the pound with the dollar as the international medium of exchange – a desire which House had discerned and told Wiseman to warn Reading about before the latter's arrival.[50] Reading met the challenge realistically:

> I have good reason to think that discussion will turn on question of dollar bills versus sterling bills. I do not see how we can successfully oppose whatever development they propose, so long as they provide money. I think it would be mistaken policy to fight what will appear to them selfish cause and which we must lose. I do not underestimate importance to London market of maintaining position of sterling bills intact. But American plans are half baked and . . . for at least a year nothing they can do will really impair position of our bills. I propose therefore . . . to give way gracefully. . . .[51]

Another point about exchange made by Crosby in October was that, were it not for the ability of bankers in some neutral countries to convert sterling into local currency in London and New York, they would have no ultimate alternative but to make advances to Britain in order to dispose of their surplus produce. Reading urged the Chancellor to consider whether he had really exhausted all possibility of borrowing money outside the USA. Crosby wanted to encourage this, and later while he was in Europe he cabled his opinion to McAdoo that the British were not doing more to raise loans outside the USA because they were borrowing from the USA at a lower rate of interest, 3½ per cent, than they could get in neutral countries. With encouragement from Reading and from the Americans the British raised loans in, for example, Denmark and the Argentine, and from their ally Japan.[52]

The question of exchange, however, was never as crucial as it had been during the summer of 1917, the Americans confining themselves, by and large, to frequent and urgent requests that the British find some other way to support the rate than through the use of American advances. They were trying to cut their expenses wherever possible throughout the whole period of Reading's visit, and Reading sympathised with their dilemma, as he made clear in a long cable to the Chancellor on 17 October:

> Treasury and their advisers are seriously alarmed at the present financial position and do not see their way to raise the enormous sums required... This general apprehensiveness is much accentuated by the outlook for the second Liberty Loan, which is at present poor... Difficulties ahead of the United States administration are gigantic and I am convinced we shall gain more by strengthening position which we are gradually establishing of confidential helpers and advisers of the United States Treasury in our joint financial problems than by too persistent and imperative presentation of our particular need for dollars.[53]

Yet, the British need for dollars was inexorable, and Reading worked to extract promises for present and future advances. This task was more difficult than it might have been because McAdoo was away for several weeks campaigning for the Liberty Loan and Crosby was apprehensive about taking too much responsibility during his absence.[54] Reading, in fact, had to wait for McAdoo's return before finally obtaining the promises he wanted.

On 9 October 1917 Reading indicated to Crosby that he needed loans of $235m. a month for three months, less the advances for Canadian wheat. Crosby demurred, and by 21 October Reading decided he would have to await McAdoo's return, expected about 26 October. He saw both men together on 26 October and formally requested $200m. for November and $235m. each for December and January. He explained to them that he wanted to make arrangements then so that he could return to Britain in time for the Inter-Allied Conference in Paris, to which Crosby was a delegate (see below). By this time it looked as though the Liberty Loan campaign would be a success (as it proved to be) and presumably McAdoo was in an easier frame of mind. At any rate, he did for Reading what he had refused to do for Lever. He approved the sums for November and December, and although he balked at promising more than $185m. for January, Reading was certain that they would provide it if it was necessary. With this agreement, he felt that he could return to Britain.[55]

Although his main financial task was thus completed satisfactorily, Reading was regretful that he had not been able to settle the question of whether or not the USA would reimburse Britain for payments made for Russian supplies or that of the Morgan overdraft. Further, he had tried to convince the Administration to set up some sort of Priority Board to determine the allocation of increasingly scarce resources between the American departments and the Allies, but in this as well he had been unsuccessful.[56]

The financial situation had been the initial motive for sending Reading to the USA, but he had another important task: to convince the President to send American representatives to an Inter-Allied Conference in Europe. The origins of this move lay in Lloyd George's anger and frustration at the outcome of the Passchendaele offensive and the prospect of stalemate on the Western Front. He wanted the Allies to adopt an 'Eastern' strategy of attacking the weaker of the Central Powers – Turkey or Austria, for example. In this he differed from General Sir William Robertson, Chief of the Imperial General Staff, and General Sir Douglas Haig, the Commander-in-Chief of the British army in France, who were adamant 'Westerners'. Lloyd George felt that he could not carry his plan in the War Cabinet, but that if the plan were presented by the USA the War Cabinet and the Allies would probably be constrained to agree. Therefore, he wanted to convene an Inter-Allied Conference to which the USA would send a representative, and he intended that Reading should convince the President to do so.[57]

Lloyd George wanted Reading to take an unofficial, personal letter from him to the President. Hankey records that on 28 August, 'All day Lloyd George was in a most capricious mood and Kerr and I drafted about ten letters from Ll.G. for Reading to take to President Wilson, but before we had finished one draft he would invariably get a "brainwave" and want a new one.'[58] This continued on 30 August, when Hankey redrafted the draft, and the completed letter was finally given to Reading on 3 September.[59] The gist of the letter was that the direction of Allied military operations lacked real unity, and that Lloyd George felt that what was required was a body to consider military problems as a whole, including alternatives to frontal assaults on the Western Front.[60] As Hankey wrote, 'in the main, it was a carefully worded plea to President Wilson to take part in the Allied Councils.'[61]

Reading gave the letter to the President on 20 September, who received it 'not without sympathy'.[62] This caution of the President was not unexpected, since Reading knew that he did not want the USA to become too closely involved with the Allies and thereby limit his freedom of action (the President considered that the USA was an 'Associate', not an 'Ally'). Reading did not realise, however, that Wiseman, whom the Prime Minister had charged with convincing House of the wisdom of the scheme, was warning House and the President to be careful: they should not become involved in Lloyd George's manoeuvres against part of the War Cabinet.[63]

Reading had to be content for some time with the knowledge that the President was considering the matter. He complained to Wiseman that the matter was not progressing quickly enough, and although Wiseman sympathised with Reading, he also reminded him that, as House had pointed out,

> the Prime Minister must remember this matter is one which he has been turning over in his mind for some time, and has no doubt been able to consider it from all sorts of angles. He can hardly expect the President to come to a decision immediately on so important a matter, or even to be prepared to express his views on the subject until he has had an opportunity for very careful thought.[64]

Reading hastily assured Wiseman that he realised that there must be some delay, and that he had seen the President that evening – 27 September – and had been 'heartened' by their talk.[65]

Wiseman and House were themselves convinced of the need for an American representative to go to the conference, and worked towards that end. When on 12 October the President, Reading, Spring Rice and House met to discuss the issue, House had already spoken to Reading and the President independently and knew what each would say to the other. The upshot was that the President intimated that he would receive favourably an invitation from the Allies to send a representative to the Inter-Allied Conference to be held in Europe in December 1917. Later that day, Reading and House conferred, and House agreed that he would be the representative (he had demurred at first, but the President would have no one else represent him).[66] The President's decision to send a representative had probably been influenced more by House and Wiseman than by Reading in his infrequent talks with the President. During these negotiations, only the President, House, Reading and Wiseman had been aware of Reading's special commission from Lloyd George.[67]

House's mission to the Inter-Allied Conference was announced on 18 October 1917. Over the course of the next two weeks it was decided that the USA would be represented also on the Inter-Allied Council by Crosby, who in fact became the chairman. In addition, House was to take Rear Admiral W. S. Benson and General Tasker H. Bliss as naval and military advisers; as civilian advisers he took, in addition to Crosby from the Treasury, Vance C. McCormick, Chairman of the War Trade Board, Bainbridge Colby, Chairman of the Shipping Board, Dr Alonzo R. Taylor of the Food Administration and Thomas N. Perkins of the War Industries Board.[68]

With House in Europe, the British were to lose their most dependable channel for encouraging the American Administration to come to a decision on any particular topic. House in fact noted of Reading that he was

> restless at being left here while I am in Europe. I think he believes there will be no way for him to get decisions, should an impasse occur... He does not wish his mission to be a failure. The truth is, in getting the President to send me to the Allied War Council, he has accomplished the main purpose of his visit. He desires to return to England with me,...[69]

The War Cabinet agreed that, if he could persuade the Treasury to promise funds in advance, Reading should return to Britain in time for the House mission.[70]

Reading had been asked to survey British representation in the United States and report back to the War Cabinet, and this most delicate of missions was, to a large extent, carried out verbally. By September 1917, when Reading went out to the USA, it was already generally realised that Spring Rice would have to be recalled. The War Cabinet on 17 September had directed Balfour to consider 'the desirability of recalling Sir Cecil Spring-Rice on leave and extending the duration of Lord Reading's stay in the United States',[71] and, in the USA, House and Reading agreed a few days later that Spring Rice would have to return to Britain.[72] In the British government the Treasury was especially conscious of the damage Spring Rice could do and of the way in which he could hamper the British mission representatives. His treatment of Lever had been so bad that it had been considered by the War Cabinet. Reading's arrival, not surprisingly, had been greeted by both Blackett and Lever with enthusiasm, Lever going so far as to suggest that Reading be put in complete authority over all the British representatives in the USA.[73] It remained, however, for Keynes to put the worst possible gloss on Spring Rice's activities. It was perhaps unfortunate for Spring Rice that he had mistreated Reading on his arrival, and that Reading had brought Keynes with him. Keynes was one of the most trenchant memorandum-writers in the Treasury. When he returned to Britain he wrote down, at the Chancellor's request, a description of the difficulties Reading had encountered, and included an evaluation of Spring Rice:

> Col. A. Murray, Col. Swinton...and I came independently to the conclusion that in his present nervous condition Sir C. Spring-Rice could not be regarded as entirely mentally responsible. It is certain that his excitability, his nervousness, his frequent indiscretion, and also his absent-mindedness render the proper conduct of his business almost impossible... But at... times he would act in a manner universally adjudged to be unworthy of his position. I formed the impression that 2 of the dominant impulses of his mind – namely dislike of the present U.S. Administration and jealousy of whatever emissary HMG might send out from this country – often impelled him subconsciously in a manner of which his normal self was not properly and sanely aware. But whatever the explanation, the effects are a matter of universal comment throughout Washington.[74]

Keynes's considered comment that Spring Rice was mad – and that political Washington knew it – could not but have had an effect on the Chancellor, and doubtless this opinion seeped out of the Treasury. The question of who was to replace him, however, would have to wait upon Reading's return.

Reading sailed for Britain on 3 November 1917, and was followed shortly thereafter by the House mission. House and Reading had spoken of a successor to Spring Rice in September, and House, as usual, had urged that Grey be sent out as Ambassador; if that were not possible, the British government should send Lord Robert Cecil or Asquith – although they agreed that Mrs Asquith would present some difficulty. The British government dutifully asked Grey to take up the post, but he declined, although Drummond told House in London that they hoped House could persuade Grey to change his mind. House could not, and early in December, having made an obeisance to House, the British government named the obvious choice: Lord Reading.[75]

The designation of Reading as Ambassador Extraordinary and High Commissioner on Special Mission to the United States represented the determination of the British government to come to grips with the splintered state of its representation in the USA. The argument for thus combining the duties of both Northcliffe and Spring Rice was cogently put by Wiseman: 'Nowadays most diplomatic questions at Washington concern supplies, and all questions of supplies when other than mere routine become matters for diplomatic negotiation.'[76] In a memorandum he wrote for the Prime Minister on his return, Reading set out the position which he felt a supreme British representative in the USA should occupy and the power he should wield, and this anticipated quite closely Reading's actual position in America in 1918:

there should be one supreme authority representing [HMG] in the United States... At Washington this representative of [HMG] should be the sole means of communication between the British Government or Departments and the President or individual ministers of the U.S. Administration in all matters affecting [HMG]. An industrial mission like the BWM or any other which may be sent to the United States should bring matters of policy or of serious difficulty to the notice of the British Representative who would then take up the matter with the United States Government. The management of the Mission should, of course, be left to its President or Chairman and only matters of real importance should be brought to the Head Representative of

[HMG]. This Head Representative should conduct all diplomatic negotiations and conferences and he should be invested with the fullest authority to act on behalf of [HMG].[77]

Although appointed in December 1917, Reading did not go out to the USA until February 1918; apparently he was determined not to go until he was certain that Northcliffe would not be going back to America and would no longer have any direct influence on the BWM.[78] In the interim he made as certain as he could that he would be the one sole channel through which all communications would flow to the American government. Further, he acted on a warning cabled by Wiseman: 'Some trouble is being caused by large number of British officials coming to this country under no control.... Earnestly suggest that you should arrange with Government that no British officials or propagandists come to this country without being first submitted to you.'[79] Cecil brought up the problem at the meeting of the War Cabinet on 30 January 1918, during which the position of the British missions, as affected by the appointment of Reading, was considered. The Cabinet decided that since Reading was to be responsible for the whole of the missions there it was right that he should be consulted before anyone was sent out from Britain to take part in them: 'All Departments should, in the first instance, communicate to Lord Reading by telegraph the name of the official they propose to send, and...in due course, if no reply was received from Lord Reading, application should be made for the necessary passport'.[80] Thus on 1 February 1918, the scope of his powers having been determined, Reading departed for the United States.

On 9 February 1918 Reading arrived in New York to take up his new position.[81] He brought a small personal staff with him: a Private Secretary from the Foreign Office, Hubert Montgomery; Colonel Swinton (who had come out with Reading in 1917) and Grimwood Mears, an old friend at the Bar, who were to act as his assistants in military and civil matters respectively; and Lt-Col. C. K. Craufurd-Stuart of the Indian army, who was to act as Comptroller of the House-hold and social secretary.[82] (Wiseman later wrote that it had been a mistake for Reading to bring Swinton and Craufurd-Stuart: everybody liked them, but 'it is a mistake for an Ambassador to have a military suite... Moreover there is no real place for them in his organisation, as the heads of the departments naturally declined to work through a military Secretary.'[83] Further, militarism was not popular in the USA, but Swinton's military experience was eventually put to use when he was removed from his embarrassing position in Washington and sent out on lecture tours for the Liberty Loan.)[84]

This time, at least, there was no mistake about Reading's powers and responsibilities, since he was clearly in charge both of the Embassy and of the mission. The American government was pleased that he was coming: Wiseman cabled, after talking to the President on 24 January, that the President was 'delighted Reading is coming and thinks his advice will be most helpful',[85] and it has been demonstrated that House and McAdoo thought highly of him. In fact there were only two disaffected sections of opinion: the British Embassy, and those members of the BWM who had personal loyalties to Northcliffe. For the members of the Embassy, it was an institutional outrage:

> To appoint anyone not a diplomat *de carriere* was most exceptional . . . and those amongst them who were members of the Diplomatic Service had been so greatly disturbed at the appointment of an Ambassador from outside the Service that they had at first felt some resentment at the establishing of a precedent likely, if extended, to block their own and their colleagues' advancement to the higher posts in their profession.[86]

The Embassy adjusted, however:

> They were . . . wise enough after the first flush of indignation to recognize that the times were without parallel and justified departure from normal usage, and, having accepted the situation, they devoted themselves to serving the new Ambassador with unqualified loyalty and zeal. But the tempo of work in the Embassy increased with such vigor that at the outset they found themselves somewhat breathless and bewildered.[87]

Reading in 1917 had had unsettling relations with Spring Rice and the Embassy staff, and he would have realised that the staff would resent an outsider coming in as Ambassador; he therefore presumably took care to establish his authority over the staff to preclude insubordination. Wiseman wrote to Drummond on 14 March that 'Reading, on his arrival, was faced with a number of awkward and unpleasant personal questions which you heard nothing about, but which had to be settled before he could get his machine to run smoothly. I do not suppose they are by any means all settled yet, but the organisation has certainly improved.'[88]

The other difficulty was the British War Mission itself. It will be recalled that Northcliffe had brought out members of his personal organisation from London to act as administrators, and these, by and large, had remained after he had left. There were complaints when Reading replaced Northcliffe,[89] and some of Northcliffe's lieutenants, such as Louis Tracy, went as far as to continue to write reports to Northcliffe (in his capacity as Chairman of the BWM in London), in which personal loyalty to Northcliffe was asserted.[90] However, since there is no evidence of sabotage, it is probable that postwar employment prospects motived much of this activity.

The main problem Reading faced with his dual assignment, once control over the Embassy staff had been established, was forcing the two organisations to work in harness. Reading 'found a good deal of confusion when he arrived owing to the Northcliffe regime at the War Mission and the entire lack of co-operation between the Embassy and the Mission.'[91] It is impossible to know for certain just what steps Reading took to remedy matters, but by July 1918, when Reading returned to Britain, there was no doubt of his success:

> At the Embassy the staff like Reading and admire him, but are a bit afraid of him... Barclay [Minister at the Embassy] accepts the situation at the Embassy most loyally and continues to do all routine work most conscientiously. He is eminently safe and reliable, but quite terrified of Reading... There has really been remarkably little friction between the many missions here; I think that this is partly due to the fact that they are all a little afraid of Reading.[92]

The greater interest during this period lies in Reading's work as Ambassador: there he was mainly concerned with getting American troops to Europe (including where they were to go), and persuading the President to support Allied intervention in Russia so as to set up an Eastern Front and thereby draw German troops away from France. Those negotiations took up the bulk of his time, and he dealt with BWM affairs only when a crisis arose or there was a major change in its structure. Thus he dealt with a food crisis on his arrival, urged the change in the War Industries Board (WIB) which enabled it to deal with priority matters, approved changes in the military missions and dealt with financial affairs when they threatened to become critical once again; but by and large Reading as High Commissioner of the British War Mission tended to leave the running of the missions to those in charge of them at the executive level, interfering only when his intellect and diplomacy were needed.

When Reading arrived in Washington in the second week of February 1918, he had already decided that the most urgent problem he had to deal with was food. The British government had become extremely worried because January and February shipments were wholly inadequate, and in France and Italy the soldiers had already suffered a cut in rations.[93] There had been an earlier difficulty, one of finance, and Lord Rhondda had even accused the Treasury of supporting the exchange with funds advanced by the USA for food.[94] In January 1918, however, the Chancellor supported Rhondda who was trying to get effective priority of finance for food (as he had earlier won priority of tonnage), and on 16 January 1918 the War Cabinet accepted Rhondda's view.[95]

The major difficulty now lay with the inadequate railway system in the USA. In January 1918 Wilson had taken control of all the American railways for the duration of the war, and he had put McAdoo in charge of the new Railway Administration. McAdoo remained Secretary of the Treasury, however, and, partially because of his inability to delegate authority, and partially because of the dismal condition of the railways themselves, he had not made much progress in co-ordinating railway traffic. The most important problem was the misuse of railway cars. Since in prewar America imports and exports had been roughly equal, railway companies had formed the habit of sending cars to the seaboard with exports and then leaving them there until they were full of imports, whereupon they were then sent to the other parts of the country. Now, however, there were relatively few imports, with the result that an estimated 145,000 railway cars waited, empty, at the Eastern sea-ports, while grain and meat waited in depots around the country to be picked up and carried to the seaboard.[96]

Reading spent 18 February going over the papers on the subject, and on 19 February he met with the Italian Ambassador and the French High Commissioner to discuss tactics, during which meeting they asked him to take the lead. The difficulty was that the Administration was then subject to attacks by Republicans for inefficiency and dilatoriness in its war preparations, and was very much on edge and touchy about criticism. Aware of the risk of destroying the good relations with the Americans which he had built up in 1917, Reading drafted a letter of delicacy and tact in which he sympathised with the Railway Administration and its problems while underlining the urgency of the problem. He then made a number of suggestions, the most important of which was that all empty railway cars should be brought back from the seaboard and sent to pick up food and then given absolute priority on the tracks. McAdoo agreed to all of the suggestions and implemented them at once. Hoover was later brought in, and after some urging, agreed to release 300,000 tons of grain from the reserves to send to France and Italy, at the risk of the Americans themselves going short. There was no shortage of tonnage, since the Allies had delayed munitions to free ships for food, and once the railway cars were moving steadily, the crisis eased.[97] By June 1918 both Hoover and Reading could report that the Allies and the Americans would have plenty of food during the next twelve months.[98]

The history of the various missions comprising the British War Mission in 1918 lacks the excitement engendered by the crises of 1917 (the Treasury mission, as usual, excepted). The missions in 1918, although often frustrated over lacks of materials, did not often come into dangerous conflict with the Americans. As High Commissioner, Reading held to his decision not to take part in the daily routine of the missions. Reading's responsibility did include naming the heads of the missions with the departments' agreement; as well, he reorganised the BWM in May 1918. The other main change in 1918 was in the field of priorities, dear to Reading's heart, namely, the giving of increased powers to the War Industries Board (as Reading had unsuccessfully argued in 1917).

On the day before he left Britain Reading wrote to the Foreign Office about his proposed arrangements in the USA. Sir Frederick Black had been named temporary Head of the BWM in October 1917 when Northcliffe was arranging to visit England, but the Cabinet at that time had not felt that he was a big enough man to hold the post permanently. Reading proposed to appoint Sir Henry Babington Smith, who had gone out with him on the Anglo-French Loan Mission in 1915, as Assistant Commissioner of the BWM, save as to finance. Once in the USA Reading found that Lever had some objection, which he met by naming Lever Assistant Commissioner for Finance. He also named

Grimwood Mears head of the food mission, and T. Ashley Sparks head of the shipping mission.[99]

The Ministry of Munitions mission was the largest of the missions, and it had the most frequent opportunities for conflict with the Americans. Its very size apparently bred insensitivity, and Reading found it necessary to complain to Churchill that 'I find sometimes that the conditions here are not sufficiently realised, and there is consequently a tendency to treat questions from a purely English point of view.'[100] Reading's remedy was an interchange of men at the top; he sent R. H. Brand back to the ministry, and Charles F. Whigham of Morgan Grenfell came out to replace him. In May Reading reorganised those branches of the BWM which dealt with war supplies for the Ministry of Munitions, Admiralty, War Office, Board of Trade and Air Board into a Department of War Supplies. Gordon, as head of the mission, became Director-General of War Supplies, and Reading was 'quite satisfied' with his work, commenting that 'I find fewer signs of friction with American authorities than I was led to expect.'[101] (This was perhaps because Gordon was no longer primarily responsible for negotiations with the Americans over munitions supplies.) When Whigham came out, he became Deputy Director-General under Gordon.[102] This was the final organisational change of note during the war.

The Allied Purchasing Commission of the WIB, with which the BWM had to deal, went through an important change in March 1918. It had been set up during the Northcliffe period, and although it was without much power, the Allies struggled to make it useful, since it was the only purchasing channel available. When Reading visited the United States in 1917 he had spent some little time trying to convince the American government to set up a board to determine priorities between the American government departments and the Allies, since the army and navy were ordering supplies right and left and the Allies were in danger of being squeezed out of the market. He had however been unable to accomplish anything before leaving the USA in November 1917.[103]

There was a priorities committee in the WIB, headed by Robert Lovett, but he was intimidated by the lack of legal sanctions in the hands of the WIB to enforce its decisions, and although a priority order was issued on steel in September 1917, only two others followed in the next several months. There was some difficulty in convincing the military services that central determination of priorities by a civilian agency was a good thing. But, as the historian of the WIB writes,

By the beginning of 1918, confusion in military procurement had become so acute that the services themselves consented to a verbal agreement permitting the priorities committee [of the WIB] to adjust cases between the two departments. Officials in the military purchasing bureau were first to try to resolve conflicts among themselves, and if this proved impossible, they were to allow the priorities committee to step in. Further appeal could then be made to the army and navy members of the WIB; if that failed, the priorities commissioner would make the final determination. The priorities committee wanted to go further than this and take initiative away from the military bureaus altogether.[104]

The President finally agreed to the change desired by Reading as well as by the priorities committee, and on 4 March 1918 he made the WIB responsible for 'the determination, wherever necessary, of priorities of production and delivery and of the proportions of any given article to be made immediately accessible to the several purchasing agencies when the supply of that article is insufficient, either temporarily or permanently.'[105] There was a new priorities board created on 27 March, on which Alexander Legge, head of the Allied Purchasing Commission, had a seat. The priorities administration made real gains: it made fifty-six orders in the next six months, tightened restrictions on non-war industries, tried to limit unnecessary building construction and developed a preference list of plants considered to be of exceptional importance to the war effort. In September 1918 it formally gained the power to co-ordinate all commandeering orders, although it had made an informal agreement with the services in June. Even so, it still suffered from a lack of enforcement power, and from a lack of control over means of transport, since McAdoo kept jealous control over the railways. Further, the programme of restrictions which it proclaimed went far beyond what it could administer.[106] As in so many other areas of the war effort, the war ended before the machinery could be perfected.

Nevertheless, the reorganisation of both the BWM and the WIB made for a more efficient relationship and supply problems between the two countries were now resolved in a reasonably amicable and efficient manner. Yet relations between the WIB and the British government began to deteriorate, especially after Reading returned to Britain in July 1918: the cause was apparently the growing suspicions of Baruch, the

Chairman of the WIB, about Britain's postwar economic plans.[107] This was, however, beyond the scope of the BWM to remedy.

During the Northcliffe period, there had been some discussion of a military mission coming out, and it had been settled that instead a new military attaché, General McLachlan, should be sent out. Now, in March 1918, the War Office decided to send a mission. Reading at first tried to discourage this plan, but the War Office insisted.

On 20 March, Lord Derby, the Secretary of State for War, cabled to Reading:

> I should like to send you a senior military officer who would be in charge of and co-ordinate the work of all the British military missions at present in the United States namely (1) the Military Attaché and officers acting under him, (2) the Training mission under Brig.-Gen. Trotter, and (3) the Recruiting Mission under Brig.-Gen. White so long as it remains in America. For this post I consider Maj.-Gen. G. T. M. Bridges eminently suitable... The Army Council and myself are convinced that the presence in America of a senior officer of practical experience at the front and with the latest information from the War Office concerning the questions of organisations training and transport, is absolutely necessary, and I am hopeful you will agree with this view.[108]

Reading found this inexplicable: Maj.-Gen. McLachlan, the military attaché, was doing his work efficiently and he certainly had the confidence of the Americans and of the Allied military attaché; why should he be reduced to what would effectively be an assistant attaché?[109] After further explanation, Reading cabled his approval on 1 April 1918, with the proviso that Bridges was subject to him; Derby agreed that Bridges was responsible to Reading and was to be attached to the Embassy.[110]

That was not how Bridges understood matters. In his autobiography he wrote that because of the acute manpower problems after Passchendaele, and because of the objections of General Pershing, the American Commander, to brigading American troops in British formations, Lloyd George had sent for him and told him to go to the USA. Ostensibly his mission was to control the military missions and act as military adviser to Reading, but in reality he was 'tactfully but firmly to bring home to the American Administration the extremely critical nature of the situation and to do my utmost to increase the flow of real bayonets and not administrative troops to Europe. Most important of all, I was to be independent of Reading and if I found things moving too slowly I was to use my own initiative as to how to convince President Wilson of the seriousness of the crisis.'[111] There is no doubt that Reading did not know of these instructions: not only was there no mention of this topic in the terms of Bridges's mission cabled to him by Derby, but he would not have tolerated Bridges's independence, especially with regard to communicating with the President. And, unless Derby was deliberately concealing these instructions from Reading, it must be assumed that he did not know of them either.[112]

Bridges and the other members of the mission arrived on 17 April 1918. He was accompanied by Maj.-Gen. Robert Hutchinson, who was to assist the American authorities in organising the dispatch of troops to the Western Front; Sir Graeme Thomson, Controller of Shipping and Railways, who was given powers to control all shipping under the Allied flags and facilitate the dispatch of food, munitions and men to France; and Sir Guy Granet, representing both the Army Council and the Food Controller, who was to ensure that supplies of food from the USA to Europe should meet the needs of both the civil population and the fresh troops from the USA.[113] Bridges and Hutchinson saw House in New York on 19 April, and then travelled on to Washington, where arrangements were made for Bridges to see the President on 22 April.

Bridges's approach to the Administration was described by a member of the Embassy military staff to Arthur Murray (now back in London): 'When General Bridges arrived he was all for using the big stick on the Americans, and we had a hard time at first keeping him away from the War Dept. I believe he thought at first that we did not wrench enough information out of them, and he was quite impatient.'[114] Bridges described the President as being 'even more unapproachable' about the war than he had been in 1917; he accepted the Prime Minister's communication about the need for troops quickly, but told Bridges to give all details to House or Baker, since he preferred to receive all information through his staff.[115] Bridges and Reading saw House on 24 April and they discussed the brigading of American troops with the British.[116] Thereafter Bridges spent most of his time in discussion with the War Department about artillery and ammunition. While he was in the USA the War Office directed him to urge the plan for intervention in Russia, and he spoke to House about the matter. Reading and Wiseman, however, were primarily responsible for negotiations over this.[117] Yet on 25 July 1918, just before Bridges returned to Britain, he wrote a strong letter to Baker, which was also seen by the President, wherein he stated the arguments in favour of intervention in Russia. The President intensely disliked receiving unsolicited information – and especially from foreigners – and the upshot of Bridges's last throw was to make him *persona non grata* with the President, as Barclay later wrote: 'I think I ought to warn you that there appears to be a good deal of feeling here against [Bridges], particularly on account of some letter he wrote to Baker before leaving, which is said to have caused the President also great irritation.'[118]

It is unclear just what Bridges accomplished by his mission, although presumably the other members were useful in dispatching American soldiers. 300,000 American soldiers a month were sent to the Western Front over a three-month period. After Bridges's departure, McLachlan resumed the direction of the military missions in the USA. The number of British personnel in the USA declined after the decision of the American government in September 1918 to dispense with all foreign training missions and to replace the officers with American officers from the front.[119]

When Reading had come out in February 1918, Wiseman recorded what many surely expected: 'I am hoping a lot from Reading. He has a wonderful chance. If he is well backed up from home with a constant stream of information, and his recommendations are promptly acted upon, he can assume a great position in Washington and do very much to guide the Administration.'[120] Reading doubtless hoped to assume some such position, and he equally hoped to have free access to the President. He began, perhaps, to go too freely, arguing that he could get nothing from Lansing, but thereby jeopardising his position.[121] The breaking point came in mid-June when Reading, at the instance of the Prime Minister, asked to see the President, and was refused an audience. Even House admitted that the President had acted rudely.[122] At any rate, the incident crystallised Reading's desire to return to Britain, even if only temporarily. Wiseman analysed his actions as follows:

> Reading feels that he came out here not as ordinary Ambassador, or High Commissioner, but because he thought, owing to his close connection with the Cabinet at home and his friendships on this side with members of the Administration, that he would gain

the President's confidence to such an extent that he would be able
to discuss with him and consult with him on important questions
affecting the war. He has now come to the conclusion that it is
quite impossible to break down the barrier between the President
and the foreign representatives and that he is unable to do more
than any ordinary Ambassador could accomplish. In this I think
he is quite wrong, and I have told him so . . . He is worried too,
about the Chief Justiceship. He feels more and more that if he
stays out here any longer he must resign his position, and, that
would be a terrible wrench for him. . . . [123]

Reading felt that he had failed in his primary aim, but Wiseman disagreed. He felt that Reading had achieved far more with the President
than anyone else whom the government could have sent out, and that
furthermore he did not realise that the many problems of supply and
finance which he had settled with comparative ease would have
presented real difficulties to anyone else, and would probably have led
to friction. This was probably because 'He has a particular gift for
putting his case in a way that will appeal to the American officials and a
very nice sense of how far he can go without causing trouble'.[124]
Wiseman discussed the whole situation with House and the State
Department and 'The opinion is unanimous that it would be a disaster
to the Allied cause if Reading did not remain here until the war is
over'.[125] But, as Wiseman later wrote to Drummond, 'You may find it
difficult to persuade Reading to return here permanently . . . In all
respects he has been an unqualified success – the French and Italian
representatives just follow after him. He has raised our influence and
prestige right throughout the country'.[126]

Reading kept an eye on Anglo-American relations after he returned to
London in July, and Wiseman fed him all the news from America in
telegrams and letters. Both he and Lloyd George eventually felt that he
should return to the USA, and Reading planned at first to sail on
17 September 1918, but he later decided that it was not practicable. He
was again planning to return in mid-October, but because of the
discussions with the Allies and the Germans, Lloyd George sent him to
Paris instead. Reading did not return to America until February 1919,
and then he stayed only long enough to wind up various matters before
returning to Britain.[127] In July 1919 Grey was finally named as British
Ambassador to the United States.

Once the Armistice was proclaimed, the change in conditions in the

USA was rapid indeed. The war machinery began 'melting away like snow',[128] with the War Industries Board itself terminating on 1 January 1919, although many of the commodities sections had simply disintegrated by that time.[129] The winding up of the BWM proceeded rapidly, and Babington Smith, the Assistant Commissioner, asked to come home at the end of January 1919, on the ground that any further questions could be dealt with by the Embassy or Gordon. The Washington office of the BWM closed on 14 June 1919, and all further communications went to Gordon as Director-General of War Supplies in the offices of the Ministry of Munitions in New York. A few months later, this office was wound up as well.[130] The British War Mission had ended, and it would leave, as such, only an obscure group memoir.[131]

9

Financial Relations, 1917–1918: Crisis, Humiliation and Chagrin

British political missions to the USA might come and go, but the Treasury mission had little respite in its restless search for American aid with which to sustain the British financial position. Lever, as head of the Treasury mission, carried the brunt of the work, and his relations with McAdoo worsened over the duration of the war. There were a number of different points at issue between the two countries, but in general they fell into four major areas of disagreement: (1) whether or not Britain could secure, in advance, agreement to a schedule of monthly payments from the USA; (2) whether or not American funds could be used to support the rate of exchange of the pound; (3) whether or not the American Treasury would repay the Morgan overdraft (demand loan); and (4) whether or not the American Treasury would assume control over British securities in the USA. In essence, Britain was reasonably satisfied with the results obtained in the first three areas, but in the fight over control of her assets Britain suffered total defeat.

It was a period of painful adjustment for both governments. The American Treasury had to learn on the job how to finance an alliance. Beyond that, McAdoo in particular had to learn how far he could use his power to force unpalatable decisions on another sovereign nation. Conversely, the Chancellor of the Exchequer and Lever had to come to terms – not always too successfully on Lever's part – with Britain's weakened condition, and to endure the indignities (as Lever saw it) forced on Britain by the American government.

This chapter looks at the financial negotiations taking place alongside the other political and economic negotiations carried out by the North-cliffe and Reading missions. The third major party alongside the two governments was the House of Morgan, and a minor theme of the period is the change in the American government's perceptions of Morgan: from hindrance to helpmate.

For the Treasury mission, the period June–September 1917 was one of disappointment and frustration and narrowly averted disaster. Advances from the American government were crucial to Britain in making payments in the USA, and the spectre of default loomed again in June as it had in May. The American government was acutely worried by the scale of Allied requests for funds and looked around for ways to cut down on them – and in particular turned its attention to British use of funds for the maintenance of the exchange rate. The request of Morgan's and the British that the USA advance money to pay off the overdraft run up by the British at Morgan's was the last straw. Adjustments might have been easier if Lever and McAdoo had been able to establish a good working relationship; but they did not, and by August things were at such a pass that the British government had to agree to send out a financial envoy – Lord Reading – to rescue matters.

Lever's original plan had been to return to Britain in July 1917, but on 12 June the Chancellor cabled and asked if he would continue to represent the Treasury in the USA. Lever agreed, provided that someone from the Treasury was sent out to help him (McFadyean had returned to Britain with the Balfour mission) – he had not had a holiday in two years. The Chancellor suggested Basil Blackett, Lever asked that he be sent as soon as possible and Blackett arrived on 11 July 1917.[1]

Meanwhile Lever had to contend with a crisis of confidence in the American Treasury over its own ability to help the Allies to the extent that had been expected. On 13 June 1917 Lever learned from Crawford that $25m. which had been promised for 12 June by McAdoo had not in fact been handed over, and further, that McAdoo had queried the British exchange operations. Since this was a period of heavy pressure on the exchange Lever was annoyed, but, expecting to be able to talk McAdoo into providing the money, he made arrangements to travel to Washington.[2] The following day in Washington he met Crawford, who described his interview the day before with McAdoo and Crosby, saying that 'he had found them extremely difficult and much over-wrought. He could not fathom what was in their minds, but he did not at all like the way in which he was received.'[3] Lever and Crawford called on Crosby, and they found Crosby

in a nervous condition. He was unable to control himself fully in many ways, and showed...that he was under a severe strain. [Lever]...gave him a general summary of the expenditure for [April and May]. He again impressed on [Lever] the fact that in the West there were a number of enquiries being made as to the reasons for the United States advancing such large sums of money to Britain as against the other Allies. He states that he was not going to allow McAdoo to be 'crucified'. . . yet he did not see how the United States were to continue to finance our requirements and those of our Allies in the amounts which we had requested. He at last consented to release $25m to us that day, . . .[4]

The strain under which Crosby and McAdoo were labouring was probably caused by worry over the Liberty Loan, the means by which the Treasury was raising the money for the Allies, as well as for the American army and navy. The $2 billion worth of bonds had been offered on 14 May 1917 at 3½ per cent interest, a rate slightly lower than that available from bank deposits. McAdoo had insisted on this against most financial advice, since he believed that people would purchase the bonds out of patriotism with little regard for interest rates. (As well, some banks had feared that a high rate of interest on the bonds would cause too great a drain of funds from their banks.) The consequence was that 'At first the bonds sold poorly. One week before the subscription books were closed, New York appeared to be the only district meeting its quota, but thereafter sales picked up . . . When the subscriptions were totalled all districts but three had exceeded their quotas, and $3,035,226,850 had been subscribed, an oversubscription of 52 per cent'.[5] On 13 June McAdoo himself had just returned from a swing through the West touting the loan, and he was sick with worry and overwork.[6] Sales had not yet started to pick up, and thus the American Treasury was quite legitimately worried about its ability to supply all the funds the Allies said they required.

Lever warned the Chancellor on 16 June 1917 that, because there would almost certainly be Congressional inquiries into American advances to Britain for exchange, there was continual opposition by the American Treasury to exchange purchases. He therefore asked for confirmation that the Chancellor wished 'exchange protected . . . by all means at my disposal, gold included'.[7] Sir Richard Chalmers, one of the Joint Permanent Secretaries at the Treasury, confirmed this, and informed him that further British government purchases would be made in dollars rather than in pounds in New York,[8] which would relieve pressure on the exchange. Lever meanwhile was attempting to pin down the American Treasury on what funds the British could expect. On 16 June he asked Crawford and Northcliffe to see McAdoo and try to get a further advance of funds early the following week (he had forborne to ask Crosby on 14 June, since the latter had been in such a state), but Crawford reported later that McAdoo had refused.[9] (Northcliffe reported that it was not pleasant to see Crawford 'practically begging for financial assistance from McAdoo'.)[10] Lever asked Crawford to try again on 18 June, and this time McAdoo agreed to a further $35m. Lever went to Washington and he and Crawford met Crosby on 20 June, and Lever again insisted that he must have definite information on the funds available for the next two months; further, that he wanted without fail $50m. on 25 June.[11] 'Interview resulted in Crosby saying that he would discuss matter with McAdoo, that it was impossible for them to meet demands of Allies, that they were subject of criticism by politicians and particularly French for large (?advances) they were making to [British] and that while he could make no promise now he hoped to let [British] have a reply this week.'[12]

By 26 June the expected funds had not materialised and only $15m. had been approved.[13] The sticking point was exchange, as Crawford made clear in a cable to the Foreign Office:

> I asked [McAdoo] early last week for an emergency advance...to provide for dollar exchange against withdrawal by U.S. banks of sterling balances in London [to purchase Liberty Bonds]. After considerable discussion Mr. McAdoo concluded that he would hardly be justified in establishing a credit for above purpose. He hesitated to regard advances for maintenance of British exchange as falling (?within) purposes [of defence and prosecuting the war]. His colleague at Treasury [Crosby] thought we had sentimental regard for our exchange in excess of its real importance in present situation.[14]

McAdoo asked Crawford to convey his sentiments to London so that the British government might comment on them.[15]

McAdoo agreed to give $35m. to Britain, but he coupled this with the stricture that the British 'had no right to assume that $85m would be forthcoming' just because they had written a letter requesting it.[16] A further $15m. was advanced, but when on 27 June 1917 there was still no promise for the future after further unsatisfactory talks with Crosby by Crawford, Lever cabled to the Chancellor asking him to approach Page, the American Ambassador in London, since 'I can make no further headway here' with the American government.[17] Northcliffe

backed him up by cabling to the Prime Minister that 'it will be imperative to take up subject with the United States Government through
diplomatic channels'.[18] Fortunately, in the proverbial nick of time, help
came, as Crawford described it to the Foreign Office:

> June 26 [Crosby] informed me...McAdoo...had authorised
> advance of only $15mil. out of balance of $50mil. standing on our
> June application. In reply to my protest Mr. Crosby said that
> Secretary insisted on time to consider situation before meeting
> our requirements in full. I urged unreasonableness of withholding
> $35mil. at such short notice. Crosby replied that McAdoo would
> not give way on this point as he felt that our demands were too
> insistent and deprived him of exercise of his discretion under the
> Act. I at once telephoned Lever who informed me that unless
> balance of $35mil. were provided he would have to stop payment
> on...June 28... I saw Crosby who got into communication
> with McAdoo and informed me late last night that the latter
> would not modify his decision. Later and again this morning I
> discussed the whole situation with [Polk], who subsequently
> conferred with Lansing and McAdoo. I saw Lansing by appoint-
> ment this afternoon and after a long conference he communicated
> with [McAdoo] who finally consented to advance $35mil.
> tomorrow June 28 provided he received a communication from
> [Spring Rice] confirming urgency of the situation and agreeing
> that McAdoo's action in this case will not commit him any
> further.[19]

Crawford's cable was not received in London until 29 June, and on 28
June Balfour, the Chancellor and his Treasury advisers met with Page.
As Page cabled to Lansing that evening,

> It was disclosed that financial disaster to all the European Allies is
> imminent unless the United States Government advances to the
> British enough money to pay for British purchases in the United
> States as they fall due. Bonar Law reports that only half enough
> has been advanced for June and that the British agents in the
> United States now have enough money to keep the exchange up
> for only one day more. If exchange with England fall, exchange
> with all European Allies also will immediately fall and there will
> be a general collapse...I am convinced that these men are not

overstating their case. Unless we come to their rescue we are all in danger of disaster.[20]

The same day Balfour sent an appeal to House that 'we seem on the edge of a financial disaster which would be worse than a defeat in the field', adding that 'You know that I am not an alarmist: but this is really serious' and asking House to intercede with the President.[21] House immediately telephoned Washington and arranged for the cable to be given to the President, and then he tried to find out the difficulty:

> I have been on the phone for hours talking first to the State Department, then to New York, trying to unravel the tangle. There seems to have been bad judgment on both sides. Sir Wm [Wiseman] Lever and Sir R. Crawford do not work closely together. Crawford works with our people and Lever has a tendency to work with J. P. Morgan & Co., and it is not certain that Morgan does not want such a crisis as has arisen in order to force themselves again into the situation from which they have been ejected by the Government.[22]

Balfour also sent a long memorandum to Spring Rice for the American government, in which he ascribed Britain's difficulties with exchange to the fact that Britain was still supporting Russian expenditure in the USA (in spite of American promises that the American government would take over the support of the Allies in the USA), and to the withdrawals of sterling by American banks in London. He detailed what resources Britain had left and asked that (1) Russian repayments of British loans for American expenditure since 1 April 1917 should be paid, (2) financial assistance for July and August should be definitely settled and (3) that the British overdraft at Morgan's should be paid out of the Liberty Loan proceeds (see below). The memorandum concluded:

> Mr. Balfour desires me to add that the friendly nature of the discussion which he had on these matters with the statesmen of this country [during the Balfour mission] did not leave him in any doubt as to the intentions of the [US] Government to meet this situation and that the first and third requests which are now put forward merely embody in a formal manner points which he fully understood to express the settled intentions of the [US] Government.[23]

As described in Chapter 6, the first point was never met. The question of money for July and August led to a great deal of activity in Washington. Arrangements were made for Northcliffe to see the President, and the President himself met with Polk, Lansing and Crawford. By 29 June Lever heard that they would receive $10m. on 30 June and $25m. on 2 July; he ordered more gold from Ottawa to purchase exchange, and asked for $100m. for 5 July.[24] To try to settle matters over the longer range, Northcliffe and Crawford met McAdoo on 3 July.

McAdoo's main complaint on 3 July was that he was not getting enough information; he was bound to furnish expenditure only for war-related uses, and he required much more detailed reasons for certain items on the British programme of needs. He particularly wanted a reasoned statement on the desirability of maintaining the exchange at £1 = $4.76.[25] The President backed McAdoo's request for more information.[26] Meanwhile McAdoo advanced the requested $100m. on 5 July 1917.[27]

McAdoo truly suffered from a lack of information about the Allies, and especially about the burden Britain had been carrying for the others. What he knew was that from 24 April to 6 July 1917 the Treasury had loaned Britain $685m., and that she was requesting at least $185m. a month for the next four months[28] – and that he had only $2 billion to loan to all of the Allies. Britain, in other words, wanted seven-tenths of the total. Britain repeated that her financial troubles in America were largely caused by the burden of the Allies, but neglected to give the information to McAdoo in enough detail to substantiate this claim. Thus McAdoo declared in a cable to Balfour on 12 July 1917 that

American financial policy will be dictated by a desire to cooperate to the fullest extent possible with the several powers making war in common against Germany, but America's cooperation cannot mean that America can assume the entire burden of financing the war. It means that America will use her available resources to the extent that the Congress may, from time to time, authorize for the purpose of supplementing the resources of the Allied powers. In order that this may be done effectively, the financial resources of the governments seeking loans from the United States should be frankly disclosed...in order to furnish an intelligent basis for the decisions of the United States Treasury in this vital matter.[29]

This cable – and possibly the urgings of Northcliffe, House and Willert that the British government be more frank[30] – jolted the Treasury into facing the range of McAdoo's ignorance and the need to remedy it as quickly as possible. The Chancellor replied to the cable on 23 July 1917 in the following terms:

> We have never desired or intended to keep any reserves from him with regards to our financial position. On the other hand, it has been our preoccupation to bring home to him exactly what that position is. Any specific question we will answer... McAdoo points out 'that America's cooperation cannot mean that America can assume the entire burden of financing the war'. How much less than this is in fact asked of her is exemplified in the following table [which showed in summary that from 1 April to 14 July 1917 the USA had given the Allies £90m. while Britain had given the Allies nearly £194m.]... The Chancellor...gratefully acknowledges that the United States Treasury have advanced $685m [nearly £145m.] to the United Kingdom in addition to the above sums for the Allies. But he invites McAdoo's particular attention to the fact that even since America came into the war financial assistance afforded to the other Allies by the United Kingdom has been *more than double* the assistance afforded them by the United States, and that the assistance the United Kingdom has afforded these other Allies much exceeds the assistance she has herself received from the United States.

The Chancellor further pointed out that while the USA had limited assistance to expenditure incurred by the Allies in the USA, the British government 'have been unable to adopt this attitude to their Allies, but have supported the burden of their expenditure in all parts of the world'. He pointed out that this burden to the Exchequer had begun in July 1914, and that to date Britain had spent over £5,000m. on the war: 'It is *after* having supported an expenditure of this magnitude for three years that the United Kingdom ventures to appeal to the [USA] for sympathetic consideration in financial discussions, where the excessive urgency of her need and the precariousness of her position may sometimes import a tone of insistence to her requests for assistance which would be out of place in ordinary circumstances.' The Chancellor included a great deal of detailed information on how Britain had raised the £5,000m., how money had been expended and especially how the expenditure of the British government in the USA had been financed and on what it had been spent. He then concluded that 'In short our resources available for payments in America are exhausted. Unless the United States Government can meet in full our expenses in the United States, including exchange, the whole financial fabric of the Alliance will collapse. This conclusion will be a matter not of months but of days.'[31] This cable had the desired effect, and for the following months financial aid came in agreed monthly advances – $185m. announced on 25 July for August and $400m. in late August for September.[32]

The question of using American funds to maintain the exchange had still to be settled. Pressure on exchange had been heavy all through July, and several times McAdoo had queried the appropriateness of using American advances to prop up the rate. The Treasury spent most of July preparing a memorandum answering McAdoo's queries.

Late in the month matters again became desperate. Since the beginning of the war Britain had exported to the USA a total of £305m. in actual gold, and the Chancellor had warned McAdoo on 23 July that no more could be sent without destroying British credit – that is, by lowering the Currency Reserves. Lever had been maintaining the rate in New York by, among other things, importing gold held for the Treasury in Ottawa, but by 23 July there was only £10m. in gold left for this purpose.[33] Keynes finally grasped the nettle and suggested the heretofore unthinkable (even to him – see Chapter 5): in a choice between the rate of exchange and the remaining gold, the rate would have to give way:

I submit...that the only safe policy is the following: (1) To instruct Lever that he is to support the exchange as long as he has any dollars in his account...(2) That he is in no circumstances to order more gold from Ottawa. (3) That if on any day he has no dollars in his account available for the support of exchange and he has been unable to obtain any, after making representations to the U.S. Treasury, he should forthwith suspend the further purchase of sterling through Morgans. The above is a cut-and-dried policy consistent with the expectation of hesitating answers from the U.S. Government and calculated to maintain the position as long as possible, to throw the onus of responsibility in the last resort on the U.S. Government and to protect our final reserves of specie.[34]

Chalmers aeed with Keynes, adding only that the American government ought to be told of this policy beforehand.[35]

It had been intended that Northcliffe would take to the President the memorandum on exchange which the Treasury had prepared, but the Cabinet decided that McAdoo would be offended if the British government went over his head. On 30 July 1917 Lloyd George cabled Northcliffe that exchange was to be supported only as far as resources in New York allowed, without recourse to gold from Ottawa. Thus it was that Spring Rice and Crawford took the memorandum to McAdoo and Crosby on 31 July 1917, at the same time conveying a verbal warning of the imminent change in the British policy on exchange.[36]

This memorandum, as McAdoo had requested, was drawn up in great detail. From May to July 1917 the cost of maintaining the rate had averaged $40m. a week: the fluctuations had been mainly due to the movement of American banking funds to and from London, and to the cost of Allied wheat purchases. The future cost would probably not be less than $25m. a week. The Chancellor argued that if the American government ceased to support British exchange (which, he argued, was really Allied exchange), 'the collapse, not only of the Allied exchanges in New York, but also of their exchanges on all neutral countries is to be expected... It is likely that exchange quotations would not only fall heavily but would become nominal – that is to say, there would, for the moment, be no exchange offering at any price and business would be at a standstill.' The Chancellor went on to say that the consequences of such a state of affairs would be partly material and partly psychological:

> On the material side exporters from the United States to the United Kingdon, other Allied countries, Australia, India and South Africa would be unable to sell their sterling bills on London. New business would be interrupted at the source, and vessels would be delayed in port by reason of shippers being unable to obtain delivery of goods without paying for them. From the American point of view this would involve a breakdown for the time being of the mechanism of a great part of her export trade, the paralysis of business and the congestion of her ports.

The initial disorganisation caused by the collapse of exchange would, of course, interrupt supplies to the Allies until remedial measures were taken, but, the Chancellor calculated, even when exchange was re-stabilised, the loss of worldwide purchasing power by the Allies 'would largely exceed' the $100m. monthly required to maintain the current rate. The Chancellor then continued:

> Turning to the psychological consequences, the results would be plainly disastrous . . . Chief of all there is the effect on the mind of the enemy . . . The encouragement and corroboration of their hopes which they discover in the abandonment of the exchanges would, therefore, be enormous . . . It would be said that with the collapse of their exchanges the Allies cannot endure six months more . . . We have constantly proclaimed to the world that it is the cornerstone of our policy. To point out the depreciation of the German exchanges and the stability of our own has been a favourite form of propaganda in all parts of the world.

The Chancellor ended with an appeal to the American government to help in this – and to let them know the decision quickly.[37]

Spring Rice had a sympathetic hearing from McAdoo. McAdoo emphasised that for the next month he would be faced with the difficult task of explaining to Congress the payments for sustaining exchange (the Congressional committees had some very hostile members), and he urged that Spring Rice explain his political problems to the British government. He 'begged' Spring Rice to find out how long Britain could continue to sustain the rate of exchange, since he hoped in a month or two to be able to help more effectively.[38] Upon receiving this cable Balfour immediately cabled back sympathetically that 'You may assure McAdoo that from their own continuing experience [HMG] appreciates fully the difficulties which American Government has to meet in presenting huge estimates of expenditure to Congress . . . Please assure McAdoo that we are most grateful for the desire which he shows to assist us at this critical juncture.'[39] According to Spring Rice this had the desired effect: 'Your appreciation of the political difficulty which faces McAdoo in Congress has been so full and sympathetic that it has cleared the atmosphere.'[40] Northcliffe certainly felt that 'after the usual amount of haggling the Government will agree to assist us',[41] and in fact the following day Crosby informed Spring Rice that McAdoo would make an additional advance of $50m. for August to meet the exchange situation. He added, however, that when Britain made the formal application for it they should say it was for 'general purposes', since McAdoo could not yet commit himself to supporting the exchange.[42] In his formal answer of 16 August 1917 to the Chancellor's cable of 23 July, McAdoo reiterated that he could not guarantee funds to maintain the exchange, but he stated that the probability of furnishing the necessary financial support would be much increased if the Allied governments would co-ordinate their proposals for loans in 'conformity with the general plan outlined' for the Inter-Allied Council[43] (Chapter 7). This was as close as McAdoo ever came to promising support for British exchange, but arguments over its utility lessened, and the rate in fact remained at 4.76 for the duration of the war (see Appendix I).

Probably more acrimony between the Treasury mission and the American Treasury was caused by the argument over the British overdraft with Morgan's of $400m. than by any other issue. It will be remembered that on 27 June 1917 the crisis over advances for July was coming to a head, when both Lever and Northcliffe were urging that the British government appeal through Page to the President. On that same day H. P. Davison, one of the Morgan partners, precipitated another crisis, when, as Crosby described it,

> Davison . . . called at this office, and asked whether there could be any doubt as to an engagement . . . having been made between Mr Balfour and Lord Cunliffe on the one hand and Lansing on the other . . . to the effect that $400,000,000 would be loaned to the British Government on the first of July . . . Crawford was present at the time this conversation took place. Both he and I stated that we knew nothing of any such engagement. Mr. Davison stated that his knowledge of it was based upon perfectly specified statements made to him personally by Lord Cunliffe and . . . Lever. It is a matter of the first importance that such a misunderstanding . . . should be removed.[44]

Crawford informed Lever of the incident, telling him that Davison had taken a very aggressive attitude, and that the result upon the Treasury was 'very disastrous'.[45]

The overdraft had grown up largely in the early part of 1917 when, as earlier described, the British had refrained from floating a loan at the request of McAdoo, who had wished the markets left clear for the Liberty Loan. On 2 May 1917, when Balfour, Cunliffe and Lever had met McAdoo, Crosby and other American officials, Balfour had mentioned the overdraft and McAdoo had agreed that it could be put on the list of requirements Britain would like to be met out of the proceeds of the Liberty Loan. Unfortunately, what McAdoo saw as a general expression of goodwill and a desire to help was taken by the British to be a binding commitment to pay – and equally unfortunately, nothing was written down.[46] From what Lever had told them, Morgan's understood that while no fixed date had been given them for the repayment, the $400m. would be a first charge on the Liberty Loan and that repayment would commence on 2 July 1917. Further, Morgan's said that it was not, as everyone thought, an indefinitely renewable overdraft, but was a time loan; that it was shared amongst sixty-seven banks, some of whom now wanted their money; and that they must begin selling collateral and applying the proceeds against the overdraft on 5 July.[47]

The British first attempted to convince McAdoo to help with the overdraft (an attempt which may have been undermined by Northcliffe when he told Crosby on 5 July that repayment of the overdraft was a British affair and would not come up to McAdoo).[48] McAdoo was never very encouraging – Northcliffe quoted him as warning that 'I do not propose to allow NY bankers and their allies to use the British Government as a club to beat the U.S. Treasury with'[49] – and by 31 July he had absolutely refused. When Morgan's heard this they panicked and gave notice that they would immediately begin selling collateral deposited with them by the British government, collateral largely made up of American securities deposited on loan with the British Treasury by British citizens. The first Morgan partner to recover was J. P. Morgan, who spent a good deal of the following day apologising to Lever and the Chancellor for the hasty action. The sale of collateral began quietly on 10 August 1917. Morgan, Lever and the Chancellor then decided to float short-term Treasury paper which would be taken up by the participants in the overdraft as payment. McAdoo gave his approval and the immediate crisis was relieved.[50]

House as well was consulted, and he came up with the suggestion that the French should request $100–200m. more than they needed from McAdoo, who would give it to them on the understanding that they turned it over to Britain, who would then use it to pay off part of the overdraft. The Chancellor approved, as did the French government, but McAdoo remained cool to the idea, through fear of what Congress would say if they found out; the issue was not yet settled when Reading came out in September to take over the financial negotiations.[51]

During the period November 1917 to February 1918, while Reading was in Britain, Lever resumed control of Treasury business in the USA. The situation was different now, since with Crosby in Britain and France with the House mission, discussions about advances for Britain took place largely in Europe; although Lever negotiated with McAdoo over advances for January and February, McAdoo tended to follow Crosby's recommendations. Lever was more concerned with the Morgan overdraft or demand loan, with attempts to apply the ship money against it and with the need for American help to retire Treasury bills issued to refund some of the overdraft and pay for supplies.

It will be recalled that in July 1917 McAdoo had refused to help with the British overdraft at Morgan's. It will also be recalled that on 3 August 1917 the American government had issued a requisition order for the ships being built to British order in American shipyards. The question was, to what use would the British government put the money that the American government was to pay them for the ships? McAdoo and Crosby naturally wished it to be used for current expenditures, thus lessening the amount required to be advanced by the Treasury, and McAdoo proposed this to Reading before he returned to Britain. Reading firmly answered that

> I fully agree that the question of the application of these funds should be discussed with you . . . I should, however, point out that from the first it has been assumed by my Government that any moneys reimbursed in respect of its expenditure on ships would be applicable to a special purpose, viz: the reduction of the Call loan or overdraft . . . and I have always understood that the matter was discussed with you on this basis.[52]

McAdoo had little choice but to accept this argument. As Thomas Lamont of Morgan's, who was in London, cabled to Morgan on 22 November, 'For your confidential information, Crosby told me last night that he could of course offer no objection to the British Treasury disposing of the shipping monies as it saw fit. Further, he did not want me to think that he had forgotten the suggestion that McAdoo and he made to me last July that these shipping monies would all be available for the Demand Loan.' . . .[53] Nevertheless McAdoo decided to make a condition: he would assent to the ship money's being applied to the overdraft provided the American Treasury was subrogated to the rights of the British Treasury with respect to a proportionate part of the collateral securing the overdraft; that is, the American government would take over the rights of the British government over the deposited securities. He cabled this view to Crosby, who conveyed it to the British Treasury. Crosby ascertained that the British did desire that the ship money be applied against the overdraft, even at the risk of smaller advances in the future.[54] In a further cable sent the same day he assured McAdoo that 'There will be no difficulty in having subrogation to collateral held against obligations thus met', but added that his proposal was that the ship money should be applied against British notes maturing in February, which had been partly issued in payment to certain manufacturers such as DuPont.[55]

The concept of subrogation was one which the British found a bit confusing and – when they had to accede to it – somewhat humiliating. The collateral concerned were British-owned American and other securities which had been deposited with the British Treasury under threat of penal taxation, and which the Treasury had deposited with Morgan's in America as security for the $400m. overdraft. The American proposal was that, if the British used money paid by the USA for the requisitioned British ships to retire part of the overdraft instead of spending it on current account, the American Treasury should be entitled to take over all rights to the collateral which the British possessed, including the right to utilise and even to sell them. The British argument was that the ships had been British, the money to be paid for them by the American government was not a loan and therefore the Americans had no right to attach conditions as to its use.[56]

McAdoo cabled his answer to Crosby on 4 December 1917: 'Willing that funds paid [HMG] by Shipping Board should be applied to Morgan overdraft but insist upon subrogation... With reference to DuPont notes and collateral notes maturing 1 February, prefer not to interfere or make suggestions as to these matters which should be taken care of by [HMG] and their bankers independently.'[57] Nevertheless, the question of advancing money to enable the British to pay off the $94m. worth of 5½ per cent bonds maturing February 1918 was not to be evaded so easily, as Crosby cabled from London on 16 December: 'Great Britain will undoubtedly ask funds to meet $94m maturing 1 February. Though I have explained your attitude, apparently no way now known to Treasury here of meeting this debt, ship money having been promised for overdraft, Lamont thinks release this promise impracticable.'[58] Lever supported this appreciation of the situation when he cabled to the Chancellor on 20 December Morgan's opinion that '1 February maturity cannot be dealt with in New York unless at least $200m is repaid on account of the overdraft during early part of January.'[59]

Thus, the questions of the overdraft, the February maturities, the ship money, subrogation and the state of American finances were all interconnected. The American Treasury had given in over the use of the ship money to retire part of the overdraft, and would soon agree to advance funds to retire the February maturities, but the price to be exacted – subrogation – would serve to preserve McAdoo against Congress and public opinion. He had agreed to the use of the ship money on the understanding that the February maturities would be taken care of by the British; by the end of December, however, he had decided that the steady sale of collateral by the British was harming American financial measures, and he was ready to reconsider his opinion. Lever and Blackett held discussions with American Treasury officials through January, and the negotiations eventually centred on the question of subrogation. The most extreme proposal of the American Treasury was for the British to transfer to the custody of the American government as large a part as possible of the American and other securities held in the USA, to be used at the discretion of the Secretary of the Treasury. It became clear, however, that the American officials were split over this – Strauss was for it, Leffingwell opposed it – and Leffingwell finally asked only for a general statement of the readiness of the British Treasury to co-operate with the American Secretary in dealing with the securities. Lever felt that the American Treasury was within its rights in asking for this assurance. However, he jibbed at a suggestion that British securities should be used to secure loans for the Allies. (France, for example, had refused to mobilise the securities of her citizens, as Britain had done, and Britain did not see why British securities should be used to secure loans for France.)[60]

By 23 January 1918 McAdoo had indicated to the British that he would pay over the ship money for the British to apply against the overdraft and would advance funds for the purpose of retiring the February maturities. But in addition to asking for subrogation with respect to the collateral to be released by the ship money – which he still assumed, on the basis of Crosby's assurance of 21 November 1917, that the British accepted – he also asked for subrogation with respect to the collateral which would be released by the payment of the February maturities.[61] By 27 January relations between Lever and McAdoo had deteriorated once again: there was deadlock over the February maturities, and McAdoo went so far as to request Wiseman to take over the negotiations, which he refused to do. Wiseman suggested, instead, that McAdoo cable Crosby to confer with the London side.[62] For the last days of January, then, there were two sets of negotiations going on.

The deadlock was caused by Lever's refusal to agree to subrogation. He understood why McAdoo desired it:

> the Secretary of the Treasury is chiefly concerned with providing himself with a political defence against attacks which he expects when it becomes known he is providing funds to repay Wall St. for advances made to Great Britain before the United States entered the war. His main defence will be that it is necessary in the interests of next Liberty Loan and of general financial position to relieve Banks. But he is anxious to be able to point to some definite quid pro quo obtained from us for his help.[63]

To help McAdoo, he was willing, as described above, to give a general assurance of co-operation to McAdoo; but he refused to agree to turn over complete control of the securities to the American Treasury. McAdoo, however, issued an ultimatum, as Lever cabled to the Chancellor on 27 January:

> McAdoo insists that he must subrogate to the rights of holders of maturity of February 1st as a *sine qua non* of an advance for meeting it. In other words United States Treasury now comes out into the open and insists on a pledge of our securities... It was intimated that the [US] Treasury would allow as much latitude as possible in arrangements of details of subrogation...I am... of opinion if subrogation is agreed to in respect of securities released by repayment Feb. 1st maturity I can obtain leave to apply ship money to call loan without any conditions.[64]

Following a suggestion by Lever, the Chancellor on 28 January 1918 cabled a personal appeal to McAdoo in which he objected to subrogation, emphasising his own political difficulties if British-owned securities were pledged to the American Treasury, since there was no parallel in Britain's own dealings with the Allies.[65] McAdoo asked House's advice on the maturities, saying there was some difference over the collateral, and House advised being generous.[66] On 29 January 1918 McAdoo grudgingly withdrew his insistence on subrogation:

I have received your personal message with regard to the February 1 maturity and the ship money...I am constrained with great reluctance to defer to your wishes in this matter although I cannot alter my judgment that the course proposed by me is wise and right in aid of the general situation and would have been welcomed in this country as indicating a readiness on the part of Great Britain to deal not less liberally with the Government than with the banks...I have received from the British representatives here certain assurances in respect to the securities owned or controlled by the British Government. These assurances are more restricted in form than I had expected.[67]

On 30 January 1918 Lever was able to report that 'Final settlement has been reached. United States Treasury will make an advance 95m on 1 Feb. and on same day ship money approximately 81m will be paid. Latter will be applied to Call Loan and former to Feb. 1 maturity. Subrogation is dropped.'[68] In place of subrogation Lever gave only the general assurance of co-operation with the American Treasury in the use of the deposited securities.

However, there appears to have been a very considerable misunderstanding between the Chancellor and Crosby. Curiously, Crosby sent a cable to McAdoo on 30 January suggesting that the Chancellor was in fact willing to agree to subrogation (although this cable presumably arrived too late to affect the outcome of the negotiations as reported by Lever):

Difficulty here over arrangement proposed by you for dealing with Feb. 1 maturity caused by misunderstanding... Chancellor of Exchequer anxious that any announcement shall make plain that arrangement is a special one providing in effect for continuing previous secured loans thus explaining use of collateral and that United States Treasury is not changing its policy of not requiring collateral for its regular loans to Great Britain. This especially desired because Great Britain has not received collateral for loans to Allies.[69]

The Chancellor on the other hand had gained from Crosby the impression that the 'proposed arrangements cover a much wider field';[70] that is, that the American Treasury had in mind eventually taking care of the entire overdraft, and Lever made inquiries at the Treasury.[71]

McAdoo responded to these inquiries by cabling to the Chancellor on 5 February that

> Crosby was mistaken in supposing that the proposed arrangements make provision for the overdraft beyond what the ship money would suffice to pay. On the contrary, I am obliged to ask that such moneys as may be made available to the British Government in the United States by the Japanese or the Danish Government or by shipments of gold shall be applied in reduction of your demands for current purposes rather than to retirement of capital liabilities.[72]

Presumably very concerned by the threatening tone of this cable, the Chancellor, on 6 February 1918, effectively rescinded the agreement of 30 January. In a cable to Lever, the Chancellor stated that he was 'convinced by further communications that there have been misunderstandings and that to place ourselves in McAdoo's hands is our only proper course...McAdoo must not be left by us with any feeling of grievance even though it may be ill-founded.'[73] To McAdoo he cabled,

> The last thing I should have thought of would have been that I should make conditions as to financial assistance accorded us by the United States Government. You have to bear great burden of Allied finance in the United States and you rightly rely on our co-operation in every way and to leave you a free hand as to proper solution of current problems. I am giving instructions that you are to be subrogated to lien of former lenders upon securities previously pledged to holders of one year notes and that these securities as well as other securities pledged to secure overdraft will be dealt with according to your instructions.[74]

No concession on the ship money was made, however.[75]

The Chancellor's immediate reward was a message from McAdoo expressing profound appreciation;[76] the ultimate reward, it was devoutly hoped, would be further help with the capital liabilities.

The British Treasury, therefore, agreed to the subrogation of the rights of its collateral – a humiliating submission to the USA, it was considered by the Treasury[77] – in order to convince the American Treasury of its good faith and willingness to co-operate when it could in the common effort, giving up its rights in order to make it easier for the American Treasury to help Britain. As well, it gave in to *force majeure*, to the implied threat that if Britain did not allow the subrogation, the USA would in no way help Britain with her alarming capital liabilities. It was symbolic also of the changed financial relationship of the two countries: no one doubted any longer who held the whip hand, and this led to growing fear in the British Treasury during 1918 that the USA would not hesitate to use it.[78]

During the remainder of the war the Treasury mission in the USA played only a supporting role in financial negotiations. This was only partly due to McAdoo's dislike of Lever; more important was the fact that Crosby, on whom McAdoo depended, was in Europe a good deal of the time, acting as chairman of the Inter-Allied Council on War Purchases and Finance, and he naturally discussed questions directly with the British Treasury. Further, Reading's time was largely taken up with negotiations on troops and intervention in Russia, although he took time in April 1918 to capitulate to American financial demands, directly contrary to the instructions of the Chancellor. There were lengthy negotiations over reimbursements for payments for the Allies and over wheat finance, but the more important discussions took place in London; on the whole, negotiations in Washington were by now of a pretty routine nature.

During the final stage of the negotiations over subrogation in February, when McAdoo had thought that the Chancellor would not consent to it, he had sent a message to the Chancellor in which he had stated that 'I am obliged to ask that such moneys as may be made available to the British Government in the United States by the Japanese or the Danish Government or by shipments of gold shall be applied in reduction of your demands for current purposes rather than to retirement of capital liabilities.'[79] By 'capital liabilities' McAdoo was mainly referring to the Morgan overdraft and Treasury bills issued to retire part of it. Once he had conciliated McAdoo, the Chancellor no longer took this threat seriously:

> Demand that proceeds of Japanese and Danish loans and of gold shipments should be met by us to meet current outgoings... probably made in a fit of annoyance. My last message to McAdoo agreeing to do what he wanted as regards our American securities may have modified his attitude... In any case...point out to him that if he perseveres with above demand he necessarily makes himself entirely responsible for meeting our capital liabilities as

they mature. If he cuts us off from every opportunity of meeting them by our own efforts the responsibility for them becomes his. Indeed I cannot believe that his words were meant seriously.[80]

Unfortunately for the British Treasury, McAdoo meant them very seriously indeed. In calculating the advances to Britain needed to enable her to meet current expenditure in March, McAdoo deducted from the predicted expenditure the amount of a loan which Britain had negotiated with Japan.[81] Because of delays in deliveries, the American advances in fact proved adequate for the March expenditure and in April the British still held the proceeds of the Japanese loan. At this point the Americans forced the issue of what was to be done with the money. On 24 April 1918 Reading cabled to the Chancellor that

> Leffingwell has asked me to use money obtained from Japan and other loans for current expenditure so as to reduce at the moment the amount required from United States Treasury. . . . I said we were keeping this money to meet accruing capital liabilities and that if we use the same for current expenditure we had no undertaking that United States Treasury would meet our capital liabilities but that you would be prepared to hand over all such monies if United States Treasury would give a definite undertaking to this effect. . . . I think it impolitic to hold out against request for use of capital sums provided United States Treasury will in writing undertake to replace these sums when required by us for capital expenditure in repayment of loans.[82]

The sum in question was $24m.[83] The Chancellor replied on 28 April agreeing to the use of the money for current expenditure, provided that Reading received a written agreement from the American Treasury to replace the sums when required by Britain for the repayment of loans, adding that 'I regard such an undertaking as essential'.[84] The Chancellor's reaction may be imagined when he received Reading's next cable: Reading had agreed that the proceeds from the Japanese loan would be used for current expenditure – and he had required no written undertaking in return. His argument was that McAdoo had felt that the Japanese loan should have been used for current expenditure immediately upon receipt, that Britain's not so doing had caused underlying irritation and that Britain should let the matter go and not reopen the question by asking for a letter from McAdoo. When McAdoo returned to Washington Reading could take up other outstanding matters with greater advantage.[85]

The Treasury was outraged. McFadyean minuted that 'Lord Reading's courage seems to have forsaken him'[86] and that it was 'intolerable',[87] and Keynes agreed with him.[88] The Chancellor then received a personal cable from Reading, in which he wrote that 'my interview with Leffingwell has resulted in clearing the atmosphere and will I am sure be of assistance in the future discussions with McAdoo. It is useless now to go over the old ground and I hope you will just accept it from me that the only possible course in your interest was the one I took.'[89] Keynes drafted the Chancellor's reply to Reading, which began

> I cannot but acquiesce in the course you have taken and trust that your concession will be a useful introduction to the major discussions you are about to initiate. If these discussions are successful we can afford to let go all the minor issues, although the action of the U.S. Treasury has been in my opinion unreasonable.

The draft then contained a paragraph which, while not sent, certainly described the Treasury's true feelings about the matter:

> Coupled with their action earlier in the year over subrogation and paying off our maturing obligations it almost looks as if they took a satisfaction in reducing us to a position of complete financial helplessness and dependence in which the call loan is around our necks like a noose and whenever obligations of ours mature in future we shall have to submit to any conditions they may choose to impose. I resent also their habit of refusing all understandings in writing and telling us to accept vague oral assurances, especially in view of the frequently changing personnel of the U.S. Treasury and our Russian experience.

The cable sent to Reading then continued,

> I acquiesce because I agree with you that the U.S. authorities will very likely combine smallmindedness over minor issues with generosity of outlook when a matter is brought to them as one of large policy. I attach therefore the greatest possible importance to the impending discussions on the finance of the Allies. Our future relations with the U.S. Treasury very much depend on their treatment of this issue.[90]

The 'impending discussions' to which the cable referred were negotiations over a new manner of computing reimbursements to Britain for advances spent for France and Italy. The British argument was that the amount of money lent to them by the USA could be greatly reduced if it was in the first instance treated as an advance to France or Italy – if that was what, in fact, it was – rather than as an advance to Britain. The Chancellor held discussions in London with Crosby and Paul D. Cravath (the American adviser to the I-AC, of whom the British Treasury thought extremely highly), and then Crosby took memoranda back to the USA and discussed matters with his colleagues at the Treasury. Crosby then returned to London on 6 July 1918 and discussions resumed there.[91] Eventually the Allies adopted the 'theory of constructive delivery and redelivery', 'a formula which allowed, for example, wheat bought by Italy from a mutual country to be paid for with dollar credits by means of a three-cornered exchange – the United States selling wheat to Norway, to be paid for with fish supplied to Italy, leaving Italy debtor to the United States for the American wheat exported.'[92]

The other set of negotiations during these months was over the financing of wheat bought in America for the Allies. Britain treated the whole of the world supply of wheat purchased for the Allies as one unit, while the Americans wished American wheat treated separately, because of their desire to restrict advances to purchases in the USA. Discussions went on in Washington, mainly between Blackett and members of the American Treasury, at the same time as in Europe. The I-AC set up a special committee, on which Keynes sat, to reconsider methods of purchasing and financing cereals, and negotiations went on for most of the year; agreement to a complex formula was finally reached in the last week of October 1918.[93]

On 1 September 1918 the British government secured loan of $192m. came to maturity, and the American Treasury advanced funds to meet it, on the same basis as for 1 February 1918 maturities – that the American Treasury would be subrogated to the rights of the collateral securing the loan. It had been considered in June, with Leffingwell writing that

> I do not think that . . . it will be possible for the British to finance a renewal of this loan on reasonable terms . . . I think the borrowing on the part of the British Government on our markets on extortionate terms would be injurious to British credit, create an unfavourable impression as to the extent of the sympathy between

the two governments, and impair our own position because of the discredit it would throw upon the credit of our largest debtor.[94]

The extortionate terms to which Leffingwell referred were an interest rate of 6 per cent for a loan of 2½ years' duration, and the privilege of conversion into a long-term bond at 6 per cent. J. P. Morgan himself admitted that the terms were 'extremely onerous', but he argued that there was 'very intense competition for the comparatively small amount of money available for investment in other directions than Liberty Bonds'. Morgan indeed hoped that Britain would be able to find the money elsewhere than on the New York money market. So of course did the British government. The only three choices they had were to borrow as above, to sell collateral, or to convince the American Treasury to advance them the money. McAdoo agreed with Leffingwell that Britain should not be forced to borrow on terms such as Morgan's had said were necessary. He also continued to dislike the idea of Britain's selling collateral, since it would absorb funds which, he felt, should be used to purchase Liberty Bonds. As the only acceptable alternative, he agreed to advance the money to the British government to retire the maturities, with the American government's being subrogated to the rights of the pledged collateral. Shortly after his return to London, therefore, Reading was able to cable gratefully to McAdoo on behalf of the Chancellor that 'It is a great satisfaction to him to know that you share his views that the terms proposed by Morgan's were impossible of acceptance'.[95]

It should not be assumed that Reading's comment implied dissatisfaction in general with Morgan's, or that he was necessarily pandering to McAdoo's well-known dislike of Morgan's (although there was probably a touch of the latter). Morgan's had given their best advice as to the terms on which the New York market would renew the loan, and the British government realised this: they simply did not want to pay the rate of interest required. The real change of attitude towards Morgan's had been Crosby's. Going abroad often changes perceptions of the home country, and Crosby's trip to Europe in November 1917 had clearly done so. Once in London he increasingly turned to Thomas Lamont, a New York Morgan partner, for help, as Lamont wrote on 13 November: 'This morning I had an hour's chat with Crosby, who expressed satisfaction that I was visiting London and Paris at this time. I am to see him again this afternoon. He thinks I may have some banking information of value to his deliberations abroad.'[96] He wrote again on 18 December: 'Upon my return to America I shall be carrying with me many personal oral messages from Crosby to W. G. McAdoo that he has been unable to cover by cable or letter. He has, in accordance with your guess, entrusted me with his confidence ever since my arrival.'[97] This is worth noting because of Crosby's importance in interallied financial negotiations. Crosby's willingness to utilise Morgan expertise and willingness to help was in contrast to McAdoo's continuing suspicions of Morgan's.[98] But the usefulness of various Morgan partners was increasingly recognised by the Administration over the months of the war: by February 1918 Stettinius had been named Surveyor General of Supplies for the US army,[99] by late April D. W. Morrow's work in Paris was considered indispensable by General John Pershing, the Commander of the American Expeditionary Force in France,[100] and Lamont himself was an alternate member of the American delegation to the Commission on the Reparation of Damages at the Peace Conference.[101]

However little he liked Morgan partners, McAdoo liked Lever even less. Relations between the two men had broken down in July 1917 and again in January 1918, and in late February House noted in his Diary that 'I told Sir William [Wiseman] that Lever of the British Treasury Dep't, who is now on Reading's staff, was *persona non grata* to McAdoo and he wished for a change. I urged Wiseman to attend to this promptly, giving the reasons for McAdoo's attitude. Wiseman saw Reading and the change was agreed upon, Reading endorsing McAdoo's opinion of Lever.'[102] Nothing was done, however, and Lever remained head of the Treasury mission. After Reading's departure for London in July 1918, matters apparently worsened: on 19 October Albert Rathbone drafted a cable for McAdoo to Crosby which stated that 'I am not willing to discuss matters with Lever or have him transact business with the Treasury. If necessary will write formal letter requesting his recall.'[103] The cable was not sent, however, Rathbone arguing that

> While the difficulties of doing business with Lever are fully appreciated it may be that he can do more harm if he is recalled than if he remains here. If recalled he will probably be retained by the British Treasury in some position of more or less importance, and may be considered an authority in regard to affairs in the United States... If we inaugurate the practice of asking recalls, not accompanied by charges, it might be that it would open the

door for a request of a change in the Special Finance Commissioner of the United States in Europe [Crosby]. As there are no specific grounds of complaint against Lever that have not existed for months, it seems inadvisable to base a request for his recall on any grounds other than that he is *persona non grata*. On the whole I believe it would be better not to suggest Lever's recall.[104]

Lever, clearly, was there for the duration.

However, McAdoo had his revenge (in a sense) for the trouble Lever had caused. A week after the Armistice he announced his resignation, with the consequence that American Treasury officials refused to take any decisions,[105] but by 27 November 1918 Lever realised that there was in fact one important decision which McAdoo had made before his resignation, and which would bedevil the British Treasury: 'It has now become clear beyond shadow of doubt that it has been McAdoo's deliberate policy to place the United States Treasury in such a position at the end of the war as to enable it to force the sale in United States markets of the whole of the British-owned American securities brought over here.'[106] Lever's mistake was in blaming the decision wholly on McAdoo. Other Treasury officials certainly agreed with the policy, as Morgan's made clear in a cable to Grenfell:

> Leffingwell also expressed the opinion that British obligations in this country should be reduced as rapidly as possible through the continuous sale of American securities for account of British Treasury. T. W. Lamont pointed out that the bulk of such securities still held might be under a moral commitment to be returned to their original owners, but Leffingwell felt that the course outlined should be urged as the natural one to be pursued by the British Treasury.[107]

Yet eventually even this problem was settled in favour of Britain: some $700m. of British securities physically in the USA were returned to Britain, and in 1923, at the time of the funding agreement, some $300m. of British collateral subrogated to the USA were released and returned to Britain.[108] It only remains to add that in July 1918 the American Treasury had given permission to the British to begin quietly to sell the collateral securing the Morgan overdraft (the Americans had resisted this before for fear of pre-empting money which would otherwise go for Liberty bonds), and by July 1919 the whole loan had been liquidated. Lever then returned to Britain.[109]

Epilogue
Did History Come to a Full Stop?

America was clearly top nation, and History came to a .
Sellar and Yeatman, *1066 and All That*[1]

It was not, in fact, wholly clear in 1918 that America *was* top nation. The British Empire after all continued in existence, and would soon be even larger, with the addition of former German colonies in Africa and former Turkish provinces in the Middle East added to Britain's imperial responsibilities. Was the USA, then, an even more powerful or important nation? This is, in fact, an impossible question to answer, but the Sellar and Yeatman quote is useful for summing up a certain rueful outlook that obtained in many quarters in Britain. The postwar period was one of adjustment for both nations, as Britain fought to recover or maintain her position in traditional areas of dominance and the USA varied between an aggressive assertion of new-found power and a self-absorbed isolation.

Britain, not for the last time, was caught between Europe and the USA, sharing the dissatisfaction of the European nations at American activities, or lack of them, while at the same time sharing in the American disinclination to become too involved in Europe. One constant theme of British policy since the turn of the century – to co-opt American power to further British policies – was difficult to implement during the interwar period where it was most important to Britain that she do so. It did not ultimately matter to Britain that the USA reigned supreme in the Caribbean or that Britain had to give way somewhat in China or even that they eventually would have to share control over oil in the Middle East with American interests. What did matter increasingly was that the USA was reluctant to involve herself in Europe at all. Frustration at what they considered to be American stupidity and shortsightedness was a recurring theme when British officials wrote on foreign or defence policy or on questions of international trade and finance during the interwar period.

In order to be a Great Power, at least two qualities were required of a country: that it have the capacity, and that it have the will. The USA in 1914 had neither. What it had was potential, and with the First World War it had the opportunity – even the necessity – to develop that potential. By 1918 the USA certainly possessed the capacity for power, financial, industrial and military (and demographic), but whether it had the sustained will to act as a Great Power was more problematical. The USA expected her wishes to be taken into account on a number of foreign policy issues, such as possible intervention in Russia or the establishment of a League of Nations; indeed, on both of these questions her power ensured that her wishes would be respected. But she retreated from most joint activities, refusing to join her wartime associates in any postwar control of financial or raw material resources. This desire for complete independence on the part of the USA was impossible for the European nations to ignore, since the USA more or less turned her back on the European continent for some years. In short, in the Great Power arena of the time, the American government refused to play.

Now, it could be argued that by showing herself able to ignore the other Powers, the USA was demonstrating that she was indeed powerful enough to go it alone. But she did lay herself open to the charge in the 1920s of wanting this power without responsibility, at least if power is defined as the ability to achieve a desired outcome. She was ready and eager to build on the financial and industrial position gained by her exertions during the war, but successive American presidents believed that it was not within the proper sphere of government to become involved in rebuilding the European economy – this, rather, was the duty of private business. Nor was it believed wise to become involved in European power politics, beyond urging disarmament policies on all sides. And even if presidents had wanted to become involved, the Congress would have ensured that the American government remained uninvolved.

For the Europeans, the question which tested American maturity was that of the war debts. As far as the American government was concerned, the Europeans had hired the money, and they were now duty-bound to repay it. The fact that in comparison with the other belligerents the USA had suffered significantly in neither human nor economic terms was held to be irrelevant to the sanctity of contracts. The European governments found American views on the matter both incomprehensible and deeply repulsive, and explicable only with reference to profound American selfishness or ignorance of the international facts of life. European politicians and newspaper writers were not shy of saying so in a hundred different ways, and American policymakers, wounded by the ingratitude of the Europeans and less inclined than ever to get involved in European affairs, thankfully washed their hands of European problems. By 1923, according to one historian, the American government had officially determined that the stability of Europe, while of importance to the USA, was not a vital American interest.[2]

The British government after the war tended to see themselves in precisely the opposite manner: they had responsibilities without enough power, and Britain was unable to opt out of European affairs. Compared to America's loss of 100,000 men, Britain had lost 950,000, with another 2 million wounded (the number of American wounded is unknown), and this was out of a population two-and-a-half times smaller than America's. The British government was in debt to the American government for nearly $5 billion, and Britain had liquidated a good proportion of her overseas assets in order to help pay for the war. By 1928, 40 per cent of the British budget would be going towards paying off war debts of one sort or another, and between the debt burden, and the need to prepare the British economy to return to gold and then to keep it there, the British economy was not in the best of health.

Nevertheless, Britain still seemed to be in better shape than many of the European nations, and she was frequently looked to to provide leadership on the Continent. She in turn looked to the USA to work with her in reconstructing Europe, in sorting out the power-political impasse between France and Germany, and in general to try to re-establish the stability of Europe. The American government, as noted above, refused to become officially involved. What she did do was to encourage the American private sector to help with European recovery, and an important theme of Anglo-American relations during the 1920s was the strength and multiplicity of private financial and trading links between the two countries. If the American government would not officially aid in European reconstruction, the Federal Reserve Bank of New York and the House of Morgan, among others, did.[3] The American government did, however, have a recurring interest in encouraging arms limitation. It can be argued, in fact, that as the Europeans judged the USA by its actions on the war debt question, so the Americans tended to judge the European countries by their moves towards disarmament. But again, it was just these American efforts to further disarmament which so infuriated many Europeans, since the USA consistently refused in return to promise any security guarantees. American attempts at arms limitation were a special source of conflict between Britain and the USA, since in this context it took the form of American attempts to cut down the size of the Royal Navy. As far as Britain was concerned, this was merely a blatant attempt by the American navy to gain naval superiority on the cheap. In short, on the official level, American relations with Europe were beset with misunderstanding and ill feeling.

Yet, between the USA and Britain there continued to be the same links of common language and literature, heritage and sentiment, which had proved to be so powerful before and during the war. These links proved to be especially strong in the Anglo-American financial community, when the support of, for example, Morgan's and the Federal Reserve Bank of New York under Benjamin Strong was of particular help both in enabling Britain to return to gold in 1925 (a not unmixed blessing) and in furthering British foreign economic policy both in Europe and the Dominions. It is probable that the success of British foreign policy during the 1920s owes more to the support of the House of Morgan than has ever been acknowledged.

This mixture of public and private agencies, and the intrusion on to centre stage in foreign policy of financial and economic matters which had before the war been largely confined to colonial policy, combined with the broken European state system, made the 1920s in particular a confusing and unpredictable decade. This is the context in which Anglo-American relations after 1918 must be viewed. Britain wanted American aid without American dominance, while the Americans preferred not to become involved in situations over which they would have little control. Each viewed the other warily and with a certain mistrust, while continuing to regard each other as their most dependable colleague. If the period from 1900 to 1945 is viewed as a whole, the major trend is obvious – the decline of Britain and the rise of the USA – but to contemporaries the view was rather less clear. The rise and decline are linked, but not in any simple causal manner. Britain had protected the USA during the nineteenth century, even if not for altruistic motives; during the First World War Britain, as the dominant power, encouraged the USA to assume the role of a Great Power in the old international system, even if, as she hoped, a subordinate one; during the postwar period the two competed and co-operated in varying measure; and during and after the Second World War the USA finally acted as the dominant power, protecting in her turn the weaker power. Britain strove to yoke American power to British policies, while the USA repeatedly feared that her power would be so manipulated: this, in sum, has been the central pattern of Anglo-American relations during the twentieth century.

Notes

Introduction: Anglo-American Relations, 1895–1918

1 For details see J. A. S. Grenville, *Lord Salisbury and Foreign Policy. The Close of the Nineteenth Century* (London: Athlone Press, paperback edn, 1970), ch. 3. For further discussion of the themes of this introduction, see A. E. Campbell, *Great Britain and the United States 1895–1903* (London: Longman, 1960); Akira Iriye, *From Nationalism to Internationalism: U.S. Foreign Policy to 1914* (London: Routledge & Kegan Paul, 1977); and Bradford Perkins, *The Great Rapprochement: England and the United States 1895–1914* (London: Gollancz, 1969).

2 Wiseman to Drummond, draft cable (not sent), probably late Dec. 1917 or early Jan. 1918, Drawer 90, file 43, William Wiseman Papers, Yale University Library, New Haven, Conn.

Chapter 1: British Purchasing 1914–1915

1 Kitchener told Lord Esher on 12 August that 'the war might last two or three years at least'. Entry for 13 August 1914, diary of Lord Esher (original manuscript), Vol. 2, folder 13, Esher Papers, Churchill College, Cambridge. Reginald McKenna, then Home Secretary, later confirmed Kitchener's prescience, writing in 1927 that 'He [Kitchener] was the first, and at the time the only member of the Cabinet, who took the view that the war would last at least three years'. McKenna is probably referring to late August 1914. 'Memorandum', 20 March 1927, Box 3, folder 7, Beaverbrook Papers, House of Lords Record Office, London. I am indebted to Dr David French for these references. See also his *British Economic and Strategic Planning 1905–1915* (London: Allen & Unwin, 1982), pp. 124–5, and Michael and Eleanor Brock (eds), *H. H. Asquith Letters to Venetia Stanley* (Oxford: Oxford University Press, 1982), p. 295.

2 Ministry of Munitions, *Official History of the Ministry of Munitions*, 12 vols (London: HMSO, 1921–2), i. 53.

3 *ibid.*, i. 57–8.

4 The first order for munitions in the United States was placed in October 1914. *Hist. of Min. of Mun.*, i. 5.

5 Department of State, *Papers Relating to the Foreign Relations of the United States, 1914*, Supplement, *The World War* (Washington, DC: US Government Printing Office, 1928), pp. 573–4.

6 Major Burdon and two assistant foremen were sent from Woolwich in September 1914 to inspect certain Bain and Studebaker wagons before shipment to England. Major Farmar was sent out concurrently to inspect small arms ammunition and in October he received the assistance of nine examiners. *Hist. of Min. of Mun.*, i. 94.

7 The War Office representative was probably Major Farmar. David Lloyd George, *War Memoirs*, 2 vols (London: Odhams, 1938), i. 89. *Hist. of Min. of Mun.*, i. 93–8. The members of the Cabinet Committee on Munitions were the Secretary of State for War (Lord Kitchener), the Lord Chancellor (Lord Haldane), the Chancellor of the Exchequer (David Lloyd George), the First Lord of the Admiralty (Winston Churchill), the Home Secretary (Reginald McKenna), the President of the Board of Trade (Walter Runciman) and the President of the Board of Agriculture (Lord Lucas). The committee met six times between 12 October 1914 and 1 January 1915 and took the initiative on the more important questions of policy and procedure which arose.

8 War Office to Foreign Office, 23 Oct. 1914, no. 62392, Series 371, vol. 2225, Foreign Office Papers (hereafter FO), Public Record Office, London.

9 *ibid.*; Bennett to Foreign Office, 24 Oct. 1914, no. 62742, War Office to Foreign Office, 24 Oct. 1914, no. 62808, Heffer to Hopwood, 26 Oct. 1914, no. 63189. all FO 371/2225.

10 Kathleen Burk, 'The Treasury; from impotence to power', in Burk (ed.), *War and the State: The Transformation of British Government, 1914–1919* (London: Allen & Unwin, 1982), pp. 91–2. Grenfell to Morgan, 5 Nov. 1914, Series C, Vol. 1, file 1, no. 30(a), David Lloyd George Papers, House of Lords Record Office, London.

11 Morgan to Grenfell, 7 Nov. 1914, C/1/1/31; Morgan to Grenfell, 11 Nov. 1914, C/1/1/32, Lloyd George Papers.

12 von Donop to Lloyd George, 12 Nov. 1914, C/5/7/6; Morgan to Grenfell, 12 Nov. 1914, C/1/1/33(a), Lloyd George Papers.

13 Grenfell to Lloyd George, 13 Nov. 1914, C/1/1/33, Lloyd George Papers.

14 Lloyd George to Grenfell, 13 Nov. 1914, C/1/1/34; Grenfell to Lloyd George, 26 Nov. 1914, C/1/1/35(a), Lloyd George Papers.

15 War Office to Foreign Office, 17 Nov. 1914, no. 72337, FO 371/2225.

16 Spring Rice to Foreign Office, 27 Oct. 1914, no. 63616, FO 371/2224. Grenfell to Lloyd George, 13 Nov. 1914, C/1/1/33, Lloyd George Papers. Basil Blackett, 'The purchase of war supplies in the United States', 27 Nov. 1914, Series II, Vol. 26, ff. 166–74, Asquith Papers, Bodleian Library, Oxford.

17 E. R. Stettinius to Wainwright, 'Memorandum', 17 April 1922, Box 82, folder 773, E. R. Stettinius Papers, Alderman Library, University of Virginia. 'The Allied Governments and their representatives experienced all the difficulties caused by ignorance of American markets, of American concerns and their standing, credit and ability to perform. Also, they lacked experience with business usages, customs and procedure in the United States and the French, Italians and Russians had additional hardship imposed by the use of a foreign tongue.' *ibid.*

18 Basil Blackett, 'The purchase of war supplies in the United States', 27 Nov. 1914, II, 26, ff. 166–74, Asquith Papers.

19 *ibid.*

20 Bennett to Foreign Office, 31 Oct. 1914, no. 65380; Spring Rice to Foreign Office, 2 Nov. 1914, no. 66175; War Office to Foreign Office, 9 Nov. 1914, no. 68708, all FO 371/2224.

21 Spring Rice to Foreign Office and Minute by Sir Edward Grey, 2 Nov. 1914, no. 66175: Foreign Office to Spring Rice, 7 Nov. 1914, no. 67380, both FO 371/2224. Grey was the Secretary of State for Foreign Affairs.

22 Duncan Crow, *A Man of Push and Go: The Life of George Macaulay Booth* (London: Hart-Davis, 1965), p. 75.

23 Crow, *Booth*, pp. 79–80. Colin Simpson, *The Lusitania* (Harmondsworth: Penguin, 1974), pp. 52-3. War Office to Foreign Office, 9 Nov. 1914, no. 68708, FO 371/2224. Arthur Willert to Geoffrey Robinson, 20 Nov. 1914, File USA 1911–1914, Arthur Willert Papers, *The Times* Archives, London. Willert was the Washington correspondent for *The Times* and very *au fait* with the Washington political scene. Robinson later changed his name to Dawson, upon receipt of his inheritance.

24 Spring Rice to Grey, 21 Oct. 1914, no. 61688; 27 Oct. 1914, no. 63616, both FO 371/2224. Spring Rice had been best man at J. P. Morgan Jr's wedding. Morgan Jr, known as Jack, had been head of the firm since his father's death in 1913.

25 War Office to Foreign Office, 3 Nov. 1914, no. 67608; Admiralty to Foreign Office, 30 Oct. 1914, no. 65078; Wyldbore Smith, 'Purchase of stores in the U.S.', 11 Nov. 1914, no. 69599, all FO 371/2224.

26   Spring Rice to Foreign Office, 12 Nov. 1914, no. 70005, FO 371/2224.
27   Simpson, *Lusitania*, pp. 52–3. His contact at the Board of Trade was probably the Permanent Secretary, Sir Hubert Llewellyn Smith, who was an old friend. See Crow, *Booth*, pp. 25, 66–7.
28   United States Senate, *Munitions Industry. Supplemental Report...of the Special Committee on Investigation of the Munitions Industry* (74th Congress, 2nd Session, Senate Report 944, 1936), vi. 67.
29   J. P. Morgan to E. C. Grenfell, cable, 2 Nov. 1914, File 5, Box History 1, Morgan Grenfell Papers, Morgan Grenfell & Co. Ltd., London.
30   Grenfell to Morgan, cable, 2 Nov. 1914, F. 5, Box Hist. 1, Morgan Grenfell Papers.
31   Grenfell to Morgan, 13 Nov. 1914, F. 6/2, Box BG Loan 7, Morgan Grenfell Papers.
32   H. P. Davison to Grenfell, 18 Nov. 1914, no. 218, F. 2, Box 68; Grenfell to Davison, 24 Nov. 1914, no. 255, and Davison to Grenfell, 25 Nov. 1914, n.n., F. 5, Box Hist. 1, all Morgan Grenfell Papers.
33   Basil Blackett, 'Purchase of war supplies in the United States', 27 Nov. 1914, II, 26, ff. 166–74, Asquith Papers.
34   Davison to J. P. Morgan & Co., 16 Dec. 1914, Folder J. P. Morgan & Co. – Cables 1914–1919, Dwight Morrow Papers, Amherst College, Connecticut. I am grateful to Dr Priscilla Roberts for allowing me to use her transcripts of the Morrow Papers. Edwin S. Montagu, Financial Secretary to the Treasury, also supported the idea of a Morgan agency. John Douglas Forbes, *Stettinius, Sr.: Portrait of a Morgan Partner* (Charlottesville, Va: University Press of Virginia, 1974), p. 46. Davison to J. P. Morgan & Co., 19 Dec. 1914, US Senate, *Munitions Industry*, exhibit no. 2166, xxvi. 7800.
35   Forbes, *Stettinius*, p. 46.
36   E. R. Stettinius, 'Memorandum', 20 Dec. 1921, Box 82, folder 773, Stettinius Papers.
37   Forbes, *Stettinius*, p. 46.
38   For the Stonehenge donation see File JPM Misc. 7, Morgan Grenfell Papers. For the French request see Forbes, *Stettinius*, p. 46.
39   US Senate, *Munitions Industry*, vi. 67. Grey to Spring Rice, 19 Dec. 1914, f. 465, FO 800/84. It should be noted that Kitchener had spoken immediately after taking office to Runciman about the need for central purchasing. Crow, *Booth*, p. 71.
40   Spring Rice to Grey, 30 Dec. 1914, f. 501, FO 800/84.
41   Spring Rice to Grey, 20 Jan. 1915, f. 60, FO 800/85.
42   D/12/2/1, Lloyd George Papers.
43   *ibid.*
44   *ibid.*
45   'The joke was current at the time on Wall Street that this brokerage arrangement with a percentage – though still undetermined – of the gross amount of purchases going to Stettinius was potentially so advantageous to him that the partners of J. P. Morgan hastily revised the agreement lest he earn more than they.' A comparison of Stettinius's income tax returns for 1914 and 1915 gives credence to the joke: in 1914 his net income was reported as $97,173.49; in 1915 his net income was $858,856.84, of which $500,000 was commission from the Commercial Agency. Forbes, *Stettinius*, pp. 48–9.
46   Forbes, *Stettinius*, pp. 47–52. Davison to Grenfell, 27 Feb. 1915, no. 1323; Davison to Morgan Grenfell & Co., 1 March 1915, no. 1332, F. 5, Box Hist. 1, Morgan Grenfell Papers. These citations form the basis for the entire paragraph.
47   Crow, *Booth*, p. 122.
48   'The Departments at that time concerned (viz. War Office, Ministry of Munitions

and their various sub-departments) on their own initiative invited C.F.W. to attend their discussions and sought his advice in the initial stages of each of the more important transactions. In this way C.F.W. was able to take an active and constructive part in the conduct of the Government's business in U.S.A., apart from the mere routine work of conducting the cable correspondence.' Grenfell to Morgan, 18 March 1918, no. 52388, F. 17, Box Hist. 3, Morgan Grenfell Papers.

49 George Booth, quoted in Crow, *Booth*, p. 123.

50 Grenfell to Lamont, 14 Oct. 1915, F. 12, Box Hist. 11 – Letters, Morgan Grenfell Papers.

51 Forbes, *Stettinius*, p. 53.

52 E. R. Stettinius, 'Memorandum', 17 April 1922, Box 82, folder 773, Stettinius Papers.

53 Grenfell to Lloyd George, 8 March 1915, C/1/2/9, Lloyd George Papers. *Hist. of Min. of Mun.*, iii. 15–16, 22–9.

54 *Hist. of Min. of Mun.*, iii. 30–1.

55 Spring Rice to Grey, 16 March 1915, ff. 121–2, FO 800/85.

56 *Hist. of Min. of Mun.*, iii. 21. Spring Rice to Russell, 20 May 1915, ff. 175–6, FO 800/85.

57 Nevertheless, on 26 March 1915 Whigham wrote to Davison in New York about the difficulties of dealing with the War Office: there was no 'want of loyalty on the part of that august body, but because there is no one head with whom to deal, and most of the individual departments who arrange the contracts for various classes of supply have never even read the Commercial Agency Contract (indeed, some of them have never even seen it) and have merely received a general instruction to deal, for American supplies, through J.P.M. & Co...how very difficult it is to carry out the contract on the lines which we originally imagined, viz., that the War Office was a definite entity with whom we should have to deal.' F. 13, B. Hist. 11 – Letters, Morgan Grenfell Papers.

58 *Hist. of Min. of Mun.*, iii. 19, 17–21.

59 *ibid.*, iii. 21.

60 D. A. Thomas, 'Draft report', 9 Dec. 1915, D/12/2/22, Lloyd George Papers.

61 See, for example, the US Senate Report no. 944 on the *Munitions Industry*, cited earlier; Charles Tansill, *America Goes to War* (Boston, Mass.: Little, Brown, 1938), p. 193, is one example of this argument.

62 Thomas Lamont, 'Historical memorandum', 12 Sept. 1939, Series II, File 84–19, Thomas Lamont Papers, Harvard Business School, Boston, Mass. Sent to Lord Lothian.

63 R. S. Sayers, *The Bank of England 1891–1944*, 3 vols (Cambridge: Cambridge University Press, 1976), ii. 86. Total payments made by Morgan's on behalf of the British government alone during the war rose to $18,000m., in addition to $6,000m. for the French. *ibid.*, 87.

64 Forbes, *Stettinius*, p. 61. Morgan's placed orders in more than 500 firms for Great Britain and in more than 525 for France; in only fourteen of those did any of the Morgan firms, or their partners, hold stock. The maximum amount owned was 3 per cent of the total outstanding capital stock of any one firm. *Munitions Industry*, xxvi. 8097.

65 US Senate, *Munitions Industry*. v. 71.

66 *ibid.*, 75.

Chapter 2: Munitions Purchasing, 1915–1917

1 'Some further considerations on the conduct of the war', Cab 42/1/39; the memorandum may also be found in Cab 37/124/40. French, *British Economic and*

Strategic Planning, ch. 10.

2 Asquith to Kitchener, 8 April 1915, quoted in R. J. Q. Adams, *Arms and the Wizard: Lloyd George and the Ministry of Munitions, 1915–1916* (London: Cassell, 1978), p. 26.

3 The May Crisis has engaged historians for years. See, for example, Lord Beaverbrook, *Politicians and the War* (London: Archon Books, 1968; first published in 2 vols 1928–32); Stephen Koss, *Lord Haldane, Scapegoat for Liberalism* (New York: Columbia University Press, 1969); Cameron Hazlehurst, *Politicians at War, 1914–1915* (London: Cape, 1971); M. D. Pugh, 'Asquith, Bonar Law and the First Coalition', *Historical Journal*, vol. xvii, no. 4 (December 1974), pp. 813–36; David French, 'The military background to the "Shell Crisis" of May 1915', *Journal of Strategic Studies*, vol. II, no. 2 (September 1979), pp. 192–205; Martin Pugh, *The Making of Modern British Politics, 1867–1939* (Oxford: Blackwell, 1982), and Michael and Eleanor Brock (eds), *Asquith*.

4 See, for example, Sir Hubert Llewellyn Smith, Permanent Secretary to the Board of Trade, to Lloyd George, 21 May 1915: 'Up to now we have . . . had to do our best to get along with a fundamentally impossible situation. Now, however, the turn of events has made possible a really comprehensive reform which even a week ago seemed impossible. The all important matter is not to let the opportunity slip, by failing to take all the necessary steps.' C/7/5/21, Lloyd George Papers. Chris Wrigley, 'The Ministry of Munitions: an innovatory department', in Burk (ed.), *War and the State*, pp. 32–41.

5 Lloyd George to D. A. Thomas, 14 June 1915, D/12/1/3, Lloyd George Papers.

6 Thomas to Lloyd George, 12 June 1915, D/12/1/2; Lloyd George to Thomas, 14 June 1915, D/12/1/3; Thomas to Lloyd George, 15 June 1915, D/12/1/5, all Lloyd George Papers. Adm. Sir Guy Gaunt, *The Yield of the Years* (London: Hutchinson, 1940), pp. 212–14.

7 John Grigg, *The Young Lloyd George* (London: Eyre Methuen, 1973), pp. 94–5.

8 72 *House of Commons Debates* 5 s., 23 June 1915, cols 1191–2.

9 Davies to Percy, 19 June 1915, no. 80688, FO 371/2589.

10 Thomas to Lloyd George, 15 July 1915, D/12/1/9; D. A. Thomas, 'Draft report', 9 Dec. 1915, D/12/2/22, both Lloyd George Papers.

11 Thomas to Spring Rice, 14 Jan. 1916, File CASR 1/65, Sir Cecil Spring Rice Papers, Churchill College Library, Cambridge. Davies to Percy, 19 June 1915, no. 80608, FO 371/2589. Spring Rice to Foreign Office, 6 July 1915, no. 89844, FO 371/2590.

12 D. A. Thomas, 'Draft report', 9 Dec. 1915, D/12/2/22, Lloyd George Papers.

13 19 June 1915, no. 80688, FO 371/2589.

14 30 June 1915, no. 86699, FO 371/2590.

15 Davison to Morgan, 22 June 1915, no. 4907, F. 5. Box Hist. 1, Morgan Grenfell Papers.

16 *Hist. of Min. of Mun.*, iii. 43–4. D. A. Thomas, 'Draft report', 9 Dec. 1915, D/12/2/22, Lloyd George Papers.

17 'Organisation of Mr Geddes' department', 19 Oct. 1915, D/1/3/9, Lloyd George Papers. *Hist. of Min. of Mun.*, iii. 44.

18 Thomas to Spring Rice, 15 Dec. 1915, CASR 1/65, Spring Rice Papers. Thomas to Cecil, 13 Dec. 1915, FO 371/2589.

19 D. A. Thomas, 'Draft report', 9 Dec. 1915, D/12/2/22, Lloyd George Papers.

20 Thomas to Spring Rice, 14 Jan. 1916, CASR 1/65, Spring Rice Papers. *Hist. of Min. of Mun.*, iii. 45.

21 Moir to Lloyd George, 6 Nov. 1915, D/12/1/17, Lloyd George Papers.

22 Moir to Lloyd George, 6 Nov. 1915, D/12/1/18; Moir to Lloyd George, 22 Nov. 1915, D/12/1/20, both Lloyd George Papers.

23 Spring Rice to Grey, 28 Jan. 1916, D/12/1/23, Lloyd George Papers.
24 Minutes by Sir Frederick Black, Eric Geddes and Lloyd George on Spring Rice to Grey, 28 Jan. 1916, D/12/1/23, Lloyd George Papers. A contrary view about Moir's activities is presented by Forbes, who had access to a private and secret history of Morgan's purchasing activities (F. Carrington Weems, *America and Munitions*, 2 vols, New York, privately printed, 1923, of which only six copies were produced); he writes bluntly that 'The Moir-Pearson group proceeded to move in and engage in actual purchasing, thus disrupting the delicate mechanism so carefully built up by the Morgan firm.' Forbes, *Stettinius*, p. 59. Stettinius went over the documentary material carefully with Weems while he was writing the book, and thus this statement must be taken seriously. Further, Moir had his own contacts in the USA – he had been purchasing in New York in November 1914 – and he was probably exploiting them. On the other hand, he had joined Booth in urging the British government to utilise an American purchasing agent rather than War Office inspectors in late 1914 (Crow, *Booth*, p. 122); it was therefore unlikely that he was deliberately undermining Morgan's position.
25 Stettinius and J. P. Morgan had sailed for Britain on 19 February 1916. Forbes, *Stettinius*, p. 59. *Hist. of Min, of Mun.*, iii. 46–8.
26 Moir to Lloyd George, 31 March 1916, Box 29, Christopher Addison Papers, Bodleian Library, Oxford.
27 Sir E. W. Moir, 'Notes on some points of interest about the formation of the Ministry of Munitions', Dec. 1922, G/240, Lloyd George Papers.
28 *Hist. of the Min. of Mun.*, iii. 45.
29 D. A. Thomas, 'Draft report', 9 Dec. 1915, D/12/2/22, Lloyd George Papers. Moir to Lloyd George, 31 March 1916, Box 29, Addison Papers.
30 *Hist. of Min. of Mun.*, iii. 55–6.
31 Lloyd George to Black, Lee and Herbert, 20 March 1916, D/3/2/62, Lloyd George Papers.
32 *Hist. of Min. of Mun.*, iii. 56.
33 Moir to Lloyd George, 31 March 1916, Box 29, Addison Papers.
34 Moir to Addison, 1 April 1916, Box 29, Addison Papers.
35 *Hist. of Min. of Mun.*, iii. 56.
36 Moir to Lloyd George, 16 May 1916, Box 29, Addison Papers.
37 Sir E. W. Moir, 'Notes on some points of interest about the formation of the Ministry of Munitions', Dec. 1922, G/240, Lloyd George Papers.
38 *Hist. of Min. of Mun.*, iii. 56.
39 Admiralty Transport Department to Foreign Office, 17 Oct. 1916, and Minute by Sperling thereon; Foreign Office to Admiralty Transport Department, 2 Nov. 1916, both no. 207981, FO 371/2800.
40 Diary, 19 Sept. 1916, Box 29, Addison Papers.
41 *Hist. of Min. of Mun.*, iii. 48–9.
42 Booth to Addison, 29 Dec. 1916, Box 29, Addison Papers.
43 *ibid.*
44 Stevenson to Black, 4 Feb. 1916, D/12/3/1; Spring Rice to Grey, 28 Jan. 1916, sent to Lloyd George 18 Feb. 1916, D/12/1/23, both Lloyd George Papers. The diary of Chandler P. Anderson illuminates the conflict between American exporters and the British government. Anderson was a well-connected lawyer, a protégé of Elihu Roots's, who sometimes acted as legal adviser to the State Department. From 5 January to 2 May 1916 he acted as counsel in London for a group of American meat-packers in their attempt to win compensation from the British government; 150 pages of his diary document the negotiations, as well as other discussions with British officials. Diary, Box 1, folder 3, Chandler P. Anderson Papers, Library of Congress, Washington, DC.

45 Willert to Robinson, 14 March 1916, File 1916, Arthur Willert Papers, *The Times* Archive, London. Spring Rice to Grey, 25 June 1916, no. 122446; 26 June 1916, no. 122693; 6 July 1916, no. 128251; Ministry of Munitions to FO, 29 June 1916, no. 125672; War Office to FO, 7 July 1916, no. 131232: and Minute on War Office to FO, 14 July 1916, all FO 371/2852.

46 Arthur S. Link, *Wilson: Campaigns for Progressivism and Peace, 1916–1917* (Princeton, NJ: Princeton University Press, 1965), pp. 61–7.

47 Minutes of the War Committee, 20 Sept. 1916, Cab. 42/20/6.

48 Diary, 5 May 1916, Box 29, Addison Papers. Recall that Lloyd George, as Chancellor, had given the same instructions to the War Office in October 1914.

49 Morgan to Ministry of Munitions, 19 May 1916, Minute by Black, 20 May 1916, Box 8, Addison Papers. Moir to Lloyd George, 9 June 1916, D/12/1/31; Moir to Lloyd George, 22 June 1916, D/12/1/32; Lloyd George to Black, 24 Sept. 1916, D/3/2/7, all Lloyd George Papers.

50 Christopher Addison, *Four and a Half Years: A Personal Diary from June 1914 to January 1919*, 2 vols (London: Hutchinson, 1934), i. 209.

51 Markham to Lloyd George, 2 June 1916, D/20/2/99, Lloyd George Papers.

52 Diary, 19 Sept. 1916, Box 29, Addison Papers.

53 'Experience with British rifle contracts...demonstrated that ample financial resources, adequate technical facilities, satisfactory production and inspection arrangements were not enough to guarantee acceptable results. Unstandardized designs and frequent modifications proved quite sufficient to render impossible a successful performance of these contracts. And this was the case even where contractors had long-established reputations as producers of sporting rifles and were possessed of ample resources.' 'Memorandum regarding activities of J. P. Morgan & Co. as purchasing agents for the British and French governments', ?1922, Box 82, folder 773, Stettinius Papers.

54 Minutes of the War Committee, 18 Oct. 1916, Cab. 42/22/2.

55 *Hist. of Min. of Mun.*, iii. 54.

56 Spring Rice to Grey, 21 Sept. 1916, no. 188562; Treasury to Foreign Office, 27 Sept. 1916, no. 193282; Spring Rice to Grey, 17 Oct. 1916, no. 208320; Crawford to Foreign Office, 4 Nov. 1916, no. 222088, all FO 371/2800.

Chapter 3: Purchasing and the Allies, 1914–1917

1 'Memorandum on the establishment and functions of the C.I.R.', n.d., Series 60, Vol. 72, Ministry of Agriculture, Fisheries and Food Papers, PRO, London.

2 Elizabeth Johnson (ed.), *The Collected Writings of John Maynard Keynes*, Vol. XVI, Activities 1914–*1919: The Treasury and Versailles* (London: Macmillan and the Royal Economic Society, 1971), p. 187.

3 André Tardieu, *France and America: Some Experiences in Co-Operation* (Boston, Mass.: Houghton Mifflin, 1927), p. 236. There was a branch of the Morgan firm in Paris, Morgan, Harjes et Cie. Franco-Morgan relations were, over the years, considerably more rocky than Anglo-Morgan relations.

4 Johnson (ed.), *Keynes*, xvi. 67. The Agreement broke down almost immediately and France financed only Russian expenditure in France, Britain furnishing the funds for expenditure in the rest of the world. *ibid.*, p. 230.

5 'Notes on agreement prepared by the British Ministry of Munitions after the conference of 30th August', n.d., no. 198048, FO 371/2852.

6 *ibid.*

7 Diary, 8 May 1916, Box 29, Addison Papers. J. M. Keynes, 'Note on the financial arrangements between the United Kingdom and the Allies', 9 April 1917, Series 172, Vol. 422, Treasury Papers, PRO, London.

8   Minutes of the War Policy Cabinet Committee, 23 August 1915, Cab. 37/133/9.
9   J. M. Keynes, 'The financial prospects of this financial year', 9 Sept. 1915, Cab. 37/134/12.
10 Johnson (ed.), *Keynes*, xvi. 149–50.
11 'Note on the financial arrangements between the United Kingdom and the Allies', 9 April 1917, T. 172/422.
12 Minute by Percy on Spring Rice to Foreign Office, 11 Nov. 1914, no. 69910, FO 371/2224.
13 Prime Minister to Russian Minister of War, 24 Nov. 1915, no. 177109, FO 371/2584. Johnson (ed.), *Keynes* xvi. 129. For elucidation on the Russian position in the CIR and on her need for funds see Keith Neilson, *Strategy and Supply: The Anglo-Russian Alliance, 1914–1917* (London: Allen & Unwin, 1984), chs 2–3.
14 Johnson (ed.), *Keynes* xvi. 133–4.
15 Britain did not do so. Buchanan to Foreign Office, 27 July 1916, no. 146988 and Treasury to Foreign Office, 4 Aug. 1916, no. 152563, both FO 371/2846.
16 Military Attaché, Petrograd, to War Office, 11 Sept. 1915 and War Office to Military Attaché, 16 Sept. 1915, both no. 134777, FO 371/2583.
17 Buchanan to Foreign Office, 6 Dec. 1915, no. 184996, FO 371/2584. Neilson, *Strategy and Supply*, ch. 5 and footnote 5.
18 Morgan to Grenfell, 24 Nov. 1915, no. 178802, FO 371/2584.
19 War Office to Military Attaché, Petrograd, 11 Dec. 1915, no. 189394, FO 371/2584. Neilson, *Strategy and Supply*, ch. 5.
20 *Who's Who in the British War Mission to the United States of America, 1917* (New York: Edward J. Clode, 1917), pp. vii, 10.
21 Spring Rice to Grey, 21 June 1915, no. 119312, FO 371/2852.
22 13 July 1916, no. 137651 , FO 371/2846.
23 'Note of the financial arrangements between the United Kingdom and the Allies', 9 April 1917, T. 172/422. For a systematic discussion of the Russians' difficulties, see Neilson, *Strategy and Supply*, ch. 3.
24 'Note of the financial arrangements between the United Kingdom and the Allies', 9 April 1917, T. 172/422.
25 The Cabinet Committee included Reginald McKenna (Home Secretary and chairman of the committee), Walter Runciman (President of the Board of Trade), Lord Lucas (President of the Board of Agriculture) and Edwin Montagu (Financial Secretary to the Treasury). CID Historical Section, 'Report on the opening of the war', 1 Nov. 1914, Cab. 17/102B. José Harris, 'Bureaucrats and businessmen in British food control, 1916–19', in Burk (ed.), *War and the State,* pp. 136–7. French, *British Economic and Strategic Planning*, pp. 101–2.
26 69 *House of Commons Debates* 5 s., col. 1178.
27 French, *British Economic and Strategic Planning*, p. 103.
28 *ibid.*, pp. 102–3.
29 Lord Selborne, 'Memorandum', 21 July 1915, Cab. 37/131/30. Lois Margaret Barnett, 'Government food policies in Britain during World War I' (PhD thesis, Columbia University, 1982), pp. 48–9.
30 R. Henry Rew, *Food Supplies in Peace and War* (London: Longman, 1920), p. 45.
31 'Memorandum in answer to the Circular of the C.I.D. of 25 July 1916', n.d., Series PRO 30, vol. 68, file 2, Sir Alan Anderson Papers: Royal Commission on Wheat Supplies, PRO, London.
32 'History of commodities control', p. 168, MAF 60/7.
33 Harris, 'Bureaucrats and businessmen', in Burk (ed.), *War and the State,* p. 138.
34 'Memorandum in answer to the Circular of the C.I.D. of 25 July 1916', PRO 30/68/2.

35 'History...', p. 168, MAF 60/7.
36 *ibid.*
37 'History', MAF 60/1. 'Control of sugar', MAF 60/6. Barnett, 'Government food policies', pp. 49–50.
38 'Memorandum in reply to the Circular of the C.I.D. of 25 July 1916', PRO 30/68/2.
39 'History...', p. 169, MAF 60/7. 'Memorandum in reply to the Circular of the C.I.D. of 25 July 1916', PRO 30/68/2.
40 *Who's Who in the British War Mission*, pp. 15, 41.
41 'History...', p. 171, MAF 60/7. 'Memorandum in answer to the Circular of the C.I.D. of 25 July 1916' and Thomson to Wheat Commission, 28 Dec. 1916, both PRO 30/68/2. Arthur Salter, *Slave of the Lamp: A Public Servant's Notebook* (London: Weidenfeld & Nicolson, 1967), pp. 76–7.
42 'History: General memorandum', MAF 60/1.
43 'History...', pp. 168–9, MAF 60/7. Harris, 'Bureaucrats and businessmen', in Burk (ed.), *War and the State*, pp. 145–6.
44 Sir Alan Anderson, 'Report', 5 Jan. 1922, PRO 30/68/11.

Chapter 4: Financial Relations, 1914–1915

1 A. R. Hall, *The Export of Capital from Britain, 1870–1914* (London: Methuen, 1968), pp. 23–7.
2 For the August 1914 financial crisis in London see Burk (ed.), *War and the State*, pp. 19, 25, 86–7. John J. Broesamle, *William Gibbs McAdoo: A Passion for Change, 1867–1917* (Port Washington, NY: Kennikat Press, 1973), pp. 189–95. Paish to McAdoo, 23 Oct. 1914, Box 125, William G. McAdoo Papers, Library of Congress, Washington, DC.
3 Broesamle, *McAdoo*, pp. 190–8, 215–16. The European Exchanges were already closed and the London Exchange closed on 31 July. The New York Stock Exchange remained closed until 13 November 1914, when it reopened for restricted trading in municipal bonds; unrestricted trading recommenced in April 1915.
4 Broesamle, *McAdoo*, pp. 174–8. See also 'The Cotton Crisis, the South, and Anglo-American diplomacy, 1914–15' in Arthur S. Link, *The Higher Realism of Woodrow Wilson and Other Essays* (Nashville, Tenn.: Vanderbilt University Press, 1971), pp. 309–29.
5 Spring Rice to Grey, 28 Sept. 1914, f. 297 and Tyrrell to Spring Rice, 2 Oct. 1914, f. 321, both FO 800/84. J. P. Morgan & Co. to Morgan Grenfell & Co., 26 Sept. 1914, no. 127 and Grenfell to Morgan, 26 Sept. 1914, no. 137, both F. 5, Box Hist. 1. Whigham to Morgan, 2 Oct. 1914 and Grenfell to Morgan, 6 Oct. 1914, both F. 12, Box Hist. 11 – Letters, Morgan Grenfell Papers. There was some suggestion about sending Lord Reading, which Spring Rice deprecated. Spring Rice to Grey, 29 Sept. 1914, f. 303; Grey to Spring Rice, 30 Sept. 1914, f. 306; Spring Rice to Grey, 30 Sept. 1914, f. 313, all FO 800/84. For further information on Paish see Avner Offer, 'Empire and social reform: British overseas investment and domestic politics, 1908–1914', *Historical Journal*, vol. xxvi, no. 1 (March 1983), pp. 119–38.
6 Broesamle, *McAdoo*, p. 146. For a detailed discussion of the development of the legislation establishing the Federal Reserve Board, and the fight over its personnel and status, see Broesamle, chs 6 and 7.
7 *ibid.*, pp. 120–4. By the end of 1915 McAdoo's contempt for the Warburg faction was apparent, with his distaste for Miller bordering on sheer hatred. Broesamle, p. 134. Oddly enough, Spring Rice, Arthur Willert, *The Times*'s correspondent in

Washington, and Blackett all regarded McAdoo as under the domination of Warburg. Spring Rice to Grey, 3 Nov. 1914, f. 309c, FO 800/84. Willert to Robinson, 3 Nov. 1914, File USA 1911–1914, Arthur Willert Papers, *The Times* Archive, New Printing House Square, London. Blackett to Bradbury, 27 Nov. 1914, ff. 182–7, II, 26, Asquith Papers.

8 Broesamle, *McAdoo*, p. 106.

9 Diary, vol. 4: 5 Dec. 1917, Charles Hamlin Papers, Library of Congress, Washington, DC

10 Diary, vol. 11: 7 Aug. 1917, E. M. House Papers, Yale University Library, New Haven, Conn. In this entry House writes eloquently of McAdoo's attempts to gather in more and more responsibility in the wartime government, ending, 'When you sum it up, it means he would be in complete control of the Government'.

11 Blackett to Bradbury, 27 Nov. 1914, ff. 182–7, II, 26, Asquith Papers.

12 Diary, vol. 2: 24 Oct. 1914, Hamlin Papers. Hamlin's entry on the 23 Oct. meeting mentions only a discussion on the price of American gold eagles in Montreal. Blackett to Bradbury, 27 Nov. 1914, ff. 182–7, II, 26, Asquith Papers.

13 Diary, vol. 2: 24 Oct. 1914, Hamlin Papers.

14 J. P. Morgan & Co. to Grenfell, 11 Nov. 1914, no. 200, F. 2, Box 68, Morgan Grenfell Papers. Diary, vol. 2; 30 Nov. 1914, Hamlin Papers. Blackett to Bradbury, 27 Nov. 1914, ff. 182–7, II, 26, Asquith Papers. Hamlin to McAdoo, 31 Oct. 1914, Box 125, McAdoo Papers. Sir George Paish, 'Memorandum', n.d., ff. 188–93e, II, 26, Asquith Papers.

15 Paish to McAdoo, 6 Nov. 1914, Box 126, McAdoo Papers. Diary, vol. 2: 20 Nov. 1914, Hamlin Papers.

16 Diary, vol. 2: 20 Nov. 1914, Hamlin Papers. Blackett to Bradbury, 27 Nov. 1914, ff. 182–7, II, 26, Asquith Papers.

17 Blackett to Bradbury, 27 Nov. 1914, ff. 182–7, II, 26, Asquith Papers.

18 Benjamin Strong to McAdoo, 23 Nov. 1914, Box 127, McAdoo Papers. Strong was Governor of the New York Federal Reserve Bank. Brown Bros.' London house was Brown Shipley, the firm of which Montagu Norman was a member 1894–1915.

19 Box 127, McAdoo Papers.

20 Blackett to Bradbury, 27 Nov. 1914, ff. 182–7, II, 26, Asquith Papers.

21 Hamlin to McAdoo, 2 Jan. 1915, enclosing telegram from Grey to Spring Rice of that date, Box 129, McAdoo Papers. Spring Rice to Blackett, 6 Sept. 1915, ff. 348–51, FO 800/85. Negotiations in London on the plan were carried on mainly by Davison and Brown who had a decisive meeting on 9 December 1914 with Lloyd George, Lord Reading and Bradbury. At the end of the day they all agreed on the following plan: a 'mutual reciprocity credit' of an amount to be determined would be arranged in London or New York for the benefit of either party; thus if, for example, exchange were adverse to New York and gold had been shipped to the danger line, a credit would be established in London for a syndicate which would be formed in New York – or vice versa. The emphasis was on the plan's being one between private bankers on both sides, with neither government becoming involved. Davison to J. P. Morgan & Co., 9 Dec. 1914, Folder J. P. Morgan & Co. – Cables 1914–1919, Morrow Papers. McAdoo was notified, as was Strong. The plan was approved, but it was several days before the text of the announcement could be agreed. J. P. Morgan & Co. to Davison, 12 Dec. 1914; Davison to J. P. Morgan & Co., 17 Dec. 1914; J. P. Morgan & Co. to Davison, 17 Dec. 1914; Davison to J. P. Morgan & Co., 19 Dec. 1914; Davison to J. P. Morgan & Co., 24 Dec. 1914, all Folder J. P. Morgan & Co. – Cables 1914–1919, Morrow Papers.

22 Spring Rice to Blackett, 6 Sept. 1915, ff. 348–51, FO 800/85.

23 Sir George Paish, 'Memorandum', n.d., ff. 188–93e, II, 26, Asquith Papers. 'Moreover it was by urging the danger of undue depletion of gold reserves that a pro-German banker at Washington tried to persuade both bankers and the Government to prevent and to prohibit the sales of American securities by Europe in the United States.' *ibid.*, f. 193a.

24 Sir John Bradbury, 'The war and finance', 17 March 1915, Cab. 37/126/12. Lloyd George, *War Memoirs*, i. 71–2. Henry F. Grady, *British War Finance, 1914–1919* (New York: AMS Reprint, 1969; first published 1927), pp. 126–9. For gold production, imports and exports see E. Victor Morgan, *Studies in British Financial Policy, 1914–25* (London: Macmillan, 1952), pp. 218, 335–7. Treasury bills were usually for ninety days; six-month and twelve-month Treasury bills were a wartime innovation.

25 Churchill was one of the few to do so. Minutes of the War Cabinet Policy Committee, 23 Aug. 1915, Cab. 37/133/9.

26 By August 1915 the German exchange at New York was 15.3 per cent below par. H.W., 'Memorandum', 9 Dec. 1915, T. 170/67.

27 War Cabinet 193, 23 July 1917, Cab. 23/3. Chancellor of the Exchequer (hereafter Chancellor) to McAdoo, 30 July 1917, no. 150751, FO 371/3115.

28 Board of Trade, 'A brief note on the dependence of the United Kingdom on United States supplies', 6 Nov. 1916, Cab. 42/23/7.

29 Sir John Bradbury, 'The war and finance', 17 March 1915, Cab. 37/126/12. Bradbury was Joint Permanent Secretary to the Treasury.

30 *George Peabody & Co., J. S. Morgan & Co., Morgan Grenfell & Co., Morgan Grenfell & Co. Ltd, 1838–1958* (London: Oxford University Press, 1958), p. 14. This is a very short company history printed for private circulation. E. C. Grenfell, 'Memorandum', 20 July 1915, T. 170/62.

31 US Senate, *Munitions Industry*, v. 169–70.

32 Morgan to Davison, 1 April 1915, no. 2686; Morgan to Davison, 19 April 1915, no. 2916; Davison to Grenfell, 4 June 1915, no. 3626; Davison to Morgan, 23 June 1915, no. 4925; J. P. Morgan & Co. to Davison, 25 June 1915, no. 3998, all F. 5, Box Hist. 1, Morgan Grenfell Papers. Diary, 18 June, 26 June 1915, File 2, Box 1, Anderson Papers.

33 Memorandum by E. C. Grenfell for the War Office, 20 July 1915, sent to the Treasury 17 Aug. 1915, T. 170/62.

34 Reginald McKenna, 'Memorandum', 22 July 1915, Cab. 37/131/37. McKenna as Chancellor was certainly more concerned about the exchange than Lloyd George, but he did not carry nearly the same weight in Cabinet.

35 Morgan Grenfell & Co. to Lloyd George, 14 Aug. 1915, D/12/1/11, Lloyd George Papers.

36 Morgan Grenfell & Co. to Lloyd George, 14 Aug. 1915, D/12/1/11, Lloyd George Papers.

37 Asquith to the king, 18 Aug. 1915, f. 10, I, 8, Asquith Papers.

38 J. M. Keynes, 'A summary of the gold position', in Johnson (ed.), *Keynes*, xvi. 109. Morgan, *British Financial Policy*, pp. 336–7. 'Protocol', 22 Aug. 1915, T. 172/256.

39 Asquith to the king, 25 Aug. 1915, f. 11, I, 8, Asquith Papers.

40 H. Montgomery Hyde, *Lord Reading* (London: Heinemann, 1967), p. 187.

41 Basil Blackett, 'Memorandum', 5 Jan. 1915, Series F, vol. 188, file 112, Reading Papers, India Office Library, London. H.W., 'The financial position in June 1915', 8 July 1915, T. 170/67. E. C. Grenfell, 'Memorandum', 20 July 1915, T. 170/62.

42 Arthur S. Link, *Woodrow Wilson and the Progressive Era, 1910–1917* (New York: Harper & Row, 1963), p. 151. Department of State, *Foreign Relations, 1914... World War*, p. 580.

43 Department of State, *Papers Relating to the Foreign Relations of the United States, The Lansing Papers, 1914–1920*, 2 vols (Washington, DC: US Government Printing Office, 1939–40), i. 146.
44 Link, *Wilson*, p. 152.
45 Arthur S. Link, *Wilson: The Struggle for Neutrality, 1914–1915* (Princeton, NJ: Princeton University Press, 1960), pp. 619–22. Dept of State, *Lansing Papers*, i. 141–4. Link, *Wilson*, p. 172. Forgan's letter was possibly sent in response to Strong's urging. Strong to McAdoo, 28 Aug. 1915, Box 143, McAdoo Papers.
46 McAdoo to House, 15 Aug. 1915, Box 73, House Papers.
47 Dept of State, *Lansing Papers*, i. 141–4.
48 *ibid.*, i. 147.
49 McAdoo to Strong, 2 Sept. 1915, Box 143, McAdoo Papers.
50 Link, *Struggle for Neutrality*, pp. 624–5.
51 Spring Rice to Grey, 18 Aug. 1915, no. 114616, FO 371/2589. H.W., 'The financial position in June 1915', 8 July 1915, T. 170/67. US Senate, *Munitions Industry*, v. 170, 171–3. Spring Rice to Grey, 10 June 1915, no. 81800, FO 371/2589.
52 US Senate, *Munitions Industry*, v. 173–4.
53 *ibid.*, pp. 174–5.
54 Montgomery Hyde, *Reading*, pp. 186–7. US Senate, *Munitions Industry*, v. 175.
55 Reading to McKenna, 8 Sept. 1915, ff. 12–13 and Reading to McKenna, 25 Sept. 1915, ff. 15–16. both File 5/6, Reginald McKenna Papers, Churchill College Library, Cambridge. When Grenfell complained about Cassel's presence, the Chancellor assured him that Cassel's sailing on the same ship as the mission was a coincidence; once he had decided to go he had (as Reading's friend) joined their table on board. Grenfell to Morgan, 3 Sept. 1915, F. 4, Box 68, Morgan Grenfell Papers. Cassel's arrangement was clearly a private one with Reading.
56 Marquess of Reading, *Rufus Isaacs, First Marquess of Reading, 1914–1935* (London: Hutchinson, 1945), pp. 32, 43.
57 Spring Rice to Grey, 19 Aug. 1915, no. 115261, FO 371/2589. Willert to Robinson, 9 Sept. 1915, 5 Oct. 1915, both File 1915, Willert Papers (*Times*).
58 Morgan to Reading, 9 Sept. 1915, F. 118/112, Reading Papers.
59 Reading, *Reading*, p. 37.
60 Blackett to Bradbury, 2 Oct. 1915, T. 170/62. Reading to Chancellor, 8 Oct. 1915, no. 146316, FO 371/2589.
61 Reading to Chancellor, 13 Sept. 1915, no. 130133, FO 371/2589.
62 Reading to Chancellor, 14 Sept. 1915, no. 131217, FO 371/2589.
63 Chancellor to Reading, 18 Sept. 1915, no. 134637; Reading to Chancellor, 23 Sept. 1915, no. 137121; and Reading to Chancellor, 25 Sept. 1915, no. 138370, all FO 371/2589. Midwestern bankers took the lead in the negotiations. Link, *Struggle for Neutrality*, p. 625.
64 Reading to Chancellor, 17 Sept. 1915, no. 133431, FO 371/2589.
65 Reading, *Reading*, p. 43. Blackett to Bradbury, 2 Oct. 1915, T. 170/62. Reading to Chancellor, 18 Sept. 1915, no. 133674, FO 371/2589.
66 Chancellor to Reading, 18 Sept. 1915, no. 134637, FO 371/2589.
67 *ibid.* Chancellor to Reading, 21 Sept. 1915, no. 135252, FO 371/2589.
68 Reading to Chancellor, 23 Sept. 1915, no. 137121, FO 371/2589. J. P. Morgan & Co. to Grenfell, 23 Sept. 1915, no. 7722, f. 106, Box Hist. 1, Morgan Grenfell Papers.
69 Scrawled note on paper headed 'Mr Morgan's Library New York', n.d., F. 118/112, Reading Papers. Reading to Chancellor, 24 Sept. 1915, no. 137540, FO 371/2589. J. P. Morgan & Co. to Grenfell, 24 Sept. 1915, no. 7772, ff. 112–13, F. 7, Box Hist. 1, Morgan Grenfell Papers.

70   Chancellor to Reading, 25 Sept. 1915, no. 138211, FO 371/2589.
71   Reading to Chancellor, 25 Sept. 1915, no. 138370, FO 371/2589.
72   Reading to McKenna, 25 Sept. 1915, f. 14, File 5/6, McKenna Papers.
73   25 Sept. 1915, ff. 15–16, File 5/6, McKenna Papers. The Morgan partners wrote confidentially to Grenfell that 'Our greatest difficulty with Commission is personality and characteristics of Holden, who is sometimes offensive, sometimes only foolish, but at all times discursive and long-winded to an almost unbearable degree.' Grenfell showed the cable to the Governor of the Bank of England. 23 Sept. 1915, no. 7722, f. 108, F. 7, Box Hist. 1, Morgan Grenfell Papers. The Chancellor later claimed (to Grenfell) that the choice of Holden had been forced on him by 'the other Bankers' in the City; he had been forced to give in to their wishes because of a 'general attitude of hostility and jealousy to Morgans.' Grenfell to Morgan, 14 Jan. 1916, E.C.G.'s Letter Book 1897–1930, Morgan Grenfell Papers.
74   Blackett to Bradbury, 2 Oct. 1915, T. 170/62.
75   Reading to Chancellor, 26 Sept. 1915, no. 138879, FO 371/2589.
76   Reading to Chancellor, 27 Sept. 1915, no. 139593, FO 371/2589.
77   f. 12, I, 8, Asquith Papers.
78   The House of Commons had risen on 30 September – for lack of anything to do – and were not due back until 12 October. The Bill went through in one sitting on 13 October. Reading to Chancellor, 1 Oct. 1915, no. 142139; Reading to Chancellor, 5 Oct. 1915, no. 144740; Chancellor to Reading, 6 Oct. 1915, no. 145286; Reading to Chancellor, 7 Oct. 1915, no. 145733: Chancellor to Reading, 8 Oct. 1915, no. 146173; Chancellor to Reading, 13 Oct. 1915, no. 149316; Chancellor to Reading, 14 Oct. 1915, no. 150444, all FO 371/2589.
79   Chancellor to Reading, 6 Oct. 1915, no. 145286, FO 371/2589.
80   Reading to Chancellor, 7 Oct. 1915, no. 145443 and Chancellor to Reading, 8 Oct. 1915, no. 146299, both FO 371/2589.
81   Blackett to Bradbury, 2 Oct. 1915, T. 170/62. Reading to Chancellor, 7 Oct. 1915, no. 145734, FO 371/2589.
82   Chancellor to Reading, 8 Oct. 1915, no. 146299, FO 371/2589.
83   Montgomery Hyde, *Reading*, p. 190. Diary, vol. 7: 2 Oct., 7 Oct., 16 Oct. 1915, House Papers. Reading to Prime Minister, 3 Oct. 1915, no. 143272, FO 371/2589.
84   Reading to McKenna, 25 Sept. 1915, f. 14, File 5/6, McKenna Papers, James Brown to Reading, 12 Oct. 1915, F. 118/112, Reading Papers. Lord Reading, 'Memorandum', 29 Oct. 1915, Cab. 37/136/39. Blackett to Bradbury, 27 Oct. 1915, T. 170/62. Reading to Chancellor, 9 Oct. 1915, no. 147134, FO 371/2589.
85   Lord Reading, 'Memorandum', 29 Oct. 1915, Cab. 37/136/39. Harvey to Bradbury, 2 Nov. 1915, no. 162883 and Bradbury to Harvey, 6 Nov. 1915, no. 165409, both FO 371/2589. J. P. Morgan & Co. to Morgan Grenfell & Co., 2 Nov. 1915, no. 9638; 6 Nov. 1915, no. 9700; 9 Nov. 1915, no. 9777; and 11 Nov. 1915, no. 9823, all F. 4, Box 68, Morgan Grenfell Papers.
86   Spring Rice to Grey, 8 Oct. 1915, no. 153857, FO 371/2589. Willert to Robinson, 5 Oct. 1915, File 1915, Willert Papers (*Times*). Reading to Prime Minister, 3 Oct. 1915, no. 143272 and Spring Rice to Grey, 8 Oct. 1915, no. 153857, both FO 371/2589. Lord Reading, 'Memorandum', 29 Oct. 1915, Cab. 37/136/39. Frederick C. Luebke, *Bonds of Loyalty: German Americans and World War I* (DeKalb, Ill.: Northern Illinois University Press, 1974), pp. 149–50.
87   Link, *Struggle for Neutrality*, pp. 626–7.
88   Blackett to Bradbury, 20 Oct. 1915, no. 153996, FO 371/2589. Blackett to Bradbury, 27 Oct. 1915, T. 170/62. Reading to Homberg, 6 Nov. 1915: Harvey to Bradbury, 20 Nov. 1915; and Spring Rice to ?Grey, Private, 29 Nov. 1915, all T. 170/63.

89 Harvey to Bradbury, 1 Dec. 1915, no. 182063, FO 371/2590. Davison to Grenfell, 30 Nov. 1915, no. 11171, f. 17, F. 8, Box Hist. 1, Morgan Grenfell Papers.
90 Harvey to Bradbury, 4 Dec. 1915, no. 184607, FO 371/2590.
91 J. P. Morgan & Co. to Morgan Grenfell & Co., 3 Dec. 1915, no. 11240, ff. 32–3 and E. C. Grenfell to J. P. Morgan & Co., 9 Dec. 1915, no. 10840, f. 47, both F. 8, Box Hist. 1, Morgan Grenfell Papers. Treasury to Morgan Grenfell & Co., 10 Dec. 1915, no. 188946, FO 371/2590.
92 Cabinet Committee on the Co-Ordination of Military and Financial Effort, 'Memorandum', 31 Jan. 1916, Cab. 37/141/38. Link, *Struggle for Neutrality*, p. 628.
93 Cabinet Committee on the Co-Ordination of Military and Financial Effort, 'Memorandum', 31 Jan. 1916, Cab. 37/141/38.
94 2 Oct. 1915, T. 170/62.
95 H. Babington Smith and Sir Richard Crawford, the Commercial Attaché at the Embassy in Washington, were also considered. Reading to Chancellor, 5 Oct. 1915, no. 144740; Chancellor to Reading, 7 Oct. 1915, no. 145570; Reading to Chancellor, 8 Oct. 1915, no. 146315; and Chancellor to Reading, 14 Oct. 1915, no. 150445, all FO 371/2589. Spring Rice to Grey, Personal, 17 Oct. 1915, f. 294 and Grey to Spring Rice, 19 Oct. 1915, no f. no., both FO 800/85.
96 Grey to Spring Rice, 19 Oct. 1915, no f. no., FO 800/85. Grey to Spring Rice, 20 Oct. 1915, no. 153782 and Bradbury to Reading, 15 Oct. 1915, no. 150906, both FO 371/2589.
97 Harvey to Bradbury, 2 Nov. 1915, T. 170/63, for example. Bradbury to Harvey, 8 Nov. 1915, no. 166746 and Harvey to Bradbury, 2 Dec. 1915, no. 182858, both FO 371/2590. Spring Rice wrote that Homberg disliked Morgan's methods, and that Davison's proceedings had not been altogether satisfactory. Spring Rice to Grey, 2 Dec. 1915, ff. 484–5, FO 800/85. Harvey to Bradbury, 23 Nov. 1915, T. 170/63.
98 Harvey to Bradbury, 4 Dec. 1915, no. 184607, FO 371/2590.

Chapter 5: Financial Relations, 1916–1917

1 Lloyd George, *War Memoirs*, i. 80.
2 Note by Lloyd George, 29 June 1916, Cab. 42/15/14.
3 Diary, 5 May 1916, Box 29, Addison Papers.
4 Cab. 37/148/6.
5 Addison to Lloyd George, 23 June 1916, Box 29, Addison Papers.
6 Box 29, Addison Papers.
7 Johnson (ed.), *Keynes*, xvi. 188.
8 Cab. 37/151/9.
9 J. P. Morgan & Co. to Grenfell, 18 July 1916, no. 23206; J. P. Morgan & Co. to Grenfell, 26 July 1916, no. 23422; Governor of Bank of England to J. P. Morgan, 28 July 1916, no. 20650; Davison to Grenfell, 3 Aug. 1916, no. 23656, all F. 10, Box Hist. 2, Morgan Grenfell Papers. Although Morgan's do not specify a reason, the lack of success of the Allies during the Battle of the Somme, which had begun 1 July 1916, probably contributed to the poor showing of the French loan.
10 Davison to Grenfell, 3 Aug. 1916, no. 23656, F. 10, Box Hist. 2, Morgan Grenfell Papers.
11 Morgan Grenfell & Co. to J. P. Morgan & Co., 4 Aug. 1916, no. 20816, F. 10, Box Hist. 2, Morgan Grenfell Papers.
12 Morgan and Davison to Grenfell, 30 Aug. 1916, no. 25542, F. 11, Box Hist. 2, Morgan Grenfell Papers. Treasury to FO, 17 Aug. 1916, no. 161500, FO 371/2852. Grady, *British War Finance*, p. 133.

13 Arthur S. Link, *Wilson: Campaigns for Progressivism and Peace, 1916–1917* (Princeton, NJ: Princeton University Press, 1965), pp. 10–15, 65. Thomas A. Bailey, 'The United States and the blacklist during the Great War', *Journal of Modern History*, vol. VI. no. 1 (1934), pp. 14–35. J. P. Morgan & Co. wrote to Grenfell on 5 Aug. that 'In our opinion there is really strong feeling here with reference to Black List and we do not believe this feeling is political.' no. 23733, F. 11, Box Hist. 2, Morgan Grenfell Papers.

14 Box 121, House Papers.

15 House to Wilson, 25 July 1916, Box 121, House Papers.

16 Cab. 37/158/3.

17 Lloyd George, *War Memoirs*, i. 510.

18 Cab. 42/23/7.

19 Morgan and Davison to Grenfell, 22 Aug. 1916, no. 25301, F. 11 and Morgan to Davison, 14 Sept. 1916, no. 27003, F. 12, both Box Hist. 2, Morgan Grenfell Papers. The French members of the committee were Messrs Homberg, Sergent and de Peyster; the British members were Lord Reading, Sir Robert Chalmers (Joint Permanent Secretary to the Treasury), Brien Cokayne (Deputy Governor of the Bank of England and member of the London Exchange Committee) and Keynes as secretary. The Morgan representatives, besides Morgan and Davison of the New York firm, were Grenfell and Herman Harjes, partner in the Paris firm. Johnson (ed.), *Keynes*, xvi. 198, 201.

20 Cab. 37/157/40.

21 Davison to Lamont, 6 Oct. 1916, no. 24324, F. 12, Box Hist. 2, Morgan Grenfell Papers.

22 Treasury to FO, 20 Oct. 1916, no. 210679, FO 371/2800. The collateral consisted of Canadian and American railroad securities, a few British railroad stocks and government securities of the Dominions, some South American countries, Cuba, Japan, India and Egypt. Grady, *British War Finance*, p. 134. Grenfell had warned Davison in August that the British government would probably require another loan in October. 23 Aug. 1916, no. 22281, F. 11, Box Hist. 2, Morgan Grenfell Papers.

23 The Chancellor regarded the 'early issue of unsecured loan as of gravest importance.' Morgan in London to Davison in New York, 23 Nov. 1916, no. 26591; but Davison and Lamont had emphasised to Morgan the previous day that 'At present we do feel time inopportune to discuss any collateral Loan Issue and most certainly an unsecured Loan. Should hardly look for change of condition by January 10th.' 22 Nov. 1916, no. 31458, both File Nov.–Dec. 1916, Box Brit. Govt Loan 3, Morgan Grenfell Papers.

24 Davison to Grenfell, 7 Nov. 1916, no. 29868, F. 13, Box Hist. 2, Morgan Grenfell Papers. Cab. 37/161/9. Memorandum by Crawford, enclosed in Spring Rice to Grey, 5 Dec. 1916, no. 255636, FO 371/2800.

25 US Senate, *Munitions Industry*, v. 200–1. Crawford to Grey, 1 Dec. 1916, no. 242886, FO 371/2800. Davison to Morgan, 21 Nov. 1916, no. 31415, F. 13, Box Hist. 2, Morgan Grenfell Papers.

26 Diary, vol. 4: 19 Nov. 1916, Hamlin Papers. US Senate, *Munitions Industry*, v. 204–5. The Governor of the Bank of England had encouraged Morgan on 30 October to issue Treasury bills, on the grounds that the Bank did so very successfully: they kept a supply of unsecured, three-month bills on hand, and discounted them 'as fast as the market would take them.' Morgan to J. P. Morgan & Co., 30 Oct. 1916, no. 24877, F. 12, Box Hist. 2, Morgan Grenfell Papers.

27 Diary, vol. 4: 24 Nov. 1916, Hamlin Papers.

28 no. 31592, F. 13, Box Hist. 2, Morgan Grenfell Papers.

29 J. P. Morgan & Co. to Morgan Grenfell & Co., 25 Nov. 1916, no. 31646, F. 13, Box Hist. 2, Morgan Grenfell Papers.

30 Diary, vol. 4: 25 Nov., 27 Nov. 1916, Hamlin Papers. Delano thought that the warning would have been printed only in the Federal Reserve *Bulletin*, but that Lamont's insistence that the plan would go ahead forced the Board's hand. US Senate, *Munitions Industry*, v. 205.

31 *New York Times*, 28 Nov. 1916.

32 US Senate, *Munitions Industry*, vi. 132.

33 *ibid.*, v. 200−2.

34 Spring Rice to Grey, 5 Dec. 1916, no. 255636, FO 371/2800.

35 J. P. Morgan & Co. to Grenfell, 29 Nov. 1916, no. 31778, F. 13, Box Hist. 2. Copies went to the Chancellor, the Governor of the Bank and Montagu Norman. Chancellor to J. P. Morgan & Co., 29 Nov. 1916, no. 26788, F. 13, Box Hist. 2, Morgan Grenfell Papers. Diary, vol. 4; 1 Dec. 1916, Hamlin Papers.

36 *ibid.*, 29 Nov., 1 Dec. 1916. Crawford to Grey, 30 Nov. 1916, no. 242886 and Spring Rice to Grey, 30 Nov. 1916, no. 242887, both FO 371/2800.

37 Crawford to Grey, 30 Nov. 1916, no. 242886, FO 371/2800.

38 Crawford to Grey, 2 Dec. 1916, no. 243908, FO 371/2800. Diary, vol. 4: 1 Dec. 1916, Hamlin Papers.

39 Spring Rice to Grey, 2 Dec. 1916, no. 243975, FO 371/2800.

40 Crawford to Balfour, Personal, 16 Dec. 1916, no. 255116, FO 371/2800.

41 Minutes of the War Committee, 28 Nov. 1916, Cab. 42/26/2.

42 Asquith to the king, 30 Nov. 1916, f. 16, I, 8, Asquith Papers.

43 Johnson (ed.), *Keynes*, xvi. 211.

44 Grenfell felt it necessary to write to Davison on 7 December that 'during Cabinet crisis none of the leading Ministers can really give proper attention to the matter in hand... No one therefore will take any responsibility...for any policy which may be reversed in the next few days by a new Administration.' no. 28038, F. 13, Box Hist. 2, Morgan Grenfell Papers.

45 Johnson (ed.), *Keynes*, xvi. 211. Keynes's memory was only slightly at fault: the true figures were $17m., $8m. and $4m. Minutes of the War Cabinet, 9 December 1916, Cab. 37/161/9. Purchases of £ exchange by J. P. Morgan & Co. for the British government:
   Quarter ending Sept. 1916 $150m.
   Quarter ending Dec. 1916   (nearly) $350m.
   'British government Treasury accounts in America', n.n., n.d., File JPM & C. Misc. 18E/1, Morgan Grenfell Papers.

46 Foreign Office minutes on French government to British government, 4 Dec. 1916, no. 245051, FO 371/2800.

47 Diary, vol. 4: 4 Jan. 1917, Hamlin Papers.

48 Minute by Sperling, 14 Dec. 1916, on Spring Rice to FO, 1 Dec 1916, no. 250107, FO 371/2800.

49 Diary, vol. 4: 29 Nov. 1916, Hamlin Papers. Warburg to Strong, 23 Nov. 1916; quoted in US Senate, *Munitions Industry*, v. 197.

50 Crawford to Grey, 30 Nov. 1916, no. 242886, FO 371/2800.

51 Willert to Robinson, 1 Dec 1916, File 1916, Willert Papers (*Times*). US Senate, *Munitions Industry*, v. 198−9.

52 Spring Rice to Grey, 5 Dec. 1916, no. 255636, FO 371/2800. McAdoo was in California and had nothing to do with the crisis. *ibid.* The identity of these 'intimate friends' is unknown. Morgan's certainly agreed, since Davison cabled to Grenfell on 30 Nov. that 'I have conviction that he [the President] is not in sympathy with Federal Reserve Board'. no. 31803, F. 13, Box Hist. 2, Morgan Grenfell Papers.

53 Lever's Diary, 27 Feb. 1917, ff. 50–1, T. 172/429.
54 Minutes of the War Committee, Cab. 42/26/2.
55 Diary, vol. 4: 30 Nov. 1916, Hamlin Papers.
56 Crawford to Grey, 30 Nov. 1916, no. 242886, FO 371/2800. Harding told Crawford that Warburg had prompted the reference to private investors; to say the least, that was a gloss on the text.
57 Lever's Diary, 23 March 1917, f. 76, T. 172/429.
58 Index to Diary: 4 Dec. 1917, Hamlin Papers. Williams to the President, 6 Dec. 1916, quoted in US Senate, *Munitions Industry*, v. 213.
59 Link, *Progressivism and Peace*, p. 204.
60 Minutes of the War Committee, Cab. 42/26/2.
61 Willert to Robinson, 1 Dec. 1916, File 1916, Willert Papers (*Times*).
62 Diary, vol. 4: 29 Nov. 1916, Hamlin Papers.
63 *ibid.*: 30 Dec. 1916.
64 US Senate, *Munitions Industry*, v. 204–5.
65 FO Minutes, 20 Dec. 1916, on Spring Rice to Grey, 5 Dec. 1916, no. 255636, FO 371/2800.
66 Minute by Sperling, *ibid.*
67 This opinion was definitely a minority one, which could probably be ascribed to Treasury pride, since Lever found him very useful when he went to the USA. Lever's Diary, 19 Feb. 1917, ff. 6–16, T. 172/429. Minute by de Bunsen on Spring Rice to Balfour, 27 Dec. 1916, no. 262194, FO 371/2800 for Chalmers on Crawford.
68 no. 11101, FO 371/3070. The third Joint Permanent Secretary was Sir Thomas Heath.
69 Treasury to Balfour to Spring Rice, 1 Feb. 1917, no. 25944, FO 371//3070.
70 Addison to Bonar Law, 14 Dec. 1916, Box 22, Addison Papers.
71 Treasury to Balfour to Spring Rice, 1 Feb. 1917, no. 25944, FO 371/3070. Sir Andrew McFadyean, *Recollected in Tranquillity* (London: Pall Mall, 1964), pp. 55–6.
72 Grenfell to Morgan or Lamont, 23 Jan. 1917, no. 30360, F. 14, Box Hist. 2, Morgan Grenfell Papers.
73 Morgan and Lamont to Grenfell, 24 Jan. 1917, no. 35818, F. 14, Box Hist. 2, Morgan Grenfell Papers. Lamont wrote to Dwight Morrow, a Morgan partner, on 17 February 1917 that 'Lever is an old New York friend of mine'. Series II, File 113–13, Lamont Papers.
74 Grenfell to Morgan, 11 Dec. 1916, no. 28136, F. 13, Box Hist. 2, Morgan Grenfell Papers.
75 Morgan Grenfell & Co. to J. P. Morgan & Co., 12 March 1917, no. 32803, F. 15, Box Hist. 2, Morgan Grenfell Papers.
76 J. P. Morgan & Co. to Morgan Grenfell & Co., 14 March 1917, no. 39688, F. 15, Box Hist. 2, Morgan Grenfell Papers.
77 Morgan Grenfell & Co. to J. P. Morgan & Co., 14 March 1917, no. 32885, F. 15, Box Hist. 2, Morgan Grenfell Papers.
78 Writing to Morgan on 11 May 1917, Grenfell recalled that ever since October 1916 'we have found this gentleman [Chalmers] opposed to Morgans in everything, and he has never missed a chance of abusing us.' E.C.G.'s Letter Book 1897–1930, Morgan Grenfell Papers.
79 Morgan Grenfell & Co. to J. P. Morgan & Co., 14 March 1917, no. 32885, F. 15, Box Hist. 2, Morgan Grenfell Papers.
80 Grady, *British War Finance*, p. 133
81 Balfour to Spring Rice, 24 Feb. 1917, no. 41794, FO 371/3118.
82 Grady, *British War Finance*, pp. 50–9.

83 Crawford to Balfour, 18 Jan. 1917, no. 15848, FO 371/3070. Lever's Diary, 27 Feb. 1917, ff. 50–1, T. 172/429.
84 Crawford to Balfour, 27 Jan. 1917, no. 22121, FO 371/3070. Crawford felt that McAdoo had been 'within an ace' of publishing a notice intended to smash the issue, because of lack of information from the British. Lever's Diary, 19 Feb. 1917, ff. 6–16, T. 172/429.
85 Grady, *British War Finance*, p. 133. It was secured by the deposit of $300m. collateral, consisting of one-half American and Canadian stocks and bonds, and one-half British colonial, South American and Japanese securities.
86 Lever's Diary, 12 Feb. 1917, ff. 30–3, T. 172/429.
87 Spring Rice to Balfour, 6 Feb. 1917, no. 28828, FO 371/3112. Spring Rice to Balfour, 7 Feb. 1917, no. 29503, FO 371/3114.
88 Balfour to Spring Rice, 14 Feb. 1917, no. 33351, FO 371/3117.
89 Lever's Diary, 12 Feb. 1917, ff. 30–3; 17 Feb. 1917, ff. 5–6; 19 Feb. 1917, ff. 6–16, all T. 172/429.
90 Lever's Diary, 19 Feb. 1917, ff. 6–16, T. 172/429.
91 *ibid.*
92 J. M. Keynes, 'Statement of resources and liabilities in America', 17 March 1917, ff. 2–4, T. 172/422.
93 Lever's Diary, 27 Feb. 1917, ff. 50–1 and 28 Feb. 1917, ff. 51–2, both T. 172/429.
94 Lever's Diary, 5 March 1917, ff. 58–9, T. 172/429.
95 *ibid.* US Senate, *Munitions Industry*, vii. 149. The overdraft reached $437m., its highest point, on 25 April 1917. J. P. Morgan & Co. to Morgan Grenfell & Co., 21 July 1917, no. 47888, F. 16, Box Hist. 2, Morgan Grenfell Papers.
96 Diary, vol. 4: 14 Feb., 15 Feb. 1917, Hamlin Papers.
97 Spring Rice to Balfour, 19 Feb. 1917, no. 39286, FO 371/3114.
98 Spring Rice to Balfour, 6 March 1917, no. 49220, FO 371/3114.
99 Crawford to Balfour, 27 Jan. 1917, no. 22122, FO 371/3070. Lever's Diary, 6 Mar. 1917, ff. 56–60 and 27 Feb. 1917, ff. 50–1, both T. 172/429.
100 Lever's Diary, 9 March 1917, ff. 61–2, T. 172/429.
101 Lever to Chancellor, 9 March 1917, ff. 18–20, T. 172/429.
102 J. M. Keynes, 'Statement of resources and liabilities in America', 17 March 1917, ff. 2–4, T. 172/422.
103 Diary, vol. 4: 21 March 1917, Hamlin Papers.
104 Lever's Diary, 23 March, 25 March 1917, both f. 76, T. 172/429.
105 Lever's Diary, 28 March 1917, f. 79, T. 172/429. Between August 1914 and July 1917 the Treasury sold $750m. worth of securities in New York; large amounts were also disposed of through private sales and sales by the Bank of England. Johnson (ed.), *Keynes*, xvi. 249–50. Between the beginning of the war and mid-1917 Britain had exported £305m. (somewhat less than $1,500m.) in gold to the USA; this included gold borrowed or purchased from France and Russia. *ibid.*, p. 249.
106 'Mr Bonar Law's statement on finance at the seventh meeting of the Imperial War Cabinet held...on the 3rd April, 1917', Cab. 23/40.
107 Johnson (ed.), *Keynes*, xvi. 224.

Chapter 6: The Balfour Mission

1 Lloyd George, *War Memoirs*, i. 991.
2 Imp. War Cab. 7, 3 April 1917, Cab. 23/40. Burton J. Hendrick, *The Life and Letters of Walter H. Page*, 2 vols (London: Heinemann, 1923), ii. 253.
3 War Cab. 113, 4 April 1917, Cab. 23/2.

4 War Cab. 115, 5 April 1917, Cab. 23/2. House to Wilson, 5 April 1917, Box 121, House Papers.
5 House to Wilson, 6 April 1917, Box 121, House Papers.
6 *ibid.*
7 House to Wilson, 8 April, 9 April 1917, Box 121, House Papers.
8 War Cab. 116, 10 April 1917, Cab. 23/2. War Cabinet Office to Oliphant, 12 April 1917, ff. 239–42. FO 800/208.
9 Charles Hanson Towne, *The Balfour Visit* (New York: George H. Dolan, 1917), pp. 15–22.
10 Diary, 12 April 1917, File 3, Box 1, and 'War missions, 1917', File Ac. 9739, Box 213, both Breckinridge Long Papers, Library of Congress.
11 Diary, vol. 10: 21 April 1917, House Papers.
12 Diary, vol. 10: 14 April 1917, House Papers.
13 See W. B. Fowler, *British-American Relations, 1917–1918: The Role of Sir William Wiseman* (Princeton, NJ: Princeton University Press, 1969), 334 pp.
14 Diary, vol. 10: 15 April 1917, House Papers.
15 Diary, vol. 10: 22 April 1917, House Papers.
16 *ibid.*
17 Diary, vol. 10: 22 April 1917, and House to Wilson, 22 April 1917, Box 121, both House Papers. Gaunt was head of British Naval Intelligence in the USA and until he was supplanted by Wiseman, the main British liaison officer with Colonel House. See Michael Sanders and Philip M. Taylor, *British Propaganda during the First World War, 1914–18* (London: Macmillan, 1982), pp. 178–81.
18 Towne, *The Balfour Visit*, pp. 60–72. Blanche E. C. Dugdale, *Arthur James Balfour, 1906–1930* (London: Hutchinson, 1936), pp. 200–8. Sir Arthur Willert, *The Road to Safety: A Study in Anglo-American Relations* (London: Derek Verschoyle, 1952), pp. 73–80.
19 David F. Houston, *Eight Years with Wilson's Cabinet, 1913 to 1920*, 2 vols (Garden City, NY: Doubleday, Page, 1926), i. 276.
20 Dugdale, *Balfour*, p. 202.
21 Balfour to Lloyd George, 26 April 1917, no. 86512, FO 371/3119.
22 Diary, vol. 10: 26 April 1917, House Papers.
23 *ibid.*
24 Diary, vol. 10: 28 April 1917, House Papers.
25 Diary, vol. 10: 30 April 1917, House Papers.
26 Diary, vol. 10: 13 May 1917, House Papers. House to Wilson, 13 May 1917, Series 2, Reel 87, Woodrow Wilson Papers, Library of Congress. Balfour to Lloyd George, 14 May 1917, no. 97867 (A), FO 371/3119.
27 Towne, *The Balfour Visit*, pp. 60, 67, Dugdale, *Balfour*, p. 202.
28 Wilson to Lansing, 10 April 1917, 841d.00/103, State Department Papers, National Archives, Washington, DC.
29 War Cab. 116, 10 April 1917, Cab. 23/2. Balfour had been Chief Secretary for Ireland 1887–91, when he had acquired the sobriquet 'Bloody Balfour'.
30 Robert Lansing, *War Memoirs* (Indianapolis, Ind.: Bobbs-Merrill, 1935), p. 277.
31 Balfour to Lloyd George, 5 May 1917, FO 115/2244. Alan J. Ward, *Ireland and Anglo-American Relations, 1899–1921* (London: Weidenfeld & Nicolson, 1969), pp. 146–9.
32 Willert, *Road to Safety*, p. 76.
33 Diary, vol. 10: 6 May 1917, House Papers.
34 'War trade questions', n.s., n.d., ff. 256–68, FO 800/208.
35 Arthur C. Murray, *Master and Brother: Murrays of Elibank* (London: Murray, 1945), pp. 145–6.

36 McKenna to Chairman of War Trade Intelligence Dept, 22 May 1917, no. 158680, FO 371/3073. Lord Eustace Percy, 'Export prohibitions and trading with the enemy', n.d., ff. 284–5, FO 800/208.
37 Diary, 4 May 1917, Box 65, Robert Lansing Papers, Library of Congress. Diary, 5 May 1917, Drawer 55, File 71, Gordon Auchincloss Papers, Yale University Library.
38 Lansing to Wilson, 5 May 1917, 763.72/4524½a, and Wilson to Lansing, 7 May 1917, 763.72/4525½, both State Dept.
39 State Dept, *Foreign Relations, 1917*, Supplement 2: pp. 828–38.
40 Diary, 8 May 1917, Drawer 88, File 2, Frank Polk Papers, Yale University Library.
41 State Dept, *Foreign Relations, 1917*, Supplement 2: pp. 838–9.
42 Balfour to Russell, f. 173, FO 800/208.
43 Willert to Robinson, File 1917–18, Willert Papers (*Times*).
44 State Dept, *Foreign Relations, 1917*, Supplement 2: pp. 846–65.
45 *ibid.*, pp. 865–70.
46 Luebke, *Bonds of Loyalty*, pp. 28, 210–12.
47 'Memorandum on subjects for agreement between the U.S. and Britain', 17 May 1917, f. 193. Addit. MSS 49748 (A. J. Balfour Papers), British Library, London. State Dept, *Foreign Relations, 1917*, Supplement 2: pp. 871, 873–4.
48 State Dept, *Foreign Relations, 1917*, Supplement 2: pp. 871–2.
49 State Dept, *Foreign Relations, 1917*, Supplement 2: pp. 875–6.
50 McKenna to Chairman of War Trade Intelligence Dept, 22 May 1917 and F. P. Robinson, 'Memorandum', 8 June 1917, both no. 158680, FO 371/3073.
51 'Importance of U.S. co-operation in shipping matters', 3 April 1917, ff. 224–5, FO 800/208. Page to Lansing, 6 April 1917, 763.72/3701, State Dept.
52 'Minute', 4 April 1917, ff. 220–3, FO 800/208.
53 Salter, *Slave of the Lamp*, p. 62. 'Shipping (economy and supply)', 26 April 1917, ff. 269–73, FO 800/208. Alan G. Anderson, 'Report', 5 Jan. 1922, PRO 30/68/11. Frederick, 'Memorandum on transportation. Urgency measure no. 1', n.d., ff. 293–5 and 'Transportation no. 2', n.d., f. 296, both FO 800/208.
54 'Memorandum', n.d., n.s. (but Percy), ff. 314–15, FO 800/208. Balfour to FO, 26 April 1917, no. 86529, FO 371/3119.
55 Diary, 1 May 1917, Box 65, Lansing Papers.
56 Diary, 7 May, 10 May 1917, Box 65, Lansing Papers.
57 Cecil to Balfour, 25 April 1917, f. 161; Lloyd George to Balfour, 1 May 1917, f. 171A; and Balfour to Lansing, 9 May 1917, ff. 10–11, all FO 800/208.
58 Balfour to Lloyd George, 4 May 1917, f. 171, FO 800/208.
59 n.d., ff. 314–15, FO 800/208.
60 F. P. Robinson, 'Memorandum', 8 June 1917, no. 158680, FO 371/3073. Salter, *Slave of the Lamp*, p. 65.
61 Crawford to Balfour, 27 May 1917, f. 128; Percy to Drummond, 27 May 1917, f. 129; Malone to Drummond, 29 May 1917, f. 2; Wiseman to Drummond, 30 May 1917, f. 141, all FO 800/208. Drummond to House, 28 May 1917, Box 40, House Papers.
62 'Memorandum', 8 June 1917, no. 158680, FO 371/3073.
63 Alan G. Anderson, 'Report', 5 Jan. 1922, PRO 30/68/11.
64 Alan G. Anderson, 'Memorandum', 22 June 1917, no. 158680, FO 371/3073.
65 *ibid.* Balfour to Lloyd George, ? April 1917, f. 167, FO 800/208. Wheat Comm. to Anderson, 23 April 1917, PRO 30/68/10.
66 H. D. Vigor, 'Report on visit to North America, April to August 1917', 4 Sept. 1917, PRO 30/68/11. Alan G. Anderson, 'Memorandum', 22 June 1917, no. 158680, FO 371/3073.

67 Anderson to Wheat Comm., 23 April 1917, PRO 30/68/10. Crow, *Booth*, pp. 143–50. Alan G. Anderson, 'Memorandum', 22 June 1917, no. 158680, FO 371/3073.
68 'No. 1. Wheat exports: Food supply and transport', 24 April 1917, ff. 333–8, FO 800/208.
69 Anderson to Wheat Comm., 26 April 1917, PRO 30/68/10. 'Minutes of meeting with the Railway Executive Committee', 26 April 1917, ff. 286–7, FO 800/208.
70 Layton to Addison, 9 May 1917, no. 94575, FO 371/3118. Alan G. Anderson, 'Wheat Export Company Progress Report no. 10', 7 May 1917, PRO 30/68/11.
71 Layton to Addison, 9 May 1917, no. 94575, FO 371/3118.
72 Alan G. Anderson, 'Memorandum', 22 June 1917, no. 158680, FO 371/3073. The Chairman was M. Sevel in deference to French pressure, but Guthrie as Director-General had executive control. *Hist. of Min. of Mun.*, iii. 73.
73 Herbert Hoover, *An American Epic*, Vol. II: *Famine in Forty-Five Nations. Organization Behind the Front, 1914–1923* (Chicago: Regnery, 1960), pp. 29–37.
74 Anderson to Wheat Comm., 11 May 1917, PRO 30/68/10.
75 Anderson to Wheat Comm., 21 May 1917, Wheat Comm. to Anderson, 26 May 1917, and Anderson to Wheat Comm., 27 May 1917, all PRO 30/68/10.
76 Dept of Agriculture to State Dept, 1 May 1917, 763.72/13435, State Dept.
77 Alan G. Anderson, 'Report', 5 Jan. 1922, PRO 30/68/11.
78 *ibid.*
79 Alan G. Anderson, 'Agenda and report of visit to Chicago and Minneapolis, 9–13 May', n.d. ff. 317–26, FO 800/208. Alan G. Anderson, 'Report', 5 Jan. 1922, PRO 30/68/11.
80 Addison to Balfour, 5 April 1917, ff. 226–8, FO 800/208.
81 C. J. Phillips, 'Notes of discussion on 8 April 1917 with Layton by Addison', Box 29, Addison Papers. Layton to Balfour, 5 June 1917, no. 158680, FO 371/3073.
82 Baker to Phillips, 30 April 1917, File 1917 – P, Box 3, Newton Baker Papers, Library of Congress.
83 Drummond to Spring Rice, 20 April 1917, f. 165, FO 800/208.
84 Lever's Diary, 10 April 1917, ff. 86–7, T. 172/429.
85 Lever's Diary, 11 April 1917, ff. 87–8; 18 April 1917, ff. 91–2 and 17 April 1917, ff. 90–1, all T. 172/429.
86 'Report on munitions and material from America for March 1917', 18 April 1917, Box 29, Addison Papers. Lever's Diary, 19 April 1917, f. 92; 1 May 1917, f. 105: 3 May 1917, f. 107; 4 May 1917, ff. 107–10; 15 May 1917, ff. 119–21, all T. 172/429.
87 P. E. Pierce, 'Notes on a conference held between the British missions...[and] the Secretary of War, and the representatives of the War Dept and the General Munitions Board in May 1917', WCD 9971-A-47, War Department Papers, National Archives.
88 Layton to Balfour, 5 June 1917, no. 158680, FO 371/3073.
89 Frederick Palmer, *Newton D. Baker: America at War*, 2 vols (New York: Dodd, Mead, 1931), i. 154.
90 Layton to Balfour, 5 June 1917, no. 158680, FO 371/3073.
91 Daniel R. Beaver, *Newton D. Baker and the American War Effort, 1917–1919* (Lincoln, Nebr.: University of Nebraska Press, 1966), pp. 56–7.
92 Balfour to Lansing, 7 May 1917, ff. 56–7, FO 800/208.
93 Layton to Balfour, 5 June 1917, no. 158680, FO 371/3073.
94 Spring Rice to FO, 6 Feb. 1917, no. 29502 and 7 Feb 1917, no. 29790, both FO 371/3112.
95 Layton to Balfour, 5 June 1917, no. 158680, FO 371/3073.
96 *ibid.*

97 Balfour to State Dept, 24 May 1917, 763.72/4686½, State Dept.
98 Layton to Balfour, 5 June 1917, no. 158680, FO 371/3073.
99 Lever's Diary, 19 April 1917, f. 92 and 20 April 1917, ff. 93–6, both T. 172/429, for example.
100 Morgan's to British Government Departments, Box 29, Addison Papers.
101 Lever's Diary, 9 May 1917, ff. 116–17, T. 172/429.
102 Layton to Balfour, 5 June 1917, no. 158680, FO 371/3073.
103 Diary, vol. 11: 19 May 1917, House Papers. Lever's Diary, 19 May 1917, f. 123, T. 172/429. House to Wilson, 22 May 1917, enclosing Memorandum by Stettinius, 2/88, Wilson Papers.
104 Lever's Diary, 15 May 1917, ff. 119–21, T. 172/429.
105 Layton to Balfour, 5 June 1917, no. 158680, FO 371/3073.
106 *ibid.*
107 Morgan to Grenfell, 26 May 1917, ff. 13–18, T. 172/424. Lever to Chancellor, 27 May 1917, no. 106203, FO 371/3114.
108 Lever's Diary, 17 April 1917, ff. 90–1; 18 April 1917, ff. 91–2; 19 April 1917, f. 92, all T. 172/429. Oscar Crosby was Undersecretary of the Treasury.
109 Layton to Balfour, 5 June 1917, no. 158680, FO 371/3073.
110 Melvin I. Urofsky, *Big Steel and the Wilson Administration: A Study in Business-Government Relations* (Columbus, Ohio: Ohio State University Press, 1969), pp. 192–247.
111 Balfour to Lansing, 18 May 1917, f. 75, FO 800/208. Layton to Balfour, 5 June 1917, no. 158680, FO 371/3073.
112 Baker to Wilson, 2/88, Wilson Papers.
113 Layton to Balfour, 5 June 1917, no. 158680, FO 371/3073.
114 W.T. Layton, 'Work of the British mission to the United States', ? June 1917, no. 151635, FO 371/3072. Many of these boards were manned by 'dollar-a-year' men, executives or lawyers released by their organisations for war work, and their desks sometimes consisted of window ledges in corridors.
115 Tom Bridges, 'General military report of mission', n.d., no. 158680, FO 371/3073.
116 Lt-Gen. Sir Tom Bridges, *Alarms and Excursions: Reminiscences of a Soldier* (London: Longmans, Green, 1938), pp. 171–2.
117 G. T. M. Bridges to CIGS, 29 April 1917, Cab. 21/53.
118 Bridges to General Scott, 30 April 1917, 2/87, Wilson Papers.
119 Baker to Wilson, 2 May 1917, enclosed in Wilson to Baker, 3 May 1917, Box 4, Baker Papers.
120 G. T. M. Bridges to CIGS, 29 April 1917, Cab. 21/53.
121 P. E. Pierce, 'Notes on a conference held between the British missions . . . [and] the Secretary of War, and the representatives of the War Dept and the General Munitions Board in May 1917', WCD 9971-A-47, War Dept. Diary, vol. 11: 21 May 1917, House Papers. Balfour to Lansing, 24 May 1917, 763.72/4686½, State Dept.
122 Bliss to Baker, 25 May 1917, 2/88, Wilson Papers.
123 G. T. M. Bridges to CIGS, 29 April, 3 May 1917, Cab. 26/53. Wilson to Baker, 3 May 1917, Box 4, Baker Papers.
124 Baker to Wilson, 9 May 1917, 2 May 1917; Wilson to Baker, 10 May 1917, all Box 4, Baker Papers.
125 G. T. M. Bridges to CIGS, 3 May 1917, Cab. 21/53. Balfour to House, 17 May 1917, ff. 70–2, FO 800/208. Diary, vol. 11: 19 May 1917, House Papers. Tom Bridges, 'General military report of mission', n.d., no. 158680, FO 371/3073. Colonel Dansey took over control from Wiseman of British Military Intelligence in the USA. Sanders and Taylor, *British Propaganda*, p. 181.
126 Bridges, *Alarms and Excursions*, p. 182.

127 Tom Bridges, 'General military report of mission', n.d., no. 158680, FO 371/3073.
128 Cecil to Balfour, 26 April 1917, f. 93, FO 800/208. Adm. Sir Dudley deChair, *The Sea Is Strong* (London: Harrap, 1961), p. 227.
129 Browning to Admiralty, 12 April 1917, no. 76457, FO 371/3118.
130 DeChair to Admiralty, 15 May 1917, no. 158680, FO 371/3073.
131 DeChair, *The Sea Is Strong*, pp. 231–2. DeChair to Admiralty, 15 May 1917, no. 158680, FO 371/3073. Cecil to Balfour, 2 May 1917, f. 104, FO 800/208.
132 DeChair to Admiralty, 7 June 1917, no. 158680, FO 371/3073. Balfour to Lloyd George, 14 May 1917, FO 371/3119.
133 Balfour to Lloyd George, 14 May 1917, no. 97867(A), FO 371/3119.
134 Diary, vol. 10: 13 May 1917, House Papers. Balfour to Lloyd George, 14 May 1917, no. 97867(A), FO 371/3119.
135 David F. Trask, *Captains and Cabinets: Anglo-American Naval Relations, 1917–1918* (Columbia, Miss.: University of Missouri Press, 1972), pp. 115–25.
136 DeChair to Admiralty, 15 May, 7 June 1917, both no. 158680, FO 371/3073.
137 Balfour to king and War Cabinet, 30 April 1917, no. 88809, FO 371/3113.
138 Willert to Robinson, 10 May 1917, File 1917–18, Willert Papers (*Times*).
139 Lever's Diary, 9 April 1917, ff. 85–6, T. 172/429.
140 Lever's Diary, 14 April 1917, ff. 89–90, T. 172/429.
141 *ibid.*
142 Lever's Diary, 16 April 1917, f. 90, T. 172/429.
143 Lever's Diary, 17 April 1917, ff. 90–1, T. 172/429.
144 Lever's Diary, 25 April 1917, f. 100 and 21 April 1917, f. 97, both T. 172/429. Spring Rice to FO, 28 April 1917, no. 86660, FO 371/3113.
145 Lever's Diary, 23 April 1917, f. 100, T. 172/429. Diary, vol. 4: 25 April, 26 April 1917, Hamlin Papers.
146 Diary, vol. 4: 4 May, 6 May, 10 May, 15 May 1917, Hamlin Papers.
147 Cunliffe to Balfour, 11 June 1917, no. 158680, FO 371/3073.
148 Diary, vol. 4: 25 May 1917, Hamlin Papers.
149 Diary, vol. 4: 25 April 1917, Hamlin Papers.
150 Lever's Diary, 26 April 1917, ff. 101–1, T. 172/429.
151 Lever's Diary, 29 April 1917, f. 102, T. 172/429.
152 Lever's Diary, 2 May 1917, ff. 105–7, T. 172/429.
153 Lever's Diary, 12 May 1917, ff. 118–19, T. 172/429.
154 Lever's Diary, 14 May 1917, f. 119, T. 172/429.
155 Chancellor to Lever, 22 May 1917, f. 103 and Lever's Diary, 14 May 1917, f. 119, both T. 172/429. Cunliffe's lack of judgement and erratic behaviour could be ascribed to growing megalomania combined with declining health. For a description of his conflicts with the Treasury in London see Burk, 'The Treasury...', in Burk (ed.), *War and the State*, pp. 93–6.
156 Page to Lansing, 6 April 1917, 763.72/3730, State Dept.
157 J.M. Keynes, 'Note on the financial arrangements between the United Kingdom and the Allies', 9 April 1917, ff. 5–23, T. 172/422. Lever's Diary, 2 May 1917, ff. 105–7, T. 172/429.
158 Chancellor to Lever, 6 May 1917, no. 92338 and 9 May 1917, no. 93509; Lever to Chancellor, 11 May 1917, no. 96603, all FO 371/3114.
159 Lever's Diary, 12 May 1917, ff. 118–19 and 17 May 1917, f. 122, both T. 172/429.
160 Lever's Diary, 18 May 1917, ff. 122–3, T. 172/429.
161 Lever to Chancellor, 19 May 1917, no. 101271, FO 371/3114.
162 Chancellor to Lever, 22 May 1917, no. 102246, FO 371/3114.
163 Lever to Crosby, 25 May 1917 and Crosby to Lever, 28 May 1917, both File GB 132/17-3, Box 119, US Treasury Papers, National Archives. Lever's Diary, 28 May 1917, ff. 127–8, T. 172/429.

164 Lever's Diary, 17 May 1917, f. 122, T. 172/429.
165 Lever's Diary, 18 May 1917, ff. 122–3 and 21 May 1917, ff. 123–4, both T. 172/429. Lever to Chancellor, 19 May 1917, no. 101271, FO 371/3114.
166 Daphne Stassin Herzstein, 'The diplomacy of Allied credit advanced to Russia in World War I' (New York University PhD thesis, 1972), p. 303.
167 A. McFadyean, 'Memorandum on the general situation in the U.S.A.', 13 June 1917, ff. 30–2, T. 172/422.
168 Lever's Diary, 5 May 1917, ff. 111–12, T. 172/429. Lever to Chancellor, 6 May 1917, no. 92034 and 7 May 1917, no. 92531, both FO 371/3114.
169 Treasury to Lever, 7 May 1917, no. 92768, FO 371/3114, n.s., n.d., f. 332, FO 800/208.
170 Lever to Chancellor, 7 May 1917, no. 92531, FO 371/3114. Lever to Chancellor, 25 May 1917, no. 104313, FO 371/3113.
171 Lever's Diary, 9 April 1917, ff. 85–6, T. 172/429.
172 n.s., n.d. (but Lever for Balfour and Cunliffe), ff. 328A–30, FO 800/208.
173 Lever's Diary, 2 May 1917, ff. 105–7, T. 172/429.
174 Lever to Crosby, 22 May 1917, File GB 132/17-3, Box 119, US Treasury.
175 Lever's Diary, 11 May 1917, ff. 117–19, T. 172/429.
176 McAdoo to Wilson, 30 April 1917, 2/87, Wilson Papers.
177 25 May 1917, f. 39, T. 172/424.
178 Balfour to Barclay, 26 May 1917 (twice), ff. 179–80 and Balfour to Cecil, 26 May 1917, f. 178, all FO 800/208.
179 Spring Rice to FO, 2 June 1917, no. 109764 and 31 May 1917 (with American newspaper reports), no. 123144, both FO 371/3113.
180 Willert, *Road to Safety*, pp. 79–80.
181 Willert to Robinson, 17 June 1917, File 1917–18, Willert Papers (*Times*).
182 26 April, 1917, F/60/2/9, Lloyd George Papers. Cecil was Minister of Blockade.
183 Willert to Robinson, 10 May 1917, File 1917–18, Willert Papers (*Times*).
184 A. McFadyean, 'Memorandum on the general situation in the U.S.A.', 13 June 1917, ff. 30–2, T. 172/422.
185 *ibid.*
186 See Seward W. Livermore, *Woodrow Wilson and the War Congress, 1916–18* (Seattle, Wash.: University of Washington Press, paperback edn, 1968), 324 pp.

Chapter 7: The Northcliffe Mission

1   Diary, vol. 10: 22 April 1917, House Papers.
2   ff. 210–11, FO 800/208.
3   ?May 1917, ff. 212–13, FO 800/208.
4   ff. 71–2, Addit. MSS. 49738. War Cab. 136, 11 May 1917, Cab. 21/54.
5   Cecil to Balfour, 17 May 1917, ff. 77–83, Addit. MSS. 49738. Grey's eyesight was also beginning to deteriorate.
6   *ibid.*
7   Cecil to Balfour, 21 May 1917, f. 142 and Balfour to Cecil, 22 May 1917, f. 206, both FO. 800/208.
8   Vol. 1, book 3, Maurice Hankey Papers, Churchill College Library, Cambridge.
9   Trevor Wilson (ed.), *The Political Diaries of C. P. Scott, 1911–1928* (London: Collins, 1970), p. 296.
10 Balfour to Cecil, 22 May 1917, f. 206, FO 800/208.
11 War Cab. 147, 25 May 1917, Cab. 21/54.
12 *ibid.* Foreign Office to Balfour and Spring Rice, 26 May 1917, *ibid.*
13 Balfour to king and War Cabinet, 28 May 1917, Cab. 21/54.
14 War Cab. 151, 30 May 1917, Cab. 23/2.

15 War Cab. 152, 31 May 1917, Cab. 23/2.
16 Diary, vol. 11: 31 May 1917, House Papers.
17 House to Wilson, 31 May 1917, 2/88, Wilson Papers.
18 Wilson to House, 1 June 1917, Box 121, House Papers.
19 Lansing to Page, 6 June 1917, 763.72/5163a, State Dept.
20 House to Wilson, 7 June 1917, 2/88, Wilson Papers.
21 Diary, col. 11: 15 July 1917, House Papers.
22 War Cab. 152, 31 May 1917, Cab. 23/2. Addison, *Personal Diary*, ii. 396. Reginald Pound and Geoffrey Harmsworth, *Northcliffe* (London: Cassell, 1959), p. 529. J. M. McEwen has argued that the idea appealed to Northcliffe 'immensely'. 'Northcliffe and Lloyd George at war', *Historical Journal*, vol. XXIV, no. 3 (September 1981), p. 666.
23 War Cab. 153, 31 May 1917, Cab. 21/54.
24 File 1917, Northcliffe Papers, *The Times* Archive.
25 House to Wilson, 12 June 1917, 2/88, Wilson Papers.
26 House to Wilson, 12 June 1917, 2/88, Wilson Papers. Spring Rice to FO, 12 June 1917, plus Minutes, no. 117120, FO 371/3120. Dawson to Northcliffe, ?date; Northcliffe to Dawson, ?12 June 1917; Dawson to Willert, 13 June 1917, File 1917, Northcliffe Papers (*Times*). Ian Malcolm, writing to Spring Rice, said that Curzon in the Lords' debate on Northcliffe's mission 'rather rasped the gilt off the gingerbread for Lord Northcliffe', 22 June 1917, CASR 1/50, Spring Rice Papers.
27 Northcliffe to Lloyd George, 20 June 1917, File 1917, Northcliffe Papers (*Times*). Diary, vol. 11: 19 June 1917, House Papers.
28 Drummond to Percy, 21 June 1917, f. 162, FO 800/209.
29 Percy to Drummond, ff. 163–4, FO 800/209.
30 Mary Rambo Kihl, 'A failure of ambassadorial diplomacy: the case of Page and Spring-Rice, 1914–1917' (PhD thesis, Pennsylvania State University, 1968), p. 217.
31 War Cab. 153, 31 May 1917, Cab. 21/54.
32 Diary, vol. 11, House Papers.
33 2/88, Wilson Papers.
34 Wilson to Daniels, 4 June 1917, 2/88, Wilson Papers.
35 Northcliffe to Lloyd George, 20 June 1917, File 1917, Northcliffe Papers (*Times*).
36 Diary, vol. 11, House Papers.
37 Drawer 90, File 27, William Wiseman Papers, Yale University Library.
38 Diary, vol. 11: 25 Aug. 1917, House Papers.
39 Balfour wrote to Geddes on 7 November 1917 that 'I hardly think that we should get much information from Spring-Rice about the feeling in the Navy Dep't; nor should I be inclined to pay excessive attention to the Northcliffe reports. I feel sure the best plan would be to wait for the arrival of Col. House and talk over the whole situation with him.' f. 350, FO 800/209.
40 House to Wiseman, 12 Aug. 1917, 90/26, Wiseman Papers. Diary, vol. 11: 13 Aug. 1917, House Papers.
41 Northcliffe to Chancellor, 14 June 1917, ff. 29–30, T. 172/425. Northcliffe to Lloyd George, 20 June, 25 June 1917, both File 1917, Northcliffe Papers (*Times*). Percy Daniels, 'Leather', 2 Nov. 1917; Louis Tracy, 'British War Mission – New York Office', 3 Nov. 1917, both F/210/1, Lloyd George papers.
42 Willert to Wiseman, 18 Aug. 1917, 90/4, Wiseman Papers. Northcliffe to Churchill, 29 Aug. 1917, File Northcliffe, 1917, Arthur Willert Papers, Yale University Library.
43 Northcliffe to Lloyd George, 18 July 1917, no. 142716, FO 371/3120. Northcliffe to Willert, 22 June 1917, File 11/9, Willert Papers (Yale). 'British War Mission

and British Ministry of Munitions at Washington D.C.', 1 Nov. 1917, F/210/1, Lloyd George Papers.

44 Northcliffe to Lloyd George, 5 July 1917, Cab. 21/54. Northcliffe to Lloyd George, Balfour, Bonar Law, 10 July 1917, no. 136921, FO 371/3120. Northcliffe to Davies, 14 July 1917, Series 25, vol. 22, Ministry of Transport Papers, PRO. Wiseman to Northcliffe, 10 Aug. 1917, 90/27, Wiseman Papers.

45 Northcliffe to Dawson, 1 July 1917, File 1917, Northcliffe Papers (*Times*). Diary, vol. 11: 1 Oct., 18 Oct. 1917, House Papers. Wiseman to Drummond, 4 Oct. 1917, ff. 283–5, FO 800/209. Willert, *Road to Safety*, pp. 109–11.

46 *Hist. of Min. of Mun.*, iii. 62–3. 'Memorandum on Allied supply from U.S.A.', n.n., n.d., ff. 288–90 and 'Explanatory note on clause 2', n.n., n.d., ff. 291–2, both FO 800/208.

47 Crawford to FO, 30 May 1917, MAF 60/189.

48 Phillips to Min. of Mun., 4 June 1917, Cab. 21/123.

49 War Cab. 159, 8 June 1917, Cab. 23/3.

50 Maurice Hankey, 'Inter-Ally Council in London to Co-Ordinate Requirements for American Supplies', 11 Aug. 1917, Cab. 21/123.

51 State Dept, *Foreign Relations, 1917*, Supplement 2: pp. 543–5.

52 Spring Rice to FO, 19 July 1917, MAF 60/189. FO to Spring Rice, 20 July 1917, no. 143489, FO 371/3120.

53 Spring Rice to FO, 21 July 1917, MAF 60/189.

54 Northcliffe to Balfour and Chancellor, 28 Aug. 1917, 90/26, Wiseman Papers.

55 War Cab. 176, 5 July 1917 and War Cab. 190, 19 July 1917, both Cab. 23/3. E.C.G. and H.H.D.T., 'Requirements of oil fuel and ships in U.S.A.', 11 July 1917, Cab. 21/123. FO to Spring Rice, 24 July 1917, no. 143487; Maclay to Lloyd George, 3 Aug. 1917, no. 152424; Chancellor to Northcliffe, 2 Aug. 1917, no. 152575, all FO 371/3120. Gordon to Phillips, 25 Aug. 1917, no. 49935, FO 371/3121.

56 FO to Spring Rice, 29 Aug. 1917, MAF 60/189. Curzon, 'Inter-Ally Council', 18 Sept. 1917, Cab. 21/123. Northcliffe to Balfour and Chancellor, 28 Aug. 1917, 90/26, Wiseman Papers.

57 War Cab. 239, 26 Sept. 1917, Cab. 23/4.

58 Buchanan to FO, 31 Aug. 1917, no. 171454 and Dodd to FO, 11 Sept. 1917, no. 177595, both FO 371/3121.

59 Crawford to FO, 30 May 1917, MAF 60/189. McAdoo to Baker, 7 July 1917, Box 183, McAdoo Papers.

60 State Dept, *Foreign Relations, 1917*, Supplement 2: pp. 543–5. William G. McAdoo, *Crowded Years* (London: Cape, 1932), p. 401.

61 Blackett's diary, 27 July 1917, f. 22, T. 172/430. Bernard M. Baruch, *Baruch: My Own Story* (New York: Holt, 1957), pp. 310–11.

62 Spring Rice to FO, 22 July 1917, no. 144191, FO 371/3115.

63 Northcliffe to Wiseman, 30 July 1917, 90/4, Wiseman Papers.

64 FO to Spring Rice, 24 July 1917, no. 143487 and Spring Rice to FO, 26 July 1917, no. 147270, both FO 371/3120.

65 McAdoo to Wilson, 30 July 1917, Box 523, McAdoo Papers. For details on the War Industries Board see Robert D. Cuff, *The War Industries Board: Business-Government Relations during World War I* (Baltimore, Md.: Johns Hopkins University Press, 1973), 304 pp.

66 Spring Rice to FO, 8 Aug. 1917, MAF 60/189. Spring Rice to FO, 9 Aug. 1917, f. 426, FO 800/242. Blackett's diary, 19 Aug. 1917, f. 29, T. 172/430.

67 Northcliffe to Wiseman, 25 Aug. 1917, 90/26, Wiseman Papers. 'Memorandum of an arrangement entered into…by the Secretary of the Treasury…and Lord

Northcliffe', 24 Aug. 1917, File A4, WIB9, Allied Purchasing Commission Papers, National Archives.

68 Grosvenor B. Clarkson, *Industrial America in the World War* (Boston, Mass.: Houghton Mifflin, 1923), p. 254.

69 *ibid.*, p. 256.

70 *ibid.*, p. 257.

71 Willert to Dawson, File 1917–18, Willert Papers (*Times*). J. M. Keynes, the Treasury representative on the I-AC, wrote to his mother on 15 December 1917 that 'It has been rather a hard week with endless hours absolutely wasted in a newly established monkey house called the Inter-Ally Council for War Purchases and for Finance.' Box 35, Keynes Papers, King's College, Cambridge.

72 Addison, *Personal Diary*, ii. 396. Addison described Gordon as one of a type who was 'quiet spoken', possessed 'penetrating efficiency' and might have been taken for a 'successful diplomatist', in *Politics from Within 1911–1918* (London: Herbert Jenkins, 1924), ii. 105. Gordon's appointment as head of the Ministry of Munitions was welcomed because of his knowledge of American business methods. R. H. Brand to Sir Joseph Flavelle, 29 April 1917, Series I, Case 3, Sir Joseph Flavelle Papers, Queen's University Library, Kingston, Ontario, Canada.

73 Crawford to FO, 30 May 1917, MAF 60/189.

74 Gordon to Addison, 10 July 1917, MAF 60/189.

75 Northcliffe to Chancellor, 18 July 1917, no. 142947, FO 371/3115.

76 Min. of Mun. to Northcliffe, 19 July 1917, ff. 177–8, T. 172/443.

77 F/41/7/16, Lloyd George Papers.

78 *ibid.* Black agreed to act as negotiator. Northcliffe to Churchill, 30 Aug. 1917, 90/26, Wiseman Papers.

79 29 Aug. 1917, F/41/7/16, Lloyd George Papers.

80 Northcliffe to Churchill, 30 Aug. 1917, 90/26, Wiseman Papers. Blackett's Diary, 31 Aug. 1917, f. 33, T. 172/430.

81 no. 171479, FO 371/3118.

82 N.n., 'British War Mission and the British Ministry of Munitions at Washington D.C.', 1 Nov. 1917; J. W. Woods, 'Purchasing Department of the British War Mission', 1 Nov. 1917; Col. L. R. Kenyon, 'British Munitions Inspection Department in U.S.', 2 Nov. 1917; Louis Tracy, 'British War Mission – New York office', 3 Nov. 1917, all F/210/1, Lloyd George Papers.

83 Drummond to Wiseman, 28 June 1917, f. 167, Wiseman to Drummond, 29 June 1917, f. 176 and Northcliffe to Balfour, 29 June 1917, f. 9, all FO 800/209. Diary, vol. 11: 28 June, 30 June 1917, House Papers. Northcliffe to Lloyd George, 3 July 1917, 91/91 Wiseman Papers. Northcliffe circular letter, 12 Aug. 1917, File 1917, Northcliffe Papers (*Times*).

84 Northcliffe to Long, 20 Aug. 1917, 90/26, Wiseman Papers. Walter Long had been placed in charge of a committee on oil matters. Long to Spring Rice and Northcliffe, 2 July 1917, f. 18, FO 800/209.

85 Northcliffe to Long, 12 Sept. 1917, 91/91, Wiseman Papers.

86 Sir F. Black, 'Supply of oil from the U.S.A.', 1 Nov. 1917, F/210/1, Lloyd George Papers.

87 Hankey to Northcliffe, 1 June 1917, Cab. 21/54. Northcliffe to Balfour, Lloyd George and Bonar Law, 8 July 1917, f. 20, FO 800/209. Blackett's Diary, 27 July 1917, f. 22 and 2 Aug. 1917, ff. 23–4, both T. 172/430.

88 Urofsky, *Big Steel*, p. 216. Northcliffe to Balfour, Lloyd George and Bonar Law, 8 July 1917, f. 20, FO 800/209. Min. of Mun. to Northcliffe, 19 Sept. 1917, 91/91, Wiseman Papers. Phillips to Northcliffe, 30 Aug. 1917, File Northcliffe – 1917, Willert Papers (Yale).

89   Robson to Anderson, 9 June 1917, PRO 30/68/11.
90   Hoover to Ministry of Food, 10 July 1917 and Spring Rice to FO, 27 July 1917, both MAF 60/189.
91   Royden to Food Controller, 17 Aug. 1917, MAF 60/189.
92   FO to Spring Rice and Northcliffe, 23 Aug. 1917 and Rhondda to Northcliffe, Hoover and Spring Rice, 29 Aug. 1917, both MAF 60/189.
93   Rhondda to Northcliffe, 31 Aug. 1917, MAF. 60/189.
94   Phillips to Northcliffe, 26 Sept. 1917, 91/92, Wiseman Papers.
95   Owen Hugh Smith, 'Allied Provisions Export Commission', n.d., F/210/1, Lloyd George Papers.
96   *ibid.*
97   *Who's Who in the British War Mission*, pp. 53, 21, 19, plus Chart. Spring Rice to FO, 4 Sept. 1917, no. 172447, FO 371/3121. Louis Tracy, 'British War Mission – New York Office', 3 Nov. 1917, F/210/1, Lloyd George Papers.
98   Spring Rice to FO for WO, 14 June 1917, no. 118668, FO 371/3120. Spring Rice to FO, 18 July 1917, no. 142997 and 21 July 1917, no. 144166, both FO 371/3119.
99   Balfour to Spring Rice, 21 June 1917, no. 125450, FO 371/3119. Northcliffe to Lloyd George, Balfour, Reading and Bonar Law, 17 July 1917, no. 141698, FO 371/3115. Northcliffe to Balfour, 16 Aug. 1917, ff. 45–7, FO 800/209.
100 Page to Balfour for Spring Rice, 14 July 1917, no. 140140, FO 371/3119.
101 Baker to House, 18 July 1917, Box 2, Baker Papers.
102 Spring Rice to Balfour, 28 July 1917, f. 157, Addit. MSS. 49740 (Balfour Papers), British Library. Wiseman to House, 8 Aug., 10 Aug. 1917, 90/27; House to Wiseman, 12 Aug. 1917, 90/26; and Wiseman to House, 24 Aug. 1917, 90/4, all Wiseman Papers.
103 Murray, *Master and Brother*, p. 135. Major-General Sir Ernest D. Swinton, *Over my Shoulder* (Oxford: George Ronald, 1951), p. 162.
104 Quoted in Murray, *Master and Brother*, p. 138.
105 Page to FO, no. 183028, FO 371/3119. Murray, *Master and Brother*, p. 136. Martin Gilbert, *Winston Churchill, 1914–1916* (London: Heinemann, 1971), p. 740n.
106 Min. of Mun. to FO to Barclay, 14 Jan. 1918, no. 9904, FO 371/3488. Murray, *Master and Brother*, p. 139.
107 Willert, *Road to Safety*, pp. 93–4.
108 Capt. Connop Guthrie, 'Shipping', n.d. (but Nov. 1917), F/210/1, Lloyd George Papers.
109 T. S. Catto, 'Anglo-Russian shipping', 2 Nov. 1917, F/210/1, Lloyd George Papers.
110 Spring Rice to Balfour, 24 July 1917, f. 148, Addit. MSS. 49740. Spring Rice to FO, 25 July 1917, f. 108, T. 172/443. Lloyd George, *War Memoirs*, i. 1012.
111 ?Royden to FO, 25 July 1917, f. 101, T. 172/443.
112 Maclay to Balfour, 20 Aug. 1917, f. 253 and Balfour to Maclay, 20 Aug. 1917, f. 255, both FO 800/209. Northcliffe to House, 25 Aug. 1917, Box 83a, House Papers. Drummond to Davidson, 12 July 1917, ff. 254–6, Addit. MSS. 49693 (Balfour Papers), British Library. Lloyd George, *War Memoirs*, i. 1011–12.
113 House to Wilson, 27 Aug. 1917, 2/90, Wilson Papers.
114 Auchincloss to Polk, 30 Aug. 1917, 73/44, Polk Papers.
115 T. Ashley Sparks, 'Shipbuilding programme in the U.S.', 30 Oct. 1917, F/210/1, Lloyd George Papers. USSB Minutes, 26 Sept. 1917, entry 4, United States Shipping Board Papers, National Archives.
116 Salter, *Slave of the Lamp*, p. 66.
117 Admiralty to FO to Spring Rice and Northcliffe, 14 Aug. 1917, no. 159517, FO 371/3121.

118 Salter, *Slave of the Lamp*, p. 66.
119 Prime Minister to n.n., 24 Sept. 1917, MT 25/6. House to Wilson, 14 Oct. 1917, 2/91, Wilson Papers.
120 See Robert Hessen, *Steel Titan: The Life of Charles M. Schwab* (New York: Oxford University Press, 1975), pp. 235–44.
121 Willert to Wiseman, 18 Aug. 1917, 90/4, Wiseman Papers. Spring Rice reported that McAdoo was 'resentful of...a misunderstanding arising out of some conversations with Lever'. Spring Rice to Balfour, 13 July 1917, ff. 380–6, FO 800/242. Wiseman to Drummond, 13 July 1917, ff. 203–7, FO 800/209. Diary, 9 July 1917, 88/2, Polk Papers. Diary, vol. 11: 10 July 1917, House Papers.
122 Diary, 22 July 1917, 55/72, Auchincloss Papers.
123 Chancellor to Page, 23 July 1917, no. 144764, FO 371/3120.
124 McAdoo, *Crowded Years*, p. 400.
125 Diary, vol. 11: 7 July 1917, House Papers.
126 Diary, vol. 11: 2 July 1917, House Papers.
127 *ibid.* Wiseman to Northcliffe, 3 July 1917, 90/22, Wiseman Papers.
128 Diary, vol. 11: 16 July 1917, House Papers.
129 17 July 1917, no. 141698, FO 371/3115.
130 McAdoo to House, 14 July 1917, Box 73, House Papers, for example. Wiseman to House, 24 Aug. 1917, 90/4, Wiseman Papers.
131 Stamfordham to Chancellor, 22 Aug. 1917, ff. 56–8, T. 172/434.
132 Chancellor to Stamfordham, 23 Aug. 1917, ff. 59–59a, T. 172/434.
133 Quoted in Montgomery Hyde, *Lord Reading*, p. 214. For the Marconi Scandal see Frances Donaldson, *The Marconi Scandal* (London: Hart-Davis, 1962).
134 Wiseman to Northcliffe, 16 Aug. 1917, 90/27, Wiseman Papers. Montgomery Hyde, *Lord Reading*, p. 214.
135 Montgomery Hyde, *Lord Reading*, p. 214.
136 Northcliffe to Chancellor, 21 Aug. 1917 and Northcliffe to Balfour, 23 July 1917, both 90/26, Wiseman Papers. Northcliffe to Lloyd George and Chancellor, 13 Aug. 1917, F/41/7/12, Lloyd George Papers.
137 Chancellor to Stamfordham, 23 Aug. 1917, ff. 59–59a, T. 172/434.
138 Wiseman to House, 24 Aug. 1917, 90/4, Wiseman Papers. FO to Northcliffe, 30 Aug. 1917, f. 262, FO 800/209. Diary, vol. 11: 2 Sept. 1917, House Papers.
139 House to Wilson, 27 June 1917, 2/89, Wilson Papers.
140 Spring Rice to Drummond, 9 July 1917, f. 21, FO 800/209.
141 Northcliffe circular letter to his family, 12 Aug. 1917, File 1917, Northcliffe Papers (*Times*).
142 Northcliffe to Rothermere, 7 Sept. 1917 and Phillips to Northcliffe, 21 Sept. 1917, both 91/91, Wiseman Papers. Wiseman to Drummond, 21 Sept. 1917, f. 269, FO 800/209.
143 91/92, Wiseman Papers.
144 Northcliffe to Lloyd George, 14 Oct. 1917 and Phillips to Northcliffe, 18 Oct. 1917, both 91/92, Wiseman Papers. War Cab. 251, 17 Oct. 1917, Cab. 23/4.
145 Northcliffe to Balfour, 24 Nov. 1917, ff. 68–71, FO 800/209. Diary, vol. 12: 6 Dec. 1917, House Papers. Pound and Harmsworth, *Northcliffe*, pp. 607, 609–10.
146 Sir Campbell Stuart, *Opportunity Knocks Once* (London: Collins, 1952), p. 64. Pound and Harmsworth, *Northcliffe*, p. 613. Sanders and Taylor, *British Propaganda*, pp. 89–93.

Chapter 8: The Reading Missions

1 Montgomery Hyde, *Reading*, p. 209.

2 War Cab. 222, 22 Aug. 1917, Cab. 23/3.

3 24 Aug. 1917, ff. 49–50, T. 172/434.

4 Northcliffe to Chancellor, 20 Aug. 1917, f. 47, T. 172/434.

5 Chancellor to Northcliffe, 24 Aug. 1917, f. 51, T. 172/434.

6 Northcliffe to Chancellor, 90/26, Wiseman Papers.

7 Cecil to House, 25 Aug. 1917, 90/27, Wiseman Papers. Diary, vol. 11: 25 Aug. 1917, House Papers. Diary, 25 Aug. 1917, 55/72, Auchincloss Papers. Charles Seymour (ed.), *The Intimate Papers of Colonel House*, 4 vols (Boston, Mass.: Houghton Mifflin, 1926), iii. 124–5, for a copy of the letter.

8 Chancellor to Lloyd George, 24 Aug. 1917, ff. 49–50, T. 172/434.

9 29 Aug. 1917, ff. 142–6, Addit. MSS. 49738.

10 War Cab. 225, 28 Aug. 1917, Cab. 23/3.

11 FO to Spring Rice, 2 Sept. 1917, no. 172576, FO 371/3123.

12 Northcliffe to Lloyd George and Balfour, 30 Aug. 1917, F/41/7/17, Lloyd George Papers.

13 Montgomery Hyde, *Reading*, p. 209.

14 Lord Hankey, *The Supreme Command*, 2 vols (London: Allen & Unwin, 1961), ii. 694.

15 Reading to Chancellor, 14 Sept. 1917, f. 99 and Chancellor to Reading, 16 Sept. 1917, f. 98, both T. 172/433.

16 Northcliffe to Dawson, 25 Sept. 1917, File 1917, Northcliffe Papers (*Times*).

17 Diary, vol. 11: 20 Sept. 1917, House Papers. Spring Rice to FO, 20 Sept. 1917, no. 183872, FO 371/3123. Spring Rice to Balfour, 21 Sept. 1917, ff. 458–63, FO 800/242. Willert, *Road to Safety*, p. 120.

18 22 Oct. 1917, ff. 127–8, T. 172/446.

19 Spring Rice to FO, 17 Sept. 1917, no. 182771, FO 371/3123.

20 Wiseman to Drummond, 4 Oct. 1917, ff. 283–5, FO 800/209.

21 *ibid.*

22 Diary, vol. 11, House Papers.

23 War Cab. 234, 17 Sept. 1917, Cab. 21/123.

24 Willert, *Road to Safety*, pp. 120–3.

25 File 30, Box 221, US Treas.

26 Lever to Chancellor, 6 Sept. 1917, f. 94, T. 172/435.

27 7 Sept. 1917, ff. 80–1, T. 172/435.

28 11 Sept. 1917, f. 59, T. 172/435. Britain had no more funds to spare for Canada, and Canadian liquidity problems precluded their increasing aid to Britain. Both countries therefore saw American funds for wheat (and for anything else) as vital. By 1918, in fact, Canada absolutely required British or American funds to cover its trade deficit with the USA. See Michael Bliss, *A Canadian Millionaire: The Life and Times of Sir Joseph Flavelle, Bart. 1858–1938* (Toronto: Macmillan of Canada, 1978), pp. 363–72.

29 Lever to Chancellor, 13 Sept. 1917, f. 47, T. 172/435.

30 Reading, *Reading*, ii. 63.

31 Reading to McAdoo, 18 Sept. 1917, File 30, Box 221, US Treas.

32 Crosby to Reading, 27 Sept. 1917 and Crosby to President, 24 Oct. 1917, both File GB 132.1, Box 117, US Treas.

33 28 Sept. 1917, f. 25, T. 172/433.

34 US Senate, *Munitions Industry*, vi. 164–6.

35 *ibid.*, vi. 164.

36 Crosby to President, 24 Oct. 1917, File GB 132.1, Box 117, US Treas.

37 F. 118/114, Reading Papers.

38 Reading to Chancellor, 8 Oct. 1917, ff. 105–6, T. 172/437.

39 Reading to Chancellor, 12 Oct. 1917, ff. 91–3, T. 172/437. Crosby to Reading,

17 Oct. 1917; Reading to Crosby, 23 Oct. 1917; Hoover to Crosby, 11 Oct. 1917; and Reading to Crosby, 25 Oct. 1917, all File 30, Box 221, US Treas.

40 ff. 75–6, T. 172/433.
41 Chancellor to Reading, 22 Sept. 1917, f. 61. T. 172/433.
42 Reading to Chancellor, 2 Oct. 1917, f. 139, T. 172/437.
43 Chancellor to Reading, 2 Oct. 1917, f. 143, T. 172/437.
44 McAdoo, *Crowded Years*, p. 396.
45 Reading to Chancellor, 14 Sept. 1917, f. 96, T. 172/433.
46 Chancellor to Reading, 17 Sept. 1917, ff. 88–9, T. 172/433. French Ambassador to FO, 26 Sept. 1917, no. 187062, FO 371/3123. Campbell to Swinton, 30 Sept. 1917, F. 118/114, Reading Papers.
47 Chancellor to Lever, 1 Sept. 1917, f. 135 and Lever to Chancellor, 13 Sept. 1917, f. 47, both T. 172/435.
48 F. 118/114, Reading Papers.
49 *ibid.*
50 House to Wiseman, 25 Aug. 1917, 90/26, Wiseman Papers.
51 Reading to Chancellor, 22 Sept. 1917, ff. 57–8, T. 172/433.
52 Reading to Chancellor, 17 Oct. 1917, ff. 69–73, T. 172/437. State Dept, *Foreign Relations, 1917*, Supplement 2: pp. 578–9. Chancellor to Reading, 1 Nov. 1917, ff. 7–9, T. 172/437, for partial list of such loans.
53 ff. 69–73, T. 172/437.
54 Reading to Chancellor, 21 Oct. 1917, ff. 61–2, T. 172/437.
55 Crosby to Reading, 17 Oct. 1917, File 30, Box 221, US Treas. Reading to Chancellor, 21 Oct. 1917, ff. 61–2, T. 172/437. Reading to Prime Minister, War Cabinet and Balfour, 27 Oct. 1917; Reading to Chancellor, 27 Oct. 1917; and Reading to McAdoo, 28 Oct. 1917, all F. 118/114, Reading Papers.
56 Reading to Chancellor, 27 Oct. 1917 and Reading to Prime Minister, War Cabinet and Balfour, 27 Oct. 1917, both F. 118/114, Reading Papers.
57 Lloyd George, *War Memoirs*, ii. 1405–18. David F. Trask, *The United States in the Supreme War Council* (Middletown, Conn.: Wesleyan University Press, 1961), pp. 13–15.
58 Lord Hankey, *Supreme Command*, ii. 694.
59 *ibid.*, ii. 695–6.
60 F/60/1/1, Lloyd George Papers.
61 Lord Hankey, *Supreme Command*, ii. 696.
62 Reading to Prime Minister, 21 Sept. 1917, F. 118/114, Reading Papers.
63 Fowler, *Wiseman*, pp. 71–90. House to Wilson, 18 Sept. 1917, 2/91, Wilson Papers.
64 Wiseman to Reading, 26 Sept. 1917, 91/107, Wiseman Papers.
65 Reading to Wiseman, 27 Sept. 1917, 91/107, Wiseman Papers.
66 Fowler, *Wiseman*, pp. 71–90. Reading to Prime Minister, 11 Oct., 12 Oct. 1917; and Reading to War Cabinet, Balfour and Chancellor, 12 Oct. 1917, all F. 118/114, Reading Papers. Diary, vol. 12: 12 Oct. 1917, House Papers.
67 Diary, vol. 11: 22 Sept. 1917, House Papers.
68 Reading to Prime Minister, War Cabinet and Balfour, 18 Oct. 1917, F. 118/114, Reading Papers. Seymour, *House*, iii. 207–8. Barclay to FO, 7 Nov. 1917, f. 118, T. 172/438.
69 Diary, vol. 12: 18 Oct. 1917, House Papers.
70 Balfour to Reading, ?26 Oct. 1917, f. 328, FO 800/209.
71 War Cab. 234, Cab. 21/123.
72 Diary, vol. 11: 22 Sept. 1917, House Papers.
73 War Cab. 234, 17 Sept. 1917, Cab. 21/123. Blackett to Fernau, 12 Oct. 1917, f. 147 and Lever to Chancellor, 3 Oct. 1917, ff. 104–5, both T. 172/446.

74 J. M. Keynes, 22 Oct. 1917, ff. 127−8, T. 172/446.
75 Diary, vol. 11: 22 Sept. 1917; vol. 12: 9 Nov., 10 Nov., 4 Dec. 1917, House Papers.
76 Fowler, *Wiseman,* pp. 67−8.
77 n.d., F. 118/113, Reading Papers.
78 Fowler, *Wiseman,* p. 125.
79 Wiseman to Reading, ?27 Jan. 1918, f. 61, FO 800/223.
80 War Cab. 334, Cab. 23/5.
81 Barclay to FO, 9 Feb. 1918, f. 132, T. 172/449.
82 Montgomery Hyde, *Reading,* p. 242. Reading, *Reading,* ii. 74.
83 Wiseman to Drummond, 14 March 1918, ff. 56−60, Addit. MSS. 49741 (Balfour Papers), British Library.
84 *ibid.* Swinton, *Over my Shoulder,* pp. 177−210.
85 Wiseman to Drummond, 25 Jan. 1918, ff. 313−15, FO 800/223.
86 Reading, *Reading,* ii. 68, 75.
87 *ibid.,* p. 75.
88 ff. 56−60, Addit. MSS. 49741.
89 Caird to Northcliffe, 25 Feb. 1918, vol. 36, Deposit no. 4890 (Northcliffe Papers), British Library.
90 Tracy to Northcliffe, 29 May 1918, vol. 12, Northcliffe Papers (BL), for example.
91 Wiseman to Drummond, 14 March 1918, ff. 56−60, Addit. MSS. 49741.
92 Wiseman to Drummond, 19 July 1918, ff. 100−1, Addit. MSS. 49741.
93 Reading, *Reading,* ii. 78.
94 Rhondda to Lloyd George, 4 Dec. 1917, F/43/5/44, Lloyd George Papers.
95 Chancellor of Exchequer, 'Priority of finance for Food Controller's programme in U.S.', 9 Jan. 1918, MAF 60/56. War Cab. 323, 16 Jan. 1918, Cab. 21/123.
96 Aaron A. Godfrey, *Government Operation of the Railroads 1918−1920* (Austin, Tex.: San Felipe Press, 1974), pp. 32−44, 53−6, 68−70. Reading, *Reading,* ii. 80.
97 Reading, *Reading,* ii. 78−84. Wiseman to Drummond, 14 March 1918, ff. 56−60, Addit. MSS. 49741.
98 Diary, vol. 13: 17 June 1918, House Papers. Copy of notes by Reading of conversation with Col. House, 21 June 1918, F. 118/117, Reading Papers.
99 War Cab. 251, 17 Oct. 1917, Cab. 23/4. Reading to Drummond, 31 Jan. 1918, no. 21394; Reading to Drummond, Personal, 15 Feb. 1918, no. 30516; and FO to Reading, 21 Feb. 1918, no. 30516, all FO 371/3427. State Dept, *Foreign Relations, 1918,* Supplement 1: pp. 501−2.
100 Reading to Churchill, 27 May 1918, ff. 386−8, FO 800/223.
101 *ibid.* Min. of Mun. to FO to Embassy, 31 July 1918, no. 131961, FO 371/3489.
102 Reading to Churchill, 27 May 1918, ff. 386−8, FO 800/223.
103 Reading to Prime Minister, 29 Sept. 1918 and Reading to Prime Minister, War Cab. and Balfour, 27 Oct. 1917, both F. 118/114, Reading Papers.
104 Cuff, *War Industries Board,* p. 196.
105 Printed in *ibid.*
106 Cuff, *War Industries Board,* pp. 196−8.
107 Reading to Balfour and Cecil, 14 June 1918, ff. 398−9, FO 800/223. Willert to Dawson, 24 July 1918, File 1917−18, Willert Papers (*Times*). Wiseman to Reading, 5 Sept. 1918, ff. 78−9, FO 800/225.
108 no. 52200, FO 371/3488.
109 Reading to Derby, Personal, 25 March 1918, no. 55292, FO 371/3488.
110 Reading to Derby, f. 510, FO 800/209. Derby to Reading, 9 April 1918, no. 62264, FO 371/3488.
111 Bridges, *Alarms and Excursions,* p. 200. Bridges was also the compiler of *Word from England: An Anthology of Prose and Poetry Compiled for the King's Forces*

(London: English Universities Press, 1940), 248 pp., a volume of an inspirational nature. There were sections on, for example, Times and Seasons, Living in the Country, Music and Mystery, as well as on Battle, Courage and Death. No room, unfortunately, could be found for anything by Wilfred Owen.

112   Derby to Reading, 5 April 1918, no. 60987 and Min. of Mun. to Headlam, 19 April 1918, no. 69943, both FO 371/3488.
113   Diary, vol. 13: 19 April 1918, House Papers. Derby to Reading, 9 April 1918, no. 63901, FO 371/3488. Bridges, *Alarms and Excursions*, p. 202.
114   Printed in Murray, *Master and Brother*, pp. 142–4.
115   Bridges, *Alarms and Excursions*, p. 203.
116   Diary, vol. 13: 24 April 1918, House Papers.
117   Bridges, *Alarms and Excursions*, pp. 204–14. Diary, vol. 13: 12 June 1918, House Papers. Fowler, *Wiseman*, pp. 164–97.
118   Barclay to Reading, 17 Sept. 1918, f. 457, FO 800/223. Palmer, *Baker*, ii. 319–21.
119   Bridges, *Alarms and Excursions*, pp. 210–11. Barclay to FO, 27 Sept. 1918, no. 164084, FO 371/3488.
120   Wiseman to Drummond, 25 Jan. 1918, ff. 9–13, Addit. MSS. 49741.
121   Diary, vol. 13: 9 May, 20 June 1918, House Papers.
122   Diary, vol. 13: 20 June, 21 June 1918, House Papers.
123   Wiseman to Murray, 4 July 1918, 91/85, Wiseman Papers.
124   *ibid.*
125   Wiseman to Murray, 4 July 1918, 91/85, Wiseman Papers.
126   19 July 1918, ff. 100–1, Addit. MSS. 49741.
127   Montgomery Hyde, *Reading*, pp. 293, 295–6, 299, 311. Reading to Geddes, 5 Sept. 1918, f. 122, FO 800/225,
128   Babington Smith to Reading, 4 Dec. 1918, ff. 487–90, FO 800/223.
129   Cuff, *War Industries Board*, pp. 259–60.
130   Babington Smith to Reading, 21 Jan. 1919, f. 497, FO 800/223. File GB 132.3, Box 116, US Treas.
131   W. G. Lyddon, *British War Missions to the U.S., 1914–1918* (London: Oxford University Press, 1938).

Chapter 9: Financial Relations, 1917–1918

1   Chancellor to Lever, 12 June 1917, no. 117527 and Lever to Chancellor, 15 June 1917, no. 119400, both FO 371/3114. Chancellor to Lever, 19 June 1917, no. 122444 and Lever to Chancellor, 21 June 1917, no. 123375, both FO 371/3115. Bagley to Drummond, 11 July 1917, f. 3, T. 172/426.
2   Lever's Diary, 13 June 1917, ff. 138–9, T. 172/429. Lever to Chancellor, 13 June 1917, no. 118515, FO 371/3114.
3   Lever's Diary, 14 June 1917, ff. 139–40, T. 172/429.
4   *ibid.* Crosby was often nervous. Morgan wrote to Lamont when the latter was in London with Crosby in November that 'I judge...Crosby considerably more frightened than anyone else in the Treasury Department...what he needs is a footwarmer.' 22 Nov. 1917, no. 55811, F. 16, Box Hist. 2, Morgan Grenfell Papers.
5   Charles Gilbert, *American Financing of World War I* (Westport, Conn.: Greenwood, 1970), pp. 122–3.
6   Lever's Diary, 14 June 1917, ff. 139–40, T. 172/429.
7   Lever to Chancellor, 16 June 1917, no. 120057 and Lever to Chancellor, 16 June 1917, no. 120056, both FO 371/3114. Quotation from no. 120056.
8   Chancellor to Lever, 21 June 1917, no. 123871, FO 371/3115.
9   Lever's Diary, 16 June 1917, ff. 141–2 and 14 June 1917, ff. 139–40, both T. 172/429.

10 Northcliffe to Lloyd George, 20 June 1917, File 1917, Northcliffe Papers (*Times*).
11 Northcliffe and Lever to Chancellor, 22 June 1917, no. 123825, FO 371/3115. Lever's Diary, 18 June 1917, ff. 142–4 and 20 June 1917, f. 146, both T. 172/429. Lever to Chancellor, 19 June 1917, no. 122119, FO 371/3114.
12 Northcliffe and Lever to Chancellor, 22 June 1917, no. 123825, FO 371/3115.
13 Lever to Chancellor, 26 June 1917, no. 126704 and 27 June 1917, no. 127554, both FO 371/3115. Crosby to President, 26 June 1917, 2/89, Wilson Papers.
14 Crawford to FO, 26 June 1917, no. 126709, FO 371/3115.
15 *ibid.*
16 Lever's Diary, 25 June 1917, ff. 147–8, T. 172/429. Crawford to FO, 26 June 1917, no. 126709, FO 371/3115.
17 no. 127554, FO 371/3115.
18 27 June 1917, no. 127324, FO 371/3120.
19 Crawford to FO, 27 June 1917, no. 128545, FO 371/3115.
20 State Dept, *Foreign Relations, 1917,* Supplement 2: pp. 532–3.
21 Balfour to Wiseman for House, 28 June 1917, f. 174, FO 800/209.
22 Diary, vol. 11: 29 June 1917, House Papers.
23 State Dept, *Foreign Relations, 1917,* Supplement 2: pp. 533–5.
24 Northcliffe to Balfour and Davies, 29 June 1917, ff. 9, 13, FO 800/209. Diary, 29 June 1917: Box 65, Lansing Papers. Lever to Chancellor, 30 June 1917, no. 129885, FO 371/3115.
25 Crawford to FO, 3 July 1917, no. 132675, FO 371/3115.
26 Spring Rice to FO, 3 July 1917, Cab. 21/123.
27 Lever's Diary, 5 July 1917, ff. 153–4, T. 172/429.
28 State Dept, *Foreign Relations, 1917,* Supplement 2: p. 536. Northcliffe to McAdoo, 7 July 1917, File GB 132/17-3, Box 119, US Treas.
29 State Dept, *Foreign Relations, 1917,* Supplement 2: pp. 543–5.
30 Lever's Diary, 17 July 1917, f. 2, T. 172/430. Willert to Robinson, 17 July 1917, File 1917–18, Willert Papers (*Times*).
31 Chancellor to Page, 23 July 1917, no. 144764, FO 371/3120.
32 Northcliffe to Chancellor, 26 July 1917, no. 148490, FO 371/3115. McAdoo to President, 26 Aug. 1917, 4/194, Wilson Papers. 33, Lever's Diary, 20 July 1917, f. 4, T. 172/430. Treasury to Cabinet Secretariat, 7 July 1917, Cab. 21/123. Chancellor to Page, 23 July 1917, no. 144764, FO 371/3120.
34 Keynes to Chalmers to Chancellor, prob. 28 July 1917, ff. 61–2, T. 172/443. For further implications of this crisis see Kathleen Burk, 'J. M. Keynes and the Exchange Rate Crisis of July 1917', *Economic History Review,* 2nd ser., vol. XXXII, no. 3 (August 1979), pp. 405–16.
35 Minute by Chalmers to Chancellor, 28 July 1917, f. 62, T. 172/443.
36 War Cab. 199, 30 July 1917, Cab. 23/3. Lloyd George to Northcliffe, 30 July 1917, no. 151220 and Spring Rice to FO, 31 July 1917, no. 150755, both FO 371/3116.
37 Chancellor to McAdoo and Northcliffe, 30 July 1917, no. 150751, FO 371/3115.
38 Spring Rice to FO, 31 July 1917, no. 150755, FO 371/3116.
39 Balfour to Spring Rice, 2 Aug. 1917, no. 152541, FO 371/3116.
40 Spring Rice to Balfour, 3 Aug. 1917, ff. 413–20, FO 800/242.
41 Northcliffe to FO, 3 Aug. 1917, no. 153044, FO 371/3116.
42 Spring Rice to FO, 4 Aug. 1917, no. 153791, FO 371/3116.
43 McAdoo to Page for Chancellor, 16 Aug. 1917, no. 161482, FO 371/3121.
44 Crosby to Lansing, 28 June 1917, GB 132/17-3, Box 119, US Treas.
45 Lever's Diary, 28 June 1917, ff. 151–2, T. 172/429.
46 Crawford to FO, 4 July 1917, no. 132717, FO 371/3115. *Foreign Relations, 1917,* Supplement 2: pp. 539–43. Grenfell wrote to the New York partners on 4 July 1917: 'Have seen Balfour, who is not at all clear in reference to the arrangements for repayment as his attention was not fixed on financial matters. Cunliffe

distinctly understood from McAdoo that you were to be repaid $400m or thereabouts out of the first proceeds of the Liberty Loan. He cannot be sure that any mention was actually made of the date 2nd July. He believes Crosby was present. He pressed to have the arrangement put in writing, but he did not obtain written confirmation. . . .' no. 38709, F. 16, Box Hist. 2, Morgan Grenfell Papers.

47 Lever's Diary, 29 June 1917, f. 152, T. 172/429. J.P.M. & Co. to E.C.G., 30 June 1917, no. 47339, and J.P.M. & Co. to M.G. & Co., copies for Chancellor, Governor and Deputy-Governor of the Bank of England, 3 July 1917, no. 47404, both F. 16, Box Hist. 2, Morgan Grenfell Papers. Chancellor to Northcliffe, 3 July 1917, no. 132300, FO 371/3115.

48 'Memorandum of conference held in Crosby's office', 5 July 1917, File GB 132-4, Box 116, US Treasury.

49 Northcliffe to Chancellor, 5 July 1917, 91/91, Wiseman Papers.

50 For Lamont's discussion with McAdoo see New York partners to Grenfell, 3 Aug. 1917, no. 49272, F.16, Box Hist. 2, Morgan Grenfell Papers. Lever to Chancellor, 1 Aug. 1917, no. 152320, FO 371/3116. Blackett's Diary, 31 July 1917, f. 23; Lever's Diary, 1 Aug. 1917, f. 23; Blackett's Diary, 10 Aug. 1917, f. 26; and Blackett's Diary, 22 Aug. 1917, f. 30, all T. 172/430. Lever to Chancellor, 15 Aug. 1917, no. 160989, FO 371/3116. J. P. Morgan to McAdoo, 16 Aug. 1917 and McAdoo to Morgan, 20 Aug. 1917, both Box 185, McAdoo Papers. McAdoo agreed to $150m. of British government ninety-day Treasury bills. Morgan to Grenfell, 17 Aug. 1917, no. 49662, F. 16, Box Hist. 2, Morgan Grenfell Papers.

51 Diary, vol. 11: 25 Aug., 31 Aug. 1917, House Papers. House to Wiseman, 25 Aug. 1917, 90/26, Wiseman Papers. Chancellor to Northcliffe, 28 Aug. 1917, f. 41, T. 172/434. Spring Rice to Balfour, 1 Sept. 1917, f. 193, Addit. MSS. 49740.

52 Reading to McAdoo, 1 Nov. 1917, File GB 132/17-10, Box 119, US Treas.

53 no. 44975, F. 17, Box Hist. 3, Morgan Grenfell Papers. Crosby himself reminded McAdoo of his promise to Lamont. Crosby to McAdoo, 21 Nov. 1917, File GB 132/14-10, Box 119, US Treas.

54 State Dept, *Foreign Relations, 1917*, Supplement 2: pp. 579–80. Crosby to McAdoo, 21 Nov. 1917, File GB 132/14-10, Box 119, US Treas.

55 21 Nov. 1917, File GB 132/17-10, Box 119, US Treas.

56 Chancellor to Lever for McAdoo, 28 Jan. 1918, ff. 17–18, T. 172/448. Chancellor to Reading, 8 May 1918, ff. 11–14, T. 172/445.

57 State Dept, *Foreign Relations, 1917*, Supplement 2: p. 587.

58 *ibid.*, pp. 589–90.

59 F. 52, T. 172/439.

60 State Dept, *Foreign Relations, 1917*, Supplement 2: pp. 590–2. Lever to Chancellor, 11 Jan. 1918, ff. 19–21, T. 172/444. Lever to Chancellor, 19 Jan. 1918, ff. 58–60 and Chancellor to Lever, 23 Jan. 1918, f. 42, both T. 172/448.

61 McAdoo to Crosby, 23 Jan. 1918, 89/91, Polk Papers.

62 Wiseman to Reading, ?27 Jan. 1918, f. 61, FO 800/223. The Treasury Department the last week of January must have been thick with the smoke of battle. On 21 January 1918 Lamont could write to Grenfell that 'Fortunately relations between . . . Lever and Federal Treasury are on such a basis that all such questions can be handled – we are convinced – without difficulty as they may arise.' no. 61200. Only seven days later he was writing that 'I fear that his [Lever's] attitude in this matter of handling the securities to be released may be somewhat rigid and that he is failing to urge upon the Chancellor a policy of being extremely broad in its attitude to Federal Treasury on this point . . . the Federal treasury officials are beginning to feel hurt and are likely to wind up the whole negotiation and abandon the theory of trying to pay off the Call Loan'. Lamont to Grenfell, 28 Jan. 1918, no. 61473, both F. 17, Box Hist 3, Morgan Grenfell Papers.

63 Lever to Chancellor, 19 Jan. 1918, ff. 58–60, T. 172/448.
64 ff. 25–6, T. 172/448.
65 Lever to Chancellor, 27 Jan. 1918, ff. 23–4 and Chancellor to Lever for McAdoo, 28 Jan. 1918, ff. 17–18, both T. 172/448.
66 Diary, vol. 13: 29 Jan. 1918, House Papers.
67 McAdoo to the Chancellor, 29 Jan. 1918, File GB 132.5/17-11, Box 115, US Treas.
68 Lever to Chancellor, f. 200, T. 172/449.
69 f. 212, T. 172/449, copy for Reading.
70 Lever to Chalmers, 31 Jan. 1918, f. 197, T. 172/449.
71 *ibid.*
72 no. 22506, FO 371/3489.
73 Chancellor to Lever, 6 Feb. 1918, f. 160, T. 172/449.
74 Reading, *Reading*, ii. 130.
75 *ibid.*
76 Quoted in Chancellor to Reading, 16 Feb. 1918, ff. 92–3, T. 172/449.
77 Chancellor to Reading, 8 May 1918, ff. 11–14, T. 172/445.
78 *ibid.*
79 McAdoo to Chancellor, 5 Feb. 1918, no. 22506, FO 371/3489.
80 Chancellor to Reading, 16 Feb. 1918, ff. 92–3, T. 172/449.
81 McAdoo to President, 6 March 1918, File GB 132.1, Box 117, US Treas.
82 ff. 24–6, T. 172/445.
83 *ibid.*
84 Chancellor to Reading, f. 22, T. 172/445.
85 29 April 1918, ff. 20–1, T. 172/445.
86 Johnson (ed.), *Keynes*, xvi. 287.
87 Minute on Reading to Chancellor, 29 April 1918, ff. 20–1, T. 172/445.
88 *ibid.*
89 3 May 1918, f. 8, T. 172/444.
90 Chancellor to Reading, 8 May 1918, ff. 11–14, T. 172/445.
91 *ibid.* Reading to Chancellor, 3 July 1918, ff. 39–40, T. 172/446.
92 Johnson (ed.), *Keynes*, xvi. 286.
93 A. Rathbone, 'Memorandum of conversation with Mr Blackett February 23', 23 Feb. 1918, File GB 132/17-10, Box 119, US Treas. G. O. May, 'Memorandum re: cereals', 7 March 1918; Crosby to Hoover, 22 June 1918; McAdoo to Reading, 12 Aug. 1918; Lever to McAdoo, 10 Sept. 1918; and Rathbone to Crosby, 24 Oct. 1918, all File 30, Box 221, US Treas.
94 Leffingwell to McAdoo, 10 June 1918, File GB 132.5/17-11, Box 115, US Treas.
95 J. P. Morgan to Reading, 16 July 1918, copy to American Treasury, and McAdoo to the President, 26 Aug. 1918, both File GB 132.5/17-11, Box 115, US Treas. Reading to McAdoo, 29 July 1918, f. 427, FO 800/223.
96 Lamont to Morgan, no. 44683, F. 16, Box Hist. 2, Morgan Grenfell Papers.
97 Lamont to Morgan, no. 46687, F. 17, Box Hist. 3, Morgan Grenfell Papers.
98 See the handwritten letter from McAdoo to the President, 27 Jan. 1918, as quoted in Forbes, *Stettinius*, pp. 71–2.
99 Forbes, *Stettinius*, pp. 71–3.
100 Cravath to Lamont, 22 May 1918, no. 56556, F. 18, Box Hist. 3, Morgan Grenfell Papers, for example.
101 Seth P. Tillman, *Anglo-American Relations at the Paris Peace Conference of 1919* (Princeton, NJ: Princeton University Press, 1961), p. 233.
102 Diary, vol. 13: 28 Feb. 1918, House Papers.
103 File GB 132.3, Box 116, US Treas.
104 Rathbone to McAdoo, 18 Oct. 1918, File GB 132.3, Box 116, US Treas.

105   Lever to Chancellor, 24 Nov. 1918, ff. 70–2, T. 172/447.
106   Lever to Chancellor, 27 Nov. 1918, ff. 61–9, T. 172/447.
107   J.P.M. & Co. to Grenfell, 27 Nov. 1918, no. 81973, F.19, Box Hist. 3, Morgan Grenfell Papers.
108   US Senate, *Munitions Industry*, viii. 177.
109   Montgomery Hyde, *Reading*, p. 311. File GB 132.3, Box 116, US Treas.

Epilogue: Did History Come to a Full Stop?

  1   W. C. Sellar and R. J. Yeatman, *1066 and All That* (London: Methuen, 1930), p. 115.
  2   Melvyn P. Leffler, *The Elusive Quest: America's Pursuit of European Stability and French Security, 1919–1933* (Chapel Hill, NC: University of North Carolina Press, 1979), p. 81.
  3   Stephen V. O. Clarke, *Central Bank Cooperation, 1924–31* (New York: Federal Reserve Bank of New York, 1967) and Kathleen Burk, 'Diplomacy and the private banker: the case of the House of Morgan', in Gustav Schmidt (ed.), *Konstellationen internationaler Politik – politische und wirtschaftliche Faktoren in den Beziehungen zwischen Westeuropa und den USA, 1924–1932* (Bochum: Studienverlag Dr. N. Brockmeyer, 1983), pp. 25–40.

Appendix I

London Exchange Rate on New York – End of Month – US$ to £

	Jan.	Feb.	Mar.	April	May	June	July	Aug.	Sept.	Oct.	Nov.	Dec.
1915	4.85³/₄	4.81¹/₄	4.80¹/₂	4.80	4.79¹/₂	4.77³/₈	4.77¹/₄	4.61	4.72	4.66¹/₂	4.71	4.75
1916	4.77³/₈	4.77³/₈	4.77¹/₄	4.77	4.76⁵/₈	4.76⁵/₈	4.76³/₄	4.76⁹/₁₆	4.76¹/₂	4.76¹/₂	4.76³/₈	4.76⁷/₁₆
1917	4.76⁷/₁₆	4.76⁷/₁₆	4.76⁷/₁₆	4.76⁷/₁₆	4.76⁷/₁₆	4.76⁷/₁₆	4.76¹/₂	4.76⁷/₁₆	4.76⁷/₁₆	4.76⁷/₁₆	4.76⁷/₁₆	4.76⁷/₁₆
1918	4.76⁷/₁₆	4.76⁷/₁₆	4.76⁷/₁₆	4.76⁷/₁₆	4.76⁷/₁₆	4.76⁷/₁₆	4.76¹/₂	4.76⁵/₈	4.76⁹/₁₆	4.76⁵/₈	4.76⁷/₁₆	4.76⁹/₁₅

Source: Morgan, British Financial Policy, pp. 307–9. Morgan notes pp. 345–8.

Appendix II

British War Loans Publicly Issued in the United States

Nature of loan	Amount ($)	Issued	Rate %	Issue price	Matured
Anglo-French Loan	250m.	10.15	5	98	15.10.20
2-Year Collateral Notes	250m.	9.16	5	99	1. 9.18
3-Year Collateral Notes	150m.	10.16	5½	99¼	1.11.19
5-Year Collateral Notes	150m.	10.16	5½	98½	1.11.21
1-Year Collateral Notes	100m.	1.17	5½	99½	1. 2.18
2-Year Collateral Notes	150m.	1.17	5½	99	1. 2.19
3-Year Collateral Notes[1]	250m.	11.19	5½	98	3.11.22
10-Year Collateral Notes[1]			5½	96¼	1.11.29

Total—$1,300,000,000

Note: 1   Refunding loan.

Appendix III

British Debt in the United States, Financial Years 1915–16 to 1919–20

Description of Loan	Amounts outstanding at end of financial years (£m.)				
	1915–16	*1916–17*	*1917–18*	*1918–19*	*1919–20*
Anglo-French loan	51.4[1]	51.4	51.4	51.4	51.4
American government			513.7	840.8	865.7
collateral notes[2]		143.2	122.3	53.3	47.4
20-year bonds			0.2	29.5	29.5
$ Treasury bills:					
Dutch Petroleum Co.		2.9	2.9	2.9	
Rifles, etc., notes		8.3	14.6	6.7	
Morgan Demand Loan[3]		73.0	26.5	14.9	
$ Treasury bills			18.3	19.2	9.3
Central Argentine RR		3.1	3.1	3.1	3.1
Danish government $ loan			3.3	5.5	
10-year bonds					30.5
English Sewing Cotton Co.[4]		1.0	1.0		
London Exchange Committee loan[5]	10.3	10.3			
Maitland Coppell		0.8			
DuPont		9.6			
Total	61.7	303.6	757.3	1,027.3	1,036.9
Total in USA plus Canada, Japan, Holland, Norway and 9 others:	70.9	473.3	1,048.7	1,364.8	1,278.7

Notes:
1 British share of the £100m., at par (£51,370,000).
2 Total amount of issues 1915–17 = $800m., but only $697m. outstanding on 31 March 1917, probably because issues were undersubscribed.
3 Overdraft of Treasury and London Exchange Committee with Morgan's. Began modestly in May 1916 but amounted to $398.5m. in May 1917.
4 In December 1916 the company borrowed $4,900,000 from Morgan's and re-lent it to the British government against collateral of £1m. of Treasury bills.
5 In June 1915 the London Exchange Committee raised a loan of $50m., this was taken over by the British government and was repaid in June 1917 by the export of gold.

Source: Morgan, *British Financial Policy*, pp. 320–35.

Appendix IV

Expenditure in the United States of Dollars Loaned to the British Government by the American Government

Cash advanced	$4,277,000,000.00
Less refunds and repayments	80,181,641.56
Net	4,196,818,358.44
Expenditures:	
Munitions and remounts	$1,330,607,883.09
Munitions for other governments	205,495,801.10
Exchange and cotton	1,682,419,875.31
Cereals	1,375,379,343.57
Other foods	1,169,153,585.05
Tobacco	99,174,858.34
Other supplies	215,331,787.01
Shipping	48,890,000.00
Reimbursements	19,302,357.55
Interest	387,732,633.50
Maturities	353,501,561.66
Relief	16,000,000.00
Silver	261,643,388.81
Food for Northern Russia	7,029,965.94
Miscellaneous	47,745,629.01
Total reported expenditure	7,219,408,669.94
Less:	
Reimbursement from American credits to other governments	1,853,612,246.37
American government payments for pounds	449,496,227.55
Proceeds of rupee credits and gold from India	81,352.908.06
Total deductions	2,384,461,381.98
Net expenditures	$4,834,947,287.96

Source: Secretary of the Treasury, *Annual Report* (Washington, DC: US Government Printing Office, 1920).

Appendix V

Summary of British Imports from and Exports to the United States

Summary of cost of imports from the USA (£m.)

1911–13	*1914*	*1915*	*1916*	*1917*	*1918*	*1919*	*1920*	*1921*
133.0	138.6	237.8	291.8	376.3	515.4	541.6	563.3	274.8

Summary of imports from the USA as a proportion of total UK imports (£m.)

	Total UK imports	*Imports from USA*	*US proportion*
1911–13	731.2	133.0	18.2%
1918	1316.2	515.4	39.2%
1920	1932.6	563.3	29.1%
1925	1320.7	245.3	18.6%

Summary of cost of exports to the USA (£m.)

1911–13	*1914*	*1915*	*1916*	*1917*	*1918*	*1919*	*1920*	*1921*
60.1	64.6	56.5	64.5	60.1	27.8	65.5	131.1	64.3

Summary of exports to the USA as a proportion of total UK exports (£m.)

	Total UK exports	*Exports to USA*	*US proportion*
1911–13	596.9	60.1	10.1%
1918	532.4	27.8	5.2%
1920	1557.2	131.1	8.4%
1925	927.4	83.2	9.0%

Summary of adverse trade balance with the USA (£m.)

1911–13	*1914*	*1915*	*1916*	*1917*	*1918*	*1919*	*1920*	*1921*
72.9	74.0	181.3	227.3	316.2	487.6	476.1	432.2	210.5

Source: Morgan, *British Financial Policy*, pp. 307–9. that figures are not precise, owing to differences in HMG departments' criteria of accounting.

Appendix VI

Summary of Exchequer Revenue and Expenditure of the UK,
1913–14 to 1918–19 (£m).

	1913–14	1914–15	1915–16	1916–17	1917–18	1918–19
Revenue	198.2	226.7	336.8	573.4	707.2	889.0
Expenditure	197.5	560.5	1,559.2	2,198.1	2,696.2	2,579.3
Surplus (+) or Deficit (−)	+0.7	−333.8	−1,222.4	−1,624.7	−1,989.0	−1,690.3

Source: Morgan, *British Financial Policy*, p. 98.

Select Bibliography

Only works referred to in the notes or which were found to be particularly useful are listed here.

I MANUSCRIPTS

A. American

1 Private

Chandler P. Anderson Papers, Yale University Library, New Haven, Conn.

Gordon Auchincloss Papers, Library of Congress, Washington, DC

Newton D. Baker Papers, Library of Congress, Washington, DC

Oscar T. Crosby Papers, Library of Congress, Washington, DC

Charles S. Hamlin Papers, Library of Congress, Washington, DC

Edward M. House Papers, Yale University Library, New Haven, Conn.

Thomas Lamont Papers, Harvard Business School, Boston, Mass.

Robert Lansing Papers, Library of Congress, Washington, DC

Breckinridge Long Papers, Library of Congress, Washington, DC

William G. McAdoo Papers, Library of Congress, Washington, DC

Dwight Morrow Papers, Amherst College, Conn.

William Phillips Papers, Harvard University Library, Cambridge, Mass.

Frank L. Polk Papers, Yale University Library, New Haven, Conn.

E. R. Stettinius Papers, University of Virginia, Charlottesville, Va

Woodrow Wilson Papers, Library of Congress, Washington, DC

2 Public – National Archives, Washington, DC

Allied Purchasing Commission Records

Department of State Records

Department of the Treasury Records

Department of War Records

United States Shipping Board Records

B. British and Canadian

1 Private

Christopher Addison Papers, Bodleian Library, Oxford

Herbert Henry Asquith Papers, Bodleian Library, Oxford

Arthur James Balfour Papers, British Library, London

Arthur James Balfour Papers, Public Record Office, London

Lord Beaverbrook Papers, House of Lords Record Office, London

Andrew Bonar Law Papers, House of Lords Record Office, London

Lord Robert Cecil Papers, British Library, London

Lord Robert Cecil Papers, Public Record Office, London
Admiral Sir Dudley deChair Papers, Imperial War Museum, London
Lord Esher Papers, Churchill College, Cambridge
Sir Joseph Flavelle Papers, Queen's University, Kingston, Ontario
Sir Edward Grey Papers, Public Record Office, London
Sir Maurice Hankey Papers, Churchill College, Cambridge
J. M. Keynes Papers, King's College, Cambridge
David Lloyd George Papers, House of Lords Record Office, London
Reginald McKenna Papers, Churchill College, Cambridge
Morgan Grenfell & Co. Ltd Papers, London
Lord Northcliffe Papers, British Library, London
Lord Northcliffe Papers, *The Times* Archive, London
Lord Reading Papers, India Office Library, London
Lord Reading Papers, Public Record Office, London
Sir Cecil Spring Rice Papers, Churchill College, Cambridge
Sir Cecil Spring Rice Papers, Public Record Office, London
Arthur Willert Papers, *The Times* Archive, London
Arthur Willert Papers, Yale University Library, New Haven, Conn.
Sir William Wiseman Papers, Yale University Library, New Haven,
    Conn.

2 *Public – Public Record Office, London*
Cabinet Records
Foreign Office Records
Ministry of Food Records
Ministry of Shipping Records
Royal Commission on Wheat Supplies Records
Treasury Records

II *Printed Sources*

A. *Primary Sources*

Department of State, *Papers Relating to the Foreign Relations of the United
    States, 1917*, Supplement 2, *The World War* (Washington, DC: United
    States Government Printing Office, 1932).
Department of State, *Papers Relating to the Foreign Relations of the United
    States, 1918*, Supplement 1, *The World War*, 2 vols (Washington, DC:
    United States Government Printing Office, 1933).
Department of State, *Papers Relating to the Foreign Relations of the United
    States, The Lansing Papers, 1914–1920*, 2 vols (Washington, DC: United
    States Government Printing Office, 1939–40).
Department of the Treasury, *Annual Report of the Secretary of the
    Treasury on the State of the Finances for the Fiscal Year Ended June 30,
    1919* (Washington, DC: United States Government Printing Office,
    1920).
Hansard, *Parliamentary Debates*, 5th series.

Johnson, Elizabeth (ed.), *The Collected Writings of John Maynard Keynes*, Vol. XVI, *Activities 1914–1919* (London: Macmillan and the Royal Economic Society, 1971).

Ministry of Munitions, *Official History of the Ministry of Munitions*, 12 vols (London: HMSO, 1921–2).

United States Senate, 74th Congress, 2nd Session, Special Committee on Investigation of the Munitions Industry, *Munitions Industry*, Report no. 944, 7 vols (Washington, DC: United States Government Printing Office, 1936).

B. *Secondary Sources*

1 *Biographies and Memoirs*

(a) *American*

Baker, Ray Stannard, *Woodrow Wilson: Life and Letters*, 8 vols (London: Heinemann, 1927–39).

Baruch, Bernard M., *Baruch: My Own Story* (New York: Holt, 1957).

Baruch, Bernard M., *Baruch: The Public Years* (New York: Holt, Rinehart & Winston, 1960).

Beaver, Daniel R., *Newton D. Baker and the American War Effort, 1917–1919* (Lincoln, Nebr.: University of Nebraska Press, 1966).

Broesamle, John J., *William Gibbs McAdoo: A Passion for Change, 1867–1917* (Port Washington, Wis.: Kennikat Press, 1973).

Chandler, Leslie V., *Benjamin Strong, Central Banker* (Washington, DC: The Brookings Institution, 1958).

Daniels, Josephus, *The Wilson Era: Years of War and After, 1917–1923* (Chapel Hill, NC: University of North Carolina Press, 1946).

Forbes, John Douglas, *Stettinius, Sr.: Portrait of a Morgan Partner* (Charlottesville, Va: University Press of Virginia, 1974).

Gregory, Ross, *Walter Hines Page, Ambassador to the Court of St James* (Lexington, Ky: University Press of Kentucky, 1970).

Hendrick, Burton J., *The Life and Letters of Walter H. Page*, 2 vols (London: Heinemann, 1923).

Hessen, Robert, *Steel Titan: The Life of Charles M. Schwab* (New York: Oxford University Press, 1975).

Hoover, Herbert, *An American Epic*, 2 vols (Chicago: Regnery, 1960).

Houston, David F., *Eight Years with Wilson's Cabinet, 1913 to 1920*, 2 vols (Garden City, NY: Doubleday, Page, 1926).

Hurley, Edward N., *The Bridge to France* (Philadelphia, Pa: Lippincott, 1927).

Lansing, Robert, *War Memoirs* (Indianapolis, Ind.: Bobbs-Merrill, 1935).

Link, Arthur S., *Wilson: The Struggle for Neutrality, 1914–1915* (Princeton, NJ: Princeton University Press, 1960).

Link, Arthur S., *Wilson: Confusions and Crises, 1915–1916* (Princeton, NJ: Princeton University Press, 1962).

Link, Arthur S., *Woodrow Wilson and the Progressive Era, 1910–1917* (New York: Harper & Row, 1963).

Link, Arthur S., *Wilson: Campaigns for Progressivism and Peace, 1916–1917* (Princeton, NJ: Princeton University Press, 1965).

Link, Arthur S., *The Higher Realism of Woodrow Wilson and Other Essays* (Nashville, Tenn.: Vanderbilt University Press, 1971).

McAdoo, William Gibbs, *Crowded Years* (London: Cape, 1932).

Nicolson, Harold, *Dwight Morrow* (London: Constable, 1935).

Palmer, Frederick, *Newton D. Baker: America at War*, 2 vols (New York: Dodd, Mead, 1931).

Phillips, William, *Ventures in Diplomacy* (London: Murray, 1955).

Redfield, William C., *With Congress and Cabinet* (Garden City, NY: Doubleday, Page, 1924).

Seymour, Charles (ed.), *The Intimate Papers of Colonel House*, 4 vols (Boston, Mass.: Houghton Mifflin, 1926).

Smith, Daniel M., *Robert Lansing and American Neutrality, 1914–17* (Berkeley, Calif.: University of California Press, 1958).

Tardieu, André, *France and America: Some Experiences in Co-Operation* (Boston, Mass.: Houghton Mifflin, 1927).

Vanderlip, Frank, *From Farm Boy to Financier* (New York: Appleton-Century, 1935).

(b) *British and Canadian*

Adams, R. J. Q., *Arms and the Wizard: Lloyd George and the Ministry of Munitions, 1915–1916* (London: Cassell, 1978).

Addison, Christopher, *Four and a Half Years: A Personal Diary from June 1914 to January 1919*, 2 vols (London: Hutchinson, 1934).

Bliss, Michael, *A Canadian Millionaire: The Life and Times of Sir Joseph Flavelle, Bart, 1858–1939* (Toronto: Macmillan of Canada, 1978).

Bridges, Lt-Gen. Sir Tom, *Alarms and Excursions: Reminiscences of a Soldier* (London: Longmans, Green, 1938).

Brock, Michael, and Brock, Eleanor (eds), *H. H. Asquith Letters to Venetia Stanley* (Oxford: Oxford University Press, 1982).

Clark, Alan (ed.), *'A Good Innings': The Private Papers of Viscount Lee of Fareham* (London: Murray, 1974).

Crow, Duncan, *A Man of Push and Go: The Life of George Macaulay Booth* (London: Hart-Davis, 1965).

Davies, Joseph, *The Prime Minister's Secretariat, 1916–1920* (Newport: R. H. Johns, 1951).

deChair, Adm. Sir Dudley, *The Sea Is Strong* (London: Harrap, 1961).

Dugdale, Blanche E. C., *Arthur James Balfour, 1906–1930* (London: Hutchinson, 1936).

Fowler, W. B., *British-American Relations, 1917–1918: The Role of Sir William Wiseman* (Princeton, NJ: Princeton University Press, 1969).

Gaunt, Adm. Sir Guy, *The Yield of the Years* (London: Hutchinson, 1940).

Geddes, Auckland, *The Forging of a Family* (London: Faber, 1952).

Gilbert, Martin, *Winston Churchill, 1914–1916* (London: Heinemann, 1971).

Grey, Sir Edward, Viscount, *Twenty-Five Years, 1892–1916*, 2 vols (London: Hodder & Stoughton, 1925).

Grigg, John, *The Young Lloyd George* (London: Eyre Methuen, 1973).

Gwynn, Stephen, *The Letters and Friendships of Sir Cecil Spring Rice*, 2 vols (London: Constable, 1929).

Hankey, Lord *The Supreme Command*, 2 vols (London: Allen & Unwin, 1961).

Hardinge, Charles, Baron, *The Old Diplomacy* (London: Murray, 1947).

Harrod, R. F., *The Life of John Maynard Keynes* (Harmondsworth: Penguin, 1972).

Hyde, H. Montgomery, *Lord Reading* (London: Heinemann, 1967).

Isaacs, Gerald Rufus, Marquess of Reading, *Rufus Isaacs, First Marquess of Reading, 1914–1935* (London: Hutchinson, 1945).

James, Robert Rhodes (ed.), *Memoirs of a Conservative: J. C. C. Davidson's Memoirs and Papers, 1910–37* (New York: Macmillan, 1970).

Koss, Stephen, *Lord Haldane, Scapegoat for Liberalism* (New York: Columbia University Press, 1969).

Leslie, Shane, *Long Shadows* (London: Murray, 1966).

Lloyd George, David, *War Memoirs*, 2 vols (London: Odhams, 1938).

Lyddon, W. G., *British War Missions to the U.S., 1914–1918* (London: Oxford University Press, 1938).

McFadyean, Sir Andrew, *Recollected in Tranquillity* (London: Pall Mall, 1964).

McKenna, Stephen, *While I Remember* (London: Thornton Butterworth, 1921).

McKenna, Stephen, *Reginald McKenna, 1863–1943: A Memoir* (London: Eyre & Spottiswoode, 1948).

Murray, Arthur C., *Master and Brother: Murrays of Elibank* (London: Murray, 1945).

Murray, Arthur C., *At Close Quarters: A Sidelight on Anglo-American Diplomatic Relations* (London: Murray, 1946).

Percy, Lord Eustace, *Some Memories* (London: Eyre & Spottiswoode, 1958).

Peterson, Maurice, *Both Sides of the Curtain: An Autobiography* (London: Constable, 1950).

Pound, Reginald, and Harmsworth, Geoffrey, *Northcliffe* (London: Cassell, 1959).

Reading, Marquess of, see Isaacs.

Roskill, Stephen, *Hankey, Man of Secrets*, Vol. 1, *1877–1918* (London: Collins, 1970).

Salter, Sir Arthur, Baron, *Slave of the Lamp: A Public Servant's Notebook* (London: Weidenfeld & Nicolson, 1967).

Stuart, Sir Campbell, *Opportunity Knocks Once* (London: Collins, 1952).

Swinton, Maj.-Gen. Sir Ernest D., *Over my Shoulder* (Oxford: George Ronald, 1951).

Willert, Sir Arthur, *The Road to Safety: A Study in Anglo-American Relations* (London: Derek Verschoyle, 1952).

Willert, Sir Arthur, *Washington and Other Memories* (Boston, Mass.: Houghton Mifflin, 1972).

Wilson, Trevor (ed.), *The Political Diaries of C. P. Scott, 1911–1928* (London: Collins, 1970).

2   *General Works*

Aitken, William Maxwell, Baron Beaverbrook, *Men and Power, 1917–1918* (London: Hutchinson, 1956).

Aitken, William Maxwell, Baron Beaverbrook, *Politicians and the War* (London: Archon, 1968; first published in 2 vols 1928–32).

Bagwell, Philip, and Mingay, G. E., *Britain and America: A Study of Economic Change, 1850–1939* (London: Routledge & Kegan Paul, 1970).

Beaverbrook, Baron, see Aitken.

Bell, A. C., *The Blockade of the Central Empires, 1914–18* (London: HMSO, 1937).

Bridges, Lt-Gen. Sir Tom (ed.), *Word from England: An Anthology of Prose and Poetry Compiled for the King's Forces* (London: English Universities Press, 1940).

Burk, Kathleen (ed.), *War and the State: The Transformation of British Government, 1914–1919* (London: Allen & Unwin, 1982).

Clarke, Stephen V. O., *Central Bank Cooperation, 1924–31* (New York: Federal Reserve Bank of New York, 1967).

Clarkson, Grosvenor B., *Industrial America in the World War* (Boston, Mass.: Houghton Mifflin, 1923).

Cuff, Robert D., *The War Industries Board: Business-Government Relations during World War I* (Baltimore, Md: Johns Hopkins University Press, 1973).

Donaldson, Frances, *The Marconi Scandal* (London: Hart-Davis, 1962).

French, David, *British Economic and Strategic Planning, 1905–1915* (London: Allen & Unwin, 1982).

George Peabody & Co., J. S. Morgan & Co., Morgan Grenfell & Co., Morgan Grenfell & Co. Ltd, 1838–1958 (London: Oxford University Press, 1958).

Gilbert, Charles, *American Financing of World War I* (Westport, Conn.: Greenwood, 1970).

Godfrey, Aaron A., *Government Operation of the Railroads, 1918–1920* (Austin, Tex.: San Felipe Press, 1974).

Grady, Henry F., *British War Finance, 1914–1919* (New York: AMS Reprint, 1969; first published 1927).

Hall, A. R., *The Export of Capital from Britain, 1870–1914* (London: Methuen, 1968).

Hazlehurst, Cameron, *Politicians at War, 1914–1915* (London: Cape, 1971).

The History of The Times: The 150th Anniversary and Beyond, 1912–1948, 2 vols (Nendeln: Kraus Reprint; first published London, 1952).

Leffler, Melvyn P., *The Elusive Quest: America's Pursuit of European*

Stability and French Security, 1919–1933 (Chapel Hill, NC: University of North Carolina Press, 1979).

Livermore, Seward W., *Woodrow Wilson and the War Congress, 1916–18* (Seattle, Wash.: University of Washington Press, 1966; paperback 1968).

Luebke, Frederick C., *Bonds of Loyalty: German Americans and World War I* (DeKalb, Ill.: Northern Illinois University Press, 1974).

Morgan, E. Victor, *Studies in British Financial Policy, 1914–25* (London: Macmillan, 1952).

Neilson, Keith, *Strategy and Supply: The Anglo-Russian Alliance, 1914–1917* (London: Allen & Unwin, 1984).

Parrini, Carl P., *Heir to Empire: United States Economic Diplomacy, 1916–1923* (Pittsburgh, Pa: University of Pittsburgh Press, 1969).

Pugh, Martin, *The Making of Modern British Politics, 1867–1939* (Oxford: Blackwell, 1982).

Ramsden, John, *A History of the Conservative Party: The Age of Balfour and Baldwin, 1902–1940* (London: Longman, 1978).

Rew, R. Henry, *Food Supplies in Peace and War* (London: Longman, 1920).

Sanders, Michael, and Taylor, Philip M., *British Propaganda during the First World War, 1914–18* (London: Macmillan, 1982).

Sellar, W. C., and Yeatman, R. J., *1066 and All That* (London: Methuen, 1930).

Simpson, Colin, *The Lusitania* (Harmondsworth: Penguin, 1974).

Stone, Norman, *The Eastern Front, 1914–1917* (London: Hodder & Stoughton, 1975).

Tansill, Charles, *America Goes to War* (Boston, Mass.: Little, Brown, 1938).

Tillman, Seth P., *Anglo-American Relations at the Paris Peace Conference of 1919* (Princeton, NJ: Princeton University Press, 1961).

Towne, Charles Hanson, *The Balfour Visit* (New York: George H. Dolan, 1917).

Trask, David F., *The United States in the Supreme War Council* (Middletown, Conn.: Wesleyan University Press, 1961).

Trask, David F., *Captains and Cabinets: Anglo-American Naval Relations, 1917–1918* (Columbia, Miss.: University of Missouri Press, 1972).

Turner, John, *Lloyd George's Secretariat* (Cambridge: Cambridge University Press, 1980).

Urofsky, Melvin I., *Big Steel and the Wilson Administration: A Study in Business-Government Relations* (Columbus, Ohio: Ohio State University Press, 1969).

Ward, Alan J., *Ireland and Anglo-American Relations, 1899–1921* (London: Weidenfeld & Nicolson, 1969).

Who's Who in the British War Mission to the United States of America, 1917 (New York: Edward J. Clode, 1917).

3   *Newspapers*

The New York Times

4   *Articles*

Bailey, Thomas A., 'The United States and the blacklist during the Great War', *Journal of Modern History*, vol. VI, no. 1 (1934), pp. 14–35.

Burk, Kathleen, 'Great Britain in the United States, 1917–1918: the turning point', *International History Review*, vol. I, no. 2 (April 1979), pp. 228–45.

Burk, Kathleen, 'The diplomacy of finance: British financial missions to the United States, 1914–1918', *Historical Journal*, vol. XXII, no. 2 (June 1979), pp. 351–72.

Burk, Kathleen, 'J. M. Keynes and the exchange rate crisis of July 1917', *Economic History Review*, 2nd ser., vol. XXXII, no. 3 (August 1979), pp. 405–16.

Burk, Kathleen, 'The mobilization of Anglo-American finance during World War I', in N. F. Dreisziger (ed.), *Mobilization for Total War* (Waterloo, Quebec: Wilfrid Laurier University Press, 1981), pp. 23–42.

Burk, Kathleen, 'Diplomacy and the private banker: the case of the House of Morgan', in Gustav Schmidt (ed.), *Konstellationen internationaler Politik – politische und wirtschaftliche Faktoren in den Beziehungen zwischen Westeuropa und den USA, 1924–1932* (Bochum: Studienverlag Dr. N. Brockmeyer, 1983), pp. 25–40.

Crosby, Oscar T., 'The American war loans and justice', *Atlantic Monthly*, vol. XII, no. 1 (1922), pp. 825–32.

Dayer, Roberta, 'Strange bedfellows: J. P. Morgan & Co., Whitehall and the Wilson administration during World War I', *Business History*, vol. XVIII, no. 2 (July 1976), pp. 127–51.

French, David, 'The military background to the "Shell Crisis" of May 1915', *Journal of Strategic Studies*, vol. II, no. 2 (September 1979), pp. 192–205.

Hessen, Robert, 'The Admiralty's American ally', *History Today*, vol. 21 (March 1971), pp. 864–9.

McEwen, J. M., 'Northcliffe and Lloyd George at war', *Historical Journal*, vol. XXIV, no. 3 (September 1981), pp. 651–72.

Maurer, John H., 'American naval concentration and the German battle fleet, 1900–1918', *Journal of Strategic Studies*, vol. VI, no. 2 (June 1983), pp. 147–81.

Offer, Avner, 'Empire and social reform: British overseas investment and domestic politics, 1908–1914', *Historical Journal*, vol. XXVI, no. 1 (March 1983), pp. 119–38.

Pugh, M. D., 'Asquith, Bonar Law and the First Coalition', *Historical Journal*, vol. XVII, no. 4 (December 1974), pp. 813–36.

Rathbone, Albert, 'Making war loans to the Allies', *Foreign Affairs*, vol. III (1925), pp. 371–98.

Van Alstyne, R. W., 'Private American loans to the Allies, 1914–1916', *Pacific Historical Review*, vol. II (1933), pp. 180–93.

5 *Unpublished Theses*

Barnelt, Lois Margaret, 'Government food policies in Britain during World War I', PhD thesis, Columbia University, 1982.

Hemery, J. A., 'The emergence of Treasury influence in the management of British foreign policy, 1914–1918', M.Phil. thesis, Cambridge University, 1982, 135 pp.

Herzstein, Daphne Stassin, 'The diplomacy of Allied credit advanced to Russia in World War I', PhD thesis, New York University, 1972, 380 pp.

Kihl, Mary Rambo, 'A failure of ambassadorial diplomacy: the case of Page and Spring-Rice, 1914–1917', PhD thesis, Pennsylvania State University, 1968, 231 pp.

Select Index

Select Index